Tolley's Practical Guide to Employees' Share Schemes

by

Colin E Chamberlain ATII Solicitor
Partner, Herbert Smith

Tolley Publishing Company Ltd
A UNITED NEWSPAPERS PUBLICATION

Published by
Tolley Publishing Company Ltd
Tolley House
2 Addiscombe Road
Croydon, Surrey CR9 5AF
081-686 9141

Typeset, Printed and Bound in Great Britain by
Unwin Brothers Ltd., The Gresham Press,
Old Woking, Surrey GU22 9LH

© Tolley Publishing Company Ltd 1994

ISBN 0 85459 818-9

Preface

This book arises out of my experience over the past 15 years or so advising companies on employees' share schemes. I have been fortunate in that my work has ranged very widely from the smallest of start-up companies to the massive water and electricity privatisations.

My guiding principle in preparing this book, therefore, has been to assemble the information my clients have most commonly sought and to present it under practical and convenient subject headings. In short, I hope the book will indeed serve as 'a practical guide to employees' share schemes'.

My first acknowledgement, therefore, must be to all my clients who have never failed to raise new and intriguing points which have incidentally given me and my colleagues over the years the opportunity to explore the subject from every possible angle. I should also like to thank my secretary, Jan Paxton, who turned out the typescript in her usual efficient manner and my wife, Annabel, and children Harriet and Florence, for their patience and understanding whilst the book was in preparation.

The text of the Inland Revenue's extra-statutory concession reproduced in this book is Crown Copyright and is reproduced by kind permission of the Controller of Her Majesty's Stationery Office. Also, I would like to thank The Association of British Insurers for their permission to reproduce material.

C E Chamberlain
Herbert Smith
Exchange House
Primrose Street
London EC2A 2HS

May 1994

Contents

	Page
Abbreviations and References	*x*
Table of Cases	*xii*
Table of Statutes	*xiii*

1 Introduction   1

2 Types of Scheme Available   3
    Schemes for senior executives   3
        Executive share option schemes   3
        Restricted share schemes   5
        Phantom share option schemes   6
    Schemes for all employees   6
        Savings-related share option schemes   6
        Free offers under a profit sharing scheme   6
        Matching offers under a profit sharing scheme   7
        Sponsored PEP's   7
    Other arrangements   7
        Share purchase schemes   7
        Subsidiary company schemes   8

3 The ABI and NAPF Guidelines   9
    Current guidelines sources   9
    Historical development of the ABI Guidelines   10
    NAPF Guidelines   12
    Summary of current guidelines   12
        Scheme limits   12
        Duration of schemes   13
        Eligibility   13
        Individual participation   14
        Pricing   14
        Timing of allocations   15
        Remuneration committees   15
        Early leavers   15
        'Super' options   16
        Performance targets   17
        'Underwater' options   17
        ESOPs   17

4 Establishment of Schemes   31
    Company Law   31
    Stock Exchange Listing Rules   35
    Requirements for an approved scheme   39
        Form of resolution to establish a scheme   39
        Applying for Inland Revenue approval of such a scheme   40

Refusal of an application for approval	43
Scheme shares	44
No restrictions on the shares	46
Material interest	49
Valuation of shares	51
Duration of a scheme	54
Renewal of schemes	55
Cessation of scheme approval	56
Costs of establishment of a scheme	57
Appendix 1	59
Appendix 2	61

5 Executive Share Option Schemes — 63

Introduction	63
Eligibility criteria	65
Eligibility in approved schemes	65
Institutional investors	66
Selection of optionholders	66
Grant of options	67
Time of grant	67
Procedure	68
Price	69
Material time for valuing shares	70
Disclaimer of options	74
Non-transferability of an option	74
Individual participation limit	75
Introduction	75
Limit under an approved scheme	76
Scheme limits	80
Exercise of options	81
Exercise by employees	82
Approved schemes	82
Unapproved schemes	82
Exercise by former employees	83
Approved schemes	84
Performance targets	85
Approved schemes	86
Appendix 3	89
Appendix 4	104

6 Special Types of Executive Share Option — 109

Introduction	109
Super Options	110
Replacement Options	113
Discounted Price Options	115
Tax conditions: TA 1988, 9 Sch 28	116
1991 ABI Guidelines	117
Tax aspects of unapproved Discounted Price Options	128
Parallel Options	128

Contents

7 Restricted Share Schemes — 139
    Introduction — 139
    Types of scheme — 139
    Allocation of Shares — 140
        Income tax — 140
        Capital gains tax — 141
        Financing allocation of shares — 141
    Forfeiture — 143
    Vesting — 144
        Income tax — 144
        Capital gains tax — 144
        National insurance — 145
        Inheritance tax — 145

8 Savings-Related Share Option Schemes — 147
    Introduction — 147
    Eligibility criteria — 147
        Inland Revenue requirements — 147
        ABI Guidelines — 148
    Applications for and grant of options — 149
        Timing — 149
    Procedure — 150
        Applications and grant of options — 150
    Price — 152
    Scaling down — 153
    Board resolution to grant options — 155
    Option certificate — 157
    Employee communications — 159
    Non-transferability of options — 161
    Savings contract — 161
    Scheme limits — 166
        Inland Revenue requirements — 166
        ABI Guidelines — 166
    Exercise of options — 166
    Early exercise at retirement age — 169
        Appendix 5 — 173

9 Profit Sharing Trust — 191
    Introduction — 191
    Appointment, retirement and removal of trustees — 191
    Contributions to the trustees — 193
    Group schemes — 195
    Subscriptions for shares — 198
        CA 1985, ss 80, 89 — 199
        Private companies — 199
    Tax reliefs on unapproved shares — 200
    Appropriations of shares — 200
    Limit on the value of scheme allocations — 206
    Limit on the value of individual appropriations — 206

Contents

Tax aspects of disposals of shares	207
Disposals of shares—capital gains tax	211
Normal duties of trustees	211
Statutory duties of trustees	213
Taxation of the trustees	215
Operation of PAYE	216
Alteration of the trusts	218
Duration of the scheme	218
Appendix 6	219

10 Free and Matching Offers under a Profit Sharing Scheme 243
Introduction	243
Preparing a board proposal	248
Free offer	249
Making the offer	249
Cash alternatives	251
Problems arising from the presentation of the offer	252
Matching offer	252
Making the offer	252

11 Subsidiary Company Profit Sharing Scheme 261
Introduction	261
Single subsidiary schemes	261
Multi-subsidiary schemes	262

12 Takeovers, Reconstructions, Demergers and Dividends 265
Takeovers	265
Share purchase agreement v general offer	265
Listed companies and the Takeover Code	266
Share option schemes	267
Exercise and acceptance of the offer	267
Roll-overs of options	268
Surrender of an option for a cash consideration	271
Profit sharing schemes	272
Schemes of arrangement	276
Share options schemes	276
Profit sharing schemes	278
Voluntary winding-up	278
Share option schemes	278
Profit sharing schemes	278
Demerger	278
Share option schemes	279
Profit sharing scheme	282
Dividends	282
Share option schemes	282
Profit sharing schemes	283
Scrip dividends	284
Share option schemes	284
Profit sharing schemes	284

Contents

13 Variations of Share Capital   287
    London Stock Exchange   287
    Investment Committees   288
    Inland Revenue   288
    Rights issues   288
       Share option schemes   288
       Profit sharing scheme   290
    Capitalisation issues   297
       Share option schemes   297
       Profit sharing schemes   298
    Sub-divisions and consolidations   298
    Reduction of share capital   298
       Share option schemes   298
       Profit sharing schemes   299
    Other variations of share capital   299

14 PEPs   301
    Introduction   301
    Types of plan   301
    Release of shares from employees' share schemes   302
    Sponsored PEPs   303
       CA 1985, s 151: financial assistance   303
       FSA 1986: investment businesses   304
       FSA 1986: investment advertisements   304

15 ESOPs and Using Existing Shares   305
    What is an ESOP?   305
    Employees' share schemes linked to an ESOP   305
    Financing of ESOPs   308
       The financing of ESOPs established to gift shares   308
       The financing of ESOPs established to sell shares   309
    Establishment of an ESOP   310
    Tax aspects   312
       Tax considerations for the company   312
       Tax considerations for the trustees   314
    ESOPs and share options   318
    Qualifying Employee Share Ownership Trusts   319
    Public company ESOPs   321
       1993 Listing Rules   321
       Disclosure   322

16 Administration and Tax Returns   327
    Administration   327
       Making offers   327
       Maintaining registers   327
       Dividends   328
       Takeover offers, rights issues and other variations of
          share capital   328
       Voting rights   328

Tax returns	328
Approved schemes	330
Annual returns	330

17 Overseas Schemes and Overseas Employees — 333
    The liability of non-residents to tax on share acquisitions — 333
    Approved schemes and overseas employees — 335
    Executive share options — 335
        UK approved sub-schemes to overseas parents schemes — 336
        Extending a savings-related share option scheme to overseas employees — 337
        Extending the profit sharing scheme to overseas employees — 338
    Establishment of schemes for overseas employees — 339
    Overseas laws and the making of share offers to overseas employees — 340
    Securities laws — 341
    Taxation — 342
    Central bank requirements — 342
    Other administrative matter to be taken into account — 342
    Some overseas schemes — 343

Index — 347

Abbreviations and References

ABI	=	Association of British Insurers
ABI Guidelines	=	The ABI Guidelines on employees' share schemes published in July 1987 including the two addendums dated May 1988 and August 1991
CA	=	Companies Act 1985
DPO	=	Discounted Price Options (described at paragraphs 6.37 to 6.41)
ESOP	=	Employee Share Ownership Plan
ESOT	=	Employee Share Ownership Trust
FA	=	Finance Act
IHTA 1984	=	Inheritance Tax Act 1984
Inland Revenue Guides	=	Guides published by the Inland Revenue on Profit Sharing Schemes IR 96, Savings-Related Share Option Schemes IR 98 and Executive Share Option Schemes IR 100
Joint Guidance	=	The Joint Guidance of the ABI and NAPF on executive share option schemes published on 15 July 1993
Model Scheme	=	The specimen rules of each of the approved profit sharing scheme, savings-related share option scheme and executive share option scheme as published by the Inland Revenue from time to time
NAPF	=	National Association of Pension Funds
NAPF Guidelines	=	The NAPF Guidelines published in March 1988
NASDAQ	=	National Association of Securities Dealers Automated Quotations
Parallel Options	=	Parallel Options (described at paragraphs 6.42 to 6.47)
PEP	=	Personal Equity Plan
Remuneration Committees	=	The committee of directors now established by most listed companies comprising mostly non-executive directors which is authorised to consider directors' remuneration
Replacement Options	=	Replacement Options (described at paragraphs 6.17 to 6.23)
s	=	section

Abbreviations and References

SAYE	=	Save As You Earn
Sch	=	Schedule
Special Commissioners	=	Special Commissioners of Income Tax
STC	=	Simon's Tax Cases
Super Options	=	Super Options (described at paragraphs 6.6 to 6.16)
TA 1988 or Taxes Act 1988	=	Income and Corporation Taxes Act 1988
TCGA 1992	=	Taxation of Chargeable Gains Act 1992
USM	=	Unlisted Securities Market

Table of Cases

Paragraph

Abbott v Philbin [1960] 39 TC 82   5.2, 5.36, 6.40, 17.6
Atherton v British Insulated and Helsby Cables Ltd [1925]
   10 TC 155   7.13, 15.29

Barber v GRE, Case C–262/88 ECJ   8.94
Booth v Mirror Group Newspapers plc [1992] STC 615   12.26
Bray v Best [1988] STC 159   15.53

Carver v Duncan [1985] STC 356   13.19
Consultants Group International v John Warman Ltd [1986]
   unreported   8.98
Clark v Oceanic Contractors Inc 56 TC 183   15.53

Heather v PE Consulting Group Ltd [1972] 48 TC 293   7.14
Hogg v Cramphorn [1967] Ch 254   4.7, 15.22

IRC v Burton Group plc [1990] STC 242   5.104, 5.105
IRC v Crossman [1937] AC 26, [1936] 1 All ER 762, 52 TLR
   415, HL   2.25, 3.29
IRC v Eurocopy plc [1991] STC 707   5.104, 5.105, 12.62
IRC v Herd [1993] STC 436   12.26, 15.53
IRC v Plummer [1979] STC 793, 54 TC 1, HL   15.47

Jeffs v Ringtons Ltd [1985] 58 TC 680   7.14

Roome v Edwards [1981] 54 TC 359   7.9

Tip Europe, Re [1987] 3 BCC 647   12.44
Transfer Terminal, Re [1987] 3 BCC 647   12.44

Weight v Salmon [1935] 19 TC 174   2.21, 7.6, 7.20, 15.53, 17.3

Table of Statutes

	Paragraph
1925 Trustee Act	9.5
ss 21, 23	9.5
s 30	9.5, 9.11
1964 Perpetuities and Accumulations Act	
s 1	4.72, 9.122
1965 Contracts of Employment and Redundancy Payments Act (Northern Ireland)	9.78
1966 Finance Act	
s 25	5.2
1970 Taxes Management Act	
ss 7, 8	16.20
1972 European Communities Act	4.23, 8.97
1972 Finance Act	8.2
s 78	6.25
s 79	1.4
1973 Finance Act	
9 Sch	1.4
1974 Finance Act	8.2
1975 Social Security Act	
20 Sch	8.93
1978 Employment Protection (Consolidation) Act	8.86, App 5–8.106, 9.78, App 6–9.122
1978 Finance Act	3.4
1980 Finance Act	8.2
s 47	6.26

1984 Finance Act	3.39, 5.6, 5.7, 5.80, 6.2
s 39(8)	1.4
s 40	1.4
1984 Inheritance Act	
ss 49, 52	7.29
ss 58, 64	9.111
s 65	9.111
(1)(a)(b)	7.26
(4)	7.26
(5)	15.49
s 70(3)	7.28
s 72	15.52
(1)	7.27
(2)(a)	7.28
(b)	15.59
(5)	7.28
s 86	7.23, 7.25, 7.30, 15.44, 15.51, 15.52
(3)	7.23
(4)	7.23, 7.27
(5)	7.23
s 163(1)	5.93
1985 Companies Act	
s 3A	4.11, 15.21
s 35(2)	15.21
s 35A	15.21
s 80	4.5, 5.68, 9.39
s 89	4.6
(5)	4.6
s 95	5.68, 9.39
s 100	4.13, 4.14
s 135(2)	13.28
s 151	4.6, 9.15, 14.11
s 153(4)	4.7, App 5–8.106, 9.15, 9.16, 14.18, 15.75
s 154	9.16
s 186(11)	9.41
s 198	9.38, 15.71
s 263	12.53, 12.71
s 317	4.12

Table of Statutes

CA 1985
- s 324(2)   9.36, 9.37, 15.67, 15.68, 15.70, 15.78
- s 325   9.36, 9.37, 15.67, 15.70
- s 330   15.26
- s 425   5.94, App 3–5.106, App 5–8.106, 12.2, 12.16, 12.17, 12.41, 12.42, 12.49
- ss 428–430F App 3–5.106, App 5–8.106, App 6–9.122, 12.10, 12.13, 12.16
- s 736   App 3–5.106, App 5–8.106, App 6–9.122
- s 736A   App 3–5.106, App 5–8.106, App 6–9.122
- 4 Sch 50   15.76
-      51   15.75
- 6 Sch   15.77
- 7 Sch 2   15.78
- 13 Sch 6   15.67, 15.68

1985 Finance Act
- s 85(1)   16.15, 16.16

1986 Financial Services Act   14.3, 14.14, 15.24
- s 57   14.14

1987 Finance Act   12.21

1988 Finance Act   1.4, 4.47
- s 77(1)   16.12
-      (2)   16.17
- s 78   7.21, 16.18
- s 79   2.1, 2.29
- s 80(1)   16.18
- s 85(1)   16.11, 16.13
-      (2)   16.18
- s 86(1)   2.30
- s 87(1)   16.12
- s 162   2.1, 2.28

1988 Income and Corporation Taxes Act   3.10, 4.1, 4.8, 4.26, 4.31, 5.10, 6.39, App 5–8.106, App 6–9.122
- s 84A   9.20
- s 85   4.83, 9.18, 15.7, 15.8
- s 85A   4.83
- s 123   12.76
- s 126(2)   13.14, 13.26
- s 135   5.2, 5.6
-      (1)   5.49, 12.25, 12.64, 17.4, 17.5
-      (2)   5.36, 5.82, 12.66, 17.6
-      (3)   5.49
-      (5)   6.40
- s 136   5.2, 5.49
-      (1)   12.20, 12.66
-      (6)   16.13, 16.15
- s 140(1)   16.17
- ss 153–168   16.19, 17.11
- s 161(1)   16.19
- s 162   17.5
-      (1)(6)   16.19
- s 185   3.29, 5.35, 5.68
-      (3)   5.80
-      (b)   15.54
-      (5)   5.77, 5.79, 5.80
-      (6)   5.34, 5.92
-      (6A)   5.34
-      (6B)   5.34
- s 186   App 6–9.122
-      (3)   App 6–9.122, 12.52, 13.20
-      (4)   9.81, 12.31, 13.15, 14.5
-      (5)   App 6–9.122
-      (6)   12.31
-      (7)   13.15, 13.16
-      (8)(b)   13.17
-      (10)   9.81
-      (11)   9.109
-      (12)   13.19
- s 187(2)   App 3–5.106, App 5–8.106, App 6–9.122, 17.12
-      (3)   4.53,

Table of Statutes

App 3–5.106, 9.54, App 6–9.122	
(5)	App 6–9.122, 17.12
(7)	4.37, App 3–5.106, App 5–8.106, App 6–9.122
s 203	App 3–5.106, App 4–5.106, 17.8
s 231	12.75
s 249	12.82
s 326	2.18, 8.60, 8.77, App 5–8.106
s 349(1)	15.37
s 414	9.53, App 6–9.122
(1)	4.54, App 3–5.106, App 5–8.106, 9.53
s 415	9.53, App 6–9.122
s 416	5.56, 12.29
s 417(1)	4.53
s 686	9.109
s 688	15.42
s 770	15.36
s 786(5)	15.35
s 832(1)	App 3–5.106, App 6–9.122
s 840	App 1–4.83, App 3–5.106, App 5–8.106, 9.22, App 6–9.122
5 Sch	15.60
8 Sch 7	4.56
9 Sch	3.20, App 1–4.83 5.77, 5.90, App 3–5.106, 6.1, 8.9, 8.10, App 5–8.106, App 6–9.122, 17.8
1	4.32
(3)	App 1–4.83, 9.22
2	
(1)	4.46, 12.23
(2)	4.33, 4.81, 9.55, 12.28
(3)	4.29, 4.34, 9.26, App 6–9.122
3	4.81
(1)	4.36
(2)	4.36, 9.23
4, 5	12.12
6	16.23
7	App 5–8.106
8	9.53, 4.51, 4.54, App 3–5.106
8A	8.93
9	4.59, App 5–8.106
10	4.29, 4.36, 5.9, App 3–5.106, App 5–8.106, App 6–9.122, 11.1, 11.2, 12.9, 12.15, 12.18, 12.33
11	4.29, 4.36, 4.38, App 3–5.106, App 5–8.106, 5.9, App 6–9.122, 11.1, 12.15, 12.18, 12.19, 12.33
12	4.29, 4.36, 4.40, App 3–5.106, App 5–8.106, 5.9, App 6–9.122, 11.1, 12.15, 12.18, 12.19, 12.33
(1)(a)	13.29
(c)	4.44, 4.45, 11.1
(2)	4.40, 4.43, 5.9
13	4.29, 4.36, 5.9, App 3–5.106, App 5–8.106, App 6–9.122, 12.15, 12.18, 12.19, 12.33
(1)	4.41
(2)	4.45
(3)	4.48
14	4.29, 4.48, 4.50, 5.9, App 3–5.106, App 5–8.106, App 6–9.122, 11.1, 12.15, 12.18, 12.19, 12.33
(3)	4.48
15	12.43

Table of Statutes

ICTA 1988
(2)	App 3–5.106, App 3–5.106		App 6–9.122
(3)	App 3–5.106, App 5.106	3A	App 6–9.122
(4)	12.20	4(1)(c)	12.69
18	8.85	(2)	9.87, 9.115, App 6–9.122, 13.20
19	8.87, 8.88, 8.92	5(3)	App 6–9.122, 13.14, 13.33
20	8.92	(4)	12.33, 13.14
21(1)	12.43, 12.50	(5)	13.21, 13.26
22	8.59	(5A)	12.39
24	App 5–8.106	6(5)	9.57, 9.119
(2)	3.19, 8.16, 8.18	7	9.112, 9.114, App 6–9.123
25	3.22, 8.26, 8.27, 12.58, 13.1, 13.24, 13.33		

1989 Finance Act
ss 36–42	5.63
ss 67–74	15.9, 15.60
5 Sch	15.61

26(1)	8.4, 8.6, 8.39		
(2)	8.4		
27(1)	5.11		

1991 Finance Act
	3.10
s 38	8.95
s 39	6.27, 6.33

(2)	5.48, 5.77	
(4)	5.13	
28	5.51, 5.53, 6.28–6.32	

1992 Social Security Contributions and Benefits Act
s 122	8.93

(2)	5.54, 6.30, 17.9
(3)	6.32
(4)	5.60
30	9.3, 9.4, 9.6, 9.64, 9.73, App 6–9.122, 17.12

1992 Taxation of Chargeable Gains Act
	4.61, App 3–5.106, App 5–8.106	
s 17	7.22, 15.44, 15.54, 15.58	
s 22(1)(a)	12.64, 12.66	
(1)(c)	5.50, 12.20, 12.66	
s 24(1)	7.19	
s 68	7.9	
s 76	7.19	
s 85A	15.62	
s 86	15.48	
s 87	15.47	
s 117	12.37	
s 126(1)	13.32	
(2)(b)	13.27	
(3)	13.32	
s 135	12.32	

31	9.4
32	9.4
33	9.4, 12.74, 12.82, 13.11
34	9.4
35(1)	9.46
(2)	9.52, 11.15
36	4.81, 9.17, 9.28, 9.31, 9.45, 9.58
37	4.58
40	4.56
10 Sch	4.81, App 6–9.122
1(1)(a)-(c)	9.56, App 6–9.122, 12.29, 12.40, 12.49
2	9.56, App 6–9.122
3	9.115,

xvi

s 136	12.49, 12.69
s 137(2)	15.58
s 165	15.24, 15.45, 15.62
(2)	15.45
s 166	15.24
ss 213–218	12.70
s 238(4)	12.20
s 271(4)	8.77
s 272	9.63, 9.66, App 6–9.122, 14.7
ss 273, 274	App 6–9.122, 14.7

1994 Finance Act

s 101	12.38, 12.39
13 Sch	15.60, 15.61

Chapter 1

Introduction

1.1 Employees' share schemes now cover approximately 4,000 companies and at least 3 million employees have participated in such schemes, the vast majority in one of the three approved share schemes of which there were approximately 867 profit sharing schemes, 984 savings-related share option schemes and 3,981 executive share option schemes in operation in March 1994. Almost all listed and Unlisted Securities Market (USM) companies, and many large private companies, have some form of employees' share scheme and, without doubt, employees' share schemes are by far and away the most significant entry into share ownership for the vast majority of individuals. Even the personal equity plan which was introduced for the purpose of encouraging the private investor looks set to become a key part of the employees' share scheme arrangements of many companies.

1.2 The book is called 'Tolley's Practical Guide to Employees' Share Schemes' because the material in the book is organised, so far as possible, under the various subject headings which arise in practice. The material on tax and company law is not dealt with in separate chapters, but as it arises in relation to particular schemes.

1.3 This approach has meant that the weight given to different topics reflects their practical importance rather than their intrinsic technical complexity. It explains why a chapter is devoted to the unapproved employee share ownership plan which has become an important adjunct of many share schemes while only a passing reference is made to the statutory version, the employee share ownership trust under *FA 1989*, which has such wide conditions to be satisfied to obtain the tax relief that it is of little or no practical relevance.

1.4 The book ignores much of the historical development of the taxation of employees' share schemes, in particular the short-lived approved share option and share incentive schemes under *FA 1972* (which was repealed with effect from 27 March 1984), the provisions for tax-relieved savings-related share incentive schemes under *FA 1973, 8 Sch* (which were repealed even before they came into effect) and the arrangements for the payment of tax on option gains before

1.4 Introduction

5 April 1984 in three, and later five, instalments under *FA 1982, s 40* and *FA 1984, s 39(8)*. It also ignores the general tax treatment in *FA 1972, s 79* of acquisitions of shares by employees under unapproved employee share schemes prior to 26 October 1987 when the new legislation in *FA 1988, ss 77–89* retrospectively came into effect.

The book appears at a time when many listed companies may be considering the renewal of their approved executive share option schemes on the tenth anniversary of the passing of the *Finance Act 1984*. It includes the July 1993 'Joint Guidance' of the Investment Committees of the ABI and NAPF on performance targets in executive share option schemes and the new procedures for the approval of employees' share schemes by listed companies under the 1993 *Listing Particulars*.

This book is written for the company secretary and other managers who have responsibility for employees' share schemes, as well as for their advisers, whether lawyers, consultants or accountants.

Chapter 2

Types of Scheme Available

2.1 There are many types of employees' share schemes ranging from those where the employee pays the full value for the shares to those where he receives free shares. In between these extremes are various arrangements under which payment is deferred in some way: share option schemes and partly-paid share schemes. Partly-paid share schemes are generally out of favour at present as they involve an annual income tax liability on the unpaid proportion of the subscription price under *FA 1988, s 162.*

2.2 Generally speaking, it is possible to classify most schemes as appropriate either for key senior executives or for all employees. Schemes for key senior executives usually involve substantial numbers of shares and may involve the executive financing his purchase of shares. Schemes for all employees will usually involve smaller parcels of shares and the financing and tax aspects will be more straightforward.

Schemes for senior executives

Executive share option schemes

2.3 The most common type of share scheme for senior executives is the executive share option scheme under which the company grants a right to buy shares at the market price, exercisable between three to ten years after the date of grant, provided the executive remains in employment. Former employees are normally allowed to buy the shares within a limited period of leaving employment even if this is before the third anniversary of grant. There will also be a right of exercise on any takeover or reconstruction of the company.

2.4 The optionholder, therefore, acquires a right to buy shares at a fixed price. If the shares increase in value then he will wish to exercise the option in due course and realise the accrued gain. If the shares do not increase in value, he will not exercise the option, but he will not be out of pocket since the option will have been granted

2.5 Types of Scheme Available

under seal or for nominal consideration of, say, £1 only. The incentive for management, therefore, is to achieve the greatest possible increase in the share price by the date of exercise.

2.5 Since 1987, the Investment Committees of the Association of British Insurers and the National Association of Pension Funds have recommended that schemes are operated so that options are only exercisable if there has been sustained growth in the company and not just an inflation-linked gain.

Super options

2.6 Under ABI Guidelines, the maximum number of shares over which options may be granted to an individual is such number of shares as may have a value at the date of grant equal to four times his annual rate of earnings. To the extent that options are granted in excess of this limit, they must be granted on 'super' option terms involving a five-year performance target based on an increase in earnings per share which at least matches the upper quartile of FTSE 100 companies.

2.7 Since a participant may only hold approved options worth four times their 'relevant emoluments' as at the date of grant, it follows that if options are held under an approved scheme, any 'super' option will normally need to be granted under a separate unapproved scheme.

2.8 Under ABI Guidelines there is no specific cap on the size of super options although the 1987 ABI Guidelines state that companies should avoid granting an excessive number of options to any individual by taking into account substantial performance-related pay in determining the earnings on which options are to be based. The 1987 ABI Guidelines suggest a cap on the amount of earnings which might need to be incorporated in any scheme.

Bridging finance arrangements

2.9 Where large share options are to be exercised, employees will not usually have the financial resources to finance the exercise of their option without selling at least some of their shares. Employees may approach their bank to arrange bridging finance, but banks are often reluctant to make loans on competitive terms where they cannot obtain security over the shares, especially as option rights are usually non-transferable.

2.10 Most companies have, therefore, established arrangements under which the company's broker or some other financial institution will provide bridging finance to enable optionholders to exercise their options out of the proceeds of a sale of all or part of the shares arising on exercise of the option. The broker will rely on the company ensuring that any share certificates are held as security for the loan until it is repaid. Such arrangements will usually also enable an employee to split his holding with any spouse before sale so as to take advantage of the spouse's annual capital gains tax exemption.

Parallel or linked share option schemes

2.11 Most options are granted on the basis of a single exercise price and period of exercise. However, a scheme may provide for the exercise of options on alternative terms as to price and the period for exercise. The option may be exercisable at a price equal to the market value at the date of grant after three years, with an alternative lower price after, say, five years if a specified performance target is achieved. In some cases the alternative exercise rights are set out in different schemes with a mechanism which provides that to the extent the optionholder exercises the option under one of the schemes, he will forego his right of exercise in respect of the option under the other scheme. Such 'parallel' or 'linked' options may, of course, be granted at different times and may offer considerable flexibility in that the second option may be granted to 'plug a gap' in the rights of exercise under the first option, or to grant an alternative lower-priced option where the value of the shares has fallen.

Restricted share schemes

2.12 Restricted share schemes, which originated in the United States, involve the 'allocation' of free shares to executives on the basis that the shares will be forfeited if the employee leaves employment before the end of a specified period, or a performance target is not satisfied within a specified period. During the performance period the shares will normally be retained by trustees.

2.13 The employee is chargeable to income tax on the value of the shares at the time the restrictions on disposal are lifted. There are, therefore, no particular tax advantages in this type of scheme except for a saving in national insurance contributions as a result of receiving shares instead of cash.

2.14 One variation of this type of scheme involves employees making some form of financial contribution, usually by purchasing a number of shares for cash or by applying part of any cash bonus entitlement so as to qualify for additional free shares. Both the purchased and free shares are subject to restrictions on disposal although the restrictions applying to the purchased shares are not necessarily as onerous as those applying to the free shares.

2.15 Types of Scheme Available

2.15 Institutional investors do not have any guidelines on this type of scheme. This may be because there are very few known cases of a company seeking shareholders' approval. As in the case of any other ESOP which only uses existing shares, there is no need for a company to seek any approval from shareholders' in respect of the establishment of such schemes.

Phantom share option schemes

2.16 Phantom share option schemes are a form of cash bonus scheme made to look like a share option scheme. Such schemes will usually be established by a company which is not in a position to establish a share option scheme usually because it is a subsidiary of a non-listed company which is not prepared to allow minority interests to arise.

Schemes for all employees

2.17 A few companies have granted share options to employees on a general basis, although in most cases such an approach has not been maintained for long, usually because such schemes use shares at a far greater rate than the conventional savings-related share option schemes as not all employees are prepared to enter into long-term savings plans.

Savings-related share option schemes

2.18 Savings-related share option schemes are linked to certified contractual savings schemes under *TA 1988, s 326*. Such savings schemes can only be offered by building societies, banks or the Department for National Savings. Banks have only been able to offer such savings schemes since 1990.

2.19 Options may be granted at a discount of up to 20 per cent to market value at the date of grant.

2.20 Most companies find that about 20 to 50 per cent of employees participate. The average amount saved is about £50 a month. This means that the average participant will be able to buy shares worth at their original market value £4,312.50 after five years or £4,875 after seven years. The maximum value of shares which may be acquired after seven years on savings of £250 a month is £21,562 on the basis of the savings bonus rates applicable on 31 March 1994.

Free offers under a profit sharing scheme

2.21 An allocation of free shares is chargeable to tax on the value of the shares received under the general principles of *Schedule E*

Types of Scheme Available **2.26**

(*Weight v Salmon* (*1935*) *19 TC 174*). However, this tax charge is deferred where shares are appropriated under an approved profit sharing scheme. It is a condition of any appropriation of shares under such a scheme that the shares must be left with trustees for up to two years; any withdrawal after this period will trigger the deferred tax charge at least until the fifth anniversary when the tax will be remitted altogether. In short, the tax charge is reduced or waived altogether depending on how long the employee keeps the shares.

2.22 The maximum value of free shares which may be received each year is ten per cent of pay up to £8,000 worth of shares (*TA 1988, s 187*). The average annual size of appropriations under such schemes is about £350 per year.

Matching offers under a profit sharing scheme

2.23 Matching offers involve the offer of one or more free shares to be appropriated under an approved profit sharing scheme for every share purchased by the employee and left with the trustee (or some other person such as a PEP plan manager). Under Inland Revenue practice, any eligible employee must be able to participate by buying shares worth no more than £100 or one per cent of pay, if less.

2.24 Such arrangements are common in large flotations, particularly privatisations. A number of UK subsidiaries of US parents also like this type of scheme. In such cases, the savings contributions may be made on a rolling or continuous basis, for example, two per cent of pay per month.

Sponsored PEPs

2.25 A number of large companies have sponsored personal equity plan managers to provide plans using only the shares of the sponsoring company. Such arrangements may be attractive to employees particularly as shares emerging from an approved profit sharing or savings-related share option scheme (but not an executive share option scheme) may be transferred into the plan directly.

Other arrangements

Share purchase schemes

2.26 Some companies, usually private companies, allow employees to subscribe or purchase shares at the market price. In private companies, the articles of association may provide for shares to be offered to an employees' share trust and such shares may then be offered by the trustees to employees on regular 'offer' days. The employees' share

2.27 Types of Scheme Available

trust will usually have an overriding power to transfer shares without any pre-emption obligations.

2.27 The company may provide financial assistance both to trustees, in order to buy shares from employees, and to employees, to buy shares from the trustees. Such financial assistance will normally be lawful if given for the purposes of an employees' share scheme.

2.28 The benefit of any interest-free loan by the company to employees will be subject to income tax on the value of the notional interest foregone. Similarly, where shares are acquired on partly-paid terms, they will be treated as acquired with a loan equal to the unpaid amount and income tax will be payable on the value of the notional interest foregone under *FA 1988, s 162* (see 16.19).

Subsidiary company schemes

2.29 Subsidiary company schemes, whether share option schemes or otherwise, are relatively uncommon. This is partly due to the attitude of the Investment Committee of the ABI which is hostile to such schemes and partly because of the absence of any market in the shares. There are also very unattractive tax charges under *FA 1988, s 79* in respect of any increase in the value of the shares for up to seven years if the company is a 'dependent subsidiary'.

2.30 Under *FA 1988, s 79* all subsidiaries are presumed by reference to *FA 1988, s 86* to be 'dependent subsidiaries' for any period of account unless:

(a) the whole or substantially the whole of the company's business during the period of account is carried on with non-group members;

(b) during the period of account not more than 5 per cent of the company's growth in value is attributable to intra-group transactions (or there is no increase at all);

(c) the ultimate holding company gives a certificate to the Inspector of Taxes within two years after the end of the period of account, that the conditions in (a) and (b) above are satisfied;

(d) an auditor gives a similar certificate based on his own enquiries into the state of affairs of the company.

Chapter 3

The ABI and the NAPF Guidelines

3.1 A company with listed shares, or whose shares are traded on the Unlisted Securities Market (USM), and any private company with significant institutional shareholdings such as a management buy-out vehicle, needs to take note of the guidelines on employees' share schemes published by certain bodies representing institutional investors in order to ensure institutional support for any share scheme proposals. The best known guidelines are those published by the Association of British Insurers ('the ABI'), formerly the British Insurance Association. The National Association of Pension Funds ('the NAPF') published guidelines on share schemes for many years but no longer does so. It was a party to a joint statement with the ABI on Performance Targets in executive share option schemes and, apart from this, now merely recommends adherence to the ABI's detailed guidelines. Other bodies which have published guidelines in the past include bodies representing investment fund managers and unit trust managers, but neither of these bodies have published guidelines for at least 15 years.

Current guidelines sources

3.2 The sources for the current guidelines on employees' share schemes are, therefore, as follows:

- the ABI Guidelines published on 13 July 1987 ('the 1987 ABI Guidelines' at guideline 11)

- the ABI's Addendum to the 1987 ABI Guidelines relating to Replacement Options published on 6 May 1988 ('the 1988 ABI Guidelines')

- the ABI's Second Addendum to the 1987 ABI Guidelines relating to discounted price options and ESOPs published on 14 August 1991 ('the 1991 ABI Guidelines')

- the ABI/NAPF Joint Statement on Performance Targets in Executive Share Option Schemes published on 15 July 1993 ('the Joint Guidance')

3.3 The ABI and the NAPF Guidelines

Copies of each of the above documents are set out in 3.39 to 3.42 below.

Historical development of the ABI Guidelines

3.3 The earliest ABI Guidelines were published in the 1960s and contained just three recommendations:

(*a*) only full-time employees could participate;

(*b*) a limit on the number of shares which may be made available under share option schemes of 5 per cent of share capital over any period of ten years;

(*c*) no option could be granted over shares at a price which was less than the market value of those shares.

In the earliest guidelines there was no limit on the size of individual share options and it was not until the 1970s that a limit of four times earnings was introduced together with a 'flow rate' limit of 3 per cent of share capital in any period of three years.

3.4 The spread of profit sharing schemes in the 1970s using shares instead of cash, and eventually given statutory recognition in the *Finance Act 1978*, led to the introduction of a limit on the number of new shares which could be made available each year of 1 per cent of share capital.

3.5 An overall scheme limit of 10 per cent of share capital in ten years was put forward as a response to the growing number of all employees' share schemes in the late 1970s.

3.6 There has never been an overall limit on the number of new shares which may be made available under any savings-related share option scheme, although the limit on the amount an individual may contribute each month under his savings contract will have the effect of limiting the number of shares which may be made available. For a number of years the ABI's limit stood at £100 whilst the statutory limit was only £50; this was then replaced by a recommended limit of £150 when the statutory limit was increased to £100. Since 1991, the ABI appears to have accepted that schemes may provide for a maximum monthly savings limit linked to the current statutory limit so there is no need repeatedly to seek shareholder approval for any increase, but with the qualification, usually required in writing, that such increases will only be put into effect after the ABI has published a revised guideline limit.

3.7 Performance targets in executive share option schemes first appeared in the 1987 ABI Guidelines when companies were recommended to grant options exercisable on the achievement of a real

The ABI and the NAPF Guidelines **3.10**

growth in earnings per share over a three-year period. However, this guideline has not to date been reflected in the majority of schemes, if only because most schemes were established before the 1987 Guidelines were published. In addition, the rapid economic growth of the period made performance targets based on real growth in earnings per share seem largely irrelevant.

The ABI's 'replacement option' concession allowed companies to replace exercised options with fresh option grants (so that over any ten-year period, the value of options might exceed the ABI's normal limit of shares worth four times earnings). One condition for the grant of replacement options is that the Remuneration Committee, or at least a committee mainly comprising non-executive directors, must be satisfied there has been a significant improvement in the performance of the company. With the introduction of this indirect performance target as a condition of grant, the ABI was prepared to relax its requirement for performance targets on exercise. Only with the publication of the Joint Guidance in 1993 did it restate its requirement for a performance target as a condition of exercise of all options.

3.8 Generally speaking, therefore, the design of executive share option schemes has been affected by the timing of their introduction. Schemes established before early 1987 rarely had performance targets. Schemes established between the 1987 ABI Guidelines in mid-1987 and the 1988 ABI Guidelines in late 1988 often had a performance target of real growth in earnings per share; thereafter schemes tended to adopt the replacement option concession without any specific performance target as a condition of exercise.

3.9 The 1987 ABI Guidelines also introduced 'super options' (see 6.6 to 6.16) which were a response to the demand by some companies to grant executive options in excess of the limit of 5 per cent of share capital over any ten-year period, or to grant options to specific individuals in excess of four times their earnings to run concurrently. Under the 1987 ABI Guidelines, such options may be granted subject to five-year performance targets based on a growth in earnings per share which matches the upper quartile of FTSE 100 companies.

3.10 *FA 1991* introduced discounted price executive share options where the company has either a profit sharing or savings-related share option scheme approved under *TA 1988* (see 6.24 to 6.41). The ABI's initial response in its 1991 Guidelines was to accept such options on condition that a five-year performance target was imposed based on a growth in earnings per share of at least 110 per cent of the increase in the retail prices index over that period. The ABI also recommended that discounted price options were limited to no more than 25 per cent of an individual's total allocation of share options. However, the ABI and the NAPF now consider discounted price options as 'undesirable': see the Joint Guidance. It appears that whilst a number

3.11 *The ABI and the NAPF Guidelines*

of companies have adopted the power to grant discounted price options, only a very small minority have actually granted such options. In the event, companies have tended to be very cautious about the grant of such options especially since the publication of the Joint Guidance. Discounted price options are likely to remain unusual, at least until the economic climate changes.

NAPF Guidelines

3.11 The NAPF no longer publishes detailed guidelines. It was a party to the Joint Guidance in 1993 but apart from that merely recommends adherence to the ABI Guidelines.

Summary of current guidelines

Scheme limits

3.12 The ABI recommends 'rolling' limits on the number of new shares which may be issued based on a percentage of the issued share capital from time to time. These limits are:

(a) an overall limit under all schemes of 10 per cent in a period of ten years (1987 ABI Guidelines, introduction and paragraph 9);

(b) a 'flow rate' limit of 3 per cent in a period of three years under all schemes (1987 ABI Guidelines, paragraph 20(a)). In the year of the introduction of any savings-related share option scheme, a limit of 5 per cent in that and the previous four years is permitted provided executive options are limited to 3 per cent (1987 ABI Guidelines, paragraph 20(b));

(c) a limit on executive options of 5 per cent in a period of ten years (1987 ABI Guidelines, paragraph 9), but there are relaxations for companies with a small market capitalisation (see 1987 ABI Guidelines, paragraph 10) and for companies with 'super' options (see 1987 ABI Guidelines, paragraph 11);

(d) a limit of 1 per cent of the ordinary share capital each calendar year under profit sharing schemes (1987 ABI Guidelines, paragraph 1).

Strictly speaking, the 1 per cent limit on new shares under a profit sharing scheme is based on calendar years, but in practice a rolling limit based on the period of one year down to the proposed date of allocation will be acceptable.

Schemes often contain an alternative to the 'flow rate' limit in (b) above of 4 per cent in any three years where a savings-related share option scheme has been established, but this limit was removed from the ABI Guidelines in 1987.

3.13 Where replacement options are allowed under a scheme, the 1988 ABI Guidelines impose a limit of 2.5 per cent of the issued ordinary share capital in the four years following the adoption of the scheme (or its alteration to allow the grant of replacement options). Although the 1988 ABI Guidelines are unclear on whether this limit applies to the grant of options over existing (as well as newly issued) share capital, it is understood that the ABI are only concerned about applying this limit to new schemes (1988 ABI Guidelines, paragraph (ii)). Where the 2.5 per cent limit is incorporated in a new scheme, this leaves 2.5 per cent for the remaining six years of the ten-year life of the scheme; where replacement options are incorporated into an existing scheme, only the balance of the 5 per cent of share capital in any ten-year period is available.

3.14 In the case of a company with a small market capitalisation, a limit on executive share options of 10 per cent in ten years is allowed (in place of the normal limit of 5 per cent in ten years (see 3.12(c)). A market capitalisation is regarded as 'small' if it is £5m or less at the time of the proposed grant of options, providing the market value of the maximum number of shares available at the time of the adoption of the scheme does not exceed £500,000.

3.15 The NAPF's only guidelines (see 3.42) on limits are an overall limit of 10 per cent in ten years under all schemes and 5 per cent in ten years under executive share option schemes. Although it is not made clear whether this relates to existing share capital as well as new shares, it is understood that the limit only applies to the issue of new shares.

Duration of schemes

3.16 The 1987 ABI Guidelines provide that 'in order that shareholders may review the effectiveness of option arrangements, schemes should have a life of not more than ten years'. Executive and savings-related share option schemes are, therefore, limited to ten years (1987 ABI Guidelines, paragraphs 13 and 16). There are no limits on the duration of a profit sharing scheme under ABI Guidelines.

Eligibility

3.17 Under executive share option schemes, only directors or employees 'who are required to devote substantially the whole of their working time to the business of the grantor company or its subsidiaries' are eligible (1987 ABI Guidelines, paragraph 14). No specific eligibility criteria are laid down in relation to profit sharing and savings-related share option schemes. For many years the ABI informally indicated that participants should work at least 14 hours a week, but in practice the ABI will accept schemes which admit all part-timers.

3.18 The ABI and the NAPF Guidelines

Individual participation

3.18 The limit on executive options of shares worth four times the annual emoluments of the executive concerned (ABI Guidelines, paragraph 11). For this purpose, all options granted in the previous ten years must be counted against this limit. Executive options may be granted in excess of this limit if the conditions for either 'super' or 'replacement' options are satisfied (see 6.6 to 6.16). In recent pronouncements, the ABI has indicated that it favours 'phased' grants which appears to mean the grant of options spread over a number of years in relatively small numbers of shares.

3.19 The limit on participation in savings-related share option schemes is fixed by reference to a maximum savings contribution of £250 per month. Although this reflects the current limits in *TA 1988, 9 Sch 24(2)*, this has not always been the case (see 3.6) and the ABI reserves the right to fix a limit which may be different to the statutory limit. This means that although the ABI will now accept a provision in the scheme rules that the individual limit shall be linked to the statutory limit from time to time, companies are not expected to increase the limit unless the ABI has indicated it approves of any increase. In some cases, the ABI has sought written undertakings to this effect from companies.

Pricing

3.20 Normally, executive options must be granted by listed companies at not less than the middle market price of the shares in question at the time when the option is granted (1987 ABI Guidelines, paragraph 12). Under *TA 1988, 9 Sch*, the market value is normally construed for tax purposes as the quarter-up price.

3.21 In certain circumstances, options may be granted as a discount to the market value, but only where special conditions of exercise are imposed (see 'Discounted Price Options' in 6.24 to 6.41).

3.22 Under *TA 1988, 9 Sch 25*, approved savings-related share options may be granted at not manifestly less than 80 per cent of the market value of the same class of shares when the option is granted.

3.23 The price at which the trustees may subscribe for new shares in any profit sharing scheme is the middle market price of the shares on the dealing day immediately prior to the appropriation of profits. The number of shares appropriated should be based on such number as have a value equal to the average cost of the shares (inclusive of expenses) to the trustees (1987 ABI Guidelines, paragraph 5).

Timing of allocations

3.24 Executive share option schemes must provide for the grant of options within 42 days following the date of publication of the results of the company. Originally, it was the ABI's practice to expect employee invitations to be issued within 14 days of an announcement of results, leaving a further 30 days for the acceptance of applications and grant of options. However, the 14 day rule has fallen into disuse and the 1987 ABI Guidelines, paragraph 12 now simply refers to a grant of options within 42 days.

3.25 Since 1988 the ABI has also accepted a provision allowing the grant of executive share options at any other time the directors consider there are exceptional circumstances which justify the grant of options at that time, for example, upon the appointment of a new chief executive. The ABI has recently expressed reservations about this provision although it has condoned its insertion in many schemes over a number of years.

3.26 Generally speaking, companies may incorporate a similar 42 day grant period in savings-related share option schemes although the 1987 ABI Guidelines are silent on this.

3.27 The 1987 ABI Guidelines provide that appropriations of profits for profit sharing schemes shall be made once only by the directors after the announcement of the final results for the trading period in respect of which the appropriation is made and paid over to the trustees as soon as practicable (1987 ABI Guidelines, paragraph 3). In addition, all monies received by the trustees for the acquisition of shares must be applied so far as practicable forthwith in the subscription or purchase of shares for immediate appropriation to the individuals eligible under the scheme (1987 ABI Guidelines, paragraph 6). The ABI do not approve of the appropriation of profits being made after interim results.

Remuneration committees

3.28 The ABI and NAPF Guidelines have consistently recommended that executive options are granted by an independent committee of directors who will not themselves participate in the scheme and who will be prepared to satisfy themselves that any performance targets have been properly satisfied i.e. not as a result of accountancy manipulation.

Early leavers

3.29 In an executive share option scheme, provision may be made for the early exercise of options where a participant dies or ceases

3.30 *The ABI and the NAPF Guidelines*

employment, no distinction being made between 'good' and 'bad' leavers (1987 ABI Guidelines, paragraph 13). Options should be exercised within one year of leaving. As a concession, so that early leavers may exercise their options during a period when option gains are relieved from income tax under *TA 1988, s 185*, the ABI permits an extension of the right of exercise for early leavers 'until three and one half years from the date of grant'. In practice, the ABI accepts an extension until the latest of the following:

(*a*)   three and one-half years after the date of grant of the particular option;

(*b*)   three and one-half years after the date of grant of the latest option to be granted to the individual;

(*c*)   three and one-half years after the last tax-exempt exercise whilst the individual was in employment.

3.30 The 1987 ABI Guidelines restrict the grant of options to persons within two years of normal retirement (1987 ABI Guidelines, paragraph 13). As an unpublished alternative, the ABI allows schemes to provide for the grant of options even to persons within two years of normal retirement, but subject to a condition of exercise that the holder must have held the option for at least two years at the date he actually retires. This enables options to be granted to those directors whose actual period of service extends beyond normal retirement date.

3.31 Whilst the rights of early exercise will normally apply regardless of the achievement of any specified performance target, the ABI informally recommend that where the cessation of employment is voluntary — such as a retirement at normal retirement age — that the performance target should nevertheless apply, even if on a pro rata basis to reflect the unexpired part of the performance period.

3.32 Following, the publication of the Joint Guidance companies may need to reconsider the extent to which performance targets should apply on early exercises. Ideally, the Remuneration Committee might be able to exercise a discretion to allow exercise in whole or in part although optionholders would need to be given an absolute right of exercise without regard to performance targets where a person leaves on account of injury, disability or redundancy. This is because the Inland Revenue will only accept a discretion to allow exercise if there is an absolute right in these 'core' circumstances.

3.33 The ABI Guidelines are silent on the question of early exercise in savings-related share option schemes or profit sharing schemes.

'Super' options

3.34 'Super' options are options which may be granted in excess of normal limits on individual participation on scheme limits (see 'Super options': 6.6 to 6.16).

The ABI and the NAPF Guidelines **3.39**

Replacement options

3.35 Replacement options are described in the 1988 ABI Guidelines (see 'Replacement Options': 6.17 to 6.23). Although replacement options may only be granted on the basis of a significant improvement in the performance of the company in the previous two or three years, following the publication of the Joint Guidance, they must also contain appropriate performance targets on exercise.

Performance targets

3.36 Following the Joint Statement no specific performance targets are now put forward although Remuneration Committees are urged to impose performance targets which use a 'realistic measure of management performance'. Such reticence about the performance target to be used arises from an agreement to differ between the ABI and the NAPF about the performance measure which constitutes the best indication of long-term sustained growth of a company. The ABI prefer a performance target based on earnings per share increases whilst the NAPF prefer a measure based on a share price benchmark such as outstripping the FT Actuaries All Share Index. The ABI and NAPF are probably wise in avoiding any specific performance targets given that they can only too easily become inappropriate in changed economic conditions. In addition, the ABI and NAPF probably never expected the Inland Revenue's inflexibility towards the variation of performance targets (see 5.86). Following the Joint Guidance, Remuneration Committees are now responsible for choosing the performance targets and will bear the employees' indignation if the performance targets turn out to be inappropriate.

'Underwater' options

3.37 Both the ABI and NAPF are against the cancellation of 'underwater' options and grant of replacement options.

ESOPs

3.38 See 15.72 to 15.74 for the ABI and NAPF's attitude to ESOPs.

The 1987 ABI Guidelines

3.39 The text of the 1987 ABI Guidelines published on 13 July 1987 is as follows:

3.39 The ABI and the NAPF Guidelines

'Share Option and Profit Sharing Incentive Schemes

Summary of Revision to Guidelines to Requirements of Insurance Offices as Investors

The Association of British Insurers has reviewed the operation of the guidelines in the light of developing practice and the recent successes in persuading companies to adopt performance criteria as a condition for the exercise of options. Profit sharing arrangements are already linked to performance and the Association has sought to devise performance criteria which will require sustained improvement in the underlying performance of a company as a condition for the exercise of all options other than options linked to a savings contract.

The guidelines now make provision for the inclusion in executive share option schemes adopted in the future of a minimum performance requirement that options should only be exercisable if during the option period there has been a real growth in the company's earnings per share. Provision is also made for the grant of options by a company over more than 5% of its Ordinary share capital and in excess of four times the annual emoluments of the participant provided that such additional options shall normally be exercisable not earlier than five years from the date of grant and then only if the growth in earnings per share of the company over any five year period following the date of grant has been such as places the company in the top quartile by reference to the growth in earnings per share of the FTSE 100 companies. Arrangements which involve a participant holding options over more than four times emoluments at any one time should require performance of a specified and demanding amount in place of the minimum real growth requirement.

In all cases such arrangements are subject to the overall limit of 10% of a company's Ordinary share capital for all employee share schemes in any ten year period with a maximum participation in the same period by any one individual of eight times annual emoluments.

It has been felt sensible to incorporate a provision that in future options should be granted by an independent committee of the board and preferably by a committee of non-executive directors, who will not themselves participate in the options. It will be expected that this committee will satisfy itself with regard to options exercised, that the various performance requirements have been met on a consistent basis, i.e. the requirements are not achieved by the inclusion of extraordinary items or creative accounting.

In circumstances where the annual remuneration of senior employees already includes a substantial element of performance related pay, consideration should be given to the inclusion of an

The ABI and the NAPF Guidelines 3.39

overall cap limiting the maximum individual participation in order to avoid an excessive amount of options being granted to any one individual. Details of options granted in any one year should in future be included as a specific item in the report and accounts with a statement of the number of employees participating in a company's scheme.

It is believed that such schemes should provide a clear community of interest between employees and the shareholders and that this is best achieved by the grant of options only over the share capital of the parent equity thus ensuring that any benefit received by the employee is available equally to the shareholders. Arrangements which involve the grant of options over the share capital of a subsidiary company will normally be opposed therefore unless in the case of an overseas subsidiary the employee would be precluded by local legislation from participating or, in the case of a UK subsidiary at least 25% of its Ordinary share capital is quoted on a recognised exchange and held outside the group.

The guidelines, which replace those issued by the BIA Investment Protection Committee in April 1985, are intended to ensure that where share option arrangements are proposed there will be a real incentive to produce sustained growth in a company's performance, and a community of interest between participants and shareholders. The framework of schemes which are consistent with the spirit of the guidelines should ensure that the share capital earmarked for such schemes will be available to employees as widely as possible and be adequate to meet all reasonable needs of a company in this context. Consideration will of course be given to a situation where the circumstances are not covered by the guidelines.

Association of British Insurers Investment Committee

Share Option and Profit Sharing Incentive Schemes
Revised Guidelines to Requirements of Insurance Offices as Investors

The guidelines to employee share option schemes have been revised to reflect evolving practice and to incorporate for the first time performance requirements as a condition of the exercise of any option (other than an option granted pursuant to a SAYE scheme which is available to all employees). The requirements set out below outline the restrictions which Insurance Offices regard as essential under such schemes if excessive appropriation of the equity entitlement of Ordinary shareholders is to be avoided.

Insurance Offices have a duty on behalf of policyholders and others on whose behalf they invest to permit only those schemes which make available such an appropriation of the profits and share capital as is felt to be equitable having regard to the finance provided by the proprietors of the company in the past and their reasonable expectations of growth in the future. The Committee

3.39 The ABI and the NAPF Guidelines

believes that the method of providing incentive arrangements in any company is a matter for its management and that the directors will take account of all the interests concerned in formulating the particular schemes proposed which, in all cases involving the issue of equity capital, should be submitted to shareholders for approval. However, as judgement of the incentive effects of particular arrangements involving the equity capital of a company is essentially a matter for its shareholders, observance of all requirements set out below will not necessarily ensure support for schemes which shareholders may feel are inappropriate on other grounds. The guidelines are intended to indicate the basic provisions necessary to give general effect to the principles outlined above in the hope that any scheme proposed which is consistent with the spirit as well as the letter of the requirements will ensure a genuine community of interest between shareholders and scheme beneficiaries. The main objectives of the guidelines are to ensure that over a period of ten years no more than 10% of the shareholders' equity is utilised for schemes of all kinds and that options which are not linked to SAYE savings contracts may be exercised only if there are accompanying and genuine long-term benefits to the company. Furthermore, in order to conserve the benefits under such schemes for future participants, no more than 3% of the equity should normally be appropriated for all forms of scheme in any three year period. In order that shareholders may review the effectiveness of option arrangements, schemes should have a life of not more than ten years.

Accordingly, unless there are very exceptional circumstances, insurance Offices may be expected to oppose proposals for the adoption of any scheme which does not satisfy each of the following requirements.

(a) *Profit sharing schemes*

1. The aggregate of the amount of the equity share capital of the proposing company that may be issued in any calendar year by way of subscription under profit sharing schemes may not exceed 1 per cent of such share capital in issue on the day preceding the appropriation of profits for the purpose of the scheme as set out under Requirement 3.

2. The aggregate of the amounts that may be appropriated out of profits in any calendar year for all profit sharing arrangements involving the acquisition by subscription or purchase of the company's shares may not exceed 5 per cent of that proportion of the profits of the relevant trading period before tax and excluding any exceptional item which, in the opinion of the directors, is attributable to the operation of participating employees.

The ABI and the NAPF Guidelines 3.39

3. The appropriation of profits for profit sharing schemes shall be made once only by the directors after announcement of the final results for the trading period in respect of which the appropriation is made and paid over to the trustees of the scheme as soon as practicable.

4. The price at which shares are subscribed under Requirement 1 shall be the middle market price of the shares of the same class on the dealing day prior to the appropriation of profits under Requirement 3.

5. On any occasion when part of the appropriation under Requirement 3 is applied in the purchase of shares in the market, the price at which shares are made available to participants under the scheme shall be the average per share of the cost of the shares subscribed under Requirement 4 and the cost including expenses of the shares purchased.

6. Any monies received by the trustees for the acquisition of shares shall not be retained but shall be applied as far as practicable forthwith in the subscription or purchase of shares for immediate appropriation to the individuals eligible under the scheme.

7. Any monies received by the trustees by way of dividends on the shares held in trust shall not be retained but shall be distributed immediately to the individual to whom the relevant shares have been appropriated.

8. On any occasion when the voting rights attached to the shares held in trust fall to be exercised, the trustees shall obtain the instructions of the individuals to whom the relevant shares have been appropriated and exercise the voting rights accordingly.

(b) *Option schemes*

9. Except as provided in 10 and 11 below, the amount of Ordinary share capital issued or issuable pursuant to all option schemes, other than schemes linked to an SAYE contract, shall be limited to 5% of the Ordinary share capital at the time a participation is granted and such options should normally be exercisable only if there has been a real growth in the earnings per share of the company over a three year period following the date of grant. In appropriate circumstances up to a further 5% may be set aside for such schemes provided that any options over shares in excess of 5% of the issued Ordinary capital shall be exercisable not earlier than five years from the date of grant and normally then only if the company's growth in earnings per share over a period

3.39 The ABI and the NAPF Guidelines

of at least five years has been such as would place it in the top quartile of the FTSE 100 companies by reference to growth in earnings per share over the same period. The aggregate share capital issued or issuable by the company under all share option or profit sharing schemes within the preceding ten years must not exceed 10% of the Ordinary share capital of the company at any time when a participation is granted.

10. In the case of a company having a market capitalisation of £5 million or less, up to 10% of the equity capital when aggregated in accordance with 9 above may be issuable under the scheme provided that the market value of such capital does not exceed £500,000 at the time of the adoption of the scheme.

11. The market value at the relevant time of the share capital to be appropriated, by allotment or by options granted, to any one participant when aggregated with the market value at the time of appropriation of any share capital appropriated in the preceding ten years to that participant under the proposed or any other share option schemes (other than an SAYE linked option) must not exceed four times the participant's total annual emoluments from the companies within the scheme and there should be a condition that such options will normally be exercisable only if over any three year period from the date of grant, the company has achieved as a minimum a real growth in earnings per share.

In appropriate cases options having a market value of up to a further four times a participant's annual emoluments may be granted if such additional options are exercisable not earlier than the fifth anniversary from the date of grant and normally then only if the company's growth in earnings per share over a period of at least five years following the date of grant has been such as would place it in the top quartile of the FTSE 100 companies by reference to growth in earnings per share over the same period.

In the case of schemes approved by the Inland Revenue under the *Finance Act 1984* and which do not provide option linking arrangements, options granted up to 1 October 1979 under other schemes may, for the purpose of the individual participation limit, be disregarded and options granted under other schemes after 1 October 1979 but before the adoption of the proposed scheme may be taken into account at one half of the market value of the relevant shares at the date of the grant.

The ABI and the NAPF Guidelines 3.39

12. The price at which shares are issued to participants, or at which participants are given an option to subscribe, must not be less than the middle market price of the shares in question (or similar formula) at the time when the participation is granted which must be within a period of 42 days following the date of publication of the results of the grantor company.

13. No option may be granted for more than ten years or exercised within three years from the date of the grant in the case of those options subject to a real growth in earnings per share requirement or within five years from the date of grant for those options subject to top quartile growth in earnings per share requirements. In the event of a take-over of the grantor company or the death or cessation of employment of the participant options may be exercised or lapse within one year or within three and one half years from the date of grant, whichever is the later, unless arrangements have been made for the option to be converted, in the event of a take-over, into options of the offeror company. No option may be granted within the two years preceding the normal retirement date of the participant either under his contract of employment or otherwise and not later than ten years from the date of the adoption of the schemes.

14. Participation under the proposed scheme must be restricted to directors or employees who are required to devote substantially the whole of their working time to the business of the grantor company or its subsidiaries and options, which must be non-assignable, may normally be granted only over the share capital of the parent company. As a general rule any arrangement involving the grant of options over a subsidiary company will be opposed unless in the case of an overseas subsidiary where necessitated by local legislation or in appropriate circumstances where at least 25% of the share capital of a subsidiary is quoted on a recognised stock exchange and held outside the group.

(c) *Savings related schemes*

15. The proposed scheme must provide that in the period of ten years commencing at the date of its adoption the total amount of share capital issued or issuable under any savings related scheme when aggregated with the total amount of share capital issued or issuable under any other profit sharing or option scheme in the preceding ten years, whether or not approved under the *Finance Acts*, shall not exceed 10% of the equity share capital of the company at the time when capital is issued or issuable under the

3.39 The ABI and the NAPF Guidelines

proposed scheme. 'Issuable' share capital includes any share capital in respect of which options have been granted or rights may be exercised.

16. Participation under the proposed scheme may be granted only within a period of ten years from the date of its adoption.

17. The price at which participants are given an option to subscribe must not be less than the middle market price of the shares of the class under option at the time when the option is granted unless the scheme has received Inland Revenue approval under statutory provisions relating to contractual savings schemes in which event the option price must be not less than 80% of such middle market price.

18. No part of the equity share capital may be issued or issuable to participants for subscription out of the proceeds of a contractual savings scheme except as provided under 15 above.

19. The maximum amount that may be contracted for savings by individual participation under the scheme shall not exceed £250 per calendar month.

(d) General

20. (a) To conserve benefits for future participants all schemes must normally provide that not more than 3% of the equity capital may be appropriated for options or subscribed out of profits under all relevant schemes in any year and the two preceding years.

    (b) In the year of introduction of any scheme or schemes otherwise complying with the above requirements and linked to an SAYE contract and available to all employees generally, the restriction under 20(a) need not be observed provided that the percentage of equity capital appropriated for all options or subscribed out of profits under all relevant schemes in any year and the four preceding years does not exceed 5% and provided that options which are not linked to SAYE arrangements shall remain subject to the limit of 3% as under 20(a).

21. All options (other than linked to an SAYE Contract) should preferably be granted by a committee of non-executive directors of the company or at least by an independent committee of directors who will not themselves participate in the options. This committee will be expected to satisfy itself that

The ABI and the NAPF Guidelines **3.40**

prior to the exercise of options, relevant performance criteria have been fully satisfied on a consistent basis, i.e. they have not been achieved by 'creative accounting' or by the inclusion of inappropriate or extraordinary items, and they are accountable to shareholders for such. In appropriate circumstances it would be expected that such a committee will impose an overall cap on the maximum participation under option arrangements by any one individual.

13th July 1987
(Amended 14th August 1991)'

The 1988 ABI Guidelines

3.40 The text of the 1988 ABI Guidelines published on 6 May 1988 is as follows:

'Addendum to Share Option and Profit Sharing Schemes Guidelines

Following representations by a significant number of the larger companies in the UK, all of whom expressed complete support for the guideline limit of 5% of capital for executive share option schemes, the ABI Investment Committee has agreed to consider a relaxation of guideline 11 in certain circumstances. This would have the effect of allowing the grant following exercise of existing options of replacement options in excess of the guideline limit of four times earnings without requiring satisfaction of the top quartile eps growth provision as a condition for their exercise. Consideration would be given to the amendment of existing schemes to incorporate this revised approach.

This relaxation would be subject to the following minimum conditions:

(i) The scheme must be administered by and the grant of options supervised by a remuneration committee consisting wholly or mainly of non-executive directors.

(ii) In the case of an existing scheme the total of options granted within four years from the date of the amendment shall not exceed 2.5% of the issued ordinary share capital of the company with any balance within the overall 5% limit remaining available for the unexpired term of the scheme if any.

In the case of a new scheme it would be envisaged that the 2.5% could be utilised in the first four years of the scheme with the remaining 2.5% being available for the remaining six years.

3.41 The ABI and the NAPF Guidelines

(iii) The remuneration committee must, prior to granting replacement options, be satisfied that there has been a significant improvement in the performance of the company over the two to three years preceding the regrant.

(iv) The Chairman of a company making any such amendment should emphasise that the 5% limit for the executive share option scheme over a 10 year period is entirely appropriate and adequate for such purposes. He should also address the importance placed by offices as investors on underlying performance by a positive statement that replacement options will be granted having regard to the performance of the company.

In any cases where it is desirable, the yearly basis on which the above limit is calculated may, for the purposes of the scheme, be that of the financial reporting year'.

The 1991 ABI Guidelines

3.41 The text of the 1991 ABI Guidelines published on 14 August 1991 is as follows:

'Dear Sir,

Share Option Schemes — Finance Act 1991

There has been speculation in recent months in the press as to the reaction of institutional investors to the proposal announced by the Chancellor earlier this year extending the advantages of an Inland Revenue approved share option scheme to options granted over shares at a discount of up to 15 per cent to the current market price. The Finance Bill has been enacted and I am now able to let you have a second addendum to the ABI guidelines on share incentive schemes which addresses this development.

ABI members generally welcome the encouragement that is being given to ESOPs and other share participation arrangements which genuinely widen and deepen share ownership, and encourage employee share participation. There is concern, however, that the grant of options over share capital at a discount to market price must increase the cost of such options to existing shareholders and it is considered reasonable, therefore, that this additional cost should be acknowledged by requiring underlying and sustained real growth as a condition of exercise of such options. The second addendum reflects the desire on the part of investing institutions for sustained and real growth in companies in which they have invested.

Consideration has been given to the many requests that have been received to provide an indication of the reaction of offices to the various ESOP and ESOT arrangements that have appeared so far.

The ABI and the NAPF Guidelines 3.41

The main cause of concern for institutional investors in the context of ESOPs is if they are used other than constructively, e.g., as an anti-takeover device. The opportunity has been taken to suggest therefore that, where a company introduces an ESOP and it is the intention that that trust or plan should be permitted to hold more than 5 per cent of the issued ordinary share capital of the company at any time, it is in the spirit of good corporate governance that the Board of that company would seek prior consent of shareholders to such an arrangement. It is not the intention to issue any further guidelines on ESOPs at this point in time unless there is evidence that such arrangements are not being used primarily to widen share ownership.

Certain other amendments have been made to the guidelines, in particular to accommodate the 20 per cent discount and higher individual limit permissible under SAYE linked arrangements, and to reflect current practice.

It is hoped that the enclosed addendum, which now forms part of the complete guidelines, a copy of which is attached, will be helpful and be regarded as a constructive approach which will assist those companies wishing to offer their employees option at a discount, to do so without disturbing existing option arrangements or dramatically increasing the dilutive effect of options. If you have any queries, I or one of my colleagues will be pleased to discuss the matter further with you.

Yours faithfully,

RD Regan
Secretary
Investment Committee

Second Addendum to Share Option and Profit Sharing Scheme Guidelines

The ABI guidelines on share option and share incentive schemes are presently designed to provide a framework whereby companies will be able to operate schemes as widely as possible whilst avoiding undue dilution of the interests of existing shareholders. The Investment Committee has reviewed these guidelines on share option and incentive schemes in the light of the announcement by Government that the advantages of Inland Revenue approved executive option schemes would be extended to options granted over shares at a maximum discount of 15% to market price in those circumstances where companies also have in operation an all-employee share scheme.

The grant of options at a discount to market price must increase the cost of such options to existing ordinary shareholders. Such a grant may also create problems in circumstances where a substantial number of options have already been granted to executives under

3.42 *The ABI and the NAPF Guidelines*

an existing scheme at full market price and other executives are now to be granted options at a discount to market price.

In order to address these two points, it is felt reasonable that where companies do grant options to executives at a discount of a maximum of 15% to market price, such options should be exercisable only after a period of 5 years and be conditional upon some sustained real return to the company, for example, growth in earnings per share equal to RPI plus 2% over any 5 year period from the date of grant.

In order to avoid existing grantees being disadvantaged, the maximum number of shares subject to options granted to an individual at the 15% discount (apart from any SAYE options, etc.) should be limited to one quarter of the total options granted to him.

The additional interest which is now developing in ESOPs and ESOTs is welcomed in the context that they can genuinely result in widening share ownership. Such schemes are, however, increasingly being advocated as providing a means of building up 'an anti-takeover stake'. Anti-takeover devices are generally felt to be undesirable. It is suggested that where an ESOP or ESOT would be capable of building up a holding of more than 5% of a company's issued Ordinary share capital, the arrangements should first be submitted to shareholders for their prior approval.

It is suggested that arrangements in accordance with the foregoing will encourage companies genuinely to allocate shares earmarked for employee share arrangements as widely as possible, will avoid unnecessary tensions or disparity between option holders and will result in a genuine long-term increase in productivity and earnings which will benefit employee and shareholder alike.

14th August 1991'.

The Joint Guidance

3.42   The text of the Joint Guidance published on 15 July 1993 is as follows:

'Share Scheme Guidance

A Joint Statement from the Investment Committees of the ABI and the NAPF

The relevance of share scheme guidance

1. Although share options are just one element of employee remuneration, shareholders are required to approve the proposals for the establishment of a scheme. Guidance

The ABI and the NAPF Guidelines 3.42

issued by shareholder bodies aims to provide parameters within which companies can devise schemes with reasonable certainty of approval by major shareholders. Similarly, those shareholders generally regard schemes with increased confidence if they understand that they comply with general principles regarded as reasonable and appropriate by shareholder bodies.

Share schemes as remuneration

2. It is recognised that share schemes can be an important part of an executive's remuneration. However, executive share schemes can deliver reward to company managements even when it is judged that the company's performance has been poor. This is not in the interests of shareholders nor is it readily understandable by the public or by employees.

   It is a fundamental requirement that exercise of executive share options should be subject to some realistic measure of management performance. The difficulties of prescribing one single measurement of long-term sustained performance — which will be regarded as appropriate for all situations — is recognised. It is generally acknowledged, however, that linking the exercise of options to sustained underlying financial performance is in the best interest of the company and long term investors. Such linkage requires sustained results before any benefit can be taken by an option holder and creates a community of interest between corporate management and the shareholder.

   It is expected that the rules of any executive scheme should include prudent limits concerning the level of share option grant to any individual and concerning the timing or phasing of such grants.

   Although, by law, companies are permitted to issue executive options at a discount to the share's market price in certain circumstances, companies should note that this is viewed as undesirable.

The management of share schemes

3. It is felt that a Remuneration Committee — constituted in accordance with the 'Cadbury' Code of Best Practice — is best placed to determine how management should be motivated to produce results which further the aim of sustained financial performance. **Any company proposing a share scheme should note, therefore, that support for the proposals is unlikely to be forthcoming unless the company has in existence a properly**

3.42 The ABI and the NAPF Guidelines

constituted Remuneration Committee which has formal responsibility for the scheme. Such a Committee will be fully aware of the circumstances of the company in question and it follows that it should, therefore, be in the best position to determine the most relevant and effective performance criteria.

It is important that shareholders understand the basis on which the chosen criteria have been set. Full details of the criteria which are felt appropriate should, therefore, be disclosed both when the scheme is put forward for approval by shareholders and annually thereafter.

4. In concluding that the criteria should be set by the Remuneration Committee, it is recognised that some indication of what is looked for in such a formula would be helpful. The ABI and the NAPF are agreed that the aim of any formula should be to produce significant and sustained improvement in the underlying financial performance of the concern in question. Both will expect the formula to be based, therefore, on criteria which genuinely reflect the effort and achievement of the management in question.

Safeguards must be incorporated by the Remuneration Committee to ensure that measures chosen are appropriate to the circumstances of the company and are used consistently. Furthermore, they must not be capable of manipulation nor must they be influenced by the particular accounting treatment of various items.

5. The institutions represented by the ABI and the NAPF will be looking, therefore, at the details disclosed by Remuneration Committees to satisfy themselves that, in the circumstances of an individual company, the criteria chosen are consistent with the foregoing. The manner in which the Remuneration Committee undertakes these responsibilities will be viewed by shareholders as one of the measures of the effectiveness of a company's non-executive directors'.

Chapter 4

Establishment of Schemes

4.1 There are a number of reasons why companies establish 'employees' share schemes' rather than enter into separate agreements with each individual employee. First, convenience, since a scheme removes the need to set out the full rights of participants in a separate agreement on each occasion an option is granted. Secondly, there are considerable company law advantages. Thirdly, the tax advantages under *TA 1988* are only available in respect of 'schemes'. Fourthly, for listed companies the use of a scheme avoids the need to obtain shareholders' specific approval of each grant of an option to a director.

Company Law

Meaning of 'employees' share scheme'

4.2 An employees' share scheme is defined by *CA 1985, s 743* as follows:

'... a scheme for encouraging or facilitating the holding of shares or debentures in a company by or for the benefit of:

(*a*) the bona fide employees or former employees of the company, the company's subsidiary or holding company or a subsidiary of the company's holding company, or

(*b*) the wives, husbands, widows, widowers or children or stepchildren under the age of 18 of such employees or former employees'.

4.3 There are a number of difficulties which arise in relation to the construction of this definition. First, the legislation refers to '*the* ... employees ...' and '*the* wives ... ' and this could mean *all* such persons. However, one meaning for the word 'the' when used with a noun in the plural is 'those who are' and this seems the better construction. In other words, the definition of 'employees' share schemes' sets out the categories of persons who may be included in an employees' share scheme, but it does not lay down that all persons

4.4 Establishment of Schemes

within these categories must be included. However, it is unlikely that an arrangement intended to benefit only directors would amount to a 'scheme' unless it is the intention that participation will be widened subsequently.

4.4 Another difficulty arises where a particular scheme allows participation by persons outside the permitted categories in *CA 1985, s 743*, for instance, non-executive directors, self-employed consultants and the employees of joint venture companies or other non-subsidiaries. There is no authority on this, but in the author's view a distinction should be made between allocations to qualifying and non-qualifying persons, and the allocations to qualifying persons should be treated as made under an employees' share scheme.

Allocations to non-qualifying persons should be treated as separate arrangements and, therefore, should not enjoy the company law benefits normally available in respect of allocations under employees' share schemes (see 4.5 and 4.6 below).

Directors' authority to allot shares

4.5 *CA 1985, s 80* provides that directors shall not exercise any power of the company to allot 'relevant securities' unless they are so authorised by a resolution in general meeting or under the articles of association. Shares allotted in pursuance of an 'employees' share scheme' within the meaning of *CA 1985, s 743* are not 'relevant securities'. An 'allotment' of shares means not only the issue of new shares, but also the grant of an option over such shares.

Disapplication of pre-emption provisions

4.6 *CA 1985, s 89* gives the shareholders of a company a right to be offered any proposed allotment of 'equity securities' in priority to third parties. However, by *CA 1985, s 89(5)* such pre-emption rights do not apply to an offer of equity securities under an employees' share scheme.

Prohibition of financial assistance in the purchase of shares

4.7 *CA 1985, s 151* provides that it is unlawful for a company to give financial assistance directly or indirectly to a person for the acquisition of its shares, or shares in any holding company. Amongst the exceptions to this is 'the provision by a company, in good faith in the interests of the company, of financial assistance for the purposes of an employees' share scheme' (see *CA 1985, s 153(4)(b)*). 'Financial assistance' will be tainted if the purpose is to establish an impediment to a possible takeover (*Hogg v Cramphorn [1967] Ch 254*). 'Financial

Establishment of Schemes **4.10**

assistance' includes any loan guarantee or other financial assistance given to 'another person', such as an ESOP trustee, for the acquisition of shares.

Tax reliefs available for approved schemes

4.8 The various tax reliefs are only available in respect of 'schemes' which have been approved under the *Taxes Act 1988* by the Board of Inland Revenue. The Inland Revenue regard any scheme as comprising not only the rules, but all documentation given to employees (see 4.29 and 4.31(*a*)). The Inland Revenue wishes to see all relevant documentation upon an application for approval under *TA 1988*.

Listed companies

4.9 Under the Listing Rules, an agreement between a company and a director for the grant of an option to subscribe for shares in the company is a 'transaction with a related party' requiring an announcement to the Stock Exchange and a circular to shareholders seeking prior approval to the transaction. However, there is a dispensation where the transaction either involves the issue of shares or the grant of an option to a director of the company, its parent undertaking or any of its subsidiary undertakings in accordance with the terms of an employees' share scheme provided the scheme does not have the effect of conferring benefits only on directors of such companies.

Memorandum and articles of association

4.10 It is common for a company's memorandum of association to incorporate a power enabling the company to establish employees' share schemes. A typical form of words for such a power is as follows:

> 'To establish, maintain, manage, support and contribute to any schemes for the acquisition of shares in the Company or its holding company by or for the benefit of any individuals who are or were at any time in the employment of, or directors or officers of:
>
> (i) the Company; or
>
> (ii) any company which is or was its holding company or is or was a subsidiary of the Company or any such holding company; or
>
> (iii) any other company or former company connected or associated in any way with the Company or with the whole or any part of its undertaking,
>
> and to lend money to any such individuals or to trustees on behalf of such individuals to enable them to acquire shares in the Company or in its holding company and to establish, maintain, manage and

4.11 Establishment of Schemes

support (financially or otherwise) any schemes for sharing profits of the Company or any other such company as aforesaid with any such individuals'.

4.11 However, the absence of any such express power will not be fatal. *CA 1985, s 3A* provides that where a company's memorandum of association states that the object of the company is to carry on business as a general commercial company then the company has the power to do all such things as are incidental or conducive to the carrying on of any trade or business by it. This would include the establishment of an employees' share scheme.

Directors' fiduciary duties

4.12 Under company law, there are various provisions intended to ensure that the director acts in the best interests of the company and avoids conflicts of interest. *CA 1985, s 317* imposes a duty on a director to declare his interest in contracts in which he is interested. In most companies, the articles of association restrict a director voting at meetings of directors on matters in which he is personally interested (see *Regulation 94* of *Table A* of the *CA 1985*). In principle, every director is potentially interested in an employees' share scheme and, therefore, voting restrictions usually need to be relaxed where an employees' share scheme is to be considered at a meeting of the directors. For this reason, the resolution to establish an employees' share scheme will normally need to relax the restrictions in the articles of association on voting by directors. Strictly speaking, any such resolution should be passed as a special resolution if it is intended to override the provisions of the articles of association.

Prohibition of the allotment of shares at a discount to the nominal value

4.13 *CA 1985, s 100* provides that no shares may be allotted at a discount. In a share option scheme, this will mean that the subscription price of new shares must be fixed at a price which is not less than the nominal value.

4.14 Whilst options may not be granted at a discount to the nominal value, many share option schemes, including approved schemes, provide for the adjustment of options in the event of certain variations of share capital such as a right issue. This will normally involve a reduction in the price of the shares under option as well as an increase in the number of shares. The question arises whether any adjustment can be made such that the adjusted option price may be less than the nominal value of a share. In order to overcome the prohibition under *CA 1985, s 100*, the difference between the adjusted option price and the nominal value would need to be paid up out of

Establishment of Schemes 4.16

a capitalisation of reserves. *Table A* only allows capitalisation issues in favour of members of the company and so the company's articles of association may need to be altered to allow a specific power to capitalise reserves in favour of persons who may not be members of the company i.e. optionholders. An appropriate power is as follows:

'Where, pursuant to an employees' share scheme (within the meaning of *section 743* of the *Companies Act 1985*) the Company has granted options to subscribe for ordinary shares on terms which provide (*inter alia*) for adjustments to the subscription price payable on the exercise of such options or to the number of shares to be allotted upon such exercise in the event of any increase or reduction in or other reorganisation of the Company's issued share capital and an otherwise appropriate adjustment would result in the subscription price for any share being less than its nominal value, then, subject to the provisions of the Articles, the Directors may on the exercise of any of the options concerned and payment of the subscription price which would have applied had such adjustment been made, capitalise any profits or reserves (including share premium account and capital redemption reserve) to the extent necessary to pay up the unpaid balance of the nominal value of the shares which fall to be allotted on the exercise of such options and to apply such amount in paying up such balance and to allot shares fully paid accordingly'.

Stock Exchange Listing Rules

4.15 Listed companies proposing to establish or alter employees' share schemes need to take account of the requirements set out in *The Listing Rules* published by the London Stock Exchange and commonly known as 'The Yellow Book'. The provisions relating to employees' share schemes were substantially revised in the latest edition of *The Listing Rules* which applies from 1 December 1993. The main change in the 1993 edition of *The Listing Rules* is that the Stock Exchange no longer reviews proposed employees' share schemes in advance although six copies of the circular and two copies of the scheme documents in their final form must be lodged with the Stock Exchange no later than the time the circular is despatched to shareholders.

4.16 Preliminary drafts of the proposed 1993 Listing Rules as circulated for discussion in June 1993 had included a proposal that all employees' share schemes, as defined by *CA 1985, s 743*, whether they used new or existing shares, should in future require prior shareholders' approval. After consultation, the London Stock Exchange reinstated the previous requirements that schemes need only be submitted for shareholders' approval where they involve the issue of new shares although it is understood that this issue remains under review. It follows, therefore, that schemes using only existing

4.17 *Establishment of Schemes*

shares through an ESOP do not require shareholders' prior approval at the present time.

Shareholders' approval for the establishment of a scheme

4.17 An employees' share scheme of a listed company incorporated in the United Kingdom (and of any of its subsidiary undertakings even where that subsidiary undertaking is incorporated or operates overseas) must be approved by an ordinary resolution of the shareholders of the company in general meeting prior to its adoption if the scheme involves or may involve the issue of new shares. A company must consult the Stock Exchange on the application of this requirement to any employees' share schemes (involving the issue of new shares) which is intended to apply to employees of associated undertakings.

Contents of a circular to shareholders

4.18 Under *The Listing Rules* a circular to shareholders for the establishment of an employees' share scheme must:

(a) include either the full text of the scheme or a description of its principal terms;

(b) include, where directors of the company are trustees of the scheme, or have a direct or indirect interest in the trustees, details of such trusteeship or interest;

(c) state that the scheme cannot be altered to the advantage of the participants without the prior approval of shareholders in general meeting (except for minor amendments to benefit the administration of the scheme and the amendments to obtain or maintain favourable tax, exchange control or regulatory treatment for participants in the scheme or for the company operating the scheme or for members of its group);

(d) if the scheme is not circulated to shareholders, include a statement that it will be available for inspection at a place in or near the City of London or such other place as the Stock Exchange may determine and at the place of the meeting from the date of the despatch of the circular until the close of the shareholders' meeting which will approve the scheme;

(e) comply with the general requirements for the contents of a circular, *viz*:

  (i) provide a clear and adequate explanation of its subject matter;

  (ii) if voting or other action is required, contain all information necessary to allow the holders of the securities to make a properly informed decision;

Establishment of Schemes **4.21**

(iii) if voting or other action is required, contain a heading drawing attention to the importance of the document and to ordinary holders of securities who are in doubt as to what action to take to consult appropriate independent advisers;

(iv) state that where all the securities have been sold or transferred by the addressees, the circular and any other relevant documents should be passed to the person through whom the sale or transfer has effected, for transmission to the purchaser or transferee.

Principal features of a scheme

4.19 *The Listing Rules* contain no specific guidance on what constitutes the principal features of a scheme and it is likely, therefore, that many listed companies will continue to refer to the previous list of such matters as set out in the 1984 edition of the Yellow Book, as follows:

(*a*) the persons who will be eligible to participate;

(*b*) the maximum number of shares available under the scheme;

(*c*) the maximum individual entitlement (if the scheme is subject to any statutory maximum entitlement, that maximum from time to time);

(*d*) the amount, if any, payable on application or acceptance and the basis for determining the subscription or option price, the period on or after which payment or calls, or loans to assist in the acquisition of shares, may be paid or called;

(*e*) the voting, dividend, transfer or other rights, including rights arising on a liquidation of the company, attaching to the securities.

4.20 *The Listing Rules* do not lay down any guidelines on the number of shares which may be allocated or the rights of participants under the proposed scheme. This is a change to the 1984 edition of the Yellow Book which required certain matters to be incorporated in any proposed scheme including a fixed numerical limit on the number of shares to be made available under a scheme (as distinct from the ABI's rolling limits) and a requirement for an auditors' certificate in the event of an adjustment of options. It is likely that such provisions will disappear from future schemes.

4.21 The 1984 edition of the Yellow Book permitted adjustments of options in the event of a capitalisation or rights issue, or in the event of any sub-division, consolidation or reduction of share capital. The Stock Exchange took the view that no adjustment was appropriate

4.22 *Establishment of Schemes*

in respect of any discount element on a vendor placing although, in practice, the Stock Exchange was prepared to accept adjustments if approved by shareholders at the time. It is likely that future schemes will provide for the adjustment of options following *any other* variation of share capital without the need for shareholders' prior approval.

The resolution contained in the notice of meeting must refer either to the scheme itself or the summary of the principal terms as the case may be.

Amendments to an employees' share scheme

4.22 *The Listing Rules* provide that a company must obtain shareholders' prior approval to any amendments to an employees' share scheme unless they are:

(*a*)   not to the benefit of present or future participants;

(*b*)   minor amendments to benefit the administration of the scheme; or

(*c*)   made to obtain or maintain favourable tax, exchange control or regulatory treatment for participants or for companies operating or participating in the scheme.

Any circular must include an explanation of the effect of the proposed amendments and either set out the full text of the amendments or state that the amendments will be available for inspection at the place of the meeting or at some place in the City of London or such other place as may be agreed with the Stock Exchange. The circular must also comply with the general requirements for circulars (see 4.18(*e*) above).

4.23   The Stock Exchange's approach to the need for shareholders' approval for changes to the advantage of participants has in recent years been relaxed where the proposed change was intended to take account of (amongst other things) any changes to existing or proposed legislation. This type of 'overriding power' to make amendments was particularly useful in the mid-1980s when various changes were made to the legislation in order to 'plug' various gaps which came to light, for instance, the inclusion of the right to surrender options for replacement options in a takeover or the right of exercise in the event of a sale of a business or subsidiary under a savings-related share option scheme. More recently, this power has been relied upon to make the alterations to savings-related and profit sharing schemes to give equal treatment to men and women at retirement by removing the statutory definition of 'pensionable age' which was incorporated in all new schemes until July 1991. In this case, the legislation referred

Establishment of Schemes **4.26**

to is *Article 119* of the EC Treaty as incorporated in UK law by the *European Communities Act 1972*.

4.24 Six copies of any circular containing proposals to amend a scheme involving the issue of new shares must be lodged with the London Stock Exchange by the time of despatch.

Requirements for an approved scheme

4.25 Tax relief is only available on the application of a company which has established a 'scheme'. It is, therefore, essential that a scheme is submitted rather than a contract between an employer and a single employee. As part of the procedure for obtaining approval of a scheme, the Inland Revenue will require sight of a duly certified copy of the resolution establishing the scheme or written confirmation of its establishment from the company secretary or appropriate advisers to the company. The Inland Revenue is not under a duty to enquire whether a scheme has been validly constituted and may rely on any certificate. Obviously, any defect in the establishment of the scheme, such as insufficient notice being given of the meeting called to establish the scheme means that, as far as the Inland Revenue is concerned, the scheme does not attract approved status.

Form of resolution to establish a scheme

4.26 An appropriate form of shareholders' resolution to establish a scheme is as follows:

'THAT, [subject to the prior approval of the Board of Inland Revenue], the XYZ Scheme, the rules of which are summarised in the Chairman's letter dated ....19...... and are now produced to the Meeting (and, for the purposes of identification, signed by the Chairman) be hereby approved and adopted'.

It is common practice to include the phrase 'subject to the prior approval of the Board of Inland Revenue' although this cannot be construed as giving the directors the authority to alter the scheme in order to obtain such approval. If the directors wish to reserve the power to make amendments to obtain the Inland Revenue's approval of the scheme, a specific power is needed. A suitable form of wording is as follows:

'THAT the directors be hereby authorised to take all steps which they consider necessary or expedient to establish and carry the [scheme] into effect including making any changes which they consider appropriate to obtain the approval of the [scheme] by the Board of Inland Revenue under the provisions of the *Income and Corporation Taxes Act 1988*'.

4.27 *Establishment of Schemes*

Any shareholders' resolution to establish a scheme may also include a relaxation of the restrictions on voting in respect of the scheme by interested directors. Unless the articles of association give the directors a power to suspend or relax restrictions on voting on matters in which they are interested, the necessary resolution will need to be approved by shareholders as a special resolution (see 4.12 above).

An appropriate form of resolution is as follows:

'THAT the directors be authorised to vote as directors and be counted in a quorum on any matter connected with the [scheme] notwithstanding that they may be interested in the same save that no director may vote or be counted in a quorum on any matter solely concerning his own participation in the [scheme], and any prohibition on voting by interested directors contained in the articles of association of the Company be hereby suspended and relaxed to that extent.'

Applying for Inland Revenue approval of a scheme

4.27 The Inland Revenue has established a special unit which deals with employees' share schemes and in particular applications for approval of schemes and for processing the annual scheme returns. The work involved in approving new schemes, and any alterations to them, is allocated amongst some ten or so officers according to the type of scheme and the first letter of each company's name. These work allocations are varied from time to time and a list of current allocations can usually be obtained from the unit. The unit's current address for correspondence is:

Inland Revenue
Savings and Investment Division
(Employee Share Schemes)
First Floor, South West Wing
Bush House
London WC2B 4RD

The unit is invariably helpful in handling enquiries from companies on approved schemes and access to the various officers is available by telephone (071-438-7801, 7803 or 7771) or by fax (071-438-7095). The unit will be assuming responsibility for receiving returns in respect of unapproved employees' share schemes from April 1994.

4.28 Any company proposing to establish an approved scheme is usually well advised to submit a copy of the proposed documentation, particularly the scheme rules, to the Inland Revenue for their preliminary comments before proceeding to establish the scheme. This will enable any points of difficulty to be resolved in advance and will enable the formal application to be processed, after establishment of

Establishment of Schemes **4.29**

the scheme, with the minimum of delay. The Inland Revenue normally processes all applications for approval in order of receipt and therefore the early submission of draft documents is usually advisable.

4.29 The Inland Revenue Guides list the documents and information which must be submitted with an application for formal approval. These are:

(*a*) A certified copy of the resolution adopting the scheme:
- the certificate should be signed by the secretary of the company or any director and should contain the date on which the scheme was adopted.

(*b*) Three copies of the scheme document:
- in the case of a profit sharing scheme, this will be the trust deed (executed and stamped 50 pence) and scheme rules; in the case of a savings-related or executive share option scheme, this will be the scheme rules.

(*c*) Copies of material to be issued to participants:
- three copies of any employee guide;
- in the case of a profit sharing scheme, three copies of any application form or other document containing the undertakings to be given under *TA 1988, 9 Sch 2(2)*.

(*d*) Copies of any circular to be issued to shareholders:
- three copies in the case of a profit sharing scheme but only two copies in the case of a savings-related or executive share option scheme.

(*e*) Information relating to the proposed scheme:
- two copies of a statement in respect of the company, and each participating company, of:
    — the name;
    — the registered office;
    — corporation tax district and Inland Revenue corporation tax reference;
- a statement that all companies in the same group will participate, or alternatively explaining the grounds on which it is considered that the requirements of *TA 1988, 9 Sch 2(3)* are satisfied (see 4.34 below);
- a duly signed declaration by, say, the Company Secretary or a director on company letterhead stating that the conditions in *TA 1988, 9 Sch 10–14* (or *paragraphs 10–12* and *14*

41

4.30 *Establishment of Schemes*

in the case of profit sharing schemes) will be satisfied. (If the shares do not belong to the company setting up the scheme, or are shares in a company under the control of another company, a further declaration is needed to show how the conditions in *TA 1988, 9 Sch 10–14* are satisfied);

- a declaration that any directors' power under the articles of association to refuse registration of a proposed transfer of shares will not be exercised against proposing transferors who are employees to a greater extent than against other proposing transferors (the declaration should also confirm that employees will be told of the nature of this declaration). This, of course, is only likely to be required in relation to private companies.

(*f*) A copy of the current Memorandum and Articles of Association:

- this is required in respect of the company whose shares will be used under the scheme, not the company which establishes the scheme.

4.30 There is no time limit on the Inland Revenue within which to approve or refuse an application. In practice, if the Inland Revenue has cleared the scheme in principle prior to formal approval, it will usually deal with the application within a week or so of the date of application. If necessary, it is usually prepared to approve a scheme in even less time.

4.31 Approval is given in the form of a certificate together with a letter addressed to the Secretary of the company establishing the scheme. A copy of the letter will be sent to any professional adviser who submitted the application on behalf of the company. Each scheme will be given a specific reference number prefixed with an 'ESS' for a profit sharing scheme, or 'SRS' for a savings-related share option scheme and an 'X' for an executive share option scheme and this will be included in the approval letter. The approval letter will normally advise the company to note the following matters:

(*a*) *alterations to the scheme*: the company will be advised that approval of the scheme will automatically cease unless any alterations are first approved by the Inland Revenue. The approval letter will usually also mention that the scheme is regarded as comprising not only any rules (and any trust deed in the case of a profit sharing scheme) but also any ancillary documents (option certificates, etc.) and those provisions of the company's articles of association which regulate the rights attaching to scheme shares and any other arrangements which affect the rights and obligations of scheme participants;

(*b*) *participating companies*: the approval letter will identify the tax district, which will usually be the company's corporation tax

Establishment of Schemes **4.32**

district, which should be notified of any changes in the companies which participate in the scheme;

(c) *profit sharing schemes — the trustees special PAYE scheme.* The approval letter will also draw the attention of companies to the need to arrange for the tax district dealing with the company's PAYE scheme to set up a PAYE scheme for the trustees for cases where the tax cannot be deducted through the company's scheme e.g. because the participant has left employment;

(d) *option schemes*: the approval letter will also advise companies with a savings-related or executive share option scheme that any applications for approval of a proposed adjustment as a result of a variation of share capital will need to be submitted to the employee share schemes unit;

(e) *executive share option schemes*: in the case of executive share option schemes, the approval letter will emphasise the importance of advising participants that income tax relief is only available where an option is exercised:

　(i)　not earlier than three years, nor later than ten years after the option was granted; and

　(ii)　not earlier than three years following the latest previous exercise by the participant of an option (obtained under this or any other executive share option scheme approved under the *Income and Corporation Taxes Act 1988*) which qualifies for relief from income tax.

Refusal of an application for approval

4.32 *TA 1988, 9 Sch (1)* provides that the Inland Revenue shall approve a scheme if they are satisfied that it fulfils all relevant statutory requirements. However, they may not approve any scheme if it appears to them that it contains features which are 'neither essential nor reasonably incidental to the purpose of providing for employees and directors benefits in the nature of rights to acquire shares or, in the case of a profit sharing scheme, in the nature of interests in shares'. Two of the most common problems which arise on this are as follows:

(a) any arrangements under which cash is to be paid either as an alternative to the exercise of option rights, or where option rights lapse in any circumstances, will be regarded as 'not incidental to the acquisition of shares';

(b) any arrangements under which scheme shares may be issued and allotted upon exercise under a share option scheme in the name of a nominee rather than the participant — this can sometimes cause difficulty on a bridging finance arrangement (see 2.9 and 2.10 above). In these circumstances the Inland Revenue consider

4.46 *Establishment of Schemes*

of an executive's employment contract, as 'special restrictions' for the purposes of *paragraph 12(1)(c)*. The Model Code contains various restrictions on dealing in shares by directors of listed companies including a prohibition on dealings prior to an announcement of final or interim results.

4.46 Whilst restrictions on dealing contained in ancillary or collateral agreements are regarded as 'special restrictions' on scheme shares for the purposes of a share option scheme, this is not so in the case of a profit sharing scheme. As a result the various undertakings which are given to the trustees of a profit sharing scheme in accordance with *TA 1988, 9 Sch 2(1)* are not treated as 'special restrictions' on scheme shares.

It is acceptable, therefore, for participants in a profit sharing scheme to enter into an agreement to sell their shares conditionally upon the release of the shares from trust.

Loan arrangements

4.47 Most employees in an executive share option scheme need to borrow the money to exercise their option although this is usually only required on short-term 'bridging' terms since, upon exercise of the option, the optionholder will be able to sell his shares and repay the loan out of the proceeds. It will usually be a term of any such bridging finance that the optionholder authorises the financier to sell sufficient of the shares to cover all principal and interest on the loan. By *TA 1988, 9 Sch 13(3)*, which was first introduced in *FA 1988*, it is specifically provided that any terms in a loan agreement about how the loan is to be repaid, or the security to be given for it, is not to be treated as a 'special restriction' in relation to any executive share option scheme. As a result, the vast majority of executive share options are normally exercised with the benefit of bridging finance arrangements through the company's brokers or some other financial institution.

Widespread ownership of shares

4.48 *TA 1988, 9 Sch 14* contains various rules intended to ensure that the class of ordinary share made available under any approved scheme is owned sufficiently widely in order to reduce the risk of manipulation of its value. The rules do not apply where either there is only one class of ordinary share or, if there is more than one class, the class of shares in question are 'employee-control' shares, i.e. a class of share which gives the directors and employees (or former directors and employees) of the company, or any company now a subsidiary, control of the company.

By *TA 1988, 9 Sch 14(3)*, shares in a company are 'employee-control shares' if the persons holding the shares are, by virtue of their holdings, together able to control the company *and* these persons are or have been employees or directors of the company or of another company which is under the control of the company. Shares of a different class to those which are scheme shares are not taken into account.

4.49 If there is more than one class of ordinary share, then the majority of the class which are scheme shares must be held by persons who acquired them otherwise than as directors and employees, or as trustees on behalf of directors and employees, of the company. An exception is made for shares acquired by a director or employee in a public offer.

4.50 By *TA 1988, 9 Sch 14(1)(c)*, there is a further restriction which applies where scheme shares are in a company which has more than one class of ordinary share capital. In this case, a majority of the issued shares of the same class as are made available under the approved share scheme must not be held by a closely-controlled holding company or by a closely controlled associate company, unless the scheme shares will be in a company which is listed on a recognised stock exchange. Where the scheme shares are made available in a company which is listed it is assumed that the scope for manipulation of the price of the shares is considerably reduced.

Material interest

4.51 The legislation contains rules designed to exclude participation in an approved scheme by persons who have (or have had in the previous twelve months) a 'material interest' in certain close companies (*TA 1988, 9 Sch 8*). The purpose of this is to avoid giving income tax relief to persons acquiring an interest in companies in which they already hold a significant interest. For this purpose, 'participation' includes both the grant and exercise of an option.

4.52 A close company will be within the rule if:

(*a*) its shares are to be used under the scheme; and

(*b*) it has control of the company whose shares are to be used under the scheme; or

(*c*) it is a member of a consortium which owns the company whose shares are to be used under the scheme.

4.53 A 'material interest' is more than 25 per cent of the ordinary share capital in the case of an approved profit sharing or savings-related share option scheme, and more than 10 per cent of the ordinary share capital in the case of an approved share option scheme. In determining whether a person has a 'material interest' it is necessary

4.54 *Establishment of Schemes*

to aggregate all the shares of which he and any associate of his (relative, partner, certain trustees and certain co-beneficiaries: see 4.54 below) are the beneficial owners of, or able, directly or through the medium of other companies, or by any other indirect means, to control. By *TA 1988, s 187(3)(b)*, it is also necessary to aggregate the shares in any close company in which he or any such associate possesses, or is entitled to acquire, such rights as would, in the event of the winding-up of that company or in any other circumstances, give an entitlement to receive more than 25 per cent (or 10 per cent in the case of an approved share option scheme) of the assets which would be available for distribution amongst the participants (as defined by *TA 1988, s 417(1)*).

4.54 A 'close company' has the meaning given by *TA 1988, s 414(1)*, *viz* a company under the control of five or fewer participants, or of participants who are directors, but excluding (amongst other things) any company not resident in the United Kingdom. In order to treat participants in schemes using the shares of UK and non-UK companies alike, *TA 1988, 9 Sch 8* provides that a company which would be closely controlled if it were UK resident will be so treated for the purposes of determining whether a person has a material interest under the approved share scheme legislation.

4.55 In 4.53 above, it was noted that the shares of an 'associate' are attributed to a participator in determining whether that participator has a 'material interest' in the company concerned. In particular, where the participator is a beneficiary under a trust, or is interested in part of the estate of a deceased person, the trustee or personal representatives are treated as 'associates' of the participator.

4.56 The attribution of shares held by a trustee to a participator who is a discretionary beneficiary could potentially give rise to difficulties in the case of pension trustees or the trustees of other employee benefit trusts. In order to deal with this situation, the legislation was changed with effect from 14 March 1989 with the result that any shares held by the trustee of an employee benefit trust are disregarded when applying the 10 per cent and 25 per cent tests in determining whether any particular participator has a 'material interest' (*TA 1988, 9 Sch 40*). For these purposes, an 'employee benefit trust' is defined by *TA 1988, 8 Sch 7(5)* as a trust under which all or most employees of the company are eligible to benefit and any disposals of trust property, being either shares in the company or cash paid outright, since 14 March 1989 have either been made in the ordinary course of trust arrangement or to benefit employees, former employees and certain spouses and dependents, or are applied for charitable purposes by the trustees of a profit sharing scheme.

4.57 Any unappropriated shares held by the trustees of an approved profit sharing scheme are specifically disregarded in applying the material interest test.

4.58 The rules on employee benefit trusts and approved profit sharing schemes deal with the main situations in which the shares of trustees may be attributed to employee participators. However, employees may have a remote interest under a family discretionary trust on there being no surviving family members. By *TA 1988, 9 Sch 37* the interest of a beneficiary under such a trust who irrevocably disclaims his interest under seal is not regarded as having an interest in the shares held under such trusts. Alternatively, the trustees may exercise any power to exclude these beneficiaries. The employee must not have received any benefit from the trust in the past twelve months. These disclaimer provisions only apply from 14 November 1986 in respect of interests arising or in existence on or after that date.

Shares under option

4.59 In determining whether a participator has a material interest in the shares of a company it is necessary to include all unissued shares over which he and his associates hold options or are otherwise entitled to acquire. It would obviously be unfair if, in determining whether a person has a material interest, the total issued ordinary share capital as well as the individual's percentage interest were not diluted to reflect the number of shares that participator (and his associates) are entitled to acquire. *TA 1988, 9 Sch 9* provides for this adjustment to be made, but only in respect of unissued share which the company is contractually bound to issue to that individual in the event of the exercise of the option. Options held by any person other than the individual concerned (or his associates) are disregarded.

4.60 Shares over which options are granted, but which will be supplied by ESOP trustees on exercise of an option are not shares which the company is contractually bound to 'issue'. Such shares will be taken into account in determining the participator's percentage interest in the company, but not in determining the total issued ordinary share capital for these purposes. In short, the material interest rules may apply more harshly where the shares under option are held through an ESOP than where they will be newly issued.

Valuations of shares

Market value of shares quoted on the London Stock Exchange

4.61 Under the approved scheme legislation the market value of a share is determined in accordance with the capital gains tax rules in *Part VIII* of the *TCGA 1992*. In the case of shares listed on the London

4.62 *Establishment of Schemes*

Stock Exchange this will normally be the lesser of the 'quarter up' price or the 'mean bargain price' (if there were any recorded bargains) as quoted on the London Stock Exchange Daily Official List on the relevant date.

However, these rules do not apply where as a result of 'special circumstances' prices quoted on the London Stock Exchange are not a proper measure of market value in which case it is necessary to apply the normal 'open market' principles of valuing shares, or to use the prices quoted elsewhere than in the London Stock Exchange Daily Official List if those other prices reflect a more active market. The Revenue's Statement of Practice SP 18/80 'Securities dealt in on The Stock Exchange USM: Status and valuation for tax purposes' makes it clear that such shares are normally treated as unquoted shares for valuation purposes (see 4.64 below).

Market value of shares quoted on the New York Stock Exchange

4.62 The Inland Revenue will accept that a value representing the mean of the day's range of sales on the New York Stock Exchange can be treated as the market value without the need for any agreement with Shares Valuation Division. The Inland Revenue Guide IR 96 states that where the latest available price is the previous day's closing price, that price may be taken as the market value provided that no significant change in the company's circumstances or significant movement in the Stock Market has occurred. It is also suggested in the Inland Revenue Guide that the scheme rules should provide for this price to be converted into sterling by reference to the rates of exchange for the relevant day as shown on the first page of the London Stock Exchange Daily Official List, or to other sources acceptable to Shares Valuation Division such as the Financial Times. Shares dealt in on NASDAQ in the United States are not treated as dealt in on the New York Stock Exchange and are therefore treated as unquoted shares (see 4.64 below).

Market value of shares quoted on other recognised stock exchanges

4.63 Whilst there are specific rules valuing shares quoted on the London Stock Exchange (see 4.61 above) and on the New York Stock Exchange (see 4.62 above), all shares quoted on other 'recognised stock exchanges' are treated in the same way as other unquoted shares and values must be specifically agreed with the Shares Valuation Division on each occasion shares or options are allocated. A list of the overseas stock exchanges which are 'recognised' by the Inland Revenue is set out in Appendix 2 at 4.83 below.

Market value of unquoted shares

4.64 The market value of unquoted shares for tax purposes is the 'open market' value on a sale of the shares on the assumption there is available to any prospective purchaser all the information which a prudent prospective purchaser might reasonably require if he were proposing to purchase it from a willing vendor. In the case of approved schemes, the Revenue normally require any scheme under which unquoted shares may be allocated to provide for the market value to be agreed with the Shares Valuation Division in advance. As mentioned above, the same applies to companies whose shares are quoted on a recognised stock exchange.

4.65 Although shares dealt in on the USM or NASDAQ are treated as unquoted shares, nevertheless, where bargains in respect of the shares have been recorded with reasonable frequency during the period prior to the proposed allocation under the scheme, the Revenue will generally, in the absence of special circumstances, use the published prices in establishing the value of the shares for tax purposes. A similar approach is adopted in practice in valuing the shares of companies whose shares are dealt in under the 'over the counter' market on the Stock Exchange provided details of bargains are published in the London Stock Exchange Daily Official List or elsewhere.

Information required for the valuation of shares in unquoted companies

4.66 The information required by Shares Valuation Division to enable a value to be negotiated includes:

(*a*) a copy of the company's accounts for the last three financial years not previously seen by Shares Valuation Division and any subsequent interim statement for the current financial year;

(*b*) the relevant scheme rules;

(*c*) a valuation proposal including an explanation of how it was arrived at;

(*d*) details of any recent arm's length transactions (including the date on which they occurred, the number of shares sold and the price paid for each share).

The address of Shares Valuation Division is as follows:

Inland Revenue
Capital Taxes Office
Shares Valuation Division
(Employee Share Schemes)
Minford House
Rockley Road
London W14 0DF
Tel: 071-603 4622

4.67 *Establishment of Schemes*

In the case of companies registered in Scotland, the address for correspondence is:

Inland Revenue
Capital Taxes Office
Share Valuation Division
(Share Option Schemes)
Mulberry House
16 Picardy Place
Edinburgh EH1 3NB

Tel: 031-556 8511

4.67 In the case of companies whose shares are dealt in on the USM or are quoted on a recognised stock exchange overseas, the Shares Valuation Division may be prepared to allow the company to value its shares for the purposes of an approved scheme on the basis of recent bargains or the recent trading price and for the company to notify the Shares Valuation Division after the grant of options on appropriation of shares as the case may be. This is regarded as satisfying the usual provision in scheme rules that the market value must be approved by Shares Valuation Division.

4.68 In the case of approved schemes, the Shares Valuation Division will normally deal with any valuation proposal promptly. If all the necessary information is supplied it is normal for the Shares Valuation Division to take no more than a few days to deal with any proposals.

4.69 The Shares Valuation Division are not normally prepared to agree share values in advance in the case of an unapproved share option scheme.

4.70 Although scheme shares must be fully-paid, the remaining shares of the same class might be partly-paid as in most privatisations. In such cases, the Inland Revenue will normally accept that the market value of a fully-paid share of the class of shares which are scheme shares might be discounted in respect of the early payment of the shares, even where this is notional as in the case of unissued shares over which options have been granted.

Duration of a scheme

Share option schemes

4.71 There are no limits under either the approved scheme legislation or under Stock Exchange rules on the duration of any share option scheme. However, a maximum duration of ten years is laid down under ABI Guidelines. The 1987 Guidelines state that:

> 'In order that shareholders may review the effectiveness of option arrangements, schemes should have a life of not more than ten years'.

Profit sharing schemes

4.72 The ABI and other bodies representing institutional investors do not lay down any guideline on the duration of a profit sharing scheme, and, as in the case of share option schemes, there are no limits on the duration of a scheme in either the approved scheme legislation or under London Stock Exchange rules.

However, the Inland Revenue will only approve a scheme which will terminate not later than the expiry of the perpetuity period which must be set out in the trust deed. Under general trust law, all settlements must finally vest within certain periods. By the *Perpetuities and Accumulations Act 1964, s 1* a statutory period of 80 years is now allowed. Most profit sharing trusts are, therefore, stated to terminate upon the expiry of a period no longer than 80 years.

Renewal of schemes

Share option schemes

4.73 Where the expiry date of a share option scheme is reached, the company may extend the life of the scheme by altering the rules and inserting a new expiry date. Any such allocation can apparently be made even after the expiry of the scheme. A scheme which has expired remains approved and existing participants under the scheme are completely unaffected by the expiry of the scheme. Usually both Inland Revenue approval and, if required under the scheme rules, shareholders' approval will be required to renew a scheme.

Profit sharing schemes

4.74 Under trust law, the duration of a trust is incapable of extension beyond the end of the perpetuity period.

Inland Revenue practice

4.75 The Inland Revenue has now adopted the practice of writing to companies which have established schemes which are about to expire to remind them of the need to renew their scheme. Where the rules of an approved scheme provides for termination of the scheme

4.76 *Establishment of Schemes*

on a particular date, any allocations after that date will not be granted in accordance with the terms of an approved scheme and will not therefore attract the usual tax reliefs.

Cessation of scheme approval

Cessation of approval at the request of the company

4.76 In principle, a company which has established an approved share scheme may seek withdrawal of that approval at any time. The mechanism for achieving this is for a resolution to be passed deleting the provision incorporated in all approved schemes that any alteration of the scheme will only be effective with the prior approval of the Inland Revenue. Once the Inland Revenue have approved the alteration then the scheme will become unapproved and any further changes which may be required can be made without the prior approval of the Inland Revenue.

4.77 A scheme may also require the prior approval of the shareholders, and possibly optionholders, for any alteration to become effective. Many schemes provide that any proposed alteration which may abrogate and adversely affect optionholders, shall require the prior approval of the holders of options over such number of shares as constitute 75 per cent of the total number of shares under option. This broadly reflects the provisions of *Table A* articles of association relating to the alteration of class rights. In the author's view, a cessation or withdrawal of a scheme's approval does not abrogate or adversely affect the *rights* of optionholders even though it may affect the amount of tax payable or the timing of its payment.

4.78 Where the approval of a scheme is withdrawn at the request of the company, approved scheme tax returns will cease to be sent to it at least in respect of periods after the cessation of approval. However, the company will remain under a general obligation to make returns of acquisitions of shares by directors and employees.

Cessation of approval at the direction of the company

4.79 The Inland Revenue has a wide power to withdraw approval of a scheme.

4.80 In the case of a share option scheme (including a savings-related share option scheme) the approval of a scheme may be withdrawn with effect from the date any of the statutory requirements for approval of the scheme cease to be satisfied, or at such later date as the Inland Revenue may agree. However, the tax relief available

Establishment of Schemes **4.83**

in respect of savings-related share options granted prior to the cessation of scheme approval cannot be prejudiced. Executive share options are not treated so leniently.

4.81 In the case of a profit sharing scheme, *TA 1988, 9 Sch 3* lays down the precise circumstances in which Inland Revenue approval of a scheme may be withdrawn, as follows:

(*a*) a participant is in breach of his undertakings under *TA 1988, 9 Sch 2(2)(a)(c)(d)* to leave scheme shares with the trustees. It will be noted that the obligation not to deal in the beneficial interest in the scheme shares is excluded if only because there is no way in which the trustees might be expected to know of any such breach and it would therefore be unfair to withdraw approval of the whole scheme;

(*b*) in the operation of the scheme, there is a contravention of any of the requirements for approval of the scheme, the provisions of *TA 1988, 10 Sch*, the scheme itself or the terms of the profit sharing trust;

(*c*) any shares which have been appropriated are given different treatment to other shares of that class in respect of the dividend payable, repayment, the restrictions attaching to them and any offer of substituted or additional shares, securities or rights of any description in respect of the shares;

(*d*) in relation to approved savings-related share option schemes and approved profit sharing schemes, the Inland Revenue ceases to be satisfied that the scheme complies with the requirement that there should be no features of the scheme which would discourage participation or which only benefit higher-paid employees, or any person who is entitled to participate in the scheme under *TA 1988, 9 Sch 36*, is excluded from participation;

(*e*) the trustees or the company which established the scheme (or any past or present participating company in a group scheme) fails to furnish any information which the Inland Revenue has required it to furnish under its statutory power to require information.

4.82 The company which established the scheme is entitled to appeal any withdrawal of approval of a scheme. Appeal is by notice given to the Inland Revenue within 30 days from the date on which the company which established the scheme is notified of the withdrawal of approval. The appeal is to the Special Commissioner which will hear and determine the matter in the same way as an appeal.

Costs of establishment of a scheme

4.83 Since 1 April 1991 the expenditure incurred by a company on the establishment of an approved employees' share scheme (and a

4.83 *Establishment of Schemes*

qualifying employee share ownership trust) is deductible in computation of trading profits under Schedule D, Case I or as a management expense of certain investment companies (*TA 1988, ss 85, 85A*). The Inland Revenue will usually reject claims for relief in respect of the establishment of unapproved share option schemes or ESOP trusts. Normal expenditure on the operation and administration of the scheme will be deductible. The position is not clear as regards expenditure on the alteration of any such schemes.

Appendix 1

Extra-Statutory Concession B27

B27 Approved employee share schemes: jointly owned companies

This concession relates to the three kinds of employee share schemes (profit sharing schemes, savings related share option schemes, and other share option schemes) approved under *TA 1988, 9 Sch* and in this concession 'control' has the same meaning as in *TA 1988, s 840*.

A jointly owned company cannot participate in any employee share scheme which is a 'group scheme' established by either of its joint owners because the jointly owned company is not controlled by the company which established the scheme (the grantor) as the legislation requires (*TA 1988, 9 Sch 1(3)*). Similarly, subsidiaries of the jointly owned company cannot participate in such a group scheme.

(*a*) Upon application by the grantor of the relevant employee share scheme the Revenue, by concession, will normally give its approval to a group scheme expressed to extend to a jointly owned company where:

   (i) the jointly owned company is not under the control of any single person;

   (ii) two persons between them control the jointly owned company and one of them is the grantor of the relevant approved employee share scheme; and

   (iii) the jointly owned company has extended to it, in relation to each of the three kinds of employee share schemes approved under *TA 1988, 9 Sch*, the approved employee share schemes of that kind established by only one of the companies which control the jointly owned company.

(*b*) Upon application by the grantor of the relevant employee share scheme the Revenue, by concession, will normally give its approval to a group scheme expressed to extend to all or any of the companies controlled by a jointly owned company where:

   (i) the jointly owned company satisfies conditions (*a*)(i) and (*a*)(ii) above; and

   (ii) all the companies (jointly owned company and the companies controlled by it) in respect of which such an application is or has been made; taken together, satisfy condition (*a*)(iii) above as if that condition related to companies controlled by the jointly owned company as well as to that company.

4.83 Establishment of Schemes

Any scheme for which application is made under this concession must provide that:

(1) if the jointly owned company ceases to satisfy condition (*a*)(i) or (*a*)(ii) above the scheme no longer extends to the jointly owned company or to the companies controlled by it, unless they have thereby become controlled by the grantor of the relevant scheme; and

(2) if any of the companies controlled by the jointly owned company ceases to be so controlled the scheme no longer extends to the company which ceases to be so controlled, unless it has thereby become controlled by the grantor of the relevant scheme.

Consent to the application of the concession will only be given where an undertaking has been given by the grantor of the relevant employee share scheme to notify the Revenue of any changes in the ownership or control of:

(*a*) the grantor;

(*b*) the other company which controls the jointly owned company with the grantor;

(*c*) the jointly owned company;

(*d*) any other company to which a group scheme is expressed to extend by virtue of this concession.

Appendix 2

Recognised Stock Exchanges

Austria
Belgium
Canadian
French
Japanese
Netherlands
Norwegian
US stock exchanges registered with the SEC
Copenhagen
Helsinki
Johannesburg
Hong Kong
German
Spanish
Colombo
Portuguese
Luxemburg
Italian
Singapore
Zurich
Basle
Geneva
Stockholm
New Zealand
Australia
Greece

Note: The Stock Exchange of the Republic of Ireland is incorporated into London Stock Exchange and therefore shares are treated as quoted on the London Stock Exchange.

Chapter 5

Executive Share Option Schemes

Introduction

5.1 Executive share option schemes are by far the most common type of employees' share scheme although usually only a minority of senior executives in any company will be selected to participate. The scheme usually involves the grant of an option to acquire a specified number of shares at a fixed price during a specified period. So long as the share price rises, the optionholder will wish to exercise the option in due course in order to realise the gain on the shares. If the share price does not rise, then the optionholder will not exercise the option and it will eventually lapse and become worthless.

5.2 In the United Kingdom, as in most jurisdictions, tax is payable on the gain which accrues on the exercise rather than the grant of an option. Originally, in the decision of the House of Lords in *Abbott v Philbin HL (1960) 39 TC 82* it was held that the grant of an option was chargeable to income tax as an emolument of the employment, but no further tax was chargeable on any gain which accrued on exercise as this was treated as derived from the option rights, not the employment. However, this decision was reversed in the case of persons who are within Case I of Schedule E at the date of grant by *FA 1966, s 25* (now *TA 1988, ss 135, 136*).

5.3 Generally speaking, no tax is now payable on the grant of an option to a person who is within Case I of Schedule E except in cases where the option may be capable of exercise for more than seven years; a gain only accrues at the date of grant on a 'long-dated' option where the option is granted at a price which represents a discount to the market value of the shares at that time. Employees who are within Case II or Case III of Schedule E are chargeable to income tax at the date of grant if any gain arises, but not at the date of exercise unless they have since become chargeable to Case I.

5.4 Income tax is chargeable on any gain which accrues at the time of exercise (or for that matter upon the assignment, release or omission to exercise) an option acquired by a person as a director or employee if he was within Case I of Schedule E at the date of grant.

5.5 Executive Share Option Schemes

If income tax was paid at the time of grant, it is credited against the amount of tax payable on any gain which arises at exercise.

5.5 Where an option was granted before 6 April 1984, the optionholder may in certain circumstances elect to pay any income tax which is chargeable in respect of any gains accruing on exercise (but not any release, assignment or omission to exercise) in instalments. The option must have been granted at a price which is not less than the market value at the date of grant (or 90 per cent of the market value in the case of options granted before 6 April 1982) and at least £250 tax must have been assessed.

5.6 *FA 1984* introduced the relief from income tax for the gains accruing on the exercise of options under approved share option schemes. The relief is only available to an optionholder where the option has been held for at least three years since the date of grant or the last occasion on which the holder exercised any approved 'executive' option (which need not necessarily be under the same scheme) in tax-exempt circumstances.

5.7 When *FA 1984* was introduced, the highest rate of income tax was 60 per cent whilst capital gains tax was chargeable at only 30 per cent. Approved share option schemes, therefore, provided significant tax advantages and, not surprisingly, rapidly became very popular as an employee benefit.

5.8 Even though there are now uniform rates of income and capital gains, the vast majority of share option schemes are still established as approved schemes. There are two main reasons for this. First, the deferral of the tax charge until any sale of the shares helps executives who wish to keep their shares rather than sell them immediately following exercise. Secondly, the availability of the annual capital gains tax exemption (£5,800 in 1994/95) which can be used to mitigate capital gains tax on successive sales of the shares over several tax years. It is also possible for the capital gains tax to be mitigated further by taking advantage of any spouse's annual capital gains tax exemption.

5.9 Unapproved share option schemes are established for a number of reasons, the most common being that the scheme shares will not satisfy the conditions for approval under *TA 1988, 9 Sch 10–14*. In particular, a company which is a subsidiary of a non-quoted company will not be able to establish an approved scheme. The other main reason for establishing an unapproved share option scheme is the greater flexibility allowed in the design of the scheme particularly in relation to the rights of exercise. Normally, the Inland Revenue will only approve a scheme where the rights of exercise are set out with some degree of certainty although a right of exercise in the discretion of the directors is permitted if it is in addition to rights of

Executive Share Option Schemes 5.14

exercise in the event of leaving employment on account of injury, disability and redundancy. In the case of an unapproved scheme, however, a company can design a scheme giving complete discretion to the directors to allow the exercise of an option by employees or former employees. In practice, the attractiveness of an option which only allows exercise in the discretion of the directors is questionable and few companies go so far as establish such a scheme.

5.10 This chapter deals with the provisions of normal executive share option schemes, whether approved under the *TA 1988* or not: see also Chapter 6 below for 'Replacement Option' Schemes, 'Super Option' Schemes, 'Discounted Price Option' Schemes and 'Parallel Option' Schemes.

Eligibility criteria

Eligibility in approved schemes

5.11 Under *TA 1988, 9 Sch 27(1)* a person is only eligible to obtain rights under an approved scheme if he is a 'full-time director' or a 'qualifying employee'.

5.12 A person is treated as a 'full-time director' if he normally works at least 25 hours a week, exclusive of meal breaks, for the company regardless of whether he works under a service contract specifying at least such number of hours. A non-executive director who normally works the required number of hours for the relevant company or companies will, therefore, be treated as eligible. However, most schemes are specifically drafted so that the test must be applied by reference to the number of contractual hours.

5.13 Under *TA 1988, 9 Sch 27(4)*, a 'qualifying employee' means an employee who is not also a director and 'is required, under the terms of his employment, to work for the company for at least 20 hours a week'. The 20 hours a week test is again calculated exclusive of time allowed for meal breaks. In the case of a 'qualifying employee', the hours per week test must be satisfied by reference to contractual hours rather than merely the number of hours actually worked.

5.14 Where the scheme does not extend to other participating companies, the directorship or employment must be with the company which established the scheme. Where the scheme is extended to other participating companies, hours worked for different participating companies (but not associated companies) may be aggregated in calculating the number of hours.

5.15 Executive Share Option Schemes

5.15 It does not matter if a person who is either a full-time director or qualifying employee at the time of grant ceases to satisfy these conditions immediately following the grant of the option. An approved option may be exercised by a former employee or indeed by the personal representatives of an optionholder who has died.

5.16 There are restrictions in approved schemes on the eligibility and right to exercise options by persons with a 'material interest' (see 4.51 to 4.58).

Institutional investors

5.17 The ABI Guidelines provide that a director or employee may only participate in a share option scheme if he is required 'to devote substantially the whole of his time to the business of the Company' (see paragraph 14 of the 1987 Guidelines). This is intended to prevent directors who work for two or more groups of companies obtaining share options under each group of companies. Such directors are apparently excluded from all the schemes.

Selection of optionholders

5.18 Executive share option schemes provide for the directors to select the eligible employees who will participate in the scheme. Normally, prospective optionholders will be selected at the absolute discretion of the directors without the need to obtain the prior approval of shareholders or any other person.

Many quoted companies have established Remuneration Committees as a committee of the board of directors comprising the Chairman and mainly non-executive directors with delegated authority to grant options under any executive share option scheme. This was a development which was strongly recommended in the ABI Guidelines published in May 1987 and there are now relatively few large public companies which have not established Remuneration Committees.

Practical Pointer

Who gets options?

Each company will identify the persons who will be selected for the grant of options according to the company's own personnel policies and its own culture. Consequently, there is an enormous variety in the extent to which options are offered to less senior employees. However, there are a number of practical considerations which always need to be taken into account as follows:

- the amount of share capital available for the grant of options may be limited;
- where a company has a savings-related share option scheme, it will generally be regarded as appropriate to grant executive share options to only a limited number of senior executives;
- given the need for any optionholder to raise significant amounts of finance in order to be able to exercise an option, it is generally considered that such schemes need to be targeted at a limited group of senior executives;
- it will generally be inappropriate for share options to be granted to middle management and below if the option is only exercisable upon the satisfaction of prescribed performance targets based on share price and particularly earnings per share as recommended by institutional investors.

Grant of options

Time of grant

Model Scheme

5.19 The Revenue's Model Scheme provides for the grant of options 'at any time or times within a period of four weeks after the results of the company are announced or the date on which the scheme is approved by the Revenue'. The grant periods in the Model Scheme are merely suggestions and, in principle, there is nothing in the approved scheme legislation which prohibits the grant of options at any time (but in relation to listed companies, see ABI Guidelines and 3.24 to 3.27 above). The Model Scheme also provides that options should not be granted earlier than the date of approval of the scheme and not later than the tenth anniversary of that date, although it is the ABI Guidelines rather than the approved legislation which restricts the life of a scheme to ten years (see 3.16 in relation to listed companies).

ABI Guidelines

5.20 ABI Guidelines provide that options must be granted within a period of 42 days following the date of publication of results of the company. The reason for this is to ensure that optionholders are granted options at a time when the maximum possible financial information about the company is in the public domain (see 3.24 to 3.26). At one time, the ABI even suggested that invitations of applications for the grant of options were issued to optionholders during the period of 14 days following an announcement of results

5.21 Executive Share Option Schemes

by the company but as most companies now grant options under seal this practice is now largely academic.

5.21 The ABI also accepts the grant of options during the period of 42 days following the approval of the scheme by the shareholders where this period does not coincide with the period of 42 days following an announcement of results.

5.22 In addition, the ABI in practice accepts the grant of options at any time the directors consider there are exceptional circumstances which justify the grant of options. This provision which was originally accepted to cover circumstances such as the grant of options to a newly appointed senior executive can be used by directors in a variety of circumstances provided they are satisfied that the circumstances in fact justify a grant of options at that time.

Stock Exchange Model Code

5.23 The Stock Exchange Model Code restricts dealings by directors of listed companies. Amongst other things, it restricts the grant of options to persons who are directors or who otherwise have possession of price-sensitive information, during:

(*a*) the period of two months immediately preceding the preliminary announcement of the company's annual results or, if shorter, the period from the relevant financial year end up to and including the time of the announcement; and

(*b*) either:

  (i) where the company reports half-yearly, the period of two months immediately preceding the announcement of the half-yearly results (or from the end of the period to the announcement if shorter); or

  (ii) where the company reports quarterly, the period of one month immediately preceding a quarterly announcement (or from the end of the period to the announcement if shorter) except in the case of the announcement of annual results.

These restrictions apply to listed companies regardless of anything to the contrary contained in the scheme and apply not only to the exercise of options, but also the surrender of options, as well as sales and acquisitions of shares.

Procedure

Offer and acceptance/grants under seal

5.24 As for any other legal contract, an option will only be enforceable if consideration is given for its grant, or the option is executed as a deed.

5.25 The Model Scheme provides for the invitation of applications and for each applicant to pay £1 as consideration for the grant of his option. Generally speaking, the alternative procedure of granting an option under seal or otherwise executing it as a deed is much simpler. The grant of options under seal saves time and effort since it is not necessary to wait for the optionholder to respond to the invitation by applying for the option, or even requiring him to pay the £1 consideration. In particular, it does not matter if the proposed optionholder is absent on business or holiday. For these reasons, most companies now grant options under seal, usually involving a securities seal or even a pre-printed certificate containing a facsimile securities seal. The seal may be countersigned by a director and secretary as may be required by the company's articles of association although normally the signatories will be pre-printed as well.

5.26 Where any payment is required as consideration for the grant of an option, it will be forfeited if the option lapses or is not exercised. Any payment for the grant of an option will be deducted in calculating any gain for income tax purposes accruing on the exercise of an option (*TA 1988, s 135*).

Price

5.27 *TA 1988, 9 Sch 29(1)* provides that the price at which shares may be acquired on the exercise of an option under an approved scheme must be stated at the time of grant. The acquisition price of the shares is so fundamental to a legally binding contract that it is difficult to envisage any grant of an option without stating the exercise price.

5.28 However, a scheme can be drafted to allow for a variation of the exercise price during the life of the option. For instance, the option price may be increased each anniversary of the date of grant by an amount representing the increase in the Retail Prices Index over the previous year, or the price may increase from time to time to reflect the carrying costs of the option shares during the option period i.e. interest costs on a notional loan to purchase the shares less the amount of dividends payable on that number of shares. So long as the exercise price is determinable at any time, the requirement for the exercise price to be stated at the time of grant would be satisfied.

5.29 Options granted under approved schemes after 1 January 1992 may be granted at a discount provided the price is not manifestly less than 85 per cent of the market value of the shares provided certain conditions are satisfied (see 'Discounted Price Options' and 'Parallel Options' in Chapter 6).

5.30 Executive Share Option Schemes

Material time for valuing shares

5.30 Under approved executive share option schemes, the option price of the shares for the purposes of a proposed grant of options must be based on the market value of the shares during a fairly limited period before the date of grant. This is either the time the option is granted or, if the Inland Revenue and the grantor agree in writing, such earlier time or times as may be provided in the agreement (*TA 1988, 9 Sch 29(8)*). A provision in any scheme rules for determining the price which is approved by the Inland Revenue will be treated as made under such an agreement.

5.31 The Inland Revenue will normally not permit the exercise price to be ascertained by reference to the market value of the shares on a day earlier than 30 days prior to the date of grant where the scheme provides for the invitation of applications.

5.32 Where options are granted under seal, the Inland Revenue will not normally agree to value the shares by reference to the market value over more than five dealing days prior to the grant. Similarly, where applications for the grant of options are invited, the Inland Revenue will not normally agree to value the shares by reference to the market over more than five dealing days before the date of invitation. Any such five-day period must in any event fall within the 30 days under 5.31 above.

Grant of an option under approved schemes at less than the market value

5.33 In approved share option schemes, share options must be granted at a price which is not 'manifestly' less than the market value of the shares at the material time, or in the case of Discounted Price Options, at 85 per cent of that value (see 'Discounted Price Options' in Chapter 6). 'Manifestly' is strictly interpreted by the Inland Revenue and so, where fractions of a share are involved, the fractional amount should be rounded up. The Inland Revenue Guide on Executive Share Option Schemes (IR 100) emphasises that if an exercise price is not determined exactly in accordance with the rules of the approved scheme, the option will not qualify for income tax relief. The Inland Revenue Tax Return (Form 34) specifically seeks information of the basis on which the market value of the shares was determined including, in the case of unquoted shares and shares quoted on any overseas recognised stock exchanges, the date of the relevant agreement of the Shares Valuation Division to the market value.

5.34 By *TA 1988, s 185(6)(6A)(6B)* any grant of approved options at less than the market value is taxable to the extent the exercise price (plus anything payable for the grant of the option) is less than the

Executive Share Option Schemes 5.38

market value of the shares at the time of grant. In the case of Discounted Price Options, tax is payable to the extent the exercise price (and anything payable for the grant of the option) is less than 85 per cent of the market value.

5.35 Any undervalue on the grant of an approved option is taxable under *Schedule E* as earned income of the tax year in which the option is granted. Any amount charged to income tax under *TA 1988, s 185* is taken into account for capital gains tax purposes in determining the cost of the shares on any subsequent disposal and is deducted in calculating the income tax charge which will arise on the exercise of the option. It appears that if an approved option is granted at less than the market value of the shares then, except in the case of Discounted Price Options, the option will inevitably have been granted otherwise than in accordance with an approved scheme and any gains on exercise will, therefore, be subject to income tax.

5.36 In unapproved share option schemes, the grant of an option at less than the market value of the shares at the date of grant will, on general principles, give rise to a charge to income tax on any gain which accrues (*Abbott v Philbin HL (1960) 39 TC 82*). However, *TA 1988, s 135(2)* specifically provides that no tax shall be chargeable in respect of the grant of an option where the option is not capable of exercise for more than seven years. It is for this reason that unapproved share options should always be exercisable for a period expiring no later than the seventh anniversary of the date of grant.

Board resolution to grant options

5.37 Under most schemes, the authority to grant options is given to the board of directors or, more specifically in listed companies, the Remuneration Committee which will usually comprise the chairman and a number of non-executive directors. An appropriate form of board resolution for the grant of share options is as follows:

'Directors Resolution

IT WAS RESOLVED THAT options be hereby granted under the [   ] Executive Share Option Scheme to the following executives:

Name and Address of Optionholders	Number of Shares	Exercise Price	Terms or Performance Targets

The Secretary be hereby instructed to prepare and issue the option certificates [and to notify the London Stock Exchange] accordingly'.

5.38 Boards of directors and Remuneration Committees often agree the options to be granted in advance of the actual date of grant.

5.39 Executive Share Option Schemes

In such cases, the exercise price cannot be ascertained at the time the directors or the Remuneration Committee meets, but there is no reason why options cannot be determined in advance based on an aggregate acquisition price. An appropriate form of board resolution is as follows:

'Directors Resolution

IT WAS RESOLVED THAT with effect from [date], options be hereby granted at a price equal to the [market value]/[mid-market closing price] on [specified date of grant] under the [   ] Executive Share Option Scheme to the following executives:

Name and Address of Optionholders	Number of Shares	Exercise Price	Terms or Performance Targets

PROVIDED THAT the number of shares above shall be limited, where appropriate, to such lesser number of shares as shall not exceed any limit on the number of shares available to that individual under the Scheme rules'.

Option certificate

5.39 The Inland Revenue will expect to see some form of option certificate or statement to be given to optionholders to be submitted with any application for approval of a scheme.

5.40 A form of option certificate is to be found amongst the specimen documents included in the Inland Revenue Guide on Executive Option Schemes (IR 100). Any form of option certificate should contain the following:

- the identity of the optionholder;
- the name of the company;
- the name of the scheme;
- the maximum number of shares under option;
- the exercise price (per share);
- a statement that the shares are not transferable, and that the option rights will lapse upon the occasion of any assignment, charge, disposal or other dealing with the rights conveyed by it or in any other circumstances;
- any performance targets or special conditions of exercise (if these were not included in any invitation).

5.41 The Inland Revenue Model Rules assumes that the option will have been granted as a result of an invitation of applications and payment of nominal consideration for the grant of the option. However, most schemes now provide for the grant of options under seal.

Executive Share Option Schemes 5.43

5.42 The manner in which a company may execute a document must be ascertained from the Articles of Association. Modern public company Articles generally provide for a common seal to be used only upon the authority of a resolution of the directors or a committee of the directors, but provision will often be made for a securities seal which can be printed directly onto the form of option certificates. The directors will normally also have a discretion whether any document sealed by the company will need to be signed and, if so, by whom.

5.43 A recommended form of option certificate for options granted under seal is as follows:

[Certificate No]

SHARE OPTION CERTIFICATE
[   ] plc/Limited
EXECUTIVE SHARE OPTION SCHEME

Date of Grant	Normal First Exercise Date	Exercise Price per Share	Number of Shares

This is to certify that:

....

of ....

has been granted an Option to acquire the number of ordinary shares of [   ]p each fully paid in the Company at the exercise price shown above under the Rules of the .... Executive Share Option Scheme.

By Order of the Board

[Printed Securities Seal]

[Printed Signature]

Secretary

NOTES
(1) The Option is not transferable, and will lapse upon any assignment, charge, disposal or other dealing.
(2) A copy of the Scheme rules is available for inspection upon request to [   ].

THIS CERTIFICATE IS IMPORTANT AND SHOULD BE KEPT IN A SAFE PLACE

5.44 *Executive Share Option Schemes*

Notes on the specimen share option certificate

(1) This form is not suitable in the case of Discounted Price Options, Parallel Options, Replacement Options and Super Options (see specimen option certificate for Discounted Price Options and Parallel Options in Chapter 6).

(2) Where the option is exercisable upon satisfaction of any specific performance targets or other conditions of exercise, the terms of these should be set out in full on the option certificate or at least attached to it.

(3) As an alternative to a printed securities seal, the option certificate may be executed by the incorporation of the words 'Executed by the Company as a deed' and countersigned by a director and secretary, or in such other form as may be approved by the directors under the articles of association of the company.

(4) The company may wish to give consideration to providing a 'tear off' counterfoil for optionholders to return in the event of any change of name or address although a company may be content to place reliance on its personnel databases.

5.44 Many schemes allow the company to issue a balance certificate where an option is exercised in part; the option certificate may be called in for endorsement or cancellation and replacement in appropriate circumstances, for instance, where the number and price of option shares has been adjusted following any variation of share capital (see 'Variations of share capital' in Chapter 13).

Disclaimer of options

5.45 Many public company schemes provide for an optionholder who so wishes to disclaim an option granted to him within a specified period following the date of grant. In principle, this is unnecessary since an optionholder always has the right to unilaterally surrender his option under seal at any time.

5.46 However, express provisions in the scheme rules allowing the disclaimer of options to be made under hand has the advantage that this will avoid the need for a disclaimer to be made under seal. A written disclaimer under the provisions of the scheme need not be stamped.

Non-transferability of an option

5.47 Normally, scheme rules will provide that an option will not be capable of transfer, assignment or charge. ABI Guidelines specifically exclude any right of transfer (1987 Guidelines, paragraph 14).

Approved schemes

5.48 TA 1988, 9 Sch 27(2) specifically excludes any transfer of option rights under an approved scheme. The only exception to this is the transmission of shares to the personal representatives of a deceased participant (see 5.93 below).

Tax on transfers of option rights

5.49 Where a gain is realised by any transfer of an option, income tax under Schedule E is chargeable under the provisions of *TA 1988, s 135(1)*. For this purpose, the gain will be the excess of the market value of the shares transferred over their exercise price (*TA 1988, s 135(3)*). However, to the extent the transferee is granted a replacement option (including in another company) for the transfer of his original option, the optionholder is treated as having acquired the replacement option for a cost equal to the consideration given for the grant of the original option (*TA 1988, s 136*) i.e. he receives a roll-over for income tax purposes.

5.50 Whilst there is a roll-over for income tax purposes for an exchange of options, there is no such roll-over for capital gains tax purposes (except in certain circumstances under an approved scheme on a change of control — see 12.14 to 12.21). The disclaimer of an option is a disposal of the option for the purposes of *TCGA 1992, s 22(1)(c)*; if a replacement option is granted at a lower price in consideration of the disclaimer of the original option, the undervalue will be the consideration given for the disclaimer of the original option for the purposes of *TCGA 1992, s 22(1)(c)*.

Individual participation limit

Introduction

5.51 The limits on individual participation under an executive share option scheme are derived from two sources: the statutory limits in *TA 1988, 9 Sch 28* which apply to approved schemes regardless of whether the company is private or listed and the ABI's limits which apply only to companies with significant holdings by institutional investors.

5.52 In general, listed companies adopt a limit of shares worth up to four times earnings. However, under the 1987 ABI Guidelines, there are circumstances in which 'Super' options in excess of four times earnings may be granted (see 'Super Options' in 6.7 to 6.16).

5.53 Executive Share Option Schemes

Limit under approved schemes

5.53 An approved share option scheme must provide that no person shall obtain rights under it which, at the time they are obtained, would cause the aggregate market value of the shares comprised in subsisting options under that, or any other approved share option scheme, established by that company or by any associated company, exceeding (or further exceeding) the 'appropriate limit' (*TA 1988, 9 Sch 28*).

Appropriate limit

5.54 The appropriate limit under *TA 1988, 9 Sch 28(2)* is the greater of:

(a) £100,000 (see 5.57 below); or

(b) four times the 'relevant emoluments' for the current or preceding tax year (see 5.60 below); or

(c) where there are no 'relevant emoluments' for the preceding tax year, four times the relevant emoluments for the twelve months' period starting with the first day during the current tax year for which there are relevant emoluments.

Aggregate of market value

5.55 In order to determine whether the proposed grant of an option is within the appropriate limit, it is necessary to aggregate the market values of all the shares comprised in any options which are to be taken into account including the market value of the shares in the proposed grant. For this purpose, shares are valued at the market value as at the time of grant. Normally, this will be the market value on such day or days immediately preceding the date of grant as may be specified in the scheme, but where an option price is based on the market value shortly before invitations are granted, it will be the market value on that day.

Where Discounted Price Options are granted, the shares will be valued on the basis of their market value rather than the discounted price.

Shares under other approved schemes

5.56 The market value of subsisting options over shares under other approved share option schemes established by the company which established the scheme, or by any associated company, must be taken into account in applying the 'appropriate limit'. An 'associated

Executive Share Option Schemes 5.62

company' is defined by *TA 1988, s 416*. Broadly speaking, it includes any company which at the relevant time (or at any time in the previous twelve months) is or has been the holding company of the company which established the scheme, or any subsidiary or holding company of that company. However, the market value of shares allocated under any savings-related share option scheme are not taken into account.

The £100,000 limit

5.57 The £100,000 limit has not been increased since the introduction of approved share option schemes in 1984 and its significance has diminished with rising earnings. It was designed to provide a simple and easily calculated alternative to the limits based on relevant emoluments which require a calculation of the earnings subject to deduction of tax under PAYE.

5.58 However, the limit has been used by non-UK resident employees who, of course, have no earnings subject to deduction of tax under PAYE. Indeed, this has been the only way in which such employees can be included in an approved scheme.

5.59 The £100,000 limit is not accepted by the ABI as an alternative to the limit of four times earnings although it was originally acceptable to the NAPF under its 1984 Guidelines. The argument generally put forward by the ABI is that it would be unacceptable for a low paid employee to receive £100,000 worth of shares where this is in excess, perhaps substantially in excess, of the four times earnings limit.

Relevant emoluments

5.60 *TA 1988, 9 Sch 28(4)* defines 'relevant emoluments' as such of the emoluments of the employment by virtue of which the person in question is eligible to participate in the scheme as are liable to be paid under deduction of tax in accordance with the PAYE Regulations but excluding any amounts representing benefits in kind. Relevant emoluments will only include emoluments paid by a participating company: the emoluments paid by any company which is not participating in the scheme must be excluded even if tax is deducted under PAYE.

5.61 Any overseas earnings which are not liable to deduction of tax under PAYE cannot count as relevant emoluments.

5.62 Relevant emoluments are calculated after deducting items to which the 'net pay' arrangements apply under PAYE Regulations.

5.63 Executive Share Option Schemes

These are statutory profit-related pay, employees' superannuation contributions (including additional voluntary contributions qualifying for income tax relief) and employee payroll charitable giving arrangements (see 'Employer's Guide to PAYE', IR P7, paragraph F82).

5.63 Relevant emoluments are the emoluments *for* a tax year, not necessarily those received in that tax year, or even included in the year end certificate of tax deduction (P60). A bonus which is paid after the end of the tax year, but related back to the tax year in which the profits on which it is based were made, can be treated as part of the relevant emoluments for that tax year. This applies notwithstanding the introduction of the new 'receipts basis' for the assessment of tax under *Schedule E* contained in *FA 1989, ss 36–42*. The payment of a bonus after the tax year may, therefore, have the effect of bringing an option grant during the tax year within the appropriate limit retrospectively. Any such bonus would need to be paid as a genuine bonus, and not simply as an advance payment of salary during a subsequent tax year.

5.64 The Inland Revenue Guide on Executive Share Option Schemes gives the following example in relation to the calculation of 'relevant emoluments' for a tax year:

Example

Tax Year ended 5th April 1990

1. Salary – £30,000 a year, paid monthly
2. Bonus for the year to 5th April 1990 – £3,000 paid in June 1990
3. Car benefit – £1,000

The relevant emoluments for the tax year ended 5th April 1990 are £33,000 (1 and 2 above), although Form P60 for tax year ended 5th April 1990 will show gross pay of only £30,000 as the bonus paid for that tax year was not paid until after 5th April 1990.

ABI Guidelines

5.65 ABI Guidelines limit individual participation in executive share option schemes, approved and unapproved, to such number of shares as have an aggregate market value at the relevant date of grant equal to 'four times the participant's total annual emoluments from the companies within the scheme'. In calculating this limit, all option grants in the previous ten years are taken into account regardless of whether they have subsequently been exercised, lapsed or surrendered. The ABI is concerned that executives do not surrender and regrant

Executive Share Option Schemes **5.69**

options at any time the price falls substantially and so insist that surrendered as well as exercised options continue to be taken into account.

5.66 However, the ABI accepts two 'concessions' in respect of its normal limit of four times earnings over any ten year period. First, it allows Replacement Options (see 6.17 to 6.23) to run sequentially in excess of four times earnings in total to 'replace' options which have been exercised. Secondly, it allows the grant of Super Options to run consecutively or sequentially in excess of four times earnings.

Excess options

5.67 Options may, in error, be granted to a person in excess of either the 'appropriate limit' or any limit on the number of shares available under the scheme. Any such excess option cannot be granted 'in accordance with the provisions of an approved share option scheme' (*TA 1988, s 185(1)*). It cannot therefore enjoy the tax reliefs available to approved options even if it appears to be granted under an approved scheme.

5.68 Where an approved option is granted in excess of either the 'appropriate limit', or any scheme limit, it would appear that the position is as follows:

(*a*) no tax reliefs will be available under *TA 1988, s 185* in respect of that option;

(*b*) it would appear the option is enforceable at the instance of the optionholder on the terms of the scheme provided the option was granted under seal or for nil consideration;

(*c*) the grant of an option would seem to be made under an employees' share scheme and, therefore, no breach of *CA 1985, s 80* applies, and there is no need for any disapplication of the pre-emption provisions under *CA 1985, s 95*.

The company will need to return the grant as an unapproved share option or, if it has previously returned it as an approved option, write to the Inland Revenue explaining the position and any appropriate adjustment of the tax liability of the optionholder will be made.

5.69 It is common for a company to grant options over the maximum number of shares available which will be based on four times the relevant emoluments of the current tax year (which will not be ascertainable until after the end of the tax year). As the relevant

5.70 *Executive Share Option Schemes*

earnings to be taken into account may not be known at the date of grant it may be helpful to grant a sequence of options during the tax year as relevant emoluments become more certain. The first tier of options would be based on the relevant emoluments of the preceding tax year. The second tier of options would be based on any salary increment received during the current tax year. A third tier of options might be based on the estimate of any bonus payable in the next tax year 'for' the current tax year. If any tier turns out to be excessive, only that tier will fail to qualify for the income tax relief.

5.70 A company which has both an approved and unapproved option scheme can grant options expressed to be made so far as possible under the approved scheme, with any excess being granted under the unapproved scheme.

5.71 An alternative way of avoiding the risk of granting options in excess of the 'appropriate limit', or for that matter any scheme limit, is for the scheme to provide for any grant of options to take effect within any relevant limit. The Model Scheme incorporates such a provision as follows:

> 'Any Option . . . shall be limited to take effect so that [it does not exceed the prescribed limit]'.

Scheme limits

The London Stock Exchange

5.72 *The Listing Rules* contain no limits on the number of shares which may be made available. Since 1 December 1993 it has no longer been necessary to include a fixed numerical limit on the number of shares to be made available under any scheme.

NAPF Guidelines

5.73 The NAPF Guidelines limit executive share options to 5 per cent of the share capital over any ten year period where the options are made available to a 'restricted group'. Otherwise, the ABI's overall limit of 10 per cent in ten years applies.

ABI Guidelines

5.74 The 1987 ABI Guidelines, paragraph 9, normally limits executive share options to 5 per cent of the ordinary share capital over any

Executive Share Option Schemes 5.78

ten year period. However, there are two exceptions. First, the 1987 Guidelines, paragraph 10, includes an exception for *small companies* which are defined as companies having a market capitalisation of £5m or less. Small companies may allocate up to 10 per cent of the ordinary share capital, provided this does not exceed £0.5m of such capital at the date of the adoption of the scheme. Secondly, the 1987 Guidelines provide for the grant of Super Options up to an additional 5 per cent of share capital where certain performance targets are satisfied over a five-year period (see 6.6 to 6.16).

5.75 Under ABI Guidelines, listed companies are also required to adhere to an overall 10 per cent in ten-year limit and a flow rate limit of 3 per cent in three years (see 3.12).

5.76 In the case of 'Replacement Options' executive share options are limited to 2.5 per cent of the share capital in the four year period following the establishment of the scheme, or the date of the alteration of the scheme to allow Replacement Options (see 6.17 to 6.23).

Exercise of options

5.77 *TA 1988, 9 Sch* does not contain any rules relating to the time or manner in which approved options must be exercised except that no option may be exercised by personal representatives later than one year after the date of the optionholder's death (*TA 1988, 9 Sch 27(2)*). However, income tax applies on the exercise of an option within three years of the date of grant or within three years of the last occasion on which the optionholder exercised any approved share option (but not a savings-related share option) in circumstances which qualified for income tax relief (*TA 1988, s 185(5)*). In addition, there is no income tax relief on the exercise of an option after the tenth anniversary of grant (*TA 1988, s 185(5)*). It should be noted that whilst the income tax reliefs normally applies from the third anniversary of grant (or the third anniversary of the last tax exempt exercise) there is in fact no prohibition on the exercise of approved options before the third anniversary of grant.

ABI Guidelines

5.78 It is the ABI Guidelines which have substantially shaped the rights of exercise in normal executive share option schemes established by listed companies. It has long been a fundamental principle of the ABI Guidelines that options could not be exercised by an employee before the third anniversary of grant. However, an exception is made in the case of employees who leave employment early. In earlier ABI Guidelines, exercise was only permitted before the third anniversary of grant in the event of an 'involuntary' cessation of employment but this wording was removed in the 1987 Guidelines. However, most

5.79 *Executive Share Option Schemes*

schemes still only permit early exercise in the event of some involuntary reason for leaving employment. The 1987 ABI Guidelines provide for a maximum period of one year after leaving within which to exercise an option.

Exercise by employees

Approved schemes

5.79 The Model Scheme provides for options to be exercisable from the third anniversary of the date of grant. This simply reflects the tax rules which provide for any gains on the exercise of an approved option prior to the third anniversary of grant to be chargeable to income tax. The Model Scheme provides that an approved option will lapse on the tenth anniversary of grant as required by *TA 1988, s 185(5)*.

The three-year rule

5.80 When approved share options were introduced in *FA 1984*, the highest rate of income tax was 60 per cent and the rate of capital gains tax was only 30 per cent. There was a concern that some executives might be 'paid' in share options rather than cash. In order to avoid such an outcome, the 'three-year rule' was introduced to bring any gains made on the frequent exercise of share options within the charge to income tax. *TA 1988, s 185(5)* provides that the relief from income tax on approved option gains in *TA 1988, s 185(3)* shall not apply where an option is exercised within three years of grant or within three years of a previous tax-exempt exercise by that optionholder. The charge to income tax applies even if the previous tax-exempt exercise was in respect of an option held by the same person under a different approved share option scheme. In applying this rule, however, the exercise of two or more options on the same day will be treated as a single exercise of an option and will be treated as exempt from income tax.

5.81 Where an option has been exercised in circumstances which give rise to a liability to income tax, it is disregarded in calculating whether a subsequent option exercise will be caught by the three-year rule.

Unapproved schemes

5.82 Most unapproved share option schemes are drafted so that options lapse on the seventh anniversary at the latest. This is to ensure that there is no risk of any charge to income tax at the date of grant.

TA 1988, s 135(2) provides that no charge to income tax can arise on the grant of an unapproved option where the option is not capable of being exercised more than seven years after the date of grant.

Exercise by former employees

ABI Guidelines

5.83 Under ABI Guidelines, options may be exercised in the period of one year after a director or employee leaves employment. The 1987 ABI Guidelines, paragraph 13 states that optionholders who have left employment may exercise for up to three and one half years from the date of grant, if later than one year after leaving employment. The purpose of this special extension is to ensure that any employee who leaves employment will have a period of at least six months when he may exercise his option in tax-exempt circumstances. However, this overlooks the fact that many executives have a series of options granted in different years.

5.84 In order to ensure that any exercise by a former employee can be tax-free even where he has a series of options, the ABI allows companies to extend the period of exercise until three and one half years after the latest of the following:

(*a*) the date of grant of the option to be exercised;

(*b*) the date of grant of any other option granted since the option granted in (*a*) above;

(*c*) the last date on which he exercised an option under the scheme (or any other approved executive share option scheme) in circumstances which qualified for relief from income tax under the approved scheme legislation.

5.85 Although 1987 ABI Guidelines allow a right of exercise by all former employees regardless of their reason for leaving, most listed companies in fact still only allow exercise in involuntary circumstances:

(*a*) injury;

(*b*) disability;

(*c*) redundancy;

(*d*) early retirement with the employer's consent; or

(*e*) the employment ceasing to be with a participating company as a result of the sale or transfer of the subsidiary or business in which the optionholder works to a person who is not a participating company.

5.86 *Executive Share Option Schemes*

5.86 Exercise will also normally be allowed where an employee retires, although the 1987 ABI Guidelines at paragraph 13 provide that 'no option may be granted within the two years preceding the normal retirement date of the participant either under his contract of employment or otherwise'. In practice, this may be unfair on elderly executives who continue working beyond their normal retirement date who would be excluded under this guideline from the grant of an option. The ABI is, therefore, prepared to relax this guideline and allow schemes to provide an alternative rule to the effect that an option may only be exercised by a retired executive if it has been held for at least two years at the date of retirement.

5.87 A number of schemes provide a right of exercise in the event a person leaves employment following maternity. It is doubtful that any claim could be brought for discrimination if such a right is either given or not given in the scheme.

5.88 A minority of schemes provide for rights of exercise in the event of the dismissal of the optionholder without good cause.

5.89 A number of schemes allow optionholders who are transferred to a foreign jurisdiction in which the exercise of the option may not be practicable or tax efficient to exercise early at the discretion of the directors.

Approved schemes

5.90 There are no restrictions under *TA 1988, 9 Sch* on the rights of exercise which may be granted under an approved option scheme in respect of former employees except that the option will cease to attract income tax relief if it is exercised more than ten years after the date of grant.

5.91 The approved share option scheme legislation refers to 'the right to acquire 'shares' rather than 'options', the only reference to the word 'option' being in the title. The Inland Revenue's interpretation is that an option is merely a bundle of rights to acquire shares and that the right to acquire shares are immutable and must be specified from the outset.

5.92 The Inland Revenue are not prepared to approve a scheme which gives the directors a discretion to allow exercise in any circumstances they deem fit, arguing that the exercise of such a discretion is the creation of a new right of exercise which, if exercisable at a price which is less than the market value of the shares at that date, would be within the charge to income tax on the undervalue by virtue of *TA 1988, s 185(6)*. However, the Inland Revenue will approve a scheme which contains a discretion on the part of the directors to allow

Executive Share Option Schemes **5.97**

exercise if an absolute right of exercise is provided upon leaving employment for injury or disability or redundancy.

The Model Scheme provides for options to be exercisable by a former employee who leaves the company 'by reason of injury, or disability, or redundancy or retirement or for such other reasons as are specified in the rules. . .'.

Exercise by personal representatives

5.93 The personal representatives of a deceased optionholder will normally be allowed to exercise the option during the period following the death of the deceased. In approved schemes, a maximum period of one year is allowed. Normally, an option held at the date of death will form part of the estate of the deceased for inheritance tax purposes and in valuing any option any restrictions on transfer are disregarded (*IHTA 1984, s 163(1)*).

Takeover, etc.

5.94 Most schemes provide for a right of exercise in the event of a takeover, scheme of arrangement under *CA 1985, s 425* or a voluntary winding-up which affects the scheme shares. Since 1987 many approved schemes have also incorporated a provision for optionholders to exchange their options with the agreement of any offeror (see Chapter 12).

Performance targets

5.95 A scheme may provide that options will only be exercisable if specified conditions of exercise are satisfied. These may include the achievement of a specified performance target.

5.96 Following the publication of Joint Statement on Performance Targets in Executive Share Option Schemes in July 1993 ('the Joint Guidance': see 3.43), all public companies are now expected to include appropriate performance targets in new or renewed executive share option schemes.

5.97 The ABI has traditionally preferred a performance target based on earnings per share growth. The 1987 ABI Guidelines recommended that in normal executive share options, the test should be a growth in earnings per share which at least matches the percentage increase in the retail prices index (see 3.36). The problem with performance targets based on earnings per share is that with the introduction of FRS3 in place of SSAP3, the figure for profit before

5.98   Executive Share Option Schemes

tax in company accounts is arguably more volatile as exceptional items now vary considerably from year to year. The ABI accepts this and is prepared for companies to restate their earnings per share figure on the basis of SSAP3.

5.98   The NAPF prefers a performance target based on a share price benchmark such as the FT Actuaries All Share Index.

5.99   The Joint Guidance of the ABI and NAPF on executive share option schemes indicates that Remuneration Committees may choose such performance targets as they consider appropriate for the company. In practice, the most appropriate performance target for most trading companies will normally be either a share price benchmark or earnings per share. In the case of property and investment holding companies, a target based on net assets can be more appropriate. Mineral companies will normally need to assess performance against some index.

In many cases, an appropriate alternative target may be performance measured against the total return indices as published in the FT Actuaries Share Indices.

Approved schemes

5.100   The Inland Revenue Guide on Executive Share Option Schemes (IR 100) confirms that additional conditions of exercise may be included in approved schemes. The Guide states that such additional conditions must *either* be clearly specified in the approved scheme, *or* the rules of the scheme must contain clear 'objective guidelines' by which those additional conditions will be determined. The example given in the Inland Revenue Guide of an 'objective guideline' is that the scheme rules may provide for additional conditions to be set based on 'the attainment of targets by the optionholder which might reasonably be considered to be a fair measure of the performance of the optionholder's job, and to be attainable'. Performance targets may therefore be individually set although it would be normal for any performance target to apply to all participants.

5.101   Many listed companies would prefer not to incorporate the precise terms of any performance target in the scheme rules since any changes to such terms in future years would require shareholders' prior approval.

5.102   Ideally, scheme rules will merely contain a power for the directors to set additional objective exercise conditions to be approved by the Inland Revenue in advance. Although this may be cumbersome, particularly if there are various individual performance targets to be

Executive Share Option Schemes **5.105**

specifically approved by the Inland Revenue, nevertheless it provides the directors with the flexibility to change the performance targets in later years without resorting to shareholders on each occasion. The detailed performance targets will be set out in the documents issued to optionholders at the time of grant and it is this document which will be submitted to the Inland Revenue for approval. If the same performance target will apply to a number of different optionholders, or will apply for a succession of grants of options over several years, it need only be approved once.

Variations of performance targets

5.103 One of the areas of greatest difficulty in respect of approved share options has been the question of altering subsisting option rights, and in particular performance targets under subsisting options. The Inland Revenue's approach to option rights is that once set they cannot be varied except in accordance with their original terms.

5.104 In *IRC v Burton Group plc* [*1990*] *STC 242*, Burton Group plc had established a share option scheme and proposed to amend it so that performance conditions could be set or varied after the date on which an option had been granted under the scheme. The court held the scheme could be altered to allow performance targets to be varied in certain circumstances. In particular, the mechanism for altering the performance targets needs to be set out in the scheme rules and a variation must be made in a way which is intended to represent a fairer measure of performance. In *IRC v Eurocopy plc* [*1991*] *STC 707* the court endorsed the Inland Revenue's usual approach to the variation of option rights. The case involved a proposed alteration to a scheme to reduce the earliest date of exercise of options from nine to six years. The Inland Revenue argued that such an alteration was so fundamental to the original option that it amounted to the grant of a new right to acquire shares. The *Burton* and *Eurocopy* cases are obviously to some extent in conflict. The Inland Revenue generally construe the *Burton* case in the narrowest possible way.

5.105 The Inland Revenue Guide on Executive Share Option Schemes (IR 100) reflects the decision in the *Eurocopy* case and provides that conditions or targets may only be varied or waived after they have been set if 'it is clearly specified in the scheme (and therefore in the terms of the option itself) when and to what extent they may be varied'. The Guide states that normally the extent of any variation should be an adjustment which the directors reasonably consider would be neither more nor less difficult to satisfy than were the original conditions when first set. This requirement that any variation should be neither more nor less difficult is an attempt to reconcile the *Eurocopy* and *Burton* cases. The *Eurocopy* case makes it clear that

5.106 *Executive Share Option Schemes*

an alteration of a significant term of an option is the grant of a new right; the *Burton* case suggests that there are circumstances in which performance targets can be varied after the grant of the option. However, the Inland Revenue's view that varied rights should be no less onerous is difficult to apply in practice. In most cases the only reason why a company may wish to vary or waive a performance target is because a change in market conditions has made the satisfaction of the performance target significantly less *capable* of achievement.

5.106 The Inland Revenue Guide states that any variation should take the form of an adjustment which the *directors* reasonably consider will be no more onerous. It is not clear whether the Inland Revenue will normally be prepared to accept the variation envisaged by the directors or will apply its own judgement in respect of any application to vary performance targets.

Executive Share Option Schemes **5.106**

Appendix 3

Set out below is a precedent for an approved Executive Share Option Scheme appropriate for a listed company. Certain passages reflect ABI and NAPF Guidelines and would not necessarily be included in the scheme of a private company.

Rules of the [   ] Executive Share Option Scheme

1. Definitions

1.1 In this Scheme, the following words and expressions shall bear, unless the context otherwise requires, the meanings set forth below:

'Appropriate Period'	the meaning given by *paragraph 15 (2)* of *Schedule 9* to the *Taxes Act*;
'Associated Company'	an associated company of the Company within the meaning the expression bears in *section 187(2)* of the *Taxes Act*;
'the Auditors'	the auditors of the Company for the time being;
'the Board'	the board of directors of the Company, or a duly authorised committee thereof;
'Close Company'	a close company as defined in *section 414(1)* of the *Taxes Act* as varied by *Paragraph 8* of *Schedule 9* to the *Taxes Act*;
'the Company'	[ ] plc (registered in [ ] under No [ ]);
'Control'	the meaning given by *section 840* of the *Taxes Act*;
'Date of Grant'	the date on which the Board grants an Option;
'Dealing Day'	any day on which the London Stock Exchange is open for the transaction of business;
'Eligible Employee'	any individual who:

(a) is a director or employee of a Participating Company on terms which require him to devote substantially the whole of his time to his duties which, if he is a director, shall be at least 25 hours a week, and, if he is an

5.106 *Executive Share Option Schemes*

<table>
<tr><td></td><td colspan="2">employee, shall be at least 20 hours a week (in either case excluding meal breaks); and</td></tr>
<tr><td></td><td>(b)</td><td>has not at the Date of Grant, and has not had within the preceding twelve months, a Material Interest in a Close Company which is:</td></tr>
<tr><td></td><td></td><td>(i) the Company; or</td></tr>
<tr><td></td><td></td><td>(ii) a company which has Control of the Company or is a Member of a Consortium which owns the Company;</td></tr>
<tr><td>**'Employees' Share Scheme'**</td><td colspan="2">the meaning given by *section 743* of the *Companies Act 1985*;</td></tr>
<tr><td>**'Executive Share Option Scheme'**</td><td colspan="2">an employees' share option scheme in which participation is solely at the discretion of directors;</td></tr>
<tr><td>**'Exercise Price'**</td><td colspan="2">the amount payable in relation to the exercise of an Option, whether in whole or in part, being an amount equal to the relevant Option Price multiplied by the number of Shares in respect of which the Option is exercised;</td></tr>
<tr><td>**'Grant Period'**</td><td colspan="2">the period of 42 days commencing on the Dealing Day following any of the following:</td></tr>
<tr><td></td><td>(a)</td><td>the day on which the Scheme is approved by the Inland Revenue;</td></tr>
<tr><td></td><td>(b)</td><td>the day immediately following the day on which the Company makes an announcement of its results for the last preceding financial year, half-year or other period;</td></tr>
<tr><td></td><td>(c)</td><td>any day on which the Board resolves that exceptional circumstances exist which justify the grant of Options;</td></tr>
<tr><td>**'the London Stock Exchange'**</td><td colspan="2">The International Stock Exchange of the United Kingdom and the Republic of Ireland Limited;</td></tr>
<tr><td>**'Market Value'**</td><td colspan="2">in relation to a Share on any day:</td></tr>
<tr><td></td><td>(a)</td><td>if and so long as the Shares are listed on the London Stock Exchange, its middle market quotation (as derived</td></tr>
</table>

Executive Share Option Schemes 5.106

from the Daily Official List of the London Stock Exchange); or

(b) subject to (a) above, its market value, determined in accordance with *Part VIII* of the *Taxation of Chargeable Gains Act 1992* and agreed in advance with the Shares Valuation Division of the Inland Revenue;

'Material Interest' the meaning given by *section 187(3)* of the *Taxes Act*;

'Member of a Consortium' the meaning given by *section 187(7)* of the *Taxes Act*;

'Option' a right to acquire Shares under the Scheme which is either subsisting or (where the context so admits or requires) is proposed to be granted;

'Option Price' the price per Share, as determined by the Board, at which an Eligible Employee may acquire Shares upon the exercise of an Option being not less than:

(a) the Market Value or, where Rule 2.3 applies, 85 per cent of the Market Value of a Share:

(i) subject to (ii) and (iii) below, on the Dealing Day (being a Dealing Day within the Grant Period) immediately preceding the Date of Grant; or

(ii) if the Board so determines, averaged over the three Dealing Days (all being Dealing Days within the Grant Period) immediately preceding the Date of Grant; or

(iii) if the Board so determines, at such earlier time or times as the Board may determine (with the previous agreement in writing of the Inland Revenue); and

(b) if the Shares are to be subscribed, their nominal value,

but subject to any adjustment pursuant to Rule 8;

5.106 Executive Share Option Schemes

'Original Market Value'	in relation to any Share to be taken into account for the purposes of the limit in Rule 2.5, its Market Value as determined for the purposes of the relevant grant of options;
'Participant'	a director or employee, or former director or employee, to whom an Option has been granted or (where the context so admits or requires) the personal representatives of any such person;
'Participating Company'	(a) the Company; and
	(b) any other company which is under the Control of the Company, is a Subsidiary of the Company and is for the time being designated by the Board as a Participating Company;
'Relevant Earnings'	in relation to an Eligible Employee:
	(a) who had earnings in the preceding Year of Assessment, the amount of his earnings for the current or, if greater, for the preceding Year of Assessment;
	(b) who did not have any earnings for the preceding Year of Assessment, the amount of his earnings for the period of twelve months beginning with the first day during the current Year of Assessment in respect of which there are earnings,
	where 'earnings' shall be taken to be such emoluments of the office or employment by virtue of which he is eligible to participate in the Scheme as are liable to be paid under deduction of tax pursuant to *section 203* of the *Taxes Act* (pay as you earn) after deducting from them amounts included by virtue of *Chapter II* of *Part V* of the *Taxes Act* (certain expenses payments and benefits in kind);
'Retirement Age'	in relation to a Participant, any age at which he is either bound or entitled to retire;
'the Scheme'	the [ ] Executive Share Option Scheme

Executive Share Option Schemes 5.106

	in its present form or as from time to time amended in accordance with the provisions hereof;
'Share'	a share in the capital of the Company which satisfies the conditions specified in *Paragraphs 10 to 14* (inclusive) of *Schedule 9* to the *Taxes Act*;
'Subsidiary'	the meaning given by *sections 736* and *736A* of the *Companies Act 1985*;
'Taxes Act'	the *Income and Corporation Taxes Act 1988*;
'Year of Assessment'	a year of assessment within the meaning given by *section 832* of the *Taxes Act*.

1.2 In the Scheme, unless the context requires otherwise:

(a) the headings are inserted for convenience only and do not affect the interpretation of any Rule;

(b) a reference to a Rule is a reference to a Rule of the Scheme;

(c) a reference to a statute or statutory provision includes a reference:

  (i) to that statute or provision as from time to time consolidated, modified, re-enacted or replaced by any statute or statutory provision;

  (ii) to any repealed statute or statutory provision which it re-enacts (with or without modification); and

  (iii) to any subordinate legislation made under it;

(d) words in the singular include the plural, and vice versa;

(e) a reference to the masculine shall be treated as a reference to the feminine, and vice versa;

(f) if a period of time is specified and starts from a given day or the day of an act or event, it is to be calculated exclusive of that day;

(g) a reference to 'a year' shall be a period calculated by reference to a previous or subsequent anniversary of a particular date.

2. Grant of Options

2.1 An Option may only be granted to an Eligible Employee who is nominated at the discretion of the Board.

5.106 *Executive Share Option Schemes*

2.2 Options may only be granted during a Grant Period and shall be granted within 30 days of the earliest day by reference to which the Option Price was determined.

2.3 The following conditions must be satisfied as at the Date of Grant where an Option is to be granted at an Option Price which is less than the Market Value:

(*a*) each Participating Company of the Scheme must have established or be a participating company in one or both of a savings related share option scheme (a 'qualifying savings related scheme') or a profit sharing scheme (a 'qualifying profit sharing scheme') which is in each case at the Date of Grant approved by the Inland Revenue pursuant to the *Taxes Act* and in determining whether any such scheme is so approved any subsequent withdrawal of such approval with effect from an earlier date shall be ignored;

(*b*) every director or employee, whether of a Participating Company or not, who would, on the Date of Grant, be eligible to receive an invitation to participate in a qualifying savings related scheme, must have been notified in writing within the period of twelve months immediately preceding the Date of Grant of the existence of that qualifying scheme and such notification shall be given by one or more of any Participating Company and the company by virtue of employment with which the director or employee is eligible to participate in the qualifying savings related scheme;

(*c*) every director or employee, whether of a Participating Company or not, who would, on the Date of Grant, be eligible to participate in a qualifying profit sharing scheme, must have been notified in writing within the period of twelve months immediately preceding the Date of Grant of the existence of that qualifying scheme and such notification shall be given by one or more of any Participating Company and the company by virtue of employment with which the director or employee is eligible to participate in the qualifying profit sharing scheme.

2.4 The Board may grant an Option subject to such objective condition or conditions of exercise as it may determine provided that any such condition shall be set out in documentation which is approved in advance by the Inland Revenue.

2.5 Any Option granted to an Eligible Employee shall be limited to take effect so that immediately following such grant the aggregate of the Original Market Value of all the Shares over which he has been granted option rights in the preceding ten years under:

(*a*) the Scheme;

Executive Share Option Schemes **5.106**

(*b*) any other Executive Share Option Scheme adopted by the Company or an Associated Company,

shall not exceed in amount four times the Relevant Earnings of that Eligible Employee at that time PROVIDED THAT no account shall be taken of any such options which have been exercised and PROVIDED FURTHER THAT in the case of an Eligible Employee who has any earnings which are not Relevant Earnings the applicable limit shall be, if greater than four times the Relevant Earnings of that Eligible Employee, the lesser of £100,000 and four times his aggregate annual rate of earnings from the Company and all Subsidiaries of the Company.

2.6 In determining the limits in Rule 2.5 above no account shall be taken of any Shares where the Option was released without being exercised within 30 days of its grant.

2.7 The Company shall issue to each Participant an option certificate in such form (not inconsistent with the provisions of the Scheme) as the Board may from time to time prescribe. Each such certificate shall specify the Date of Grant of the Option, the number and class of Shares over which the Option is granted and the Option Price. The option certificate shall be sealed or executed in such other manner as to take effect in law as a deed.

2.8 Except as provided in the Scheme, every Option shall be personal to the Participant to whom it is granted and shall not be transferable.

2.9 No amount shall be paid in respect of the grant of an Option.

3. Number of Shares in respect of which Options may be granted

3.1 The number of Shares which may be allocated under the scheme on any day shall not, when added to the aggregate number of Shares which have been allocated in the previous ten years under the Scheme and any other Executive Share Option Scheme adopted by the Company, exceed such number as represents 5 per cent of the ordinary share capital of the Company in issue immediately prior to that day provided that the number of Shares which may be allocated under all Executive Share Option Schemes during the period of four years, commencing on the adoption date of the Scheme, shall not exceed 2.5 per cent of the ordinary share capital of the Company in issue from time to time.

3.2 Unless the limit set out in Rule 3.3 is and has always been complied with the number of Shares which may be allocated under the Scheme on any day shall not, when added to the aggregate of the number of Shares which have been allocated in the previous three

5.106 *Executive Share Option Schemes*

years under the Scheme and any other employees' share scheme adopted by the Company, exceed such number as represents 3 per cent of the ordinary share capital in issue immediately prior to that day.

3.3 The number of Shares which may be allocated on any day shall not, when aggregated with the number of Shares which have been allocated in the previous five years under the scheme and any other employees' share scheme adopted by the Company shall not exceed 5 per cent of the ordinary share capital of the Company in issue immediately prior to that day.

3.4 The number of Shares which may be allocated under the scheme on any day shall not, when aggregated with the number of Shares which have been allocated in the previous ten years under the scheme and any other employees' share scheme adopted by the Company, exceed 10 per cent of the ordinary share capital of the Company in issue immediately prior to that day.

3.5 In determining the above limits no account shall be taken of any Shares where the right to acquire the Shares was released, lapsed or otherwise became incapable of exercise.

3.6 References in this Rule to 'allocation' shall mean, in the case of any share option scheme, the placing of unissued Shares under option and, in relation to other types of employees' share scheme, shall mean the issue and allotment of Shares and references to 'allocated' shall be construed accordingly.

4. Rights of exercise and lapse of Options

4.1

(*a*) Save as provided in Rules 4.2, 4.3, 4.5 and Rule 5, an Option shall not be exercised earlier than the third anniversary of the Date of Grant;

(*b*) Save as provided in Rules 4.2, 4.3 and Rule 5, an Option may only be exercised by a Participant whilst he is a director or employee of a Participating Company or an Associated Company;

(*c*) An Option may not be exercised by a Participant if he has, or has had at any time within the twelve month period preceding the date of exercise, a Material Interest in the issued ordinary share capital of a Close Company which is the Company or a company which has Control of the Company or is a Member of a Consortium which owns the Company;

(*d*) Save as provided in Rules 4.2, 4.3 and Rule 5, an Option may only be exercised if any conditions pursuant to Rule 2.3 have been fulfilled to the satisfaction of the Board.

Executive Share Option Schemes **5.106**

4.2 An Option may be exercised by the personal representatives of a deceased Participant within one year following the date of his death.

4.3 An Option may be exercised within one year following the date on which the Participant ceases to hold an office or employment with a Participating Company or an Associated Company if such cessation is as a result of:

(*a*) injury or disability;

(*b*) pregnancy;

(*c*) redundancy within the meaning of the *Employment Protection (Consolidation) Act 1978*;

(*d*) retirement at normal retirement age provided the Option has been held for at least two years at the date of such retirement (or for such longer period as the Board may determine at the Date of Grant);

(*e*) early retirement by agreement with his employer;

(*f*) the company which employs him ceasing to be under the Control of the Company;

(*g*) the company which employs him (not being under the Control of the Company) ceasing to be an Associated Company;

(*h*) the transfer or sale of the undertaking or part-undertaking in which he is employed to a person who is neither under the Control of the Company nor an Associated Company;

(*i*) any other reason at the discretion of the Board.

PROVIDED THAT if the Participant ceases to hold the said office or employment as a result of any of the reasons specified in (*a*) to (*i*) above the Board may extend the period of exercise so that the Option shall remain exercisable from the date of the said cessation of office or employment until the earliest of the following to occur:

(i) the date which is six months after the third anniversary of the Date of Grant;

(ii) the date which is six months after the third anniversary after the last date on which any Option was granted under the Scheme; or

(iii) the date which is six months after the third anniversary of the last occasion (if any) on which an approved option was exercised by the Participant whilst he was a director or employee of a Participating Company or an Associated Company in circumstances which qualified for relief from income tax.

5.106 *Executive Share Option Schemes*

4.4 If a Participant, whilst continuing to hold an office or employment with a Participating Company or an Associated Company, is transferred to work in another country and as a result of that transfer the Participant will either:

(a) become subject to income tax on his remuneration in the country to which he is transferred and the Board is satisfied that as a result he will suffer a tax disadvantage upon exercising an Option; or

(b) become subject to restrictions on his ability to exercise an Option or to deal in the Shares issuable upon the exercise of that Option by reason of or in consequence of, the securities laws or exchange control laws of the country to which he is transferred,

the Participant may exercise the Option in the period commencing three months before and ending three months after the transfer takes place.

4.5 Options shall lapse upon the occurrence of the earliest of the following events:

(a) the 10th anniversary of the Date of Grant;

(b) the expiry of any of the periods specified in Rules 4.2 and 4.3 (save that if at the time any of the applicable periods under Rule 4.3 expire, time is running under the period in Rule 4.2, the Option shall not lapse by reason of this Rule 4.5(b) until the expiry of the period under Rule 4.2);

(c) the expiry of any of the periods specified in Rules 5.3, 5.4 and 5.5 save where an Option is released in consideration of the grant of a New Option over New Shares in the Acquiring Company (during one of the periods specified in Rules 5.3 and 5.4) pursuant to Rule 5.6;

(d) the Participant ceasing to hold an office or employment with a Participating Company or an Associated Company in any circumstances other than:

　(i) where the cessation of office or employment arises on any of the grounds specified in Rules 4.2 and 4.3; or

　(ii) where the cessation of office or employment arises on any ground whatsoever during any of the periods specified in Rule 5;

(e) subject to Rule 5.5, the passing of an effective resolution, or the making of an order by the Court, for the winding-up of the Company;

(f) the Participant being deprived (otherwise than on death) of the legal or beneficial ownership of the Option by operation of law,

Executive Share Option Schemes 5.106

or doing or omitting to do anything which causes him to be so deprived or becomes bankrupt.

5. Takeover, reconstruction and amalgamation, and liquidation

5.1 If any person obtains Control of the Company as a result of making an offer to acquire Shares which is either unconditional or is made on a condition such that if it is satisfied the person making the offer will have Control of the Company, an Option may be exercised within six months of the time when the person making the offer has obtained Control of the Company and any condition subject to which the offer is made has been satisfied.

5.2 For the purposes of Rule 5.1 a person shall be deemed to have obtained Control of the Company if he and others acting in concert with him have together obtained Control of it.

5.3 If any person becomes bound or entitled to acquire Shares under *Sections 428* to *430F* of the *Companies Act 1985* or Articles 421 to 423 of the Companies (Northern Ireland) Order 1986, an Option may be exercised at any time when that person remains so bound or entitled.

5.4 If, under *section 425* of the *Companies Act 1985* or Article 418 of the Companies (Northern Ireland) Order 1986, the court sanctions a compromise or arrangement proposed for the purposes of, or in connection with, a scheme for the reconstruction of the Company or its amalgamation with any other company or companies, an Option may be exercised within six months of the court sanctioning the compromise or arrangement.

5.5 If notice is duly given of a resolution for the voluntary winding-up of the Company, an Option may be exercised within two months from the date of the resolution.

5.6 If any company ('the Acquiring Company'):

(*a*) obtains Control of the Company as a result of making:

  (i) a general offer to acquire the whole of the issued ordinary share capital of the Company which is made on a condition such that if it is satisfied the Acquiring Company will have Control of the Company; or

  (ii) a general offer to acquire all the shares in the Company which are of the same class as the Shares which may be acquired by the exercise of Options,

in either case ignoring any Shares which are already owned by it or a member of the same group of companies; or

5.106 *Executive Share Option Schemes*

(b) obtains Control of the Company in pursuance of a compromise or arrangement sanctioned by the court under *section 425* of the *Companies Act 1985* or Article 418 of the Companies (Northern Ireland) Order 1986; or

(c) becomes bound or entitled to acquire Shares under *sections 428* to *430F* of the *Companies Act 1985* or Articles 421 to 423 of the Companies (Northern Ireland) Order 1986,

any Participant may at any time within the Appropriate Period, by agreement with the Acquiring Company, release any Option which has not lapsed ('the Old Option') in consideration of the grant to him of an Option ('the New Option') which (for the purposes of *paragraph 15* of *Schedule 9* to the *Taxes Act*) is equivalent to the Old Option but relates to shares in a different company (whether the Acquiring Company itself or some other company falling within *paragraph 10(b)* or (c) of *Schedule 9* to the *Taxes Act*).

5.7 The New Option shall not be regarded for the purposes of Rule 5.6 as equivalent to the Old Option unless the conditions set out in *paragraph 15(3)* of *Schedule 9* to the *Taxes Act* are satisfied, but so that the provisions of the scheme shall for this purpose be construed as if:

(a) the New Option were an option granted under the scheme at the same time as the Old Option;

(b) except for the purposes of the definitions of 'Participating Company' and 'Subsidiary' in Rule 1, the reference to [   ] plc/Limited in the definition of 'the Company' in Rule 1 were a reference to the different company mentioned in Rule 5.6;

(c) Rules 10.1 and 10.2 were omitted.

6. Manner of exercise

An Option may be exercised, in whole or in part, by the delivery to the Secretary of the Company or its duly appointed agent of an option certificate covering at least all the Shares over which the Option is then to be exercised, with the notice of exercise in the prescribed form duly completed and signed by the Participant (or by his duly authorised agent) together with a remittance for the exercise price payable in respect of the Shares over which the Option is to be exercised. If any conditions must be fulfilled before an Option may be exercised, the delivery of the option certificate shall not be treated as effecting the exercise of an Option unless and until the Board is satisfied that the conditions have been fulfilled.

7. Issue or transfer of Shares

7.1 Shares to be issued pursuant to the exercise of an Option shall be allotted within 28 days following the effective date of exercise of the Option.

Executive Share Option Schemes **5.106**

7.2 The Board shall procure the transfer of any Shares to be transferred pursuant to the exercise of an Option within 28 days following the effective date of exercise of the Option.

7.3 Shares to be issued pursuant to the Scheme will rank *pari passu* in all respects with the Shares then in issue, except that they will not rank for any rights attaching to Shares by reference to a record date preceding the date of exercise.

7.4 Shares to be transferred pursuant to the Scheme will be transferred free of all liens, charges and encumbrances and together with all rights attaching thereto, except they will not rank for any rights attaching to Shares by reference to a record date preceding the date of exercise.

7.5 If and so long as the Shares are listed on the London Stock Exchange, the Company shall apply for a listing for any Shares issued pursuant to the Scheme as soon as practicable after the allotment thereof.

8. Adjustments

8.1 The number of Shares over which an Option is granted and the Option Price thereof shall be adjusted in such manner as the Board shall determine following any capitalisation issue, rights issue, subdivision, consolidation or reduction of share capital of the Company or any other variation of share capital to the intent that (as nearly as may be without involving fractions of a Share or an Option Price calculated to more than two places of decimals) the Exercise Price payable in respect of an Option shall remain unchanged, provided that no adjustment made pursuant to this Rule 8.1 shall be made without the prior approval of the Inland Revenue (so long as the Scheme is approved by the Inland Revenue).

8.2 Subject to Rule 8.3, an adjustment may be made under Rule 8.1 which would have the effect of reducing the Option Price of unissued shares to less than the nominal value of a Share, but only if, and to the extent that, the Board shall be authorised to capitalise from the reserves of the Company a sum equal to the amount by which the nominal value of the Shares in respect of which the Option is exercisable exceeds the adjusted Exercise Price, and so that an exercise of any Option in respect of which the Option Price has been reduced, the Board shall capitalise and apply such sum (if any) as is necessary to pay up the amount by which the aggregate nominal value of the Shares in respect of which the Option is exercised exceeds the Exercise Price for such Shares.

5.106 *Executive Share Option Schemes*

8.3 Where an Option subsists over both issued and unissued Shares, an adjustment permitted by Rule 8.2 may only be made if the reduction of the Option Price of both issued and unissued Shares can be made to the same extent.

8.4 The Board may take such steps as it may consider necessary to notify Participants of any adjustment made under this Rule 8 and to call in, cancel, endorse, issue or reissue any option certificate subsequent upon such adjustment.

9. Adminstration

9.1 Any notice or other communication under, or in connection with, the scheme may be given by personal delivery or by sending the same by post, in the case of a company to its registered office, and in the case of an individual to his last known address, or, where he is a director or employee of the Company or an Associated Company, either to his last known address or to the address of the place of business at which he performs the whole or substantially the whole of the duties of his office or employment, and where a notice or other communication is given by first-class post, it shall be deemed to have been received 48 hours after it was put into the post properly addressed and stamped.

9.2 The Company may distribute to Participants copies of any notice or document normally sent by the Company to the holders of Shares.

9.3 If any option certificate shall be worn out, defaced or lost, it may be replaced on such evidence being provided as the Board may require.

9.4 The Company shall at all times keep available for allotment unissued Shares at least sufficient to satisfy all Options under which Shares may be subscribed or to procure that sufficient Shares are available for transfer to satisfy all Options under which Shares may be acquired.

9.5 The decision of the Board in any dispute relating to an Option or the due exercise thereof or any other matter in respect of the Scheme shall be final and conclusive, subject to the certification of the Auditors having been obtained when so required by Rule 8.1.

9.6 In any matter in which they are required to act hereunder the Auditors shall be deemed to be acting as experts and not as arbitrators.

9.7 The costs of introducing and administering the Scheme shall be borne by the Company.

10. Alterations

10.1 Subject to Rule 10.2, the Board may at any time alter or add to all or any of the provisions of the Scheme in any respect, provided

Executive Share Option Schemes 5.106

that if an alteration or addition is made at a time when the Scheme is approved by the Inland Revenue under *Schedule 9* to the *Taxes Act* it shall not have effect until it has been approved by the Inland Revenue.

10.2 Subject to Rule 10.3, no alteration or addition to the advantage of present or future Participants or employees shall be made under Rule 10.1 to such of the provisions of the Scheme as relate to any of the following:

(*a*)   the persons to whom Options may be granted;

(*b*)   limitations on the grant of Options;

(*c*)   the determination of the price at which Shares may be acquired by the exercise of Options;

(*d*)   the adjustment of Options;

(*e*)   the restrictions on the exercise of Options;

(*f*)   the rights to be attached upon their issue to Shares issued upon the exercise of Options;

(*g*)   the rights of Participants on the winding-up of the Company;

(*h*)   the transferability of Options; and

(*i*)   the terms of Rule 10;

without the prior approval by ordinary resolution of the members of the Company in general meeting.

10.3 Rule 10.2 shall not apply to any alteration or addition which:

(*a*)   is necessary or desirable in order to obtain or maintain Inland Revenue approval of the Scheme under *Schedule 9* to the *Taxes Act* or any other enactment, or to comply with or take account of the provisions of any proposed or existing legislation or law, to take advantage of any changes to the legislation or law, to take account of any of the events mentioned in Rule 5, or to obtain or maintain favourable taxation treatment of the Company, any Subsidiary or any Participant; and

(*b*)   does not affect the basic principles of the Scheme, the definition of 'Option Price', the limits on individual participation, or the limits in Rule 3.

10.4 No alteration or addition shall be made under Rule 10.1 which would abrogate or adversely affect the subsisting rights of a Participant unless it is made:

(*a*)   with the consent in writing of such number of Participants as hold Options under the Scheme to acquire 75 per cent of the Shares which would be issued or transferred if all Options granted and subsisting under the Scheme were exercised; or

5.106 *Executive Share Option Schemes*

(b) by a resolution at a meeting of Participants passed by not less that 75 per cent of the Participants who attend and vote either in person or by proxy,

and for the purpose of this Rule 10.4 the Participants shall be treated as the holders of a separate class of share capital and the provisions of the Articles of Association of the Company relating to class meetings shall apply *mutatis mutandis*.

10.5 Notwithstanding any other provision of the Scheme other than Rule 10.1 the Board may, in respect of Options granted to Eligible Employees who are or who may become subject to taxation outside the United Kingdom on their remuneration, amend or add to the provisions of the Scheme and the terms of Options as it considers necessary or desirable to take account of or to mitigate or to comply with relevant overseas taxation, securities or exchange control laws provided that the terms of Options granted to such Eligible Employees are not overall more favourable than the terms of Options granted to other Eligible Employees.

10.6 As soon as reasonably practicable after making any alteration or addition under Rule 10.1, the Board shall give written notice thereof to any Participant affected thereby.

11. General

11.1 The Scheme shall terminate upon the tenth anniversary of its adoption by the Company in general meeting or at any earlier time by the passing of a resolution by the Board or an ordinary resolution of the Company in general meeting. Termination of the Scheme shall be without prejudice to the subsisting rights of Participants.

11.2 The Company and any Subsidiary of the Company may provide money to the trustees of any trust or any other person to enable them or him to acquire Shares to be held for the purposes of the scheme, or enter into any guarantee or indemnity for those purposes, to the extent permitted by *section 153* of the *Companies Act 1985*, provided that any trust deed to be made for this purpose shall, at a time when the scheme is approved by the Inland Revenue under *Schedule 9* to the *Taxes Act*, have previously been submitted to the Inland Revenue.

11.3 The rights and obligations of any individual under the terms of his office or employment with the Company or a Participating Company or a Subsidiary of the Company or an Associated Company shall not be affected by his participation in the Scheme or any right which he may have to participate therein, and an individual who participates therein shall waive all and any rights to compensation or

Executive Share Option Schemes 5.106

damages in consequence of the termination of his office or employment with any such company for any reason whatsoever insofar as those rights arise or may arise from his ceasing to have rights under or be entitled to exercise any Option under the Scheme as a result of such termination, or from the loss or diminution in value of such rights or entitlements.

11.4 These Rules shall be governed by and construed in accordance with English law.

5.106 *Executive Share Option Schemes*

Appendix 4

Rules of the Overseas Executive Share Option Scheme

1. Definitions

In this Overseas Executive Scheme, the word and expressions used in the Executive Share Option Scheme shall bear, unless the context otherwise requires, the same meaning herein save to the extent these Rules shall provide to the contrary. The following expression shall bear the meaning set forth below:

'This Overseas Executive Scheme'   This Overseas Executive Share Option Scheme, as constituted by the Rules set out in this Appendix, or as amended from time to time.

2. Application of the scheme

Save as modified by Rules 3, 4 and 5 below, all the provisions in the Rules of the Scheme shall be incorporated into this Overseas Executive Scheme as if fully set out herein and so as to be part of these Rules and (for avoidance of doubt) Shares allocated under this Overseas Executive Scheme shall be taken into account for the purposes of Rule 3 of the Scheme.

3. Remuneration

The definition of 'Relevant Earnings' for the purposes of these Rules shall be applied subject to the deletion of the words 'as are liable to be paid under deduction of tax pursuant to *section 203* of the *Taxes Act* (pay as you earn) after deducting from them amounts included by virtue of *Chapter II* of *Part V* of the *Taxes Act* (certain expenses payment and benefits in kind)' and the substitution therefore of the following:

> 'excluding the value of any benefits in kind or any payments liable to reimbursement by the employing company concerned'.

4. Period of Options

The reference in Rule 4.5(*a*) of the Scheme to 'tenth anniversary' shall be treated for the purposes of these Rules as a reference to 'seventh anniversary'.

5. Revenue Approval

The requirement in the definition of 'Option Price' in Rule 1 and Rules 8 and 10.1 to obtain Inland Revenue approval shall not apply in this Overseas Executive Scheme.

6. Interpretation

The Rules of this Overseas Executive Scheme shall be construed in accordance with English law.

Chapter 6

Special Types of Executive Share Option

Replacement Options, Super Options, Discounted Price Options and Parallel Options

Introduction

6.1 Chapter 5 described the design of normal executive share option schemes as shaped by *TA 1988, 9 Sch* and, in the case of schemes established by listed companies, the ABI and NAPF Guidelines.

6.2 The ABI has devised various so-called 'concessions' to its own Guidelines in order to deal with particular pressures which have arisen. The first of these pressures was the wish on the part of some companies to grant options to run either concurrently or sequentially in excess of four times earnings. The 1987 ABI Guidelines introduced 'Super Options' to deal with this by allowing such options to be granted, but only on the basis that exercise was linked to the achievement of a stiff performance target. The 1987 ABI Guidelines recommended a growth in earnings per share over any five years at least equal to the upper quartile of FTSE 100 Companies as measured by reference to earnings per share growth. However, by 1988 when a great number of the original options granted upon the introduction of approved share options in *FA 1984* were first exercisable, many companies, whose earnings per share growth did not match the upper quartile of FTSE 100 Companies, applied pressure on the ABI to further relax its Guidelines to allow the grant of options over a further four times earnings to replace those which were becoming exercisable, i.e. in excess of four times earnings over any ten-year period. These so-called 'Replacement Options' were allowed on the basis that, amongst other things, the Remuneration Committee considers that there had been a significant improvement in the performance of the company over the previous two or three years which justifies the grant of options at that time. In short, Replacement Options involve a pre-grant performance target which is significantly less onerous than the performance targets applied as a condition of exercise in 'Super Options'.

6.3 Special Types of Executive Share Option

6.3 Following the Joint Statement on Executive Share Option Schemes by the ABI and NAPF in July 1993 ('the 1993 Joint Guidance'), all executive options of listed companies are now expected to be granted subject to appropriate performance targets as a condition of exercise and, consequently, Replacement Options are now subject to performance targets in the same way as all other options.

6.4 FA 1991 permitted the grant of approved options at up to a 15 per cent discount to the market value at the date of grant. It had long been a fundamental principle of both the ABI and NAPF Guidelines that no options may be granted at less than market value. The ABI responded to this change in the legislation by accepting Discounted Price Options on the basis that stiff performance targets were attached as a condition of exercise, again involving five-year performance periods.

6.5 Many companies have been wary of granting Discounted Price Options on an 'all or nothing' basis. Such companies have granted so-called Parallel Options which involve the grant of an option over a specified share at the full market price, but with an alternative right to exercise at a discounted price in whole or in part if a specified performance target is satisfied. Generally speaking, the discounted price terms will be first exercisable after five instead of the usual three years.

Super Options

6.6 The 1987 ABI Guidelines recognised two circumstances in which options may be granted in excess of normal limits.

6.7 The first of these circumstances is where options are granted to an employee over shares which, at the market value at the date of grant, exceed an amount equivalent to four times his annual rate of earnings. Under the ABI's normal limit on the size of executive share options, the four times earnings limit is applied taking into account all options granted by the employing group in the previous ten years including options which have been exercised, surrendered and lapsed. Under the Super Option concession, the four times earnings limit can be exceeded in either of two ways:

(i) options may subsist at any one time over shares with a total market value, at the date of grant, greater than four times earnings;

(ii) over any ten-year period further options may be granted replacing options which have been previously granted and exercised so that the combined allocations exceed four times earnings in total.

Special Types of Executive Share Option   6.10

To the extent options subsist over shares worth more than four times the participant's annual rate of earnings, ABI Guidelines lay down that such options must be granted on Super Option terms; on the other hand, where further options are to be granted to replace options which have been granted and exercised within the previous ten years, such options may be granted either as Super Options or as Replacement Options (see 6.17 to 6.23) which do not impose such stringent performance targets, but where the amount of share capital available for executive share options must be restricted to 5 per cent of share capital.

6.8 The other circumstances in which Super Options must be granted is where options are granted in excess of the ABI's scheme limit on executive share options of 5 per cent of the issued ordinary share capital over any ten-year period.

6.9 The 1987 ABI Guidelines set out the Super Option conditions which are as follows:

- the options should not be exercisable before the fifth anniversary of the date of grant;

- the options should be subject to performance targets applying over a five-year period starting at the date of grant: the 1987 ABI Guidelines suggested a growth in the company's earnings per share over the period of five years which would place the company in the top quartile of the FTSE 100 companies by reference to growth in earnings per share over the same period. However, since the publication of the 1993 Joint Guidance the setting of appropriate performance targets is now presumably a matter for the Remuneration Committee.

6.10 Although the 1987 ABI Guidelines state that Super Options should not be exercisable before the fifth anniversary of the date of grant, it is understood that the ABI accept certain relaxations of this requirement. The ABI accepts that options may be exercised without regard to any performance targets by a former employee who leaves early on account of injury, disability, redundancy or early retirement with the consent of his employer, or by the personal representatives of the optionholder following his/her death. The ABI also accepts that options may be exercised before the fifth anniversary of the date of grant where the employee retires or leaves employment for any other reason in the discretion of the directors but, in such circumstances, the directors should only allow an exercise of the option where they are satisfied that, given the amount of time which has elapsed since the grant of the option and the earnings per share performance of the company during that period, it appears likely that the company is on target to achieve the Super Option performance target at the end of the five-year period. In addition, the ABI accepts that the performance targets may be waived upon a takeover or reconstruction of the

6.11 *Special Types of Executive Share Option*

company or following a disposal of the business or subsidiary for which the optionholder still works.

6.11 The ABI's preference for any Super Option performance target is a growth in earnings per share which matches the upper quartile of FTSE 100 companies notwithstanding the publication of the 1993 Joint Guidance which gives Remuneration Committees more flexibility in setting performance targets. However, this earnings per share test can be very difficult to apply given that the identity of the upper quartile of FTSE 100 companies will change from time to time. It is probably easiest to identify the company which is 25th in order of earnings per share growth over the relevant period. In order to fund this it is necessary to make an assessment of all the earnings per share figures published by FTSE 100 companies at the end of the proposed five-year period and comparing their earnings per share figures during that period with their earnings per share figures five years earlier. Basically the figure at the end of the period should be expressed as a percentage of the earnings per share figure at the start of the period.

A company will have satisfied the performance test as its percentage increase in earnings per share at least matches the percentage increase in earnings per share of the FTSE 100 company which was 25th in terms of earnings per share growth at the end of the period.

6.12 Under the ABI Guidelines, any continuous five-year period following the date of grant may be taken, although the ABI accepts a five-year period commencing at the start of the accounting period during which the relevant option grant is made. This means that the earliest possible basis period will be the twelve month period expiring on the last accounting reference date prior to the grant of the option.

Example

date of grant of option

31.12.92   31.12.93   31.12.94

Basis Period	5 Year Performance Period

6.13 If the performance target is not satisfied at the end of the earliest five-year period, the calculation may be reworked for the following year and so on each year. The option will usually only be exercisable if the performance target has been satisfied over a five-year period expiring before the lapse of the particular option. In the final year before lapse of any option, careful examination of the rules may be necessary to decide whether an exercise of options may only

Special Types of Executive Share Option **6.18**

be allowed once the final year's accounts have been approved by shareholders or whether an exercise on the basis of draft audited accounts would be acceptable.

6.14 A difficulty which can arise with any conditions of exercise based on an increase in earnings per share is that there must be a positive earnings per share figure for both the basis and final periods or it will not be possible to calculate any percentage increase. In any year in which there is a loss per share, it will not be possible to calculate an earnings per share and so that year cannot be used as a basis period and the start of any performance period would need to be deferred.

6.15 Where Super Options are granted over shares with a total market value in excess of the approved scheme limit of four times relevant emoluments, it will be necessary for the excess shares to be comprised in a separate unapproved share option scheme.

6.16 The 1987 ABI Guidelines, paragraph 11, provide that 'options having a market value of up to a further four times a participant's annual emoluments' may be granted as 'Super' Options. It is understood that these additional options can be replaced as soon as any earlier allocations of 'Super' Options are exercised.

Replacement Options

6.17 ABI Guidelines provide for an individual limit on the grant of normal executive share options of shares having a total market value at the date of grant of four times earnings, after taking account of all options granted in the immediately preceding period of ten years (1987 ABI Guidelines, paragraph 11). In 6.4 above it was noted that the 1987 ABI Guidelines allowed a relaxation of the four times earnings limit where the options are granted on Super Option terms, that is to say, subject to stringent performance targets based on a FTSE 100 upper quartile test.

6.18 In 1988, the ABI introduced a further relaxation to allow Replacement Options. Many of the original options granted under approved schemes when they were introduced in 1984 were by 1988 due to be exercised. Many of these options had been granted to individuals up to the limit of four times earnings. Any further options to these individuals would, therefore, be restricted to relatively small grants based on recent salary increments. Under ABI Guidelines, it would be ten years from the original date of grant before options based on the original four times earnings could be replaced. Understandably, few would be prepared to wait that long and would, therefore, have had an incentive to leave employment and find a new

6.19 *Special Types of Executive Share Option*

appointment as the only way to receive a fresh grant of options on normal rather than Super Option terms.

6.19 The 1988 ABI Guidelines introduced Replacement Options. This permits a company to grant options up to a further four times earnings to replace options which have previously been exercised. The conditions for the grant of replacement options are as follows:

(a) the scheme must be administered by a Remuneration Committee comprising the chairman and a majority of non-executive directors;

(b) an additional limit on the number of shares over which options may be granted of 2.5 per cent of issued ordinary share capital. This is in addition to the normal 5 per cent limit on executive share options and applies over the period of four years commencing with the establishment of the scheme or the introduction of the concession as the case may be;

(c) the Remuneration Committee must, prior to granting Replacement Options, be satisfied that there has been a significant improvement in the performance of the company over the two or three years preceding the re-grant;

(d) the Chairman of a company making any amendment to allow Replacement Options should emphasise in the circular to shareholders that the normal 5 per cent limit for executive share options is entirely appropriate and adequate. He is also required to address the importance placed by Insurance Companies as investors on underlying performance by a positive statement that the Replacement Options will be granted having regard to the performance of the company.

6.20 The 2.5 per cent limit only applies to the extent options are granted over unissued share capital. Although this is not clearly set out in the 1988 ABI Guidelines, this must be the case since the ABI has not to date shown itself in any way concerned with the use of existing shares in employee share schemes apart from requiring prior shareholders' approval where more than 5 per cent of share capital may be held by any ESOP from time to time.

6.21 There is no established meaning given to the words 'significant improvement in the performance of the company'. The ABI usually recommends earnings per share growth as the appropriate test of company performance but it does not insist on this as a condition for the grant of Replacement Options under this relaxation. The ABI appears to leave this issue to the judgement of the Remuneration Committee.

6.22 The 1987 ABI Guidelines recommend that all options should be granted subject to a minimum performance target of real growth in earnings per share. Replacement Options, although introduced to address the issue of replacing 'exercised' options, involve the achievement of broadly subjective performance targets as a condition of the grant of an option rather than its exercise. As a result, Replacement Options have been widely taken up by UK companies more as a means of avoiding any minimum performance target than in order to provide for the grant of options in excess of four times earnings over any ten-year period. Recent surveys of larger company schemes appear to suggest that almost 50 per cent of such companies use Replacement Options.

6.23 Following the publication of the 1993 Joint Guidance, the ABI now requires performance targets to be imposed as a condition of exercise as well as the condition of their grant. The ABI now even expresses the view that Replacement Options should no longer be granted or, if they are granted, are only granted on Super Option terms.

Discounted Price Options

6.24 A Discounted Price Option is an option granted at a price which represents less than the market value of the shares at the time of grant. Until recently such options were granted only rarely and usually only by private companies. This is because it has been a fundamental principle of the ABI since the introduction of its Guidelines in the 1960s that options should be granted at the market value at the date of grant.

6.25 The 1987 Guidelines provide at paragraph 12 that:

'The price at which shares are issued to participants, or at which participants are given an option to subscribe, must not be less than the middle market price of the shares in question (or similar formula) at the time when the participation is granted....'.

The market price principle received statutory endorsement in the previous approved share option scheme legislation under *FA 1972, s 78*.

6.26 A 10 per cent discount was first allowed under approved savings-related share option schemes introduced in *FA 1980, s 47*. The ABI had little difficulty in accepting discounts in savings-related share option schemes which were designed specifically to encourage wide employee share ownership.

6.27 From 1 January 1992 approved share option schemes were first allowed to provide for the grant of options at a discount under *FA 1991, s 39*. This permitted the grant of options at up to a 15 per

6.28 *Special Types of Executive Share Option*

cent discount to the market value of the shares as determined for tax purposes. However, the ABI and NAPF have not welcomed the appearance of Discounted Price Options in executive share option schemes and indeed have attempted to attach a number of conditions to their use with a view to persuading companies only to grant such options where stiff performance targets are specified as a condition of any exercise.

Tax conditions: TA 1988, 9 Sch 28

6.28 In the case of options granted on or after 1 January 1992, a scheme may provide for options to be granted at a price which is not less than 85 per cent of the market value of shares of the same class at the material time (the date of grant or, if the Revenue and the company establishing the scheme so agree in writing, such earlier time or times in the preceding 30 days as may be agreed).

Options may be only granted if the scheme also provides that the following conditions must also be satisfied at the time the option is granted:

(*a*) the company which established the scheme (and each participating company) has either established or also participates in either an approved savings-related share option scheme or an approved profit sharing scheme (a 'qualifying scheme'); and

(*b*) every employee eligible under all such 'qualifying schemes' at the time the option is granted has at some time in the previous twelve months been 'informed' of the existence of the qualifying scheme by the company which established it or by one of its participating companies.

6.29 The intention behind the legislation is to encourage the establishment of wide employee share schemes. It therefore makes it a condition of the grant of options at a discount that eligible employees are 'informed' of the existence of a qualifying scheme. It is not a condition that a qualifying scheme is actually operated — merely employees of companies which participate in the approved share option scheme are duly informed of the existence of the qualifying scheme. Obviously employees will be 'informed' if they are actually invited to participate in the qualifying scheme during the relevant twelve month period. The Inland Revenue have indicated that 'informed' means informed in writing and that there must have been a delivery of the information to each individual. It will not be sufficient merely to put up messages on a noticeboard.

6.30 The conditions may apply differently to different groups of companies. Take, for instance, two groups of companies each

Special Types of Executive Share Option **6.33**

comprising ten subsidiaries. In Group A, only the company which established the scheme participates but in Group B all the subsidiaries participate. In applying the condition in *TA 1988, 9 Sch 29*, only the company establishing the scheme in Group A need participate in a qualifying scheme and its employees be informed of the existence of the qualifying scheme. Of course, the Inland Revenue could deny approval of the qualifying schemes if it considered the scheme had the effect of conferring benefits wholly or mainly on directors of companies in the group or on those employees of companies in the group who are in receipt of the higher or highest levels of remuneration (*TA 1988, 9 Sch 2(3)*) (see 4.34 above). However, it is difficult to see how the Inland Revenue could invoke this provision to deny relief in the case of most holding companies unless there had been a specific attempt to benefit only group directors or higher paid employees in the relevant company. On the other hand, in Group B where all subsidiaries participate in the share option scheme, the eligible employees of all the subsidiaries will need to be informed in writing of the existence of the qualifying schemes.

6.31 It may be that in both Groups A and B, only the directors of the main board participate in the share option scheme; but it will still be necessary for all the eligible employees of Group B, but not Group A, to be informed of the existence of the qualifying schemes. The 'information' condition may, therefore, have the unexpected consequence that groups of companies may be discouraged from extending participation in the share option scheme if only because of the need to inform employees of the new participating companies of the existence of a qualifying scheme. There are, for instance, many companies which established profit sharing schemes to make free or matching offers on their flotation and which have not been used since. Such companies may prefer to terminate any such schemes rather than suffer the embarrassment of informing eligible employees of its existence.

6.32 The limit of four times relevant earnings under *TA 1988, 9 Sch 28(1)(2)* is applied by reference to the market value of shares for tax purposes at the date of grant and not any discounted acquisition price of the shares where the scheme permits such options to be granted (*TA 1988, 9 Sch 28(3)*).

1991 ABI Guidelines

6.33 Following the surprise introduction of Discounted Price Options with effect from 1 January 1992 in *FA 1991, s 39*, the ABI rapidly produced guidelines on such options in August 1991. The ABI justified the new guidelines as dealing with two principal concerns.

6.34 Special Types of Executive Share Option

First, it believed the grant of such options 'must increase the cost of such options to existing ordinary shareholders' and, therefore, suggested exercise should only be allowed after five years and upon condition of some 'sustained real return to the company'. Secondly, it identified possible tensions between existing optionholders with market price options and new optionholders with discounted price options, and suggested a rationing of new Discounted Price Options so that those with existing market value options did not feel resentment at the prospect of new options being quoted on discounted price terms.

Performance conditions

6.34 Although the 1991 ABI Guidelines indicated that Discounted Price Options should be exercisable only after a period of five years and upon satisfaction of performance targets, it is understood that the ABI accepts such schemes may provide for early exercise of options without the need to satisfy the performance targets where the employee dies, or where he leaves employment on account of unforeseen circumstances such as injury, disability, redundancy or early retirement, or where the business or subsidiary for which he works is transferred or sold.

6.35 In the case of employees allowed to exercise their options for any other reason in the discretion of the directors, the ABI suggests that exercise should only be allowed where in the light of the performance of the company since the date the option was granted it appears likely that the option would be exercisable at the due date for exercise. The ABI considers that options should not be granted to executives within four years of their normal retirement date.

6.36 The performance target suggested by the 1991 ABI Guidelines is a 'growth in earnings per share equal to RPI plus 2 per cent over any five year period from the date of grant'. It is understood the ABI interprets this as meaning that, over any five-year period the growth in earnings per share must be 110 per cent of RPI rather than only 102 per cent of RPI. It is also clear that the five-year period must be consecutive and must run from the start of any financial year commencing not earlier than the start of the financial year in which the option is granted. In other words, the earliest base year against which the increase in RPI may be measured is the financial year ending immediately prior to the financial year in which the option is granted.

Rationing of Discounted Price Options

6.37 The 1991 ABI Guidelines recommend that the proportion of Discounted Price Options granted to any individual are restricted to

Special Types of Executive Share Option **6.39**

25 per cent of that individual's total holding. Allegedly this is to avoid 'tension' arising between different groups of optionholders some of whom have been granted Discounted Price Options and some who have not. Such concerns are difficult to understand if only because different groups of optionholders have long enjoyed different option prices without any apparent 'tension'. It seems more likely that the ABI just simply wishes to discourage the grant of such options, or at least ensure they assume no more than a peripheral place in a company's scheme.

6.38 The ABI's limit on Discounted Price Options to one-quarter of the total number of shares comprised in options granted to that individual applies on a ten-year rolling period, i.e. Discounted Price Options should not exceed 25 per cent of the options granted over the previous ten years.

The ABI has since issued further informal guidance as follows:

- where Replacement Options are granted (i.e. in excess of four times earnings over a ten-year period the original options should be disregarded in calculating the availability of Discounted Price Options — obviously this means that fewer Discounted Price Options may be granted since the 25 per cent limit will be based on a maximum of only four times earnings from time to time;

- where Parallel Options are granted options must be counted against the 25 per cent available for Discounted Price Options even though such options may subsequently be exercised on full market value option terms.

The ABI's informal guidance on Discounted Price Options has become so difficult to understand and apply that it is doubtful if many of the companies which have granted Discounted Price Options have done so with complete adherence to such guidance. Certainly, most companies have incorporated a minimum five-year option period and some form of performance target, but it appears the majority have not chosen to follow the 25 per cent limit on Discounted Price Options if only because few companies see any reason to believe that the tensions foreseen by the ABI between those holding Discounted Price Options and the others will in fact arise. However, many companies simply sensed that for the duration of the recession at least it may not be entirely appropriate to grant Discounted Price Options and, therefore, shelved any such proposals indefinitely.

Method of granting Discounted Price Options

6.39 Whilst the Inland Revenue will only approve changes to schemes to allow Discounted Price Options if the statutory conditions for such options are incorporated (see 6.28 above), there is, of course,

6.39 *Special Types of Executive Share Option*

no obligation to include the ABI's conditions (see 6.33 above) in the scheme rules. These can be incorporated in the ancillary documentation provided power to do so is included in the scheme. This will normally take the form of a power to include such conditions of exercise as the directors see fit subject to the prior approval of the Inland Revenue. The ancillary documentation would then be submitted to the Inland Revenue for approval. An appropriate form of option certificate, notice of exercise and employee guide are set out below:

Form of Option Certificate for a Discounted Price Option

[Certificate No]

SHARE OPTION CERTIFICATE
[   ] plc
EXECUTIVE SHARE OPTION SCHEME

Date of Grant	Normal First Exercise Date	Exercise Price per Share	Number of Shares

This is to certify that:

....

has been granted an Option to acquire the number of ordinary shares of [   ] p each fully paid in the Company at the exercise price per share shown above in accordance with and subject to the Rules of the [   ] Executive Share Option Scheme (as modified by the Appendix hereto) and subject to satisfaction of the performance target set out in paragraph 2(a) of the Appendix hereto (this is EPS growth over any 5 consecutive years at least 10 per cent greater than RPI) not earlier than [5th anniversary of grant].

By Order of the Board

[Securities Seal]

Secretary

The option is not transferable, assignable or chargeable

Special Types of Executive Share Option 6.39

Form of Option Certificate for Discounted Price Option

Appendix [attached to option certificate]

(Discounted Options — Special Restrictions on Exercise)

1. This Appendix forms part of the Rules of the [   ] Executive Share Option Scheme.

2. The following special restrictions on exercise apply in respect of an Option held by an optionholder on terms that it may be exercised at an Option Price which is less than the Market Value at the Date of Grant:

(a) Rule [   ] — *Earnings per Share Performance Target*

Pursuant to Rule 2.4, the Option may only be exercised if:

$$\frac{\text{EPSf}}{\text{EPSb}} \text{ equals or is greater than } \frac{I_2 \times 110}{I_1 \times 100}$$

Where:

EPSb equals the earnings per share of the Company for any accounting period not earlier than the accounting period ended immediately prior to the Option's Date of Grant.

EPSf equals the earnings per share of the Company for the accounting period ending five consecutive years after the last day of the accounting period taken into account for the purposes of EPSb above.

I_1 equals the Retail Prices Index (All Items) published for the month corresponding to the last month of the accounting period taken into account for the purposes of EPSb above.

I_2 equals the Retail Prices Index (All Items) published for the month corresponding to the last month of the accounting period taken into account for the purposes of EPSf above.

If, during the relevant period, the Company should alter its accounting reference date, the basis for calculating earnings per share or its share capital, the earnings per share figures for any period shall be adjusted in such manner as the Auditors shall confirm to be in their opinion fair and reasonable to take account

6.39 *Special Types of Executive Share Option*

of such alterations with the intent that the bases for determining earnings per share figures are consistent. For this purpose the Auditors shall have regard to the Statement of Standard Accounting Practice 3 instead of FRS3.

The Board will waive the above performance target where a Participant ceases employment by reason of injury, disability, pregnancy, redundancy, early retirement (but not normal retirement) and on the sale out of the subsidiary or business in which he is employed and in the event of a takeover, reconstruction or winding-up of the company over which the Option subsists.

The Board may waive, vary or amend all or any terms of this condition, in particular if it considers the earnings per share test is no longer a fair measure of the Company's performance nor reasonably attainable, but shall do so only to the extent that the Board reasonably considers that it will subsequently be no more nor less difficult for an optionholder to satisfy the condition as so adjusted than it was for him to achieve the condition in its original form when it was first set. Such waiver, variation or amendment must be agreed in advance with the Inland Revenue.

(*b*) Rule [   ] — *First Normal Exercise Date*

Pursuant to Rule [   ], the Option may not be exercised earlier than the fifth anniversary of the Date of Grant unless it is exercised by an optionholder who ceases to be a director or employee of a Participating Company on account of injury, disability, pregnancy, redundancy, early retirement (but not normal retirement) and on the sale of the subsidiary or business in which he is employed and in the event of a takeover, reconstruction or winding-up of the company over which the Option subsists.

(*c*) Rule [   ] — *Exercise at Normal Retirement Age*

Pursuant to Rule [   ], the Option may only be exercised on account of retirement (but not early retirement by agreement with the employer) if it has been held for a minimum of four years since the Date of Grant.

(*d*) Rule [   ] — *Exercise for any other Reason approved by the Directors*

In the event the Board proposes to exercise its discretion under Rule [   ], it may only do so if it considers that the increase in earnings per share to the date of exercise is in line with the performance target in (*a*) above after taking account of the period the Option has been held.

Special Types of Executive Share Option 6.39

Form of Notice of Exercise for a Discounted Price Option

[   ] plc

[   ] EXECUTIVE SHARE OPTION SCHEME

NOTICE OF EXERCISE OF OPTION

This notice is to be completed by the optionholder named [overleaf] (or by his personal representative(s) if he has died), when exercising the Option to acquire some or all of the shares shown [overleaf]. It should be returned to the Secretary, [   ] plc, [address].

To: the Directors of [   ] plc

I/We refer to the Option granted to me/the optionholder .... (insert full name) at the price of ....p per share on .... 19 .... and now:

— exercise the Option in respect of ordinary shares of [   ]p each in the Company; and

— enclose a cheque for £ ..... in favour of '[   ] plc' as payment in full; and

— request that I/We be registered as the holder(s) of such ordinary shares and a definitive certificate for such shares be sent at my/our risk to me/us at the first address below.

BLOCK CAPITALS PLEASE

FULL NAME	**Signature of optionholder**
ADDRESS	**(or first personal**
....	**representative*)**
	....
FULL NAME	**Signature of second personal**
ADDRESS	**representative***
....	....

All legal personal representatives must complete and sign the form. The grant of probate or letters of administration must be sent with this form.

6.39 Special Types of Executive Share Option

Form of Employee Guide for a Discounted Price Option

THE [   ] EXECUTIVE SHARE OPTION SCHEME

Form of Employee Guide for Optionholders granted a Discounted Price Option

1. Grant of Option

(a)   The Scheme has been approved by the Inland Revenue under the *Income and Corporation Taxes Act 1988* and accordingly should enjoy the tax reliefs explained in paragraph 8 below.

(b)   Options are granted under the Scheme at the discretion of a committee [consisting of mainly] non-executive directors.

(c)   The option is granted over shares in the Company and is exercisable at the earliest after five years at an option price representing *85 per cent* of the market value at the date of grant ('the discounted price') provided the special performance target based on earnings per share growth has been achieved.

The special performance target is attached as an appendix to your option certificate [and notice of exercise]. Briefly, the performance target is earnings per share growth over five financial years equal to 110 per cent of the rate of growth in the retail prices index over the same period. The earliest financial year you can take for comparison is [   ].

(d)   The effective date of the grant of your Option is the date shown on the [enclosed] Option Certificate. No payment is required for the grant of your Option.

2. Rights of Optionholders

(a)   The Option is personal to you and may not be transferred to any other person.

(b)   You [will] receive copies of all documents sent to shareholders generally, but unless you are already a shareholder, you are not entitled to attend shareholders' meetings.

3. Rights of exercise

(a)   The first normal exercise date for your discounted price option is the fifth anniversary of the date of grant. Options may only be exercised if the performance target attached to your option certificate is achieved.

(b)   Normally, you cannot exercise an Option if you have left employment with the Group. However, you can exercise an option

Special Types of Executive Share Option 6.39

without regard to the performance target for up to one year after leaving on account of:

  (i) injury or disability;

  (ii) pregnancy;

  (iii) redundancy;

  (iv) early retirement with the agreement of your employer;

  (v) the company for which you work ceasing to be part of the Group;

  (vi) the undertaking in which you work being transferred outside the Group.

However, if you leave employment on account of retirement (but not early retirement by agreement with your employer) then you will only be allowed to exercise the option during the period of one year after leaving if you have held it for four years. The exercise of an option on discounted terms after four years where you have retired early will only be possible if the Directors have been prepared to extend the period for the exercise of the option.

The Directors may also allow options to be exercised if you leave for any other reason approved by them. They will only allow an option to be so exercised to the extent the performance target seems likely to be achieved at the end of five years bearing in mind the actual period the option has been held.

Normally, you would have only one year to exercise your option from the date of ceasing employment for any of the above reasons. However, the Directors may extend the period of exercise so as to avoid any income tax charge upon exercise (see paragraph 8 below).

(c) You may exercise your option at the discounted price (without regard to the performance target) in the event of any takeover, reconstruction or amalgamation, or voluntary winding-up of the Company. Alternatively, you may, with the agreement of any offeror, be given the opportunity to exchange an option for an option in the offeror.

(d) Your personal representatives would be able to exercise your option at the discounted price (without regard to the performance target) within one year following the date of your death without regard to the achievement of the performance target.

(e) No option may be exercised later than ten years after the date of grant.

4. How to exercise an Option

An option may be exercised in whole or in part by the completion of the Notice of Exercise [attached to the option certificate] and its delivery to [the Company Secretary]. A remittance to cover the total

6.39 *Special Types of Executive Share Option*

price payable for the shares must be attached. As any exercise is at the discounted price it will not be effective unless the Directors are reasonably satisfied that the performance target has been achieved. Before exercising any Option you should carefully consider whether there are any tax implications (see paragraph 8 below).

5. Rights upon exercise

The shares which you acquire by the exercise of an option will be issued and allotted, or if appropriate, transferred to you, within ... days of the date of exercise. They will have exactly the same rights as all other shares in the Company, as governed by the Memorandum and Articles of Association, except that they will not rank for any rights attaching to shares in the Company by reference to a record date preceding the date of exercise.

6. The Company's [Share Transaction Rules]

Your attention is drawn to the Company's [Share Transaction Rules] which prohibit dealings in the Company's shares by the Group's directors and certain of its employees within a specified period immediately prior to an announcement of its results to the London Stock Exchange. For this purpose a dealing includes the exercise as well as the subsequent sale of the shares.

7. Rights and bonus issues

If there is a rights or bonus issue in respect of shares in the Company, or a reduction, consolidation or sub-division of the Company's share capital, or possibly an open offer, the number of shares over which your option is granted and the option price may be adjusted by the Directors so as to protect any appreciation in the value of the shares over which the option was granted. Any adjustment would be subject to approval by the Inland Revenue and confirmation from the Company's auditors that it was fair and reasonable.

8. Taxation

The following is a general summary and employees are advised to consult their own professional advisers as to their individual tax position under the Scheme.

(a) *At the date of grant*

There is no liability to tax at the date of grant. The Company will supply details of options granted to the Inland Revenue at the end of the tax year.

Special Types of Executive Share Option 6.39

(*b*) At the date of exercise

    (i) You will not be liable to any income tax as a result of the exercise of your option unless you exercise an option:

        (1) prior to the third anniversary of the date upon which it was granted; or

        (2) within three years of the date upon which you previously exercised any option granted under the Scheme or under any other approved executive share option scheme where such exercise qualified for income tax relief.

    (ii) If you are liable to income tax on an exercise of an option, any gain is calculated as the excess of the market value of the shares at the date of exercise over the sum you pay for them. The tax is payable in one lump sum at the end of the tax year in which you exercise the option. Details of the exercise will be supplied by the Company to the Inland Revenue, but you will remain under an obligation to return any gain arising on the exercise in your annual Tax Return.

    (iii) In addition, your personal representatives will not be liable to any tax as a result of their exercise of your option during the period of one year following the date of your death provided that the exercise is before the tenth anniversary of the date of grant.

(*c*) Sale of the Shares

This will usually be treated as a disposal for capital gains tax purposes, and capital gains tax will be payable on any chargeable gain. A gain will arise if the sale proceeds exceed the total acquisition price (or, if you have paid income tax on the exercise of the option, the market value of the shares on the date of exercise). However, in computing any chargeable gain you are entitled to take advantage of both the annual exemption (which, for the tax year 1994/1995, is £5,800) and the 'indexation allowance' under which the cost of the shares for capital gains tax purposes is increased in line with the rate of inflation, but only since the date of exercise.

9. Rules of the Scheme

Your rights under the Scheme are governed by the Rules which may be inspected upon request to the Company Secretary together with such additional terms and conditions of exercise as the Directors have imposed at the date of grant and which are set out in these Notes in respect of an option which is exercised at the discounted price.

Dated   19

6.40 *Special Types of Executive Share Option*

Tax aspects of unapproved Discounted Price Options

6.40 The grant of an option over shares at a price which is less than the market value of the shares at the time of grant is a benefit chargeable to tax under the general principles of *Schedule E* (*Abbott v Philbin HL (1960) 39 TC 82*). However, *TA 1988, s 135(5)* provides that the receipt of the option shall not be chargeable to income tax where the option is not capable of exercise for more than seven years. Any unapproved Discounted Price Option should therefore be granted for a maximum of seven years.

6.41 The grant of an unapproved Discounted Price Option will be a disposal of a chargeable asset, namely the option, for capital gains tax purposes. Arguably, a gain accrues equal to the amount of the discount. Whilst *TCGA 1992, s 149(A)* provides relief from capital gains tax in respect of disposals of approved share options, no such relief applies in the case of an unapproved option. Consequently, an unapproved option is deemed to have been disposed of at a price equal to the market value of the option so that the amount of any discount is treated as the amount of any gain on the disposal.

Parallel Options

6.42 A Parallel Option is an option granted over shares on alternative terms as to exercise. In particular, the alternative terms may relate to the price, the period during which the option is exercisable and any performance targets to be satisfied as a condition of exercise. Two separate options may be granted over the same shares under separate schemes. Alternatively, the two options may be granted 'in parallel' under the same scheme if the scheme so provides including an approved share option scheme. To the extent an option is exercised upon one set of terms, it may not be exercised on the alternative set of terms and vice versa.

6.43 Parallel options have had various uses over the last ten years or so but a particular use has arisen as a result of the 1991 ABI Guidelines on Discounted Price Options.

6.44 In the case of Discounted Price Options, ABI Guidelines provide that a right of exercise should only arise after five years upon achievement of an appropriate performance target which the ABI prefer should be based on an earnings per share growth at least equal to 110 per cent of the increase in the Retail Prices Index over that period. Given the 'all or nothing' nature of any such performance target, many companies concluded that it would be better to grant options on alternative terms so that if the performance target for the exercise of Discounted Price Options were not achieved, the option

Special Types of Executive Share Option **6.47**

may still be exercisable on normal share option terms after three years. In this way, the discounted price option is seen as a bonus available if the performance target can be achieved. Of course, normal terms may also be granted on the basis of performance targets, but usually these will be less stringent than the Discounted Price Option.

6.45 Since a Parallel Option is in effect two options granted on alternative terms over the same shares, the points relating to normal options in Chapter 5 and Discounted Price Options in Chapter 6 apply separately to each part of the option.

6.46 The ABI'S attitude to Parallel Options has been unenthusiastic but then its general attitude to Discounted Price Options has been generally unenthusiastic. Nevertheless, if the separate component parts of Parallel Options each satisfy ABI Guidelines then it would be churlish of the ABI to recommend that Parallel Options should not be adopted.

6.47 An appropriate form of option certificate, notice of exercise and employee guide are set out overleaf:

6.47 *Special Types of Executive Share Option*

Form of Option Certificate and Appendix for a Parallel Option

---

Date of Grant [Certificate No]

SHARE OPTION CERTIFICATE

[   ] plc/Limited

EXECUTIVE SHARE OPTION SCHEME

This is to certify that:

....

has been granted an Option to acquire the number of ordinary shares of [   ]p each fully paid in the Company in accordance with and subject to the Rules of the [   ] Executive Share Option Scheme (as modified by the Appendix hereto) on the alternative terms set out under Columns 'A' and 'B' below:

	A ('normal terms')	**B** ('discounted terms')
number of shares	[ ] less any previously exercised upon discounted terms pursuant to this option	[ ] less any previously exercised upon normal terms pursuant to this option
exercise price per share	[market value]	[85 per cent of market value]
normal first exercise date	[third anniversary of grant]	[fifth anniversary of grant]
performance target	None	The performance target set out in paragraph 2(*a*) of the Appendix hereto (this is EPS growth over any five consecutive years at least 10 per cent greater than RPI)

By Order of the Board

[Securities Seal]

Secretary

The option is not transferable, assignable or chargeable.

Special Types of Executive Share Option 6.47

Form of Option Certificate for a Parallel Option

Appendix [attached to option certificate]

(Discounted Options — Special Restrictions on Exercise)

1. This Appendix forms part of the Rules of the [   ] Executive Share Option Scheme.

2. The following special restrictions on exercise apply in respect of an Option held by a Participant on terms that it may be exercised at an Option Price which is less than the Market Value at the Date of Grant ('discounted terms'):

(a) Rule [   ] — Earnings per Share Performance Target

Pursuant to Rule [   ], no Option may be exercised on discounted terms unless:

$$\frac{\text{EPSf}}{\text{EPSb}} \text{ equals or is greater than } \frac{I_2 \times 110}{I_1 \times 100}$$

Where:

EPSb equals the earnings per share of the Company for any accounting period not earlier than the accounting period ended immediately prior to the Option's Date of Grant.

EPSf equals the earnings per share of the Company for the accounting period ending five consecutive years after the last day of the accounting period taken into account for the purposes of EPSb above.

I_1 equals the Retail Prices Index (All Items) published for the month corresponding to the last month of the accounting period taken into account for the purposes of EPSb above.

I_2 equals the Retail Prices Index (All Items) published for the month corresponding to the last month of the accounting period taken into account for the purposes of EPSf above.

If, during the relevant period, the Company should alter its accounting reference date, the basis for calculating earnings per share or its share capital, the earnings per share figures for any period shall be adjusted in such manner as the Auditors shall

6.47 Special Types of Executive Share Option

confirm to be in their opinion fair and reasonable to take account of such alterations with the intent that the bases for determining earnings per share figures are consistent. For this purpose the Auditors shall have regard to the Statement of Standard Accounting Practice 3 instead of FRS 3.

The Board will waive the above performance target [where an optionholder ceases employment by reason of injury, disability, pregnancy, redundancy, early retirement (but not normal retirement) and on the sale of the subsidiary or business in which he is employed and] in the event of a takeover, reconstruction or winding-up of the company over which the Option subsists.

The Board may waive, vary or amend all or any terms of this condition, in particular if it considers the earnings per share test is no longer a fair measure of the Company's performance nor reasonably attainable, but shall do so only to the extent that the Board reasonably considers that it will subsequently be no more nor less difficult for an optionholder to satisfy the condition as so adjusted than it was for him to achieve the condition in its original form when it was first set. Such waiver, variation or amendment must be agreed in advance with the Inland Revenue.

(b) Rule [   ] — *First Normal Exercise Date*

Pursuant to Rule [   ], no Option may be exercised on discounted terms earlier than the fifth anniversary of the Date of Grant unless it is exercised by an optionholder who ceases to be a director or employee of a Participating Company on account of injury, disability, pregnancy, redundancy, early retirement (but not normal retirement) and on the sale of the subsidiary or business in which he is employed and except in the event of a takeover, reconstruction or winding-up of the company over which the Option subsists.

(c) Rule [   ] — *Exercise at Normal Retirement Age*

Pursuant to Rule [   ], no Option may be exercised on discounted terms on account of retirement (other than early retirement by agreement with the employer) unless it has been held for a minimum of four years since the Date of Grant.

(d) Rule [   ] — *Exercise for any other Reason approved by the Directors*

In the event the Board permits the exercise of an Option pursuant to Rule [   ], an exercise on discounted terms shall only be allowed if the Board considers that the increase in earnings per share to the date of exercise is in line with the performance target in (a) above after taking account of the period the Option has been held.

Special Types of Executive Share Option 6.47

Form of Notice of Exercise for a Parallel Option

[   ] plc/Limited
[   ] EXECUTIVE SHARE OPTION SCHEME

NOTICE OF EXERCISE OF OPTION

This notice is to be completed by the optionholder named [overleaf] (or by his personal representative(s) if he has died), when exercising the Option to acquire some or all of the ordinary shares shown [overleaf]. It should be returned to the Secretary, [   ] plc, [address].

To: the Directors of [   ] plc

I/We refer to the option granted to me/the optionholder ....(insert full name) on..................... 19........ and now:

*— exercise the Option in respect of ..... ordinary shares upon *normal terms* at the price of ..... p per share; and/or

*— exercise the Option in respect of ..... ordinary shares upon *discounted terms* at the price of ..... p per share; and
(* delete as applicable)

— enclose a cheque for £ ..... in favour of '[   ] plc' as payment in full; and

— request that I/We be registered as the holders of such ordinary shares and a definitive certificate for such shares be sent at my/our risk to me/us at the first address below.

BLOCK CAPITALS PLEASE

FULL NAME .... **Signature of optionholder**
ADDRESS .... **(or first personal**
           .... **representative*)**
           ....

FULL NAME .... **Signature of second**
ADDRESS .... **personal representative***
           ....

All legal personal representatives must complete and sign the form. The grant of probate or letters of administration must be sent with this form.

6.47 *Special Types of Executive Share Option*

Form of Employee Guide for a Parallel Option

THE [   ] EXECUTIVE SHARE OPTION SCHEME

**Employee Guide
for Optionholders
granted a Parallel Option**

1. Grant of Option

(*a*)   The Scheme has been approved by the Inland Revenue under the *Income and Corporation Taxes Act 1988* and accordingly should enjoy the tax reliefs explained in paragraph 8 below.

(*b*)   Options are granted under the Scheme at the discretion of a committee [consisting of mainly] non-executive directors.

(*c*)   The option is granted over shares in the Company and is exercisable on alternative terms as follows:

— **normal terms**: after *three years* at an option price representing *100 per cent* of the market value at the date of grant; and/or

— **discounted terms**: after *five years* at an option price representing *85 per cent* of the market value at the date of grant ('the discounted price') provided the special performance target based on earnings per share growth has been achieved.

To the extent you exercise the option on normal terms, you cannot exercise the option over that number of shares on discounted terms; and vice versa.

The performance target is attached as an appendix to your option certificate [and notice of exercise]. Briefly, the performance target is earnings per share growth over five financial years equal to 110 per cent of the rate of growth in the retail prices index over the same period. The earliest financial year you can take for comparison is [   ].

(*d*)   The effective date of the grant of your option is the date shown on the [enclosed] option certificate. No payment is required for the grant of your option.

2. Rights of Optionholders

(*a*)   The option is personal to you and may not be transferred to any other person.

Special Types of Executive Share Option 6.47

(b) You [will] receive copies of all documents sent to shareholders generally, but unless you are already a shareholder, you are not entitled to attend shareholders' meetings.

3. Rights of exercise

(a) The first normal exercise date for your option is either the third or fifth anniversary of the date of grant depending upon whether the exercise is on normal or discounted terms. Options may only be exercised upon discounted terms if the performance target attached to your option certificate is achieved.

(b) Normally, you cannot exercise an option if you have left employment with the Group. However, you can exercise an option at the discounted price (without regard to the performance target) for up to one year after leaving on account of:

   (i) injury or disability;
   (ii) pregnancy;
   (iii) redundancy;
   (iv) early retirement with the agreement of your employer;
   (v) the company for which you work ceasing to be part of the Group;
   (vi) the undertaking in which you work being transferred outside the Group.

However, if you leave employment on account of retirement (but not early retirement by agreement with your employer) then you will only be allowed to exercise the option during the period of one year after leaving if on your retirement you have held it for the required period — this is two years in the case of options exercised on normal terms and four years in the case of options exercised on discounted terms. The exercise of an option on discounted terms after four years where you have retired early will only be possible if the directors have been prepared to extend the period for the exercise of the option.

The Directors may also allow the option to be exercised if you leave for any other reason approved by them. They will only allow an option to be so exercised to the extent the performance target seems likely to be achieved at the end of five years bearing in mind the actual period the option has been held.

Normally, you would have only one year to exercise your option from the date of ceasing employment for any of the above reasons. However, the Directors may extend the period of exercise so as to avoid any income tax charge upon exercise (see paragraph 8 below).

6.47 *Special Types of Executive Share Option*

(*c*) You may exercise your option at the discounted price (without regard to the performance target) in the event of any takeover, reconstruction or amalgamation, or voluntary winding-up of the Company. Alternatively, you may, with the agreement of any offeror, be given the opportunity to exchange an option for an option in the offeror.

(*d*) Your personal representatives would be able to exercise your option at the discounted price (without regard to the performance target) within one year following the date of your death without regard to the achievement of the performance target.

(*e*) No option may be exercised later than ten years after the date of grant.

4. How to exercise an Option

An Option may be exercised in whole or in part by the completion of the Notice of Exercise [attached to the option certificate] and its delivery to [the Company Secretary] — you must enter the applicable normal or discounted option price. A remittance to cover the total price payable for the shares must be attached. If the exercise is at the discounted price it will not be effective unless the Directors are reasonably satisfied that the performance target has been achieved. Before exercising any Option you should carefully consider whether there are any tax implications (see paragraph 8 below).

5. Rights upon exercise

The shares which you acquire by the exercise of an option will be issued and allotted, or if appropriate, transferred to you, within 28 days of the date of exercise. They will have exactly the same rights as all other shares in the Company, as governed by the Memorandum and Articles of Association, except that they will not rank for any rights attaching to shares in the Company by reference to a record date preceding the date of exercise.

6. The Company's [Share Transaction Rules]

Your attention is drawn to the Company's [Share Transaction Rules] which prohibit dealings in the Company's shares by the Group's directors and certain of its employees within a specified period immediately prior to an announcement of its results to the London Stock Exchange. For this purpose a dealing includes the exercise as well as the subsequent sale of the shares.

Special Types of Executive Share Option **6.47**

7. Rights and bonus issues

If there is a rights or bonus issue in respect of shares in the Company, or a reduction, consolidation or sub-division of the Company's share capital, or possibly an open offer, the number of shares over which your option is granted and the option price may be adjusted by the Directors so as to protect any appreciation in the value of the shares over which the option was granted. Any adjustment would be subject to approval by the Inland Revenue and confirmation from the Company's auditors that it was fair and reasonable.

8. Taxation

The following is a general summary and employees are advised to consult their own professional advisers as to their individual tax position under the Scheme.

(*a*) *At the date of grant*

There is no liability to tax at the date of grant. The Company will supply details of options granted to the Inland Revenue at the end of the tax year.

(*b*) *At the date of exercise*

(i) You will not be liable to any income tax as a result of the exercise of your option unless you exercise an option:

(1) prior to the third anniversary of the date upon which it was granted; or

(2) within three years of the date upon which you previously exercised any option granted under the Scheme or under any other approved executive share option scheme where such exercise qualified for income tax relief.

(ii) If you are liable to income tax on an exercise of an option, any gain is calculated as the excess of the market value of the shares at the date of exercise over the sum you pay for them. The tax is payable in one lump sum at the end of the tax year in which you exercise the option. Details of the exercise will be supplied by the Company to the Inland Revenue, but you will remain under an obligation to return any gain arising on the exercise in your annual Tax Return.

(iii) In addition, your personal representatives will not be liable to any tax as a result of their exercise of your option during the period of one year following the date of your death provided that the exercise is before the tenth anniversary of the date of grant.

6.47 Special Types of Executive Share Option

(c) *Sale of the Shares*

This will usually be treated as a disposal for capital gains tax purposes, and capital gains tax will be payable on any chargeable gain. A gain will arise if the sale proceeds exceed the total acquisition price (or, if you have paid income tax on the exercise of the option, the market value of the shares on the date of exercise). However, in computing any chargeable gain you are entitled to take advantage of both the annual exemption (which, for the tax year 1994/1995, is £5,800) and the 'indexation allowance' under which the cost of the shares for capital gains tax purposes is increased in line with the rate of inflation, but only since the date of exercise.

9. Rules of the Scheme

Your rights under the Scheme are governed by the Rules which may be inspected upon request to the Company Secretary together with such additional terms and conditions of exercise as the Directors have imposed at the date of grant and which are set out in these Notes in respect of an option which is exercised at the discounted price.

Dated   19

Chapter 7

Restricted Share Schemes

Introduction

7.1 A 'restricted share scheme' involves the free allocation of shares paid up out of profits, to employees on the basis that they will be forfeited if the employee leaves or a performance target is not achieved within a specified period of time. The shares are usually held by trustees pending the vesting of the shares, that is to say, the time the risk of forfeiture is lifted.

7.2 Restricted share schemes are an import from the United States where such schemes have been popular for many years. Under the US Internal Revenue Code, Section 83, income tax on the value of any property including shares is expressly stated to apply on the date any risk of forfeiture ceases rather than the date of allocation. In the US the shares will generally be placed in the name of the employee, rather than in the name of trustees. In the UK, therefore, restricted share schemes are a type of ESOP (see 'ESOPs' in Chapter 15 below) which is not normally the case in the US.

7.3 A significant number of large UK listed companies have established restricted share schemes in the past few years. In most cases, they have been established using existing shares and have therefore been established without shareholders' prior approval. The London Stock Exchange normally only requires shareholders' approval for schemes involving the issue of new shares. One of the few exceptions to this was the restricted share plan established in early 1990 by *Granada Group PLC* but a few other companies have since submitted their schemes for prior approval.

Types of scheme

7.4 Most restricted share schemes have involved free allocations of shares which are subject to forfeiture in the event that a performance target, usually based on earnings per share, is not achieved. Usually the performance target is set at the time of allocation but there are schemes where an unconditional allocation has been made following the achievement of a performance target over the previous year or

7.5 Restricted Share Schemes

years. In the Prudential Corporation scheme, executives have been allowed to direct that the whole or part of their annual bonuses (or shares already held by them up to the value of such bonuses) are applied in the purchase of shares, in respect of which the company makes a matching allocation of free shares to be held by the scheme trustees subject to appropriate performance targets.

Allocation of shares

7.5 An allocation of shares under UK restricted share schemes will normally involve the trustees resolving to hold shares under the scheme trusts for identified eligible employees. Such an allocation will give the participant only a contingent interest in the shares since the allocation is subject to forfeiture in certain circumstances.

Income tax

7.6 In principle, a contingent interest in shares is a benefit in money or money's worth which is chargeable to tax under the general principles of Schedule E (*TA 1988, s 131*; see *Weight v Salmon* (*1935*) *19 TC 174*). The value of any such contingent interest will be the market value at allocation of shares of the same class and then discounting that value over the period until vesting to reflect the possibility of forfeiture.

7.7 However, in practice the Inland Revenue will normally be prepared to defer any tax charge until the vesting of the shares in the same way as under US law (see 7.2 above) or for that matter under section 29 AC of the Australian Income Tax Code. Such an approach is in line with the case of *Edwards v Roberts* (*1935*) *19 TC 618* which involved a similar scheme to modern restricted share schemes. The employees were entitled to contingent interests in a 'conditional fund' made up of shares in the company and to the fund's annual income. These interests vested at the end of five years unless forfeited before that time. The employees were taxed on the value of their entitlements at the end of five years and no attempt was made to tax the conditional interest on allocation.

7.8 Where the tax is paid in respect of the allocation of shares, the charge is based on the discounted value of the shares. On the other hand, where the tax is paid by reference to the date of vesting, the tax charge will be based on the market value of the shares at the date of vesting. Most employees will prefer to be taxed at the date of vesting on the market value at that time since the shares will vest and be capable of immediate realisation so as to enable the participant to pay his tax liability.

Capital gains tax

7.9 *TCGA 1992, s 68* provides that the settled property provisions apply to all trust property except that to which *TCGA 1992, s 60* applies; this excludes property to which the beneficiary is absolutely entitled, that is to say, to which the beneficiary has 'the exclusive right... to direct how the asset shall be dealt with'. It is evident that a participant in a restricted share scheme does not have any right to direct how the asset shall be dealt with until the vesting of the shares. It follows, therefore, that even though on the allocation of shares a certain part of the trust property is appointed in favour of a particular beneficiary contingently, the trust property clearly remains part of the same settlement for capital gains tax purposes (see *Roome v Edwards HL (1981) 54 TC 359*).

It follows, therefore, that there is no disposal for capital gains tax purposes at the time of allocation. The position is not the same as the grant of an option under a share option scheme as in that case there is a separate disposal of property — namely the option (see *TCGA 1992, s 144(1)*). Consequently, there will be no charge to capital gains tax on the allocation of shares under a restricted share scheme.

Financing allocations of shares

Introduction

7.10 The trustees of a restricted share scheme will sooner or later need to be financed by outright contributions. There is no reimbursement of the acquisition costs of the shares upon the exercise of any options as there is in the case of an ESOP linked to an executive share option scheme.

7.11 The question which arises, therefore, in establishing any restricted share plan is whether the company's contributions to the trustees will be paid

(*a*)   at the time of allocation;

(*b*)   at the time of vesting; or

(*c*)   from time to time.

Obviously, to the extent that the trustees of the restricted share scheme plan to allocate shares which it does not already own outright, it will be necessary for it to borrow the acquisition price. It is likely that the only source of borrowed funds for this purpose will be the company. It follows, therefore, that the trustees will in practice often need to

7.12 Restricted Share Schemes

apply any contributions received in repayment of loans previously made to the company.

Deductibility of contributions for tax purposes

7.12 A contribution made by the company to the trustees of a restricted share scheme will only be deductible in computing trading profits if it is

(a) revenue rather than capital in nature;

(b) paid wholly and exclusively for the purposes of the company's trade.

Briefly, a series of *ad hoc* voluntary payments will normally be deductible in computation of trading profits, but a substantial payment intended to form the core of a fund will be treated as capital in nature.

7.13 Any outright payment by a company to ESOP trustees to acquire a substantial holding of shares for allocation under a restricted share scheme runs the greatest risk of challenge by the Revenue as a payment of capital. In *Atherton v British Insulated and Helsby Cable Ltd HL (1925) 10 TC 155* a contribution made to constitute a pension fund was held to be capital as it brought a capital asset into existence. A distinction might be made in the case of a contribution to ESOP trustees if the payment is one of a number of payments made over a number of years. In addition, it might also be argued that under a restricted share scheme, the immediate allocation of shares means that the expenditure incurred by the company can be directly related to the allocations of shares in favour of specific employees with the result that the contributions can be properly regarded as expenditure on the emoluments of particular employees.

7.14 The leading cases in the deductibility of payments to ESOPs indicate that a series of *ad hoc* voluntary payments intended to service the goodwill of employees and not intended to bring a capital asset into being will normally be treated as deductible in computation of trading profits (see *Heather v PE Consulting Group Ltd CA (1972) 48 TC 293*; *Jeffs v Ringtons Ltd ChD (1985) 58 TC 680*). On this basis, allocations of shares by making a series of *ad hoc* voluntary payments over a number of years should be deductible. The payments should not form part of an agreed schedule of payments as such payments may simply be regarded as instalments of capital. The best approach is for the company to make voluntary payments out of its profits each year. The ESOP trustees may always borrow any additional funds needed to acquire shares which it requires for allocation.

Restricted Share Schemes **7.19**

7.15 In any restricted share scheme, the allocation of shares will often be contingent upon the achievement of a performance target and the participant remaining an employee of the company. Where these conditions are not satisfied, the allocation of shares may be forfeited by the employee and the shares returned to the general trust fund. Given this risk of forfeiture, the most efficient means of financing the acquisition of any shares will be for the ESOP trustee to acquire the shares by means of loans and for these loans to be repaid out of monies contributed by the company once it becomes certain that the shares will be vested in the participating employee. In such cases, the contribution made to the ESOP trustees can be directly linked to the particular vesting of shares in a participant even though the immediate use of the funds may be to repay the loans made to the ESOP trustees.

7.16 For a discussion of the tax treatment of any loans made to the ESOP trustees by the company in connection with the acquisition of shares for allocation under a restricted share scheme (see 15.33 to 15.36).

Forfeiture

7.17 A restricted share plan will normally provide that where a participant leaves employment before the vesting day or where some performance target fails to be satisfied, the original allocation of shares may be forfeited.

Income tax

7.18 There will be no income tax consequences of a forfeiture. The employee merely loses a contingent interest in the allocated shares.

Capital gains tax

7.19 A forfeiture of allocated shares is in principle a disposal for capital gains tax purposes by virtue of *TCGA 1992, s 24(1)*. This provides that the extinguishment of an asset shall constitute a disposal of an asset whether or not any capital sum is received by way of compensation or otherwise.

However, no charge to tax will arise as the disposal is covered by *TCGA 1992, s 76* which relieves disposals of interests in settled property by the original beneficiaries.

7.20 Restricted Share Schemes

Vesting

Income tax

7.20 On vesting, the participant becomes absolutely entitled to the shares. On general principles, the shares represent an emolument in moneys worth (see *Weight v Salmon HL (1935) 19 TC 174*). Given that tax will normally have been assessed at the time of allocation, the Revenue will seek to charge tax at vesting on the basis of the market value of the shares at that time. However, it is assumed that if tax were charged at the time of allocation that the Revenue would allow credit for this against the tax chargeable at vesting.

7.21 *FA 1988, s 78* imposes a charge to income tax where there is (amongst other things) a removal or variation of a restriction to which shares are subject. Arguably, the lifting of the risk of forfeiture by effluxion of time upon vesting is not the 'removal or variation' of a restriction since such lifting was pre-ordained at the time of allocation. However, if the scheme provides for the premature lifting of the risk of forfeiture on any specified event, such as the participant's cessation of employment as a result of redundancy, then the sudden unforeseen occurrence of the participant's redundancy will be a chargeable event giving risk to a liability to income tax on the value which accrues from the lifting of the restriction.

Capital gains tax

7.22 At vesting, the participant becomes absolutely entitled to the shares as against the trustee. Consequently, the trustee is treated as making a disposal of the shares for capital gains tax purposes under *TCGA 1992, s 71*. A disposal is treated as made for a consideration equal to the market value of the shares since the disposal is made in connection with the participant's employment (see *TCGA 1992, s 17*).

7.23 Under (Extra-Statutory Concession D35) published on 5 December 1990, relief from capital gains tax is available on certain disposals by employee trusts where:

(*a*) the employee trust transfers the chargeable asset for no consideration (a transfer pursuant to the exercise of a share option would therefore be ineligible);

(*b*) the employee to whom the asset is transferred is chargeable to income tax on the value of the asset;

(*c*) the 'employee trust' must be an employee trust within the meaning of *IHTA 1984, s 86*, subject to two modifications. First, the restriction in *sub-section (3)* of *IHTA 1984, s 86* does not need to be satisfied, in other words, it is not necessary that the trusts property is held for 'all or most' of the employees of

Restricted Share Schemes 7.26

the company concerned. Secondly, the employee receiving the transfer of the asset must not be to a person of the kind described in *IHTA, s 28(4)* and not excluded by *sub-section (5)*, that is to say, he must not, broadly speaking, hold together with his associates 5 per cent or more of the equity of the company.

National insurance

7.24 The value received in the form of shares is not 'pay' for national insurance purposes and so no national insurance contributions are payable (see *SI 1979 No 591, reg 19(l)(m)*).

Inheritance tax

7.25 The trustee of a restricted share scheme will normally hold trust property on discretionary trusts. As for any ESOP, the inheritance tax treatment will depend upon whether it falls within *IHTA 1984, s 86* that is to say, a trust for the benefit of all or most of the company's employees.

Non-section 86 trusts

7.26 A non-*section 86* trust is subject to inheritance tax in the normal way for discretionary trusts as follows:

- where a distribution is made out of the trust (*IHTA 1984, s 65(1)(a)*);
- where value is transferred out of the trust without a distribution (*IHTA 1984, s 65(1)(b)*);
- every tenth anniversary of the trust.

However, there is relief from inheritance tax on any distribution which is subject to income tax in the hands of the recipient (an employee, former employee or relative of an employee). This will cover the vast majority of distributions at the time of vesting, but it will not apply to the original allocation of shares to the extent that this is a distribution for inheritance tax purposes. It is advisable, therefore, to ensure that allocations are made within 90 days of the establishment of the ESOP since no inheritance tax charge will arise under the relief in *IHTA 1984, s 65(4)*. In any event, any charge to inheritance tax on a distribution during the first ten years should be minimal particularly if the trustee's acquisition of shares is funded by loan and in any event the ten year charge can be avoided by distributing the trust assets shortly beforehand.

7.27 Restricted Share Schemes

Section 86 trust

7.27 A trust which qualifies as a *section 86* trust normally enjoys full relief from any inheritance tax charge where any distribution is made to a qualifying beneficiary and in respect of the ten year tax charge. However, property comprised in a 'qualifying interest in possession' will not be treated as held on exempt *section 86* trusts. An interest in 5 per cent or more of the whole of the trust will be treated as such a qualifying interest in possession (*IHTA 1984, ss 72(1), 86 (4)(b)*).

7.28 Where any allocation of shares under a restricted share scheme within *section 86* involves 5 per cent or more of the whole of the trust this will be treated as the creation of an interest in possession trust and will give rise to a charge to inheritance tax under *IHTA 1984, s 72(2)(a)*. This tax charge will only be relieved to the extent income tax is paid by the employee on the allocation (*IHTA 1984, ss 70(3), 72(5)*). However, as there is normally no income tax charge at allocation, inheritance tax will normally apply assuming the employee has an interest in possession in more than 5 per cent of the whole of the employee trust as a result of the allocation.

7.29 Furthermore, on termination of the 5 per cent interest in possession (on forfeiture or on sale of the shares for cash) the employee will be treated as making a lifetime transfer of value (*IHTA 1984, s 52*). On vesting, there will be no charge to tax since the employee is treated as beneficially entitled to the property (*IHTA 1984, s 49*).

7.30 Consequently, allocation of shares under a restricted share scheme where the property is held on trusts within *IHTA 1984, s 86* should be limited to no more than 5 per cent of the whole of the property so that such interest is not treated as the creation of a 'qualifying interest in possession' with the result that inheritance tax applies at that time.

Chapter 8

Savings-Related Share Option Schemes

Introduction

8.1 Under a savings-related share option scheme, employees enter into a SAYE savings contract to save a fixed amount each month over five years. An option is granted at the outset over the maximum number of shares which may be acquired with the total savings and bonus under the savings contract. The scheme has three features which it is generally thought makes it attractive. First, the options may be granted at up to a 20 per cent discount to the market value at the time of grant. Secondly, any gains on the exercise of the option will normally be free of income tax. Thirdly, the bonuses payable under the SAYE savings contract are also tax-free.

8.2 Although the legislation was introduced with effect from 1 July 1981 under *FA 1980*, it is substantially based on the previous approved savings-related share option scheme introduced in *FA 1972* and repealed by *FA 1974*. During the 1970s the main banks and a number of other companies continued to operate such schemes despite the high rates of income tax applying in respect of the gains accruing at exercise of the option.

8.3 Since the re-introduction of approved savings-related share option schemes in 1980, the number of schemes has grown progressively. The Inland Revenue's estimate of the number of schemes in operation in March 1992 was 984. On the assumption that the average scheme covers some seven subsidiaries, it would appear that there are about 6,500 companies currently covered by savings-related share option schemes. Certainly, most of the larger listed companies operate such schemes with only a few notable exceptions.

Eligibility criteria

Inland Revenue requirements

8.4 The scheme is specifically designed to encourage wide employee participation. *TA 1988, 9 Sch 26(1)* therefore requires the scheme to be made available to every person who:

8.5 *Savings-Related Share Option Schemes*

(*a*) is a full-time employee or a full-time director of the company which has established the scheme, or in the case of a group scheme, of a participating company; and

(*b*) has been such at all times during the five years down to the date of grant; and

(*c*) is chargeable to income tax under Case I of Schedule E in respect of the office or employment.

8.5 A person will only be eligible to apply for an option if he is a director or employee of a participating company on the date of grant. If he leaves employment before the date of grant, then any application will become invalid. This compares with approved profit sharing schemes where appropriations to certain former employees are allowed.

Discretionary participation

8.6 Although *TA 1988, 9 Sch 26(1)* provides that certain employees must be eligible to participate in any offers under the scheme, the company may extend offers of participation to other directors and employees if the scheme so allows.

8.7 Generally speaking, companies usually extend their savings-related share option scheme to all employees who work at least two years, although the trend in recent years has been to reduce the qualifying period to only one year or less.

ABI Guidelines

8.8 The ABI has not published any guidelines relating to eligibility for a savings-related share option scheme. However, for many years it considered that only persons working 14 hours a week should be eligible to participate and this has been reflected in many schemes. However, certain types of employees, such as retailers who have numerous part-time workers, have long extended savings-related shares option schemes to all employees working at least 8 hours a week. The ABI will now accept participation by all part-time employees, if only because of concerns about claims which may be made against employers for unfair discrimination against part-time employees.

8.9 There is nothing under *TA 1988, 9 Sch* which prevents participation by non-executive or part-time directors. However, the ABI's view is that non-executive directors should not participate in employees' share schemes and this view has prevailed at least amongst listed companies.

Overseas employees

8.10 In principle, there is nothing under *TA 1988, 9 Sch* which excludes participation by employees outside the scope of Case I of Schedule E i.e. overseas employees (see 17.8 below).

Applications for and grant of options

Timing

Model Scheme

8.11 The Inland Revenue Model Scheme provides for eligible employees to be invited to apply for the grant of options under the scheme during the period of four weeks following approval of the scheme by the Inland Revenue or after each announcement of the annual or half-yearly results of the company. The periods for the invitation of applications in the Model Scheme are merely indicative as there is nothing in the approved scheme legislation which requires options to be granted at any particular time. The Model Scheme also provides that no options should be invited later than the tenth anniversary of the date of grant although, again, there is nothing in the approved scheme legislation which restricts the life of a scheme to ten years.

ABI Guidelines

8.12 The only comment made in the ABI Guidelines about the timing of savings-related share option scheme offers is that options may only be granted within ten years of the establishment of the scheme. No comment is made about the timing of any invitation of applications. However, in practice listed companies generally adhere to making invitations during a period of 42 days following an announcement of results.

Exceptional invitation periods

8.13 Many schemes provide for the invitation of applications at any time there are exceptional circumstances which justify the grant of options at that time. The main circumstances which may be regarded as exceptional are the approval of the scheme and any announcement of changes to either the legislation or the rate of terminal bonuses payable under the savings contracts.

Stock Exchange Model Code

8.14 The Stock Exchange Model Code for Dealings by Directors of listed companies restricts the grant of options to persons who

8.15 *Savings-Related Share Option Schemes*

are directors, or who otherwise have possession of price sensitive information, during the period of 60 days prior to any announcement of results by a listed company. These restrictions apply to listed companies regardless of anything contained in the scheme.

Procedure

Applications and grant of options

8.15 The Model Scheme provides that invitations must state the date by which any applications are to be made, the price per share and the maximum amount an applicant may save each month.

8.16 Since 1991, the maximum amount which an optionholder may save under his savings contract each month is £250 including any amount he saves each month under any other corporate savings-related share option scheme *(TA 1988, 9 Sch 24(2)(a))*. However, a scheme will generally give the directors a discretion to fix a lower monthly savings limit. The minimum monthly savings amount is £10 and has remained unaltered since the introduction of savings-related share option schemes on 1 January 1981 (*9 Sch 24(b)*).

8.17 The Model Scheme provides for each invitation to apply for an option to be accompanied by a proposal for a savings contract and an application form which must provide for the applicant to state the monthly savings contribution he wishes to make and (if given the opportunity) whether his option is to be granted on the basis of the standard or the maximum bonus (see 8.21).

8.18 Under the form of application prescribed by HM Treasury, optionholders are required to declare that the aggregate amount they are saving under all corporate savings-related share option schemes is not more than the maximum permitted under *TA 1988, 9 Sch 24(2)* i.e. £250 a month. The Treasury's prescribed form of application also requires applicants to declare that they are eligible to participate in the scheme and are at least 18 years of age. An employee under 18 years of age only has legal capacity to enter into contracts for 'necessaries' and therefore cannot be bound by the savings contract. Consequently, minors under 18 years of age cannot participate in any offer under the scheme.

8.19 There is no obligation to supply applicants with a copy of the scheme rules, but companies which establish a scheme will normally prepare a guide for employees and this will be given to employees at the time of invitation.

Savings-Related Share Option Schemes 8.23

Choice of standard or maximum bonus

8.20 Schemes may be approved on any one or more of the following bases:

- giving employees the right to use only the standard bonus in buying shares;
- giving employees a choice of using either the standard or maximum bonus to buy shares;
- giving employees only a right to use their savings contributions to buy shares.

8.21 The Model Scheme gives employees a choice of using either the standard or maximum bonus. However, many schemes are drafted on the basis of maximum flexibility so that the directors can operate the scheme in any of the above ways. Generally speaking, only companies which have substantial numbers of shares available for the grant of options should give employees a choice of using the maximum bonus. This is because the employee is able to commence saving under a new offer during the final two years of the savings contract which obviously means a greater flow of shares will be involved than under schemes where only the standard bonus is available. A few companies only allow employees to use the savings (and not the bonus) for the acquisition of shares under the option, but this seems unfair on employees who find they are prevented from applying their bonuses in buying shares. Most of the companies with schemes which originally provided for only savings to be used to buy shares have tended in recent years to alter the scheme rules to allow for the use of bonuses.

Weekly paid employees

8.22 Application forms may need to take account of whether employees are weekly paid or four-weekly paid. Since the savings contract is based on monthly contributions, the contributions of weekly (or four-weekly) paid employees will be deducted from pay and paid over to the savings authority to await its crediting against the savings account.

Number of shares

8.23 Since the fundamental principle of any savings-related share option scheme is that the employee enters into a contract under which he agrees to save a fixed amount of his own choice, each month, offers under the scheme are not expressed in terms of the number of shares for which an employee may apply, but in terms of the monthly

8.24 Savings-Related Share Option Schemes

amount he wishes to save. Application forms usually contain a table showing the total amount of savings and bonus at the maturity of the savings contract; it is rare for this to be shown in terms of the number of shares which will be available at the option price. An employee will, of course, know the option price and he can always calculate the number of shares if this is of concern to him.

8.24 Options under savings-related share option schemes are granted in consideration of the agreement of the optionholder entering into the savings-contract with the savings body. It is not necessary, therefore, for the optionholder to make any payment as consideration for the grant.

8.25 The Model Scheme provides that optionholders must have a minimum of 14 days following the issue of invitations within which to make any application. The Inland Revenue will normally allow scheme rules to provide for a shorter period where this is appropriate, for instance, where the offer period is designed to coincide with the offer period in a flotation.

Price

8.26 *TA 1988, 9 Sch 25* provides that the option price must be stated at the time the option is granted and must not be manifestly less than 80 per cent of the market value of the shares of the same class at that time, or, if the Board of Inland Revenue and the grantor agree in writing, at such earlier time or times as may be provided in the agreement.

8.27 Since offers must be made under savings-related share option schemes by invitation of applications, the exercise price will normally, in practice, be fixed by reference to the market value of the shares shortly before the invitations are made. Where the scheme provides for the price to be fixed by reference to the market value of the shares on the business day, or an average of the market values over one or more business days, prior to the date of invitation, this will be treated as an 'agreement in writing' for the purposes of *TA 1988, 9 Sch 25*. If the scheme rules do not specify any particular days, the Inland Revenue will normally only agree the market value at the time of grant of the option. Following an announcement of results by the company, the Inland Revenue will not normally agree a market value fixed by reference to any day or days prior to such announcement.

8.28 The Inland Revenue's practice is that options should normally be granted within 30 days of any day by reference to which the price of the shares is determined. Where the price is fixed by reference to several days prior to the date of invitation, the earliest of those days

Savings-Related Share Option Schemes 8.33

must be treated as the first of the 30 days. The Inland Revenue do not normally allow the price to be fixed over more than five days.

8.29 A number of schemes provide for the price to be fixed by reference to the market value on the date of grant. Under such arrangements, applications will be invited on the basis that the price will only be announced at the date of grant.

8.30 A number of companies with a large number of employees find a period of 30 days between the fixing of the price and the date of grant as providing insufficient time for an offer under a savings-related share option scheme. Such companies will issue invitations without details of the price. The price is subsequently announced during the course of the offer period.

8.31 The legislation provides that options may be granted at a price which is not manifestly less than 80 per cent of the market value of the shares at the relevant time. The scheme may provide for the price to be fixed at any higher price and a number of companies in fact give no discount. The Inland Revenue's interpretation of 'manifestly' is applied strictly. In calculating the price of shares, the company should always round up rather than round down the price. Most companies feel it is inelegant to express the share price in fractions of a pence although there is no objection to this if it is required.

8.32 There is nothing in the legislation which provides that the price must be expressed in sterling although under the savings contract any savings must be made in sterling. A scheme using the shares of a foreign parent may provide for the grant of options expressed in sterling over a variable number of shares depending on the proceeds of the savings contract after conversion into local currency. However, the Inland Revenue will require a cap to be placed on the number of shares which may be acquired equal to the number which can be acquired on the basis of the appropriate exchange rate at the time the option was granted. As a result, any beneficial movement in the exchange rate will not lead to an increase in the underlying number of shares under option; on the other hand, any adverse movement in the exchange rate will lead to a decrease in the number of shares.

Scaling down

8.33 Most schemes contain limits on the number of new shares which may be issued under it and, even if such limits did not exist, most companies would still need to limit the number of shares which are made available under any offer. Schemes, therefore, need to contain provisions for scaling down applications where necessary.

8.34 *Savings-Related Share Option Schemes*

8.34 The Model Scheme provides successive steps to be taken to eliminate excess applications as follows:

(*a*) each election for the maximum bonus to be included in the repayment under savings contracts to be treated as an election for only the standard bonus to be included;

(*b*) the repayment under the savings contract to be deemed to be an election for no bonus to be so included;

(*c*) the excess over £10 of the monthly savings contributions chosen by each applicant to be reduced pro rata to the extent necessary;

(*d*) applications to be selected by lot, each based on a monthly savings contribution of £10 and the inclusion of no bonus in the repayment under the savings contract.

8.35 It is obviously fair to start any scaling down by treating applications for the maximum bonus as applications for the standard bonus. This is because of the 'gearing' effect of options based on the maximum bonus. Following the five-year savings period, the savings are left with the savings body to qualify for the maximum bonus after seven years. During this period, the optionholder may start saving up to £250 a month under a new savings contract.

8.36 It is clearly wasteful and unfair to treat all applications as not including any bonus. This is because on the basis of the current bonus rate of nine monthly savings contributions after five years, an optionholder would only be able to apply approximately 87 pence in respect of every £1 withdrawn from the savings contract in buying shares. It would seem fairer to scale down monthly savings so that the full proceeds can be applied in the purchase of shares, particularly when bonuses and interest rates are at relatively unattractive rates.

8.37 Scaling down the excess of an application over a stated monthly contribution can be carried out on the basis of treating repayments as including either the maximum or standard bonus, although it is usually more convenient to carry out the calculations on the basis of only the standard bonus. In particular, it has normally been the excess over £10 which has been scaled down but there is no reason why a higher threshold cannot be adopted provided the scheme has the flexibility to permit the selection of such threshold as the directors may determine from time to time. There is a certain merit in choosing a threshold amount of £30 or £40 for instance, since it guarantees applications up to this amount.

8.38 A scaling down achieved through selecting by lot is undoubtedly a last resort. It would be very unfair to apply this method unless

Savings-Related Share Option Schemes 8.43

applications had first been scaled down by applying each of the other methods first. In such a case, it may well be better to consider withdrawing the offer altogether.

8.39 The scheme rules should give the directors the flexibility to apply any or all of the above methods as they consider appropriate including agreeing with the Inland Revenue any other method of scaling down. The Inland Revenue's main concern is to ensure that all eligible employees participate on 'similar terms' as required by *TA 1988, 9 Sch 26(1)*. It will not regard the following methods of scaling down as made on 'similar terms':

- reducing all applications by the same amount e.g. £50 off every application;
- refusing applications from optionholders who are already participating in the scheme, or who are already saving a certain amount under the scheme.

8.40 Surprisingly, it is acceptable to scale down applications pro rata the remuneration of applicants on the length of their service since *TA 1988, 9 Sch 26(2)* provides that such factors would be 'similar terms'.

8.41 In order to assist any scaling down, each application form should authorise the directors to reduce the monthly savings contributions selected by the applicant. The application form in the Inland Revenue's Explanatory Notes on SAYE Share Option Schemes (IR 98) provides such an authority.

Board resolution to grant options

8.42 Once the directors have resolved to invite applications, the procedure for the acceptance of applications and grant of options should follow automatically. If any scaling down is necessary because of excess applications, the procedures can be built into the resolution to grant the options. It is not necessary for the directors to meet twice, once in order to invite applications and then later in order to accept applications. The form of resolution to invite applications can provide for the acceptance of all valid applications in full and for the resulting grant of options. If applications exceed any limit on the number of shares to be made available, any one director may be authorised to approve the scaling down of applications in accordance with the prescribed steps.

8.43 An appropriate form of resolution for the grant of options is as follows:

8.43 Savings-Related Share Option Schemes

'Resolution

1. IT WAS REPORTED to the Meeting that a proposal had been put forward of an invitation of applications to be made on [   ] 19[   ] and the following documents were produced to the Board accordingly:

(a) proof letter of invitation;

(b) proof application form;

(c) proof employee guide.

2. IT WAS PROPOSED that the following companies would participate in any offer:

[list participating companies]

3. IT WAS RESOLVED THAT invitations to apply for the grant of options under the scheme be issued on [date] to all employees and directors of the Company and the participating companies referred to on the following terms:

(i) *eligibility* — all directors and employees who work at least [   ] hours a week and who will have on [   ] [date] at least [   ] [months/years] continuous service with the Company or participating company;

(ii) *bonus offered* — eligible employees shall be invited to apply for [5 year options only]/[for 5 or 7 year options as they choose];

(iii) *maximum monthly contribution* — the maximum monthly contribution shall be [£250];

(iv) *option price* — [   ] being [80 per cent] of the middle market quotation of a share on the dealing day preceding [date of issue of invitation]/[average of the middle market quotations of a share on the 3 dealing days preceding [date of issue of invitations]] as derived from the Daily Official List of the London Stock Exchange for the relevant day;

(v) *maximum number of shares* — [   ] shares shall be available under this offer for the grant of options under the scheme; and

(vi) *date of grant* — options shall be granted on [date — not later than 30 days from price fixing date].

4. IT WAS RESOLVED that all applications for the grant of options be accepted in full save to the extent such applications exceed the limit in which event all applications shall be scaled down by a committee of any of the directors in any of the procedures which may be considered appropriate in Rule [   ] of the Scheme Rules.'

Option certificate

8.44 The Model Scheme provides for directors to issue option certificates. A pro forma option certificate will normally need to be submitted to the Inland Revenue as part of the application for approval of the scheme. A form of option certificate is to be found amongst the specimen documents included in the Inland Revenue's Guide on SAYE Share Option Schemes (IR 98). Normally, the Inland Revenue will expect the following statements to be included in any option certificate:

(*a*) the identify of the optionholder;

(*b*) the name of the company;

(*c*) the name of the scheme;

(*d*) the maximum number of shares under option;

(*e*) the date of grant;

(*f*) the exercise price (per share);

(*g*) a statement that the shares are not transferable, and the option rights will lapse upon the occasion of any assignment, charge, disposal or other dealing with the rights conveyed by it or in any other circumstances.

8.45 In addition, it may be helpful to include the following further information:

(*a*) the amount of the monthly contribution;

(*b*) the Bonus Date i.e. the date on which the option will normally become exercisable;

(*c*) the date on which deductions from pay will commence;

(*d*) the maximum proceeds including the bonus on the savings account.

8.46 A recommended form of option certificate is as overleaf:

8.46 Savings-Related Share Option Schemes

[Certificate No.   ]

SHARE OPTION CERTIFICATE

[   ] plc/Limited

SAVINGS-RELATED SHARE OPTION SCHEME

Date of Grant	Monthly Savings Contribution (weekly-paid/four-weekly paid employee - see note below)	Bonus Date (Date on which option normally becomes exercisable)	Maximum Expected Repayment under the Savings Contract	Exercise Price per Share	Number of Shares under Option

This is to certify that:

....

of ....
has been granted an Option to acquire the number of ordinary shares of [   ] p each fully paid in the Company at the exercise price per share shown above in accordance with and subject to the Rules of the .... Savings-Related Share Option Scheme

By Order of the Board

[Secretary of the Company]

Secretary

NOTES

(1) Deductions from your pay in respect of your contributions will commence on the pay date[   ] 19..... For weekly-paid employees/four-weekly paid employees deductions will commence on the pay date [   ] 19..... and will continue each week until [240/60] contributions have been made and held in a 'feeder' account pending transfer to the savings account. Transfer will be made to the savings account each month at the monthly contributions rate shown above.
(2) The Option is not transferable, and will lapse upon any assignment, charge, disposal or other dealing.
(3) A copy of the scheme rules is available for inspection upon request to [   ].

THIS CERTIFICATE IS IMPORTANT AND SHOULD BE KEPT IN A SAFE PLACE

Employee communications

Importance of employee communications

8.47 There is no doubt that clear employee communications material will increase the take-up of any offer under a scheme since the better an employee understands the value of the offer, and how the scheme works, the more likely he is to respond to any offer. Employee communications usually comprise at least one of the following:

- written guide
- company newspaper articles
- team briefings and formal presentations
- videos
- posters
- electronic mail

Key information

8.48 The key to effective employee communications in savings-related share option schemes is to focus on the limited number of decisions which an employee has to make when considering making an application to join the scheme. First, the employee needs to understand that the scheme involves entering into a five-year contract to pay a fixed sum each month and so he needs to consider whether he is prepared to enter into such a contract and, if so, the amount he is prepared to save each month. In deciding whether to save and the amount he wishes to save, he can take into account that:

(a) he will be granted the right to buy shares (without any obligation to buy) at a fixed price which will represent a discount to the market value;

(b) the rate of interest on any savings; and

(c) the tax exemptions which are applicable in respect of the bonus and the option gains.

The employee needs to take account of the implications of his not remaining an employee until the bonus date, the third anniversary of grant or even the first anniversary of the commencement of the savings contract.

8.49 The second main decision which he may need to take into account is whether he wishes to elect for the standard (five-year) bonus or the maximum (seven-year) bonus which offers a higher return.

8.50 Savings-Related Share Option Schemes

8.50 In order to keep the communications sharply focused, it is appropriate initially to ensure information on certain areas is kept to a minimum, for instance, suspension of monthly contributions, the rights of exercise or on roll-overs of options on a takeover. Information about suspending payments and the exercise procedures are best supplied after the grant of options and can be enclosed with the option certificate or included in information packs with the annual sharesave account statements each year. In any event the best time to supply information about rights of exercise on a sale of a business or a takeover is as soon as any such event occurs or appears likely to occur. The right time to supply information about rights of exercise on any sale of the shares and any transfer of the shares into a Personal Equity Plan is at the time of exercise. Such information can be included in the statements sent out by most savings bodies to warn savers of any forthcoming bonus date.

Written material

8.51 Most companies appear to provide full explanatory written material about any scheme at the time it is first launched and on subsequent offers. A few companies send shareholders' circulars and annual reports to employees.

8.52 Savings bodies send participants annual sharesave account statements each year and will usually alert participants to the bonus date shortly before this arises.

8.53 Most of the savings bodies are prepared to print explanatory guides usually in a fairly standard format although a minority of the savings bodies will contribute money towards the company's own printing costs but usually only in the case of large schemes.

Company newspaper articles

8.54 Company newspaper articles are often the most effective methods of communicating the essence of the scheme if only because such articles tend to stick to the main points and are not cluttered by inessential information.

Team briefings and formal presentations

8.55 The spread of team briefing procedures relying on managers to brief their own teams is effective in drawing the attention of employees to the existence and timing of any offers. Such informal methods always need to be supported by the provision of written material to ensure consistent and reliable information is supplied to all eligible employees. A number of companies make use of formal

Savings-Related Share Option Schemes 8.60

presentations inviting the use of specially prepared videos, slides, flip charts and scripts for speakers.

8.56 Many savings bodies will provide trained presenters to give presentations based on material prepared by the building society which may or may not be personalised for the particular client company.

Videos

8.57 Videos can be an excellent way to ensure consistent and reliable information is supplied to employees at team briefings and formal presentations. The majority of savings bodies have standard videos and indeed many companies will appoint a savings body on the basis of the material contained in the video.

Posters

8.58 Posters can be helpful in alerting employees to the timing of any offers, although with the increasing use of computer tapes for maintaining personal databases employees increasingly receive offer packages through the post at their home addresses.

Non-transferability of options

8.59 A savings-related share option scheme must exclude any right of voluntary transfer, assignment or charge in respect of option rights (*TA 1988, 9 Sch 22*). This is reflected in the form of a sharesave contract which excludes any right of voluntary transfer and makes detailed provision for the actions to be taken by a savings body which becomes aware of a purported transfer of the benefit of the savings contract (see 8.60 below).

Savings contract

Introduction

8.60 Savings-related share option schemes are linked to a contractual savings scheme which is usually with a savings body nominated by the company, but in some cases may be selected by the employee. Only contractual savings schemes certified by the Treasury under *TA 1988, s 326* and approved by the Inland Revenue may be used. These now include the Department for National Savings SAYE Issues and building society and bank Sharesave schemes. The terms of the savings contracts offered by each of these bodies are broadly identical. The prospectuses have been changed with greater frequency in recent years and it is always essential to ensure that the current prospectus

8.61 Savings-Related Share Option Schemes

approved by the Inland Revenue is to be used in any offer. References in this section to 'paragraph numbers' are to paragraph numbers in the Sharesave Scheme F prospectus which was introduced for new contracts from 1 April 1993.

Eligibility

8.61 A person may only enter into a savings contract on the basis of a declaration to the savings body if:

(a) he is not less than 16 years of age;

(b) he is eligible to participate in a savings-related share option scheme operated by his current employer;

(c) the aggregate of each monthly contribution under the proposed contract and all other approved savings contracts operated by banks, building societies and the Department for National Savings in connection with savings-related share option schemes do not exceed the *lesser* of:

   (i) £250 (or such greater sum as HM Treasury may from time to time determine); or

   (ii) the monthly contribution necessary to secure as nearly as may be repayment of an amount equal to the aggregate exercise price of the shares under the relevant savings-related share option scheme offer.

8.62 The savings body is only permitted to accept an application if it has received a copy of the Inland Revenue's certificate of approval in respect of the scheme. An extra copy of the Inland Revenue's certificate of approval is sent to the company for this purpose.

8.63 Under the terms of the prospectus, the savings body is precluded from accepting applications from persons under 16 years of age.

8.64 Paragraph 3 of the prospectus states that the savings body shall not be obliged to enter into a savings contract although it is difficult to envisage the circumstances in which any savings body would exercise this discretion. This may, of course, result in the company which has granted the option being in breach of the terms of its own scheme if any employees with a statutory right to participate in any offer under the scheme were so excluded. In such circumstances, the company would need to appoint an alternative savings body for that employee.

Savings contributions

8.65 Savings contributions can only be credited to the savings account in 60 fixed monthly amounts of between £10 and £250 a month. The fixed monthly amount may be selected by the investor and must be in a multiple of £1.

Duration of the savings period

8.66 The savings contract starts when the first contribution is credited to the savings account. After the first month, each of the remaining 59 monthly contributions are due during each successive month. Since paragraph 13 of the prospectus provides that, where interest is paid in lieu of bonus, it is deemed to run from the first day of the month the relevant savings contribution is due, it follows that savings bodies normally require deductions from pay to be received by the end of the immediately preceding month. In this way savings bodies are in a position to credit the monthly contribution to the savings account on the first day of the month to which the contribution relates. There are provisions allowing investors temporarily to suspend or stop making payments (see 8.71 below).

Contributions from employees

8.67 Paragraph 6 of the prospectus states that employees' contributions shall be made through the employing company, as the agent of the employee, from deductions from pay authorised by the employee. This means that contributions cannot be made by direct debit or standing order direct from employees' bank or building society accounts, although a number of banks justify this practice on the basis that the employees' pay was paid into their bank accounts anyhow. The requirement for contributions to be deducted from pay also seems to exclude the participation of overseas employees under arrangements whereby a lump sum is placed in a 'feeder account' in sterling from which the regular monthly contributions are transferred.

Weekly-paid employees

8.68 Many employees are paid weekly or four-weekly and it can be difficult to synchronise the deductions from pay with the crediting of contributions to the savings contract on a monthly basis. The most common way of dealing with deductions from the pay of weekly paid employees is for the deductions to be made by the employee each successive week for 240 weeks and to be transferred each week (or each four weeks) into a feeder account with the saving body. Similarly, deductions from the pay of four-weekly paid employees are transferred into the savings body feeder account each four weeks. In both cases, this will mean the deductions from pay will be ahead of the due dates for crediting the monthly contributions. Indeed, the savings body feeder accounts will normally receive the final weekly deduction after approximately four years seven months, some five months before the

8.69 Savings-Related Share Option Schemes

date on which for the 60th monthly contribution is normally due. Savings bodies vary in their practice in relation to offering interest on feeder accounts; some, such as the Halifax, offer interest automatically whilst most do not, although almost all will do so upon request. The average period of time sums are held in a feeder account is about two months and so the amounts of interest involved are relatively insignificant.

8.69 Where a company believes it is possible to cope with more frequent deductions from weekly-paid employees then there is nothing to stop the company offering a 'deduction holiday' of four consecutive weeks at the end of each calendar year or waiving all fifth deductions in any month. In this way deductions from the pay of weekly-paid employees can keep in step with the crediting of the monthly contributions to savings accounts.

8.70 A few companies even retain weekly deductions until the due date for the payment of the monthly contributions. Whenever an employer holds onto any deductions, it will, of course, be necessary for the employer to account for these deductions in the event the employee leaves employment before the transfer is made to the savings body.

Postponement and stopping contributions

8.71 The terms of savings contracts do not oblige an employee to make all 60 monthly contributions. An employee may postpone or stop making contributions. Up to six monthly contributions in total — not necessarily successive contributions — can be postponed. The effect of postponing any monthly contributions is that the period of the contract, including the bonus date, is set back by one month. If a seventh monthly contribution is postponed, the participant is treated as having given notice of an intention to stop paying contributions. Where such notice has been given, or is treated as having been given, no further contributions may be credited to the savings account and the investor is entitled to apply for repayment of his contributions in full with interest where applicable. The savings body is not automatically obliged to remit any balance on the account.

8.72 Interest is only applicable after the first anniversary of the start of the contract (or after twelve monthly contributions have been made, if later). Given that the contract only starts on the date in the first month on which the monthly contribution is 'received', care may need to be taken to ensure repayment is only obtained after that date in the month. No interest is payable after the seventh anniversary of the start of the savings contract in cases where the 60 monthly payments have not been made unless HM Treasury otherwise determine which it has not done so far. Where interest is payable upon

Savings-Related Share Option Schemes 8.76

completion of the savings contract, it is payable at the rate of 3 per cent per annum on the aggregate of the savings and bonus. Interest is calculated, in respect of each separate monthly contribution, from the first day of the month. Many schemes provide for options to lapse upon the optionholder giving notice of his intention to stop monthly payments although there is no statutory obligation to do so. If the scheme rules do not specifically provide for the lapse of options in such circumstances the option will only be exercisable to the extent the scheme rules allow, for instance, within six months of leaving employment on account of injury, disability or similar specified circumstances.

8.73 Interest on any contributions which are withdrawn before completion of the savings contract is only 3 per cent. This had been 5 per cent interest throughout the period from the introduction of savings-related share option schemes until 31 March 1993.

Bonuses

8.74 Bonuses are a lump sum paid in lieu of interest after the completion of the savings contract. They are payable upon the application of the investor to close his account. The bonus payable upon completion of 60 monthly savings is nine monthly contributions (equivalent to 5.53 per cent interest per annum). Where the savings account is closed at least two years after the bonus date, the bonus payable is 18 monthly contributions (equivalent to 5.87 per cent interest per annum). Where the savings account is closed between the bonus date and the second anniversary of the bonus date, interest is payable on the amount withdrawn (including the bonus which will have been credited to the savings account) at the rate of 3 per cent per annum in respect of each completed month since the bonus date.

Death

8.75 No more monthly contributions are payable or may be credited to the savings account after the death of an investor. Where the savings body has continued to receive any contributions after death, it is obliged to refund them and make any necessary adjustments to the savings contract. Personal representatives may withdraw the savings and any interest or bonus which is due. Where the savings contract has not been completed, no interest is payable where the account is closed before the first anniversary of the start of the contract and 5 per cent interest is payable thereafter until the seventh anniversary of the start of the contract.

No transfer of the savings contract

8.76 A savings contract cannot be transferred to another person. Any purported transfer after completing the 60 monthly savings under

8.77 *Savings-Related Share Option Schemes*

the savings contract is treated as an application for repayment of the savings and the bonus and any interest to date which must be repaid to the investor, not his transferee. Any purported transfer before completion of the savings contract is treated as notice of intention to stop paying monthly contributions and accordingly all contributions are repaid together with any interest.

Tax relief

8.77 Any bonus or interest payable under a savings contract qualifies for exemption for tax purposes under *TA 1988, s 326* and *TCGA 1992, s 271(4)*. Such bonus or interest is exempt for all tax purposes which means that the taxpayer is not required to return it in his annual tax return.

Scheme limits

Inland Revenue requirements

8.78 There are no limits under the legislation on the number of shares which may be allocated under a savings-related share option scheme or indeed any other type of approved scheme.

ABI Guidelines

8.79 The 1987 ABI Guidelines do not contain any specific limits on the number of shares issuable under savings-related share option schemes adopted by listed companies. The overall limit of 10 per cent of the issued ordinary share capital over any ten-year period and the flow-rate limit of 3 per cent over any three-year period apply. The 1987 ABI Guidelines make special provision for the year in which a savings-related share option scheme is introduced by allowing a total allocation in that and the previous four years of 5 per cent of share capital, provided all executive share options are limited to 3 per cent of share capital over any three year period.

Exercise of options

Introduction

8.80 The fundamental principle of a savings-related share option scheme is that the scheme shares are to be paid for out of the repayment and any bonus or interest payable under the linked certified savings contract.

8.81 However, the shares may only be acquired upon exercise of the options in fairly limited circumstances. The legislation sets out the circumstances in which options may be exercised.

Income tax on option gains

8.82 All gains on the exercise of an option in the circumstances set out below are exempt from income tax except where the right of exercise arises within three years of the date of grant on account of a takeover, scheme of arrangement, voluntary winding-up of the company or the disposal of the business or subsidiary in which the optionholder works.

Exercise at the bonus date

Normally, options may only be exercised during the period of six months following the bonus date. For this purpose, the bonus date is the date on which the 60th monthly contribution is credited to the savings account, or the second anniversary of that date where the optionholder elects to take the maximum bonus. This means that where an employee elects for the maximum bonus, he is not able to change his mind and exercise his option when the standard bonus is credited to this account upon completion of the savings contract; in such a case he must wait until the date the maximum bonus is due. If before the maximum bonus is due, he leaves employment (other than in the special circumstances mentioned below) he loses his rights of exercise altogether even though he has completed all 60 monthly savings contributions.

8.83 Shortly before the time the bonus becomes payable most savings bodies automatically alert optionholders of their right to obtain repayment and exercise their options.

8.84 Once the selected bonus date is reached, there is no entitlement to interest during any further period in which the savings are left with the savings body.

Early exercise in the event of death

8.85 Under *TA 1988, 9 Sch 18* a scheme must provide that, if an optionholder dies before the bonus date, any exercise of the option must normally be made within twelve months of his death. If he dies within the normal six month period allowed for exercise after the bonus date, then the personal representatives are allowed until twelve months after the bonus date within which to exercise the option.

8.86 Savings-Related Share Option Schemes

Early exercise upon leaving employment under TA 1988, 9 Sch 19

8.86 A scheme must provide for a right of exercise during the period of six months following the date on which the employee leaves in certain involuntary circumstances which are set out in the legislation. These circumstances are where the employee leaves on account of injury, disability, redundancy (within the meaning of the *Employment Protection (Consolidation) Act 1978*), retirement on reaching a particular age which has to be specified in the scheme (see 8.92 to 8.105 below) or retirement on reaching any other age at which the optionholder is bound to retire under the terms of his contract of employment.

8.87 As far as employees who leave employment before the bonus date on account of other reasons are concerned, *TA 1988, 9 Sch 19* provides that no right of exercise may be allowed before the third anniversary of the date of grant except on the personal grounds set out in 8.86 above or in the event of a takeover, scheme of arrangement, voluntary winding-up or the disposal of the business or subsidiary for which the optionholder works.

8.88 *TA 1988, 9 Sch 19* provides that so far as employees who leave after the third anniversary of the date of grant are concerned, the scheme must either exclude any right of exercise or, to the extent rights of exercise are permitted, the scheme must restrict such rights to a period of six months after leaving employment.

8.89 In addition to the statutory rights of early exercise (injury, etc. referred to above), most companies allow a right of exercise after the third anniversary on the grounds of early retirement and perhaps maternity.

8.90 A scheme may provide for a right of exercise by any director or employee who leaves employment after the third anniversary of the date of grant for any reason which may be specified in the scheme rules, including for any reason whatsoever. Given that employees who leave after three years will have saved for a fairly substantial period — the usual minimum period for the exercise of an executive share option scheme — and that the rate of interest on early withdrawals of savings have been fixed at a particularly low rate for long-term savings accounts — it is surprising that only a few companies have permitted an automatic right of exercise after the third anniversary regardless of the reasons for leaving. Even the Model Scheme is drafted on the basis that a right of exercise will be allowed after the third anniversary of grant only in specified circumstances.

8.91 Where a scheme permits only limited rights of exercise after the third anniversary but allows employees the right to elect for the maximum bonus, there is a case for the scheme providing for a

Savings-Related Share Option Schemes **8.95**

relaxation of the rights of exercise with effect from the completion of the savings contract after five years. This is because of the anomaly which arises whereby former employees who elect for the standard bonus may be entitled to exercise their options after the bonus date regardless of the reason for leaving whilst employees who elected for the maximum bonus and leave will only be able to exercise their options if they leave on account of reasons specified in the scheme rules (see 8.82 above).

Early exercise at retirement age

8.92 *TA 1988, 9 Sch 19* provides that an optionholder who ceases to hold the office or employment by virtue of which he is eligible to participate by reason of, amongst other things, retirement on reaching retirement age or any other age at which he is bound to retire in accordance with his contract of employment. *TA 1988, 9 Sch 20* additionally provides a right of exercise for an optionholder on reaching an age specified in the scheme.

8.93 In schemes approved on or after 25 July 1991, that age must be (*a*) the same for men and women, and (*b*) not less than 60 nor more than 75 years of age (*TA 1988, 9 Sch 8A*). In schemes approved before 25 July 1991, the age to be specified is the 'pensionable age' within the meaning of *Schedule 20* to the *Social Security Act 1975* (now included in the *Social Security Contributions and Benefits Act 1992, s 122*). This is 65 years of age for men and 60 for women.

8.94 The reason for the change in the legislation lies in Article 119 of the EC Treaty and the case of *Barber v GRE, Case C–262/88*. In that case, the European Court held that pension rights were 'pay' for the purposes of Article 119 which provides, amongst other things, that men and women should be treated equally in matters relating to pay. As the implications of the Barber case were considered, it was realised that the use of the term 'pensionable age' as defined for the purposes of the social security legislation probably exposed employers to liability for claims based on unequal treatment of men and women in relation to pay.

8.95 The position as regards new schemes approved on or after 25 July 1991 is dealt with by the introduction of the term 'specified age' in *FA 1991, s 38*. However, no changes were made in relation to existing schemes which, of course, initially meant nearly all such schemes. The employers in these cases were apparently unable to alter their schemes to afford equal treatment of men and women. Not surprisingly, the Inland Revenue were soon prepared to deal with this apparent oversight in the legislation by permitting companies to change the rules of schemes approved before 25 July 1991 to incorporate a specified common age instead of references to pensionable

8.96 *Savings-Related Share Option Schemes*

age. In the year or so following 25 July 1991 the Inland Revenue insisted on companies providing a legal opinion to justify the making of the change to subsisting option rights. As the numbers of legal opinions grew, the Inland Revenue decided it no longer required a legal opinion. In September 1992, the Inland Revenue wrote to many companies with schemes established before 25 July 1991, and many professional advisers, and indicated its willingness to consider proposals for changing references to 'pensionable age' to a specified age.

8.96 Companies are sometimes reluctant to make the necessary changes in schemes established before 25 July 1991 particularly if it requires prior shareholder approval. This is short-sighted since successful claims based on the unequal treatment of men and women under savings-related share option schemes seems inevitable. It is not sufficient to defend any such case on the basis that the scheme merely reflected the requirements of UK legislation at the time the scheme was established, particularly as the Inland Revenue have now written to most companies drawing their attention to the opportunity to alter subsisting option rights.

8.97 Most listed company schemes need to obtain the prior approval of shareholders for changes to the benefit of optionholders relating to the rights of exercise. However, many schemes contain an authority for the directors to make any changes which are intended to comply with or take account of any changes to the legislation or any statutory provisions. The question which arises, therefore, is whether Article 119 can be construed as 'legislation' or 'statutory provisions' for this purpose. Under the *European Communities Act 1972*, all directly enforceable provisions of the EC Treaty, including Article 119, shall be 'recognised' and available in law, and be enforced, allowed and followed accordingly. While this means that such provisions form part of English law, it does not necessarily follow from this that they should be treated as 'legislation' or 'statutory provisions'. Whether they are such is then a question of domestic law or interpretation contracts.

8.98 In the unreported Court of Appeal decision in *Consultants Group International v John Warman Ltd*, 19 December 1986, Purchas LJ held that a requirement of a consultant to obtain all necessary approvals required under current legislation except that of an 'EEC Licence', the term 'current legislation' should be interpreted as including EEC Regulations. This was on the basis that the reference to the EEC Licence would otherwise have been superfluous. In this case the draftsman thought the EEC Regulations would fall within the scope of 'legislation'.

8.99 It is a rule of construction under English law that in the absence of any indication that the context requires otherwise, words should be given their common English meaning. Applying this rule,

Savings-Related Share Option Schemes 8.103

provisions of the EC Treaty (and Regulations and Directives) are clearly 'legislation'. The Oxford Dictionary defines legislation as the 'enactments of a legislature' and this would seem to cover Article 119. Similarly, Article 119 would seem to be a 'statutory provision'. The Oxford Dictionary defines it as a 'decree, decision or law of a sovereign or legislative authority'.

8.100 It follows, therefore, that where any savings-related share option scheme contains a power for the directors to make changes to comply with or take account of any 'legislative' or 'statutory provision' that the incorporation of a reference to 'the specified age' in place of 'pensionable age' may be made without prior shareholders' approval. However, even if shareholders' prior approval is necessary, companies should still consider making the changes to avoid any risk of a claim by a male employee in respect of the unequal treatment of men and women under the scheme.

8.101 Whether a company is proposing to establish a new scheme, or to alter the reference to pensionable age in an old scheme, the difficulty facing any company is the choice of the age which is to be specified in any scheme. Most companies now have a compulsory retirement age for the majority of their employees which is common for both men and women and which is fixed at 65 years of age or at any other age at which male employees were traditionally required to retire in that company. However, employees are often entitled to retire from some earlier age, usually 60 years of age, but sometimes even 55 years of age. The problem under savings-related share option schemes is that the age at which employees normally retire as a matter of entitlement will vary and will usually be well before the age at which they are bound to retire under their contracts of employment.

8.102 The new concept of a specified age which must be the same for all employees, male and female, is highly unsatisfactory. The employee can only take advantage of an exercise of his/her option at the specified age if he/she actually retires at that precise age. The point is not clear but the employee is probably not entitled to exercise his/her option if he/she retires, say, six months after reaching the specified age and certainly not if he/she retires one year later than the specified age. Unfortunately, few actually retire at any specified age but will retire under voluntary retirement schemes usually at some age before the right of exercise arises at the compulsory retirement age.

8.103 Many schemes permit a right of exercise upon an optionholder leaving on account of early retirement with the agreement of their employer. Early retirement does not describe the situation where an employee retires at any age he is entitled to retire under a voluntary retirement scheme. Only a reference to 'retirement age' as any age at which the employee is entitled to retire under the terms of his contract

8.104 *Savings-Related Share Option Schemes*

of employment' could do that. Even where optionholders retire 'early', they are only permitted to exercise their options if they have been held for at least three years.

8.104 In the Inland Revenue's circular of September 1992, the Inland Revenue indicated that it would approve two kinds of amendments to savings-related share option schemes:

(i) the replacement of references to 'pensionable age' with reference to both age 60 and age 65, so that individual participants would have rights of exercise on reaching either age;

(ii) the replacement of references to 'pensionable age' with references to age 60, subject to transitional provisions designed to protect the interests of male participants over the age of 60 at the time of the change.

8.105 The idea of giving a right of exercise upon retirement at reaching either 60 or 65 years of age still means that the majority of employees who retire at an age between 60 and 65 will have no right to exercise at their actual retirement. The alternative amendment of allowing a right of exercise at 60 years only, subject to transitional provisions for male participants over the age of 60 at the time of the change, suffers equally from the same problem. The only long-term solution is an amendment to the legislation which allows exercise at 60 years of age or any later age regardless of whether the optionholder exercises or not.

Early exercise upon a takeover

(See 'Takeover, etc.', in Chapter 12).

Number of shares which may be acquired on exercise

8.106 The fundamental principle of a savings-related share option scheme is the linkage between the amount of savings and any interest and the number of shares which may be acquired upon an early exercise. The Model Scheme contains a requirement that any repayment under the savings contract shall exclude the repayment of any contribution on the due date for payment of which more than one month after the date on which repayment is made. This was introduced to stop an abuse which was common upon takeovers and in other circumstances on early exercise of paying up savings contracts in advance, or at least up to the 59th monthly contribution, so as to increase the number of shares which may be acquired. Even apart from that abuse, this provision means that sums held in suspense accounts with the savings body by weekly-paid employees cannot be used to acquire shares under the scheme until credited on the due date to the savings account as a monthly contribution.

Appendix 5

Set out below is a precedent for an approved savings-related share option scheme appropriate for a listed company. Certain passages reflect ABI and NAPF Guidelines and would not necessarily be included in the scheme of a private company.

Rules of the [   ] Savings Related Share Option Scheme

1. Definitions

1.1   In this Scheme, the following words and expressions shall bear, unless the context otherwise requires, the meanings set forth below:

'Appropriate Period'	the meaning given by *Paragraph 15(2)* of *Schedule 9* to the *Taxes Act*;
'Associated Company'	an associated company of the Company within the meaning that expression bears in *section 187(2)* of the *Taxes Act*;
'the Auditors'	the auditors of the Company for the time being;
'the Board'	the board of directors of the Company or a duly authorised committee thereof;
'Bonus Date'	where Repayments under the Savings Contract made in connection with an Option are taken as including the maximum bonus, the earliest date on which the maximum bonus is payable and, in any other case, the earliest date on which the standard bonus is payable under such Savings Contract;
'Close Company'	a close company as defined in *section 414(1)* of the *Taxes Act* as varied by *paragraph 8* of *Schedule 9* to the *Taxes Act*;
'the Company'	[ ] plc (registered in under No [ ]);
'Continuous Service'	the meaning given to 'continuous employment' in *Schedule 13* to the

8.106 *Savings-Related Share Option Schemes*

	Employment Protection (Consolidation) Act 1978;
'Control'	the meaning given by *section 840* of the *Taxes Act*;
'Date of Grant'	the date on which the Board accepts a duly completed form of application;
'Date of Invitation'	the date on which the Board invites applications for Options;
'Dealing Day'	any day on which the London Stock Exchange is open for the transaction of business;
'Eligible Employee'	any individual who:

    (a)   (i)   is a director or employee of a Participating Company on terms which require him to devote at least such minimum number of hours a week to his duties as the Board may determine provided that such minimum shall be not less than 8 nor more than 25 hours; and

            (ii)   is chargeable to tax in respect of his office or employment under Case I of Schedule E of the *Taxes Act*; and

            (iii)   has such qualifying period (if any) of Continuous Service (being a period commencing not earlier than five years prior to the Date of Grant) as the Board may determine; or

    (b)   is an executive director or employee and is nominated by the Board either individually or as a member of a category of such executive directors or employees;

Savings-Related Share Option Schemes 8.106

'Employees' Share Scheme'	the meaning given by *section 743* of the *Companies Act 1985*;
'Exercise Price'	the amount payable on the exercise of an Option, whether in whole or in part, being an amount equal to the relevant Option Price multiplied by the number of Shares in respect of which the Option is exercised;
'Invitation Period'	the period of 42 days commencing on any of the following:

    (a) the day on which the Scheme is approved by the Inland Revenue;

    (b) the day immediately following the day on which the Company makes an announcement of its results for the last preceding financial year, half-year or other period;

    (c) any day on which the Board resolves that exceptional circumstances exist which justify the grant of Options;

    (d) any day on which a change to the legislation affecting savings-related share option schemes approved by the Inland Revenue under the *Taxes Act* is proposed or takes effect; or

    (e) any day on which a new Savings Contract prospectus is announced or takes effect;

'the London Stock Exchange'	The International Stock Exchange of the United Kingdom and the Republic of Ireland Limited;
'Market Value'	in relation to a Share on any day:

    (a) if and so long as the Shares are listed on the London Stock Exchange, its middle market quotation (as derived from the Daily Official List of the London Stock Exchange); or

    (b) subject to (a) above, its market value, determined in accordance with *Part VIII* of the *Taxation of Chargeable*

8.106 *Savings-Related Share Option Schemes*

	Gains Act 1992 and agreed in advance with the Shares Valuation Division of the Inland Revenue;
'Material Interest'	the meaning given by *section 187(3)* of the *Taxes Act*;
'Maximum Contribution'	the lesser of: (a) £250 per month; or (b) such maximum monthly contribution as may be permitted pursuant to *paragraph 24* of *Schedule 9* to the *Taxes Act*; or (c) such maximum monthly contribution as may be determined from time to time by the Board;
'Member of a Consortium'	the meaning given by *section 187(7)* of the *Taxes Act*;
'Monthly Contributions'	monthly contributions agreed to be paid by a Participant under the Savings Contract made in connection with his Option;
'Option'	a right to acquire Shares under the Scheme which is either subsisting or (where the context so admits or requires) is proposed to be granted;
'Option Price'	the price per Share, as determined by the Board, at which an Eligible Employee may acquire Shares upon the exercise of an Option being not less than: (a) 80 per cent of the Market Value on the Dealing Day immediately preceding the Date of Invitation (or, if the Board so determines, 80 per cent of the average of the Market Values on the three Dealing Days immediately preceding the Date of Invitation or 80 per cent of the Market Value at such other time as may be agreed in advance in writing with the Inland Revenue); and

Savings-Related Share Option Schemes 8.106

	(b)	if the Shares are to be subscribed, their nominal value,
		but subject to any adjustment pursuant to Rule 10;
'Participant'		a director or employee, or former director or employee, to whom an Option has been granted, or (where the context so admits or requires) the personal representatives of any such person;
'Participating Company'	(a)	the Company; and
	(b)	any other company which is under the Control of the Company, is a Subsidiary of the Company and is for the time being designated by the Board as a Participating Company;
'Repayment'		in relation to a Savings Contract, the aggregate of the 60 Monthly Contributions which the Participant has agreed to make and any bonus due at the Bonus Date;
'Savings Contract'		a contract under a certified contractual savings scheme (within the meaning of *section 326* of the *Taxes Act*) approved by the Inland Revenue for the purpose of *Schedule 9* to the *Taxes Act*;
'the Scheme'		the [ ] Savings Related Share Option Scheme in its present form or as from time to time amended in accordance with the provisions hereof;
'Share'		a share in the capital of the Company which satisfies the conditions specified in *paragraphs 10 to 14* (inclusive) of *Schedule 9* to the *Taxes Act*;
'Specified Age'		[ ] years of age;
'Subsidiary'		the meaning given by *sections 736 and 736A* of the *Companies Act 1985*;
'Taxes Act'		the *Income and Corporation Taxes Act 1988*.

8.106 *Savings-Related Share Option Schemes*

1.2 In this Scheme, unless the context requires otherwise:

(*a*) the headings are inserted for convenience only and do not affect the interpretation of any Rule;

(*b*) a reference to a Rule is a reference to a Rule of this Scheme;

(*c*) a reference to a statute or statutory provision includes a reference:

  (i) to that statute or provision as from time to time consolidated, modified, re-enacted or replaced by any statute or statutory provision;

  (ii) to any repealed statute or statutory provision which it re-enacts (with or without modification); and

  (iii) to any subordinate legislation made under it.

(*d*) words in the singular include the plural, and vice versa;

(*e*) a reference to the masculine shall be treated as a reference to the feminine, and vice versa;

(*f*) if a period of time is specified and starts from a given day or the day of an act or event, it is to be calculated exclusive of that day;

(*g*) a reference to 'a year' shall be a period calculated by reference to a previous or subsequent anniversary of a particular date.

2. Application for Options

2.1 The Board may, during any Invitation Period, invite applications for Options from Eligible Employees, and any such invitation shall be in writing and shall include details of:

(*a*) eligibility;

(*b*) the Option Price;

(*c*) the Maximum Contribution payable;

(*d*) whether, for the purpose of determining the number of Shares over which an Option is to be granted, the Repayment under the Savings Contract is to be taken:

  (i) as including the maximum bonus;

  (ii) as including only the standard bonus; or

  (iii) as not including a bonus.

(*e*) the date by which applications made pursuant to Rule 2.3 must be received (being neither earlier than 14 days nor later than 25 days after the Date of Invitation),

and the Board may determine and include in the invitations details of the maximum number of Shares over which applications for Options are to be invited in that Invitation Period.

2.2 An application for an Option must incorporate or be accompanied by a proposal for a Savings Contract.

2.3 An application for an Option shall be in writing in such form as the Board may from time to time prescribe save that it shall provide for the applicant to state:

(a) the Monthly Contributions (being a multiple of £1 and not less than £10) which he wishes to make under the Savings Contract to be made in connection with the Option for which application is made;

(b) that his proposed Monthly Contributions (when taken together with any Monthly Contributions he makes under any other Savings Contract) will not exceed the Maximum Contribution;

(c) if Eligible Employees may elect for the Repayment under the Savings Contract to be taken as including the maximum bonus, the standard bonus, or as not including a bonus, his election in that respect.

2.4 Each application for an Option shall provide that, in the event of excess applications, each application shall be deemed to have been modified or withdrawn in accordance with the steps taken by the Board to scale down applications pursuant to Rule 3.

2.5 Proposals for a Savings Contract shall be limited to such building society or bank as the Board may designate or, if the Board so allows, the Department for National Savings.

2.6 Each application shall be deemed to be for an Option over the largest whole number of Shares which can be acquired at the Option Price with the Repayment under the Savings Contract entered into in connection with the Option.

3. Scaling down

3.1 If valid applications are received for a total number of Shares in excess of any maximum number of Shares determined by the Board pursuant to Rule 2.1, or any limitation under Rule 5, the Board shall scale down applications by taking, at its absolute discretion, any of the following steps until the number of Shares available equals or exceeds such total number of Shares applied for:

(a) by treating any elections for the maximum bonus as elections for the standard bonus and then, so far as necessary, by reducing the proposed Monthly Contributions pro rata to the excess over

8.106 Savings-Related Share Option Schemes

such amount as the Board shall determine for this purpose being not less than £10 and then, so far as necessary, selecting by lot; or

(b) by treating each election for a bonus as an election for no bonus and then, so far as necessary, by reducing the proposed Monthly Contributions pro rata to the excess over such amount as the Board shall determine for this purpose being not less than £10 and then, so far as necessary, selecting by lot; or

(c) by reducing the proposed Monthly Contributions pro rata to the excess over such amount as the Board shall determine for this purpose being not less than £10 and then, so far as necessary, selecting by lot.

3.2   If the number of Shares available is insufficient to enable an Option based on Monthly Contributions of £10 a month to be granted to each Eligible Employee making a valid application, the Board may, as an alternative to selecting by lot, determine in its absolute discretion that no Options shall be granted.

3.3   If the Board so determines, the provisions in Rule 3.1(a), (b) and (c) may be modified or applied in any manner as may be agreed in advance with the Inland Revenue.

3.4   If, in applying the scaling down provisions contained in this Rule 3, Options cannot be granted within the 30-day period referred to in Rule 4.2 below, the Board may extend that period by twelve days regardless of the expiry of the relevant Invitation Period.

4. Grant of Options

4.1   No Option shall be granted to any person if:

(a) at the Date of Grant that person shall have ceased to be an Eligible Employee; or

(b) that person has, or has had at any time within the twelve month period preceding the Date of Grant, a Material Interest in the issued ordinary share capital of a Close Company which is the Company or a company which has Control of the Company or is a Member of a Consortium which owns the Company.

4.2   Within 30 days of any Dealing Day by reference to which the Option Price was fixed (which date shall be within an Invitation Period) the Board may, subject to Rule 3 above, grant to each Eligible Employee who has submitted a valid application, an Option in respect of the number of Shares for which application has been deemed to be made under Rule 2.6.

4.3 The Company shall issue to each Participant an option certificate in such form (not inconsistent with the provisions of the Scheme) as the Board may from time to time prescribe. Each such certificate shall specify the Date of Grant of the Option, the number and class of Shares over which the Option is granted, the Option Price and the Bonus Date.

4.4 Except as otherwise provided in these Rules, every Option shall be personal to the Participant to whom it is granted and shall not be transferable.

4.5 No amount shall be paid in respect of the grant of an Option.

5. Number of Shares in respect of which Options may be granted

5.1 Unless the limit set out in Rule 5.2 is and has always been complied with, the number of Shares which may be allocated under the Scheme on any day shall not, when added to the aggregate of the number of Shares which have been allocated in the previous three years under the Scheme and any other Employees' Share Scheme adopted by the Company, exceed such number as represents 3 per cent of the ordinary share capital of the Company in issue immediately prior to that day, or 5 per cent thereof where that day falls within the period of four years commencing with the first day on which Options were granted under the Scheme.

5.2 The limit referred to in Rule 5.1 is that the number of Shares which may be allocated under the Scheme on any day shall not, when added to the aggregate of the number of Shares which have been allocated in the previous five years under the Scheme and any other Employees' Share Scheme adopted by the Company, exceed such number as represents 5 per cent of the ordinary share capital of the Company in issue immediately prior to that day.

5.3 The number of Shares which may be allocated under the Scheme on any day shall not, when added to the aggregate of the number of Shares which have been allocated in the previous ten years under the Scheme and any other Employees' Share Scheme adopted by the Company, exceed such number as represents 10 per cent of the ordinary share capital of the Company in issue immediately prior to that day.

5.4 In determining the above limits no account shall be taken of any Shares where the right to acquire such shares was released, lapsed or otherwise became incapable of exercise.

8.106 *Savings-Related Share Option Schemes*

5.5   References in this Rule to the 'allocation' of Shares shall mean, in the case of any share option scheme, the placing of unissued shares under option and, in relation to other types of Employees' Share Scheme, shall mean the issue and allotment of shares and references to 'allocated' shall be construed accordingly.

6.   Rights of exercise and lapse of Options

6.1

(a)   Save as provided in Rules 6.2, 6.3, 6.4 and Rule 7, an Option shall not be exercised earlier than the Bonus Date under the Savings Contract entered into in connection therewith.

(b)   Save as provided in Rule 6.2, an Option shall not be exercised later than six months after the Bonus Date under the Savings Contract entered into in connection therewith.

(c)   Save as provided in Rules 6.2 and 6.3, an Option may only be exercised by a Participant whilst he is a director or employee of a Participating Company.

(d)   An Option may not be exercised by a Participant if he has, or has had at any time within the twelve month period preceding the date of exercise, a Material Interest in the issued ordinary share capital of a Close Company which is the Company or a company which has Control of the Company or is a Member of a Consortium which owns the Company, nor may an Option be exercised by the personal representatives of a deceased Participant if the Participant had such a Material Interest at the date of his death.

6.2   An Option may be exercised by the personal representatives of a deceased Participant:

(a)   within twelve months following the date of his death if such death occurs before the Bonus Date;

(b)   within twelve months following the Bonus Date in the event of his death within six months after the Bonus Date.

6.3   An Option may be exercised by a Participant within six months following his ceasing to hold the office or employment by virtue of which he is eligible to participate in the Scheme by reason of:

(a)   injury, disability, redundancy within the meaning of the *Employment Protection (Consolidation) Act 1978*, or retirement on reaching the Specified Age or any other age at which he is bound to retire in accordance with the terms of his contract of employment; or

Savings-Related Share Option Schemes 8.106

(b) his office or employment being in a company of which the Company ceases to have Control; or

(c) the transfer of his contract of employment (which relates to a business or part of a business) to a person who is neither an Associated Company nor a company of which the Company has Control; or

(d) retirement at any age at which he is entitled to retire in accordance with the terms of his contract of employment (other than at the Specified Age or any age at which he is bound to retire), early retirement with the agreement of the employer, or pregnancy, in each case only if such cessation of office or employment is more than three years after the Date of Grant.

For the purposes of the Scheme, a woman who leaves employment due to pregnancy will be regarded as having left the employment on the earliest of:

(i) the date she notifies her employing company of her intention not to return;

(ii) the last day of the 29 week period of her confinement; and

(iii) any other date specified by the terms of her office or employment with her employing company.

6.4 An Option may be exercised by a Participant within six months following the date he reaches the Specified Age if he continues after that date to hold the office or employment by virtue of which he is eligible to participate in the Scheme.

6.5 No person shall be treated for the purposes of Rule 6.3 as ceasing to hold an office or employment by virtue of which that person is eligible to participate in the Scheme until that person ceases to hold any office or employment in the Company or any Associated Company or any company of which the Company has Control.

6.6 An Option granted to a Participant shall lapse upon the occurrence of the earliest of the following:

(a) subject to (b) below, six months after the Bonus Date under the Savings Contract entered into in connection with the Option;

(b) where the Participant dies before the Bonus Date, twelve months after the date of death, and where the Participant dies in the period of six months after the Bonus Date, twelve months after the Bonus Date;

(c) the expiry of any of the six month periods specified in Rule 6.3(a) to (d), save that if at the time any of such applicable periods expire, time is running under the twelve month periods specified in Rule 6.2, the Option shall not lapse by reason of

8.106 *Savings-Related Share Option Schemes*

this Rule 6.6 until the expiry of the relevant twelve month period in Rule 6.2;

(*d*) the expiry of any of the periods specified in Rules 7.3 to 7.5, save where an Option is released in consideration of the grant of a New Option over New Shares in the Acquiring Company (during one of the periods specified in Rules 7.3 and 7.4) pursuant to Rule 7.6;

(*e*) the Participant ceasing to hold any office or employment with a Participating Company or any Associated Company for any reason other than those specified in Rule 6.3 or as a result of his death;

(*f*) subject to Rule 7.5, the passing of an effective resolution, or the making of an order by the court, for the winding-up of the Company;

(*g*) the Participant being deprived (otherwise than on death) of the legal or beneficial ownership of the Option by operation of law, or doing anything or omitting to do anything which causes him to be so deprived or become bankrupt; and

(*h*) before an Option has become capable of being exercised, the Participant giving notice that he intends to stop paying Monthly Contributions, or being deemed under the terms of the Savings Contract to have given such notice, or making an application for Repayment of the Monthly Contributions.

7. Takeover, reconstruction and amalgamation, and liquidation

7.1 If any person obtains Control of the Company as a result of making an offer to acquire Shares which is either unconditional or is made on a condition such that if it is satisfied the person making the offer will have Control of the Company, an Option may be exercised within six months of the time when the person making the offer has obtained Control of the Company and any condition subject to which the offer is made has been satisfied or waived.

7.2 For the purpose of Rule 7.1 a person shall be deemed to have obtained Control of the Company if he and others acting in concert with him have together obtained Control of it.

7.3 If any person becomes bound or entitled to acquire Shares under *sections 428* to *430F* of the *Companies Act 1985* or Articles 421 to 423 of the Companies (Northern Ireland) Order 1986 an Option may be exercised at any time when that person remains so bound or entitled.

7.4 If, under *section 425* of the *Companies Act 1985* or Article 418 of the Companies (Northern Ireland) Order 1986, the court sanctions a compromise or arrangement proposed for the purposes

Savings-Related Share Option Schemes 8.106

of, or in connection with, a scheme for the reconstruction of the Company or its amalgamation with any other company or companies, an Option may be exercised within six months of the court sanctioning the compromise or arrangement.

7.5   If a resolution for the voluntary winding-up of the Company is passed, an Option may be exercised within two months from the date of the passing of the resolution.

7.6   If any company ('the Acquiring Company'):

(*a*)   obtains Control of the Company as a result of making:

   (i)   a general offer to acquire the whole of the issued ordinary share capital of the Company which is made on a condition such that if it is satisfied the Acquiring Company will have Control of the Company; or

   (ii) a general offer to acquire all the shares in the Company which are of the same class as the Shares which may be acquired by the exercise of Options,

in either case ignoring any Shares which are already owned by it or a member of the same group of companies; or

(*b*)   obtains Control of the Company in pursuance of a compromise or arrangement sanctioned by the court under *section 425* of the *Companies Act 1985* or Article 418 of the Companies (Northern Ireland) Order 1986; or

(*c*)   becomes entitled to give notice under *section 429* of the *Companies Act 1985* or Articles 421 to 423 of the Companies (Northern Ireland) Order 1986 that he desires to acquire Shares,

any Participant may at any time within the Appropriate Period, by agreement with the Acquiring Company, release any Option granted under the Scheme which has not lapsed ('the Old Option') in consideration of the grant to him of an option ('the New Option') which (for the purposes of *paragraph 15* of *Schedule 9* to the *Taxes Act*) is equivalent to the Old Option but relates to shares in a different company (whether the Acquiring Company itself or some other company falling within *paragraph 10(b)* or *(c)* of *Schedule 9* to the *Taxes Act*).

7.7   The New Option shall not be regarded for the purposes of Rule 7.6 as equivalent to the Old Option unless the conditions set out in *paragraph 15(3)* of *Schedule 9* to the *Taxes Act* are satisfied. Where the provisions of Rule 7.7 apply, the provisions of the Scheme shall be construed as if:

(*a*)   the New Option were granted under the Scheme at the same time as the Old Option;

8.106 *Savings-Related Share Option Schemes*

(*b*) except for the purposes of the definitions of 'Participating Company' and 'Subsidiary' in Rule 1, the reference to [   ] plc/ Limited in the definition of 'the Company' in Rule 1 were a reference to the different company mentioned in Rule 7.6;

(*c*) Rules 12.1 and 12.2 were omitted.

8. Manner of exercise

8.1 An Option may only be exercised during the periods specified in Rules 6 and 7, and only with monies not exceeding the amount of the Repayment under the Savings Contract entered into in connection therewith as at the date of such exercise. For this purpose, no account shall be taken of such part (if any) of the Repayment of any Monthly Contribution, the due date for the payment of which under the Savings Contract arises after the date of the Repayment.

8.2 Exercise shall be by the delivery to the Secretary of the Company or other duly appointed agent, of an option certificate covering the Shares over which the Option is then to be exercised, with the notice of exercise in the prescribed form duly completed and signed by the Participant (or by his duly authorised agent) together with any remittance for the Exercise Price payable, or authority to the Company to withdraw and apply monies equal to the Exercise Price from the Savings Contract, to acquire the Shares over which the Option is to be exercised. The effective date of exercise shall be the date of delivery of the notice of exercise.

9. Issue or transfer of Shares

9.1 Shares to be issued pursuant to the exercise of an Option shall be allotted within 28 days following the effective date of exercise of the Option.

9.2 The Board shall procure the transfer of Shares to be transferred pursuant to the exercise of an Option within 28 days following the effective date of exercise of the Option.

9.3 Shares to be issued pursuant to the Scheme will rank *pari passu* in all respects with the Shares then in issue, except that they will not rank for any rights attaching to Shares by reference to a record date preceding the date of exercise.

9.4 Shares to be transferred pursuant to the Scheme will be transferred free of all liens, charges and encumbrances and together with all rights attaching thereto, except they will not rank for any rights attaching to Shares by reference to a record date preceding the date of exercise.

Savings-Related Share Option Schemes 8.106

9.5 If, and so long as, the Shares are listed on the London Stock Exchange, the Company shall apply for a listing for any Shares issued pursuant to the Scheme as soon as practicable after the allotment thereof.

10. Adjustments

10.1 The number of Shares over which an Option is granted and the Option Price thereof shall be adjusted in such manner as the Board shall determine following any capitalisation issue, rights issue, subdivision, consolidation or reduction of share capital of the Company or any other variation of share capital to the intent that (as nearly as may be without involving fractions of a Share or an Option Price calculated to more than two places of decimals) the Exercise Price payable in respect of an Option shall remain unchanged, provided that no adjustment made pursuant to this Rule 10.1 shall be made without the prior approval of the Inland Revenue (so long as the Scheme is approved by the Inland Revenue).

10.2 Subject to Rule 10.3, an adjustment may be made under Rule 10.1 which would have the effect of reducing the Option Price of unissued Shares to less than the nominal value of a Share, but only if, and to the extent that, the Board shall be authorised to capitalise from the reserves of the Company a sum equal to the amount by which the nominal value of the Shares in respect of which the Option is exercisable exceeds the adjusted Exercise Price, and so that on exercise of any Option in respect of which the Option Price has been reduced, the Board shall capitalise and apply such sum (if any) as is necessary to pay up the amount by which the aggregate nominal value of the Shares in respect of which the Option is exercised exceeds the Exercise Price for such Shares.

10.3 Where an Option subsists over both issued and unissued Shares, an adjustment permitted by Rules 10.2 may only be made if the reduction of the Option Price of both the issued and unissued Shares can be made to the same extent.

10.4 The Board may take such steps as it may consider necessary to notify Participants of any adjustment made under this Rule 10 and to call in, cancel, endorse, issue or reissue any Option certificate consequent upon such adjustment.

11. Administration

11.1 Any notice or other communication made under, or in connection with, the Scheme may be given by personal delivery or by sending the same by post, in the case of a company to its registered office and in the case of an individual to his last known address, or, where he is

8.106 *Savings-Related Share Option Schemes*

a director or employee of the Company or an Associated Company, either to his last known address or to the address of the place of business at which he performs the whole or substantially the whole of the duties of his office or employment, and where a notice or other communication is given by first-class post, it shall be deemed to have been received 48 hours after it was put into the post properly addressed and stamped.

11.2 The Company may distribute to Participants copies of any notice or document normally sent by the Company to the holders of Shares.

11.3 If any option certificate shall be worn out, defaced or lost, it may be replaced on such evidence being provided as the Board may require.

11.4 The Company shall at all times keep available for allotment unissued Shares at least sufficient to satisfy all Options under which Shares may be subscribed or procure that sufficient Shares are available for transfer to satisfy all Options under which Shares may be acquired.

11.5 The decision of the Board in any dispute relating to an Option or the due exercise thereof or any other matter in respect of the Scheme shall be final and conclusive, subject to the certification of the Auditors having been obtained when so required by Rule 10.1.

11.6 In any matter in which they are required to act hereunder, the Auditors shall be deemed to be acting as experts and not as arbitrators.

11.7 The costs of introducing and administering the Scheme shall be borne by the Company.

12. Alterations

12.1 Subject to Rule 12.2, the Board may at any time alter or add to all or any of the provisions of the Scheme in any respect, provided that if an alteration or addition is made at a time when the Scheme is approved by the Inland Revenue under *Schedule 9* to the *Taxes Act* it shall not have effect until it has been approved by the Inland Revenue.

12.2 Subject to Rule 12.3, no alteration or addition to the advantage of present or future Participants or employees shall be made under Rule 12.1 to such of the provisions of the Scheme as relate to any of the following:

(*a*)   the persons to whom Options may be granted;

Savings-Related Share Option Schemes 8.106

(b) limitations on the grant of Options;

(c) the determination of the price at which Shares may be acquired by the exercise of Options;

(d) the Maximum Contribution payable;

(e) the adjustment of Options;

(f) the restrictions on the exercise of Options;

(g) the rights to be attached upon their issue to Shares issued upon the exercise of Options;

(h) the rights of Participants on the winding-up of the Company;

(i) the transferability of Options; and

(j) the terms of Rule 12;

without the prior approval by ordinary resolution of the members of the Company in general meeting.

12.3 Rule 12.2 shall not apply to any alteration or addition which:

(a) is necessary or desirable in order to obtain or maintain Inland Revenue approval of the Scheme under *Schedule 9* to the *Taxes Act* or any other enactment, to comply with or take account of the provisions of any proposed or existing legislation or law, to take advantage of any changes to existing legislation or law, to take account of any of the events mentioned in Rule 7, or to obtain or maintain favourable taxation treatment of the Company, any Subsidiary or any Participant; and

(b) does not affect the basic principles of the Scheme, the definition of 'Option Price', the limits on individual participation, or the limits in Rule 5.

12.4 No alteration or addition shall be made under Rule 12.1 which would abrogate or adversely affect the subsisting rights of a Participant, unless it is made:

(i) with the consent in writing of such number of Participants as hold Options to acquire not less than 75 per cent of the Shares which would be issued or transferred if all Options granted and subsisting were exercised in respect of the maximum number of Shares the subject thereof; or

(ii) by a resolution at a meeting of Participants passed by not less than 75 per cent of the Participants who attend and vote either in person or by proxy,

and for the purposes of this Rule 12.4 the Participants shall be treated as the holders of a separate class of share capital and the provisions of the Articles of Association of the Company relating to class meetings shall apply *mutatis mutandis*.

8.106 *Savings-Related Share Option Schemes*

12.5 As soon as reasonably practicable after making any alteration or addition under Rule 12.1, the Board shall give written notice thereof to any Participant affected thereby.

13. General

13.1 The Scheme shall terminate upon the tenth anniversary of its adoption by the Company in general meeting or at any earlier time by the passing of a resolution by the Board or an ordinary resolution of the Company in general meeting. Termination of the Scheme shall be without prejudice to the subsisting rights of Participants.

13.2 The Company and any Subsidiary of the Company may provide money to the trustees of any trust or any other person to enable them or him to acquire Shares to be held for the purposes of the Scheme, or enter into any guarantee or indemnity for these purposes, to the extent permitted by *section 153* of the *Companies Act 1985*, provided that any trust deed to be made for this purpose shall, at a time when the Scheme is approved by the Inland Revenue under *Schedule 9* to the *Taxes Act*, have previously been submitted to the Inland Revenue.

13.3 The rights and obligations of any individual under the terms of his office or employment with the Company, a Participating Company, a Subsidiary of the Company, or an Associated Company shall not be affected by his participation in the Scheme or any right which he may have to participate therein, and an individual who participates therein shall waive all and any rights to compensation or damages in consequence of the termination of his office or employment with any such company for any reason whatsoever insofar as those rights arise, or may arise, from his ceasing to have rights under or be entitled to exercise any Option under the Scheme as a result of such termination, or from the loss or diminution in value of such rights or entitlements.

13.4 These Rules shall be governed by and construed in accordance with English law.

Chapter 9

Profit Sharing Trust

Introduction

9.1 The approved profit sharing scheme legislation was introduced to provide tax relief on free appropriations of shares to employees made after 5 April 1979. The underlying principle is that the full tax relief is only available if the shares are left with trustees until the 'release date' at the end of five years. It is in any event a condition of an appropriation that the employee undertakes to leave his shares with the trustees for a minimum period of up to two years.

9.2 The possible bases of allocation of shares amongst employees are examined in detail at 9.58 to 9.59 and in Chapter 10. This chapter principally examines the conditions which must be satisfied to obtain approval of any profit sharing scheme.

Appointment, retirement and removal of trustees

Establishment under trust

9.3 *TA 1988, 9 Sch 30* provides that any profit sharing scheme must provide for the establishment of a body of persons resident in the United Kingdom to acquire and appropriate scheme shares. In addition, there must be a trust which is constituted under the law of a part of the United Kingdom.

Nature of appointment

9.4 The powers and duties of trustees are normally ascertained by reference to the terms of the trust deed and the general law. *TA 1988, 9 Sch 30–34* specify various duties which must be incorporated in any trust instrument as a condition of approval of any scheme under *TA 1988* (see 9.101 to 9.107).

9.5 As far as trusts expressed to be made under English law are concerned, *Part II* of the *Trustee Act 1925* sets out a number of general powers held by trustees including several which will normally apply to the trustees of a profit sharing trust, for instance, the power to

9.6 Profit Sharing Trust

deposit documents for safe custody (*TA 1925, s 21*) and the power to employ agents (*TA 1925, s 23*) which would normally be sufficient to cover the appointment of scheme registrars. In any event, trustees will normally be entitled to the benefit of the implied indemnity of trustees under *TA 1925, s 30*.

Persons who can be appointed trustees

9.6 TA 1988, 9 Sch 30 refers to 'a body of persons' who may be appointed trustees. This would seem to imply that at least two or more persons must be appointed to act but, in practice, the Inland Revenue will approve a scheme with a single company as trustee, but not a sole individual. However, any trustee must be resident in the United Kingdom and, where there is more than one trustee, the Inland Revenue will insist upon at least one of them being resident in the United Kingdom.

9.7 If a participant may be appointed trustee, the trust deed should provide that any such trustee will not be liable to account to other participants for any benefits derived from participation in the scheme.

9.8 In the case of listed companies, ABI Guidelines do not make any specific recommendations about the persons who may be appointed trustee. However, the ABI takes the view that where directors and employees are appointed trustee, at least one of the trustees should be a non-executive director or a person independent of the company. Given the restrictions on the powers of the trustees under most profit sharing trusts, the identity of the trustees is less important than under other trusts.

9.9 In the writer's opinion, it is normally best to appoint a subsidiary to act as trustee of a profit sharing trust. Any such subsidiary should have the power under its Memorandum of Association to act as a corporate trustee. The main advantage of appointing a corporate trustee is continuity as deeds of appointment will be unnecessary upon successive changes of trustee.

9.10 Nevertheless, a number of companies prefer to appoint either non-executive directors, or appoint the scheme registrars as trustees. Most large registrars will take on the trusteeship of a profit sharing scheme.

Protection of trustees

9.11 Although the trustees of a profit sharing scheme are entitled to the benefit of the statutory indemnity under the *Trustee Act 1925, s 30*, many trust deeds nevertheless contain an express indemnity of the trustees including exoneration of any liability on the part of the trustees for the negligence or fraud of any agent unless the trustee was at fault in appointing the particular agent in the first place.

9.12 The Inland Revenue's Guide on Profit Sharing Schemes (IR 96) contains an express power to this effect. Trustees have a general duty to invest trust monies even where such funds are to be held short-term. In order to obviate the need for the trustees to invest monies short-term the trust deed should specifically authorise the trustees to hold uninvested trust monies.

Retirement and removal

9.13 Most profit sharing trust deeds make detailed provision for the retirement and removal of trustees. The Model Scheme provides for existing trustees to resign at any time by giving written notice and for the company to remove an existing trustee without giving any reason and appoint a replacement by deed.

Contributions to the trustees

Voluntary payments

9.14 All contributions to the trustees should be made as voluntary payments. Arguably, payments made under a legal obligation to pay a proportion of profits each year would be annual payments and chargeable to income tax in the hands of the trustee. The Model Scheme does not suggest there is any obligation on the company to make contributions.

Financial assistance in the purchase of shares

9.15 *CA 1985, s 151* provides that it is unlawful for a company to give financial assistance for the purposes of acquiring shares in itself or its holding company. An exemption is provided in the cases of financial assistance given 'in good faith, in the interests of the company,... for the purposes of an employees' share scheme' (*CA 1985, s 153(4)(b)*).

9.16 Whilst the directors of a private company need only consider the provisions of *CA 1985, s 153(4)(b)*, the directors of a public company must also consider the provisions of *CA 1985, s 154*. This provides that a public company must either have net assets which are not reduced by the proposed financial assistance, or the proposed financial assistance must be provided out of distributable reserves. Where it is proposed to operate a profit sharing scheme by subscribing for new shares, it is unlikely there will be any reduction in the net

9.17 Profit Sharing Trust

assets of the company since the monies allocated to the profit sharing trustees will be returned to the company in the form of a subscription for shares. However, if the shares are to be purchased through the market, the monies allocated to the profit sharing scheme trustees will be used to pay third parties and will therefore represent a reduction in the assets of the company. In this case, the company will need to ensure it has distributable reserves which will cover any proposed allocation of monies. Unless the company has sufficient distributable reserves, it will not be able to operate the scheme.

Common distributable pool and bases of allocation

9.17 *TA 1988, 9 Sch 36* provides that eligible employees must participate in the scheme on 'similar terms'. The consequence of this is that eligible employees of different participating companies must participate in the scheme on an identical basis of allocation in respect of a single distributable pool. Although the relative performance of different subsidiaries may be reflected in the basis of allocation, it is not possible to determine separate distributable pools based on the relative profits of the subsidiary concerned. Similarly, it is not possible to operate different bases of allocation between different subsidiaries. Only by establishing separate profit sharing trusts for each subsidiary is it possible to properly reflect the relative performance of any subsidiary in the size of its profit sharing allocations (see Chapter 11 below).

Tax relief for contributions

9.18 Under *TA 1988, s 85*, a statutory right to tax relief is given to companies which make payments to the trustees of an approved profit sharing scheme if either of the following conditions apply:

(*a*) the payment is applied by the trustees in the acquisition of shares for appropriation to participants within nine months of the end of the accounting period in which it is charged as an expense of the company incurring the expenditure, or such longer period as the Board of Inland Revenue may allow; or

(*b*) the payment is required to meet the reasonable expenses of the trustees in running the scheme.

9.19 Strictly speaking, the tax relief is available where at the time the shares are acquired the intention is to appropriate them under the scheme. If it turns out that no appropriation is made, the tax relief still appears to be due. If any shares are sold, the proceeds of sale should be held under the trusts of the scheme and used to buy shares on a subsequent occasion if the original tax relief is not lost. The tax relief is given, in the case of a trading company, as a deduction in computation of profits or gains for the purposes of Schedule D and, in the case of an investment company, a management expense.

9.20 The tax relief is only available in proportion to the company's own employees. It is essential, therefore, that where the company which established the scheme makes a payment on behalf of employees of other participating companies, that it allocates the cost amongst each participating company to reflect the participation of their respective employees. Only the cost of the trustees' expenses can ultimately be borne by the company establishing the scheme without being shared by the participating companies. There is no tax relief where the contribution is applied in acquiring shares before the scheme has been approved by the Inland Revenue (*TA 1988, s 84A*).

Subscription for shares

9.21 The trust deed should state whether the trustees subscribe for new shares or may purchase existing shares or both.

Group schemes

9.22 *TA 1988, 9 Sch 1(3)* provides that where a company which has established a scheme has control of another company or companies, the scheme may be expressed to extend to all or any of these companies and is known as 'a group scheme'. A company which establishes a scheme cannot extend the scheme to holding companies, although the shares of a holding company may be used under its scheme. Strictly speaking, only companies under the 'control' (within the meaning of *TA 1988, s 840*) of the company which established the scheme may participate in it. However, in certain circumstances, jointly-owned companies are admitted to participate in an approved scheme (see Chapter 4, *Appendix I*).

Anti-abuse

9.23 *TA 1988, 9 Sch 3* provides that the Board of Inland Revenue must be satisfied when it approves a profit sharing scheme that, if the company which establishes the scheme is a member of a group of companies, that the scheme will not have the effect of conferring benefits wholly or mainly on directors or on higher-paid employees in group companies. If after approval of the scheme, the Inland Revenue cease to be satisfied that this condition continues to be fulfilled then it may withdraw approval of the scheme with effect from that time or some later time (*TA 1988, 9 Sch 3(2)(d)*).

Apart from this provision which is intended to avoid abuse, a company

9.24 *Profit Sharing Trust*

which establishes a scheme has a discretion as to the companies under its control which may be admitted as participating companies.

Admission of other participating companies

9.24 The Model Scheme provides for other participating companies to be admitted to the scheme by execution of a deed of adherence by which it agrees to be bound in all respects by the trust deed and rules of the scheme for so long as it remains under the control of the company which established the scheme. In practice, the Inland Revenue do not require formal deeds of adherence by participating companies and schemes may provide for the adherence of subsidiaries by board resolution. A parent company can direct any of its subsidiaries that formal deeds of adherence are unnecessary. Any deed of adherence which is executed is not liable to any stamp duty.

9.25 Where a new participating company is admitted to the scheme, the company which established the scheme should advise the Inland Revenue although many earlier letters of approval of schemes advise that only the corporation tax district need be advised. The Inland Revenue will notify the appropriate tax district.

As far as the procedures for the admission of a jointly-owned company are concerned, see Chapter 4, *Appendix I*.

Cessation of participation

9.26 The Model Scheme provides that any company which ceases to be under the control of the company which established the scheme shall cease to be a participating company. The Model Scheme also provides that the directors may resolve that a company, even if it remains under the control of the company which established the scheme, shall cease to be a participating company. The Inland Revenue will be concerned to ensure that where the directors remove any company from the scheme that this will not leave only higher paid employees in the scheme contrary to *TA 1988, 9 Sch 2(3)*. As in the case of the admission of a new participating company, the Inland Revenue which deals with the corporation tax of the company establishing the scheme should be notified of any cessation of participation.

Implications for scheme participants of a company ceasing to be a participating company

9.27 Where a participant ceases to be an employee in a participating company by reason of injury, disability or redundancy, the period of retention will end and, on any disposal of the participant's shares, tax will be restricted to 50 per cent of the initial market value of the shares. The tax relief only applies where the participant ceases to be an employee of a participating company for any of the prescribed reasons and there is no tax relief where the cessation of employment arises *after* the company ceases to be a participating company.

Multi-trust arrangements for groups

9.28 Where companies under the control of the company which established any scheme are admitted to that scheme, its employees must be eligible to participate 'on similar terms' to all other employees (*TA 1988, 9 Sch 36(1)*). The practical effect of this is that under a group scheme there must be a single distributable pool of profits and a common basis of allocation of shares amongst employees. There is very little scope for operating the scheme so that employees of different participating companies receive allocations based on the profitability of their respective employing companies, or indeed the profits are allocated amongst the employees of each participating company on a different basis. The Inland Revenue will normally accept a basis of allocation which 'weights' an employee's entitlement according to the profitability of his employing company, but will not go so far as to allow separate distributable pools for each subsidiary. This inevitably means that in a group scheme, the more profitable companies will inevitably subsidise the profit allocations of the less profitable companies in the group. The only way to achieve the flexibility of separate distributable pools and separate bases of allocation, is to set up separate trusts for each company or sub-group. Under a multi-trust arrangement, a parent company establishes a scheme which contains the overall limits on the amount of profits and number of shares which may be allocated under the various group schemes. A series of 'satellite' schemes are established by each subsidiary, with the parent company joining in each trust deed to exercise control over the operation of each individual scheme. Although separate distributable pools and bases of allocation will be operated in accordance with the wishes of the subsidiary, the parent company will remain in overall control.

9.29 The 'satellite' schemes in a multi-trust arrangement would have identical provisions so that they operate on a parallel basis in relation to the payment of dividends, scrip dividends, rights issues, capitalisation issues and voting rights. In addition, where any company or sub-group, operating its own scheme, is transferred or sold to a third party, the continuing costs of the scheme will be borne by the company operating the scheme, rather than the parent company.

9.30 Such arrangements, therefore, offer considerable flexibility compared to single 'group-wide' schemes without, in practice, substantially adding to the costs or complexity of these arrangements.

9.31 *Profit Sharing Trust*

Subscription for shares

9.31 *TA 1988, 9 Sch 30* refers to the establishment of trustees who, 'out of moneys paid to them' by the company which established the scheme, are required to acquire shares for appropriation. For many years, it was understood that a monetary consideration needed to be paid for any shares acquired by profit sharing trustees. There is nothing in the legislation which requires shares to be purchased at any particular price, and so even a nominal consideration was considered sufficient. This may only have been, as in most privatisations, a total of £1. However, there is no particular significance in the reference to 'moneys paid' in *paragraph 30* and in practice the Inland Revenue do not object to the receipt of gifts of shares by the trustees.

ABI Guidelines on subscriptions for shares

9.32 The 1987 ABI Guidelines set out the limits on the number of shares which may be subscribed and state that any subscription for shares must be made at the middle market price for shares of the same class on the dealing day prior to the appropriation day.

9.33 In addition, to the normal ABI Scheme limits of 10 per cent in any ten-year period and 3 per cent in any three-year period under all schemes, the maximum number of shares which may be newly issued under a profit sharing scheme is 1 per cent of the ordinary share capital in each calendar year (see Chapter 4).

Listed companies

9.34 The trustees of any company which is listed, or whose shares are traded in a public market, will normally purchase the shares required for any profit sharing scheme through the market subject to payment of any broker's commission and stamp duty.

9.35 The directors of listed companies and the trustees of any profit sharing scheme set up by a listed company need to consider the Model Code for Securities Transactions by Directors of Listed Companies published by The London Stock Exchange. The directors may not deal in the shares of a listed company at any time during the period of two months immediately preceding the preliminary announcement of the company's annual results or half-yearly results or at any other time when they are in possession of unpublished price sensitive information. Similarly, the trustees of any profit sharing scheme should avoid any dealing in the shares of the company at such times.

9.36 Under the *Companies Act 1985, s 324(2)* a director is under an obligation to notify the company in writing of the occurrence, while he is a director, of any event as a result of which he, amongst other things, becomes interested in shares of the company. The acquisition of shares by the trustees of a profit sharing scheme in which the director is a participant is, strictly speaking, a notifiable event under this section and the company should enter the information in its register of directors interests maintained pursuant to *CA 1985, s 325*.

9.37 Any matter relating to a director's interests in shares which is notifiable under *CA 1985, ss 324* or *325* must be disclosed to the Company Announcement Office of The London Stock Exchange. Such notification must include the nature of the transaction, the nature and extent of the director's interest in it in addition to details of the date, price and number of shares involved in the transaction.

9.38 In short, any dealings by the trustees of a profit sharing scheme in unappropriated shares will be notifiable to The London Stock Exchange as a dealing by the directors although any such notification should make it clear that the directors were not dealing personally.

In principle, the trustees would appear to have a notifiable interest under the provisions of *CA 1985, s 198* if their holdings of unappropriated shares exceeds 3 per cent of the share capital. Under *CA 1985, s 198* any increase or decrease in the holding is notifiable.

CA 1985, ss 80, 89

9.39 Since a profit sharing scheme is an employees' share scheme for the purposes of *CA, s 743*, any subscription for shares will not be treated as relevant securities 'requiring specific authority for the directors to allot' under *CA 1985, s 80* or 'equity securities' requiring specific disapplication of the pre-emption provisions under *CA 1985, s 95*.

Private companies

9.40 Any acquisition of shares by the trustees of a profit sharing scheme will require consideration of the provisions of the articles of association. Most private companies impose pre-emption rights in favour of other shareholders in respect of the shares of any proposing transferor. In order to avoid the need for all other shareholders to waive their pre-emption rights both in respect of transfers to the trustees and in respect of any transfer of scheme shares into the name of a participant, a private company should consider the incorporation

9.41 *Profit Sharing Trust*

of provisions in the pre-emption rights giving an overriding right of transfer in respect of scheme shares.

Tax reliefs on unappropriated shares

9.41 A profit sharing trust is in principle subject to tax in the same way as any other taxpayer. However, there are two special tax reliefs available to the trustees of a profit sharing scheme for up to 18 months after the acquisition of any shares:

(i) relief from income tax, including the additional rate, on all dividends received on those shares (*TA 1988, s 186(11)*);

(ii) relief from capital gains tax in respect of any gains arising on the disposal of the shares.

The relief from income tax under *TA 1988, s 186(11)* will only be given by way of discharge or repayment once the conditions have been established. In the meantime, therefore, the Inland Revenue will normally collect the additional rate of tax.

Appropriations of shares

9.42 An appropriation of shares involves a resolution of the trustees that they hold specified shares on behalf of participants under the scheme. It is not necessary for the trustees to minute full details of the appropriation as this will normally be done on their behalf by the scheme registrar on making up the register.

9.43 At the time the trustees resolve to make any appropriation under the scheme, they must already have acquired the legal title to the relevant number of shares. The Inland Revenue take the view that the legislation only refers to the appropriation of 'shares' and therefore it is not sufficient if the trustees hold only a beneficial interest in the shares or provisional letters of allotment.

Timing

9.44 The legislation does not specify the times when an appropriation may be made although the Model Scheme suggests that this would normally be following an announcement of results. The 1987 ABI Guidelines which apply to listed companies specify that only one appropriation should be made each year and that this should be made following the announcement of final results for the trading period in respect of which the appropriation is made. In practice, the ABI accepts the making of appropriations at any time during the period of 90 days from the announcement of final results. The ABI does not accept appropriations made after the announcement of interim results since the directors cannot know the year's profits for the purposes of the 5 per cent of profits test (see 9.72).

Eligibility for an appropriation

9.45 *TA 1988, 9 Sch 36(1)* provides that certain employees must be eligible to participate in any appropriation under the scheme. This is any person who:

(*a*) is a full-time employee or a full-time director of the company (or any participating company); and

(*b*) at the time of appropriation has been such a director or employee at all times during a qualifying period of up to five years; and

(*c*) is chargeable to tax in respect of his office or employment under Case I of Schedule E.

In addition, the legislation allows any other director or employee to be allowed to participate including non-executive directors and part-time employees, directors and employees who have worked for the company for less than five years, overseas directors and employees whose emoluments are chargeable to tax under Case II or III of Schedule E.

9.46 *TA 1988, 9 Sch 35(1)* allows former directors and employees who left within the preceding 18 months to participate in the scheme. This is intended to allow schemes to operate by making appropriations in respect of the last accounting period to all persons who were employees at any stage during that year.

9.47 A full-time director or employee is a person who is required to work 25 hours a week, excluding meal breaks.

9.48 In drafting the qualifying service criteria in a profit sharing scheme it is necessary to consider whether such service must be with the same participating company throughout the period, or whether only 'continuous service' is necessary. In the writer's opinion, it is fairer to base the period of qualifying service on 'continuous service'.

9.49 In early schemes, part-time employees were often excluded. The ABI originally considered that profit sharing schemes should only be made available to employees who worked at least 14 hours a week but is now prepared to accept employees working a lesser number of hours each week and indeed will normally accept the absence of any qualifying service criteria.

9.50 Most schemes set out the normal eligibility criteria but allow the directors a discretion to extend the scheme to other employees either individually or as a category of employees. Since any alteration

9.51 *Profit Sharing Trust*

of the eligibility criteria in the scheme rules will normally be a matter for prior shareholders' approval, it is important that the rules are drafted as flexibly as possible.

9.51 Where a scheme determines eligibility by reference to a qualifying period of service on a particular date, all employees who satisfy the test must be included even if they have subsequently ceased employment. This is different from savings-related share option schemes where employees must be excluded if they leave employment before the date of grant.

9.52 *TA 1988, 9 Sch 35(2)* contains a prohibition on employees participating in a scheme if an appropriation has already been made to him in the same tax year under another approved profit sharing scheme established by:

(*a*) the company which established the scheme; or

(*b*) a company which controls or is controlled by the company which established the scheme, or which is controlled by a company which also controls the company which established the scheme;

(*c*) a company which is a member of a consortium owning the company which established the scheme, or which is owned in part by the company which established the scheme as a member of a consortium.

This contrasts with savings-related share option schemes where a similar exclusion of eligibility in the original legislation was subsequently removed.

Material interests in close companies

9.53 *TA 1988, 9 Sch 8* excludes an appropriation of shares under a profit sharing scheme to a person who has, or has had within the preceding twelve months, a material interest in a close company which is either the company whose shares are to be appropriated, or which has control of the company whose shares are to be appropriated or is a member of a consortium which owns that company. A 'close company' is defined in *TA 1988, s 414*, but for these purposes, ignoring *TA 1988, ss 414(1)(a), 415*.

9.54 'Material Interest' is defined as 25 per cent of the ordinary share capital for the purposes of the profit sharing legislation (*TA 1988, s 187(3)*).

Statutory undertakings

9.55 Under *TA 1988, 9 Sch 2(2)* a profit sharing scheme must provide for every eligible employee in a profit sharing scheme to enter into an agreement with the company which established the scheme under which as consideration for participating in the scheme he undertakes:

(*a*) to permit his shares to remain in the hands of the trustees throughout the *period of retention*;

(*b*) not to assign, charge or otherwise dispose of his beneficial interest in his shares during that period; and

(*c*) if he directs the trustees to transfer the ownership of his shares to him at any time before *the release date*, to pay to the trustees before the transfer takes place a sum equal to income tax at the basic rate on the appropriate percentage of the locked-in-value of the shares at the time of the direction; and

(*d*) not to direct the trustees to dispose of his shares at any time before the release date in any other way except by sale for the best consideration in money that can reasonably be obtained at the time of the sale or, in the case of redeemable shares in a workers co-operative, by redemption.

9.56 There are certain exceptions to these undertakings.

(i) A participant is not prevented by any of the above obligations from directing the trustees to accept certain offers relating to the takeover or reconstruction of the company in respect of scheme shares held for him by the trustees. These exceptions are set out in *TA 1988, 10 Sch 1(1)(a)–(c)*.

(ii) A participant may always sell the beneficial interest in his shares to the trustees after the period of retention for a consideration equal to the best consideration in money that can reasonably be obtained at the time of the sale.

(iii) Personal representatives are not obliged to pay any sum on account of income tax where they direct the trustees to sell (*TA 1988, 10 Sch 1(2)*).

Unauthorised shares

9.57 Shares will from time to time be appropriated to a person who is ineligible to participate in the scheme or are in excess of the limit available to any person. Such shares are known as 'unauthorised' and 'excess' shares respectively. Unauthorised shares are deemed as disposed of at the release date or, if earlier, immediately before the date of the participant's death (*TA 1988, 10 Sch 6(5)*). On any deemed disposal, or on any actual disposal, unauthorised shares are treated as having a locked-in-value equal to their market value at that date. In short, income tax will be payable on the whole of the value of the shares on that date.

9.58 Profit Sharing Trust

Bases of allocation

9.58 The legislation does not lay down particular bases of allocation which must be adopted in allocating shares amongst employees although any allocations must be 'on similar terms' (*TA 1988, 9 Sch 36(1)*). It is stated in *TA 1988, 9 Sch 36(2)* that the fact that the number of shares to be appropriated to participants in a scheme varies by reference to the levels of their remuneration, the length of their service or similar factors shall not be regarded as meaning that participation will not be on similar terms.

9.59 The most common bases of allocation found in profit sharing schemes are as follows:

(*a*) an equal number or value of shares e.g. £200 worth of shares each; or

(*b*) such proportion of the total number of shares which are available as may be equal to the proportion which the participants current annual earnings bears to the aggregate current annual earnings of all participants; or

(*c*) such proportion of the total number of shares available as may be equal to the proportion which the participant's length of service bears to the aggregate length of service of all participants; or

(*d*) any or all of the above but adjusted by the proportion which the profits of the subsidiary for which the employee works bears to the aggregate profits of all members of the group.

In addition, schemes will normally allow for allocations of shares based on the matching offer principle. In any matching offer, shares are allocated to a participant on the basis of the number of shares he purchases and leaves with the trustees (see 10.29).

9.60 Most schemes give directors a discretion to select any one of the above bases of allocation so that they can vary the basis of allocation from time to time. In addition, many schemes provide for the directors to agree with the Inland Revenue any other objective basis of allocation. Such a provision in the scheme rules will usually avoid the need for a listed company to seek the prior approval of shareholders to any proposed change of the basis of allocation.

9.61 For further information on free offers and matching offers under profit sharing schemes, see Chapter 10 below.

Value of shares for tax purposes

9.62 The initial market value of shares appropriated under a profit sharing scheme needs to be identified for two reasons.

9.63 First, it is the value on which any income tax liability will arise if the shares are disposed of or transferred into the name of the participant before the release date (see 9.77). Secondly, the limit on individual participation in a scheme each tax year is determined by reference to the initial market value of the shares (see 9.73 below).

9.64 The 'initial market value' of a participant's shares means the market value of those shares at the date of appropriation, or on any earlier date or dates as may be agreed in writing between the Inland Revenue and the trustees (*TA 1988, 9 Sch 30(4)*).

Listed companies

9.65 The schemes of listed companies usually provide for the initial market value to be based on one of the following:

(*a*) the middle market price of the shares on the date of appropriation; or

(*b*) the average middle market price of the shares over the period of three or five days preceding the date of appropriation; or

(*c*) the cost of acquiring the shares whether by subscription or purchase.

9.66 Strictly speaking, the market value of quoted shares has the same meaning as in *TCGA 1992, s 272 viz* the 'quarter-up' price. However, the 1987 ABI Guidelines recommend that where shares are subscribed for under a profit sharing scheme that such subscription should be at the middle market price and the Inland Revenue's Model Scheme, surprisingly, provides for the initial market value of quoted shares to be based on the middle market price. In practice, therefore, the middle market price is usually adopted.

9.67 It is not clear why any company should prefer the market value of shares for the purpose of a profit sharing scheme to be calculated on the basis of the average price over several days rather than just one day's middle market price. Obviously, the use of several days' prices may avoid a high or low initial market value but it is not immediately obvious why this should be of concern to any company when giving away shares. Whilst under any share option scheme, the lower the value of the shares taken into account for tax purposes the better for the employee, the opposite applies in the case of profit sharing schemes where the higher the value the less the potential liability to income tax on an early disposal of the shares and the lower any potential capital gains tax liability.

9.68 However, some schemes involve the allocation of a specified amount of cash or profits each year, for instance, 'three per cent of pay' or 'three per cent of profits'. In such cases the company may

9.69 *Profit Sharing Trust*

wish to see some correspondence between the amounts spent by the trustees on acquiring the shares and the initial market value of the shares for tax purposes.

9.69 This can be largely achieved by basing the initial market value of the shares on the net cost to the trustees of purchasing the shares. The initial market value of each share will be the average cost of subscription or purchase. The only restriction the Inland Revenue place on this approach is that where the cost to the trustees of acquiring shares is to be taken into account, only purchases and subscriptions within specified periods prior to the date of appropriation should be taken into account. Only purchases through the market within the preceding 60 days and subscriptions within the preceding 30 days may be taken into account; the price of any acquisition at an earlier time must be ignored.

9.70 The Inland Revenue may be prepared to agree the market value of the shares on the basis of the price on some earlier day or days. In practice, the Inland Revenue would not normally be prepared to agree the value on the basis of any day earlier than 30 days prior to the date of appropriation.

Private companies

9.71 In a scheme established by a private company, the initial market value is based on the market value of the shares as agreed with the Shares Valuation Division.

Limit on the value of scheme allocations

9.72 There are no limits under the legislation on the amount of profits which may be allocated to a profit sharing scheme each year or the overall value of shares which may be allocated. However, the 1987 ABI Guidelines state that a maximum of 5 per cent of profits before tax and extraordinary items may be allocated in profits each year.

Limit on the value of individual appropriations

9.73 The scheme must provide that the aggregate initial market values of all the shares appropriated to any one participant in a year of assessment will not exceed 'the relevant amount' (*TA 1988, 9 Sch 30(3)*). 'The relevant amount' for 1994/1995 is defined as the higher of:

(*a*) 10 per cent of the participant's 'salary' — subject to an overall cap of £8,000; or *(b)* £3,000,

in the current or preceding tax years, whichever the greater. 'Salary' means such of his emoluments from his employment with participating companies as are liable to be paid under deduction of tax through PAYE *in* the relevant tax year.

9.74 Whilst the individual participation limit under executive share option schemes includes bonuses paid 'for' a tax year, under the profit sharing scheme bonuses are only taken into account to the extent they are liable to be paid 'in' the particular tax year. The value of any benefits in kind are disregarded and any sums paid under 'net pay' arrangements under the PAYE Regulations (for instance, employee's contributions to a pension scheme) would be deducted.

9.75 The alternative limit of £3,000 in a tax year applies regardless of the amount of earnings received from participating companies through PAYE. The limit will therefore be of relevance to the following:

(*a*) non-UK resident employees who do not have earnings subject to PAYE;

(*b*) new employees who only have a few months earnings in the current tax year;

(*c*) employees whose earnings under PAYE in 1994/1995 are less than £30,000 and are to receive a profit sharing allocation in excess of 10 per cent of their salary.

9.76 In practice, annual profit sharing allocations each tax year average approximately £300 per participant, and the average percentage of pay allocated as profit sharing is 2.5 per cent. Only in very few cases will the profit sharing scheme limit be found to restrict an allocation.

Tax aspects of disposals of shares

9.77 Under an approved profit sharing scheme the income tax charge which would otherwise arise on the value of the shares at the time of appropriation is deferred for up to five years whilst the shares are held in trust in order to 'wait and see' if the shares are disposed of during the period — in any event the participant undertakes not to dispose of them during the 'period of retention' which normally runs for up to two years after appropriation. If the participant directs the trustees to dispose of his shares — or to transfer them into his own name — during the five-year 'wait and see' period, income tax will be charged on the 'appropriate percentage' of the 'locked-in-value' of the shares, basically the initial market value of the shares as adjusted for capital receipts. At the end of the five-year 'wait and see'

9.78 Profit Sharing Trust

period the shares may be transferred into the participant's own name, or may be sold, without any liability to income tax.

Period of retention

9.78 It was noted above that it is a condition of receiving an appropriation of shares that a participant undertakes that he will (amongst other things) permit his shares to remain in the hands of the trustees throughout the period of retention. The 'period of retention' means the period beginning on the day on which the shares are appropriated to a participant and ending on the second anniversary of appropriation or, if it is earlier:

(*a*) the date on which the participant ceases to be a director or employee of a participating company in the scheme on account of:

    (i) injury or disability; or

    (ii) dismissal by reason of redundancy (within the meaning of the *Employment Protection (Consolidation) Act 1978* or the *Contracts of Employment and Redundancy Payments Act (Northern Ireland) 1965*); or

(*b*) the date the participant reaches 'the relevant age';

(*c*) the date of the participant's death;

(*d*) in the case where the participant's shares are redeemable shares in a workers' co-operative, the date on which the participant ceases to be employed by the co-operative (or any subsidiary of the co-operative).

9.79 The effect of the period of retention coming to an end for any of the above reasons is that the shares may be sold or transferred into the participant's own name. However, any such disposal or transfer of the shares will not be free of income tax consequences. (The tax consequences are explained at 9.82 below.)

9.80 The relevant age means, in the case of schemes approved before 25 July 1991, 60 years for women and 65 years for men, or, in the case of schemes approved on or after 25 July 1991, such age between 60 or 65 years of age as the scheme may specify and is common to both men and women. In schemes approved before 25 July 1991, the Inland Revenue are prepared by concession to allow the scheme to be altered, so far as the rights of participants are concerned, to provide that the period of retention ends on a common specified age in place of 60 and 65 years of age for women and men respectively. Since 30 November 1993, where a scheme approved before 25 July 1991 has been amended so that men as well as women

Profit Sharing Trust **9.83**

are entitled to withdraw shares from age 60, men may do so at that age without any income tax liability.

Disposal of shares — income tax

9.81 Where the trustees dispose of a participant's shares before the earlier of:

(*a*) the release date (which is the end of the five-year wait and see period), or

(*b*) the death of the participant,

the participant is chargeable to tax under Schedule E on the appropriate percentage of the locked-in-value of the shares at the time of disposal. The tax charge arises in the tax year in which the disposal takes place (*TA 1988, s 186(4)*). Normally, a disposal takes place at the direction of the participant — he will ask the trustees to sell. However, prior to the release date the following situations will also be treated as disposals:

(*a*) a transfer of the shares into the participant's own name; or

(*b*) a disposal of the beneficial interest in the shares (other than as a result of his insolvency or otherwise by operation of law).

In the above two cases, and where the Inland Revenue are of the opinion that any disposal has not taken place on arms-length terms, the disposal will be treated as made at the market value at the date of disposal (*TA 1988, s 186(10)*).

9.82 On a disposal of scheme shares, income tax is chargeable on the 'appropriate percentage' of the 'locked-in-value'. The appropriate percentage is normally as follows:

(*a*) 100 per cent if the disposal takes place before the fourth anniversary of appropriation; or

(*b*) 75 per cent if the disposal takes place on or after the fourth anniversary and before the release date.

However, the appropriate percentage is restricted to only 50 per cent if the participant has ceased to be a director or employee on account of injury, disability, redundancy or upon the participant reaching the relevant age (see 9.80 above).

9.83 The locked-in-value is based on the initial market value at the time of appropriation. This value will be adjusted to reflect any capital receipts (see 9.85) or capital reorganisations (see Chapter 13), and will be treated as reduced to the amount of the disposal proceeds

9.84 *Profit Sharing Trust*

in a case where the disposal proceeds are less than the locked-in-value. It would be unfair if a participant were forced to pay tax on the locked-in-value where this is higher than the sale proceeds.

9.84 The tax is normally collected through PAYE. Briefly, the procedure involves the trustees arranging for the deduction of PAYE tax on the appropriate percentage of the locked-in-value of any shares which may be sold. Where the charge to tax arises as a result of the transfer of shares into the name of the participant, the participant is obliged to account to the trustees for a sum equal to the basic rate of tax on the appropriate percentage of the locked-in-value of the shares. In such a case, the trustees will not receive a sufficient sum of money to account through PAYE for any higher rate of tax which is payable and this will be collected by direct assessment on the participant.

Capital receipt

9.85 A liability to income tax under Schedule E also falls on 'capital receipts'. A capital receipt is any money or money's worth received in respect of a scheme share prior to the release date which is not:

(i) income in the hands of the recipient;

(ii) the proceeds of a disposal; or

(iii) a new holding of shares on a company reconstruction.

The most common type of capital receipt is nil paid rights shares on a rights issue.

9.86 Capital receipts are chargeable to income tax under Schedule E in the tax year in which the entitlement arises. Income tax is payable on the appropriate percentage of so much of the amount or value of the receipt as exceeds the appropriate allowance for that tax year. The appropriate allowance for any tax year means a sum which is £20 multiplied by one plus the number of tax years in the immediately preceding five years in which shares were appropriated to participants under the scheme. Where more than one capital receipt is received in any year, they are set against the allowance in the order received.

9.87 In any rights issue, participants will often 'tail-swallow', that is to say, direct the trustees to sell such number of nil paid shares as will realise enough cash to take up the balance. By *TA 1988, 10 Sch 4(2)* the proceeds of the sale of shares in a 'tail-swallow' are not treated as a capital receipt.

9.88 In practice, the availability of the appropriate allowance will mean that only a minority of participants will usually pay income tax on any capital receipt. To the extent any capital receipt is received, the locked-in-value of the shares in respect of which it arises will be reduced by the amount of the receipt brought into charge to income tax. To the extent the aggregate amount of the capital receipts equals the locked-in-value of the shares in respect of which the entitlement arises, no further liability to income tax can arise (*TA 1988, 10 Sch 4(3)*).

Disposal of shares — capital gains tax

9.89 In addition to any liability for income tax on a disposal of shares, it is also necessary to consider whether a chargeable gain may arise on any disposal. Although any scheme shares are held in the name of the trustees, the participant is nevertheless treated as the beneficial owner of the shares for capital gains tax purposes from the moment of appropriation (*TCGA 1992, s 238(1)*) and accordingly he will be treated as making any such disposal.

9.90 In computing any chargeable gains, all profit sharing scheme shares held by the trustees on behalf of an employee are treated as a separate pool (*TCGA 1992, s 104(4)*). In effect, therefore, on any disposal of shares held by the trustees of a profit sharing scheme, any gain will be calculated by reference to the average of the initial market values of the scheme shares.

Normal duties of trustees

9.91 The trustees are subject to all the normal duties imposed upon trustees under the general law quite apart from the special statutory duties which are imposed under the profit sharing scheme legislation.

9.92 A trustee is in a fiduciary relationship with the beneficiaries. The practical effect of this is that the trustees must act in the best interests of scheme participants, and is liable to the scheme participants, not the company, for any breach of trust. Any claims which the company may have against the trustees can normally only be founded on a breach of contract based on their terms of appointment. For this reason, companies should consider carefully the terms on which they appoint persons to be trustees and enter into an appropriate written contract.

Unappropriated assets

9.93 Where assets are held prior to appropriation, the trust deed would normally provide for dividends to be retained by the trustees and applied in the payment of expenses and for the trustees to have discretion in relation to any offers for the shares or any other rights arising in respect of the shares.

9.94 Profit Sharing Trust

9.94 Under the *Trustee Investment Act 1961*, trustees are only permitted to hold one-half of any capital monies received in equities and therefore an appropriate power is required to allow them to hold the trust assets wholly in the form of shares in the company although this will normally be inferred from the profit sharing scheme. Profit sharing trust deeds need to provide for the trustees to invest trust assets in bank deposits including non-interest bearing accounts where this is considered appropriate by the trustee.

Appropriated shares

9.95 Where the trustees have appropriated shares to scheme participants, the shares are retained by them for the scheme participants as beneficial owners in accordance with the contractual obligations under *TA 1988, 9 Sch 2(2)* to leave shares with the trustees. This means that most of the share rights will be exercised or enjoyed through the trustees. The trustees will receive all dividends, and will exercise voting rights at the direction of the scheme participants. Most schemes will set out these rights expressly but the rights will apply even where the trust deed is silent.

Dividends from UK companies

9.96 Where the trustees hold scheme shares on behalf of participants, the company will normally pay a single dividend cheque to the trustees as the registered holder of all the shares. Alternatively, dividends may be mandated to individual scheme participants so that future dividends are paid directly to them.

9.97 Trustees will normally supply individual tax vouchers to scheme participants and will normally use Form R185E although a substitution form can usually be agreed with Inland Revenue, Claims (Bootle), St John's House, Merton Road, Stanley Precinct, Bootle, Merseyside L69 4EJ (tel: 051-922 6363).

Dividends from overseas companies

9.98 Where the trustees receive dividends from overseas companies, UK tax at the basic rate will normally be deducted by any UK paying agent (after giving credit for any overseas tax deducted at source). The trustees are required to supply scheme participants with a certificate of deduction of tax on Form R189C showing details of the holding of shares, dividend and tax deducted.

9.99 If the trustees receive a dividend from an overseas company without deduction of UK basic rate tax, the trustee is treated as the UK paying agent and must deduct UK basic rate tax (after giving

Profit Sharing Trust **9.103**

relief for any overseas tax deducted at source) and account for the tax to the Inspector of Foreign Dividends, Surrey KT7 0DP. When distributing the dividends the trustee is required to supply each participant with a certificate of deduction of tax on Form R189.

9.100 Overseas participants may be able to obtain repayment of any basic rate tax deducted from the Inspector of Foreign Dividends.

Statutory duties of trustees

Notice of appropriation

9.101 The trust deed must impose upon trustees an obligation to notify participants, as soon as practicable after any appropriation, of the number and description of shares and stating their initial market value (*TA 1988, 9 Sch 31*).

Obligation to hold scheme shares during the period of retention

9.102 The trust deed must contain a provision prohibiting the trustees from disposing of any scheme shares during the period of retention unless directed by the participant in the event of any takeover or reconstruction offer (*TA 1988, 9 Sch 32*). This mirrors the contractual obligation imposed on the participant to leave his shares with the trustees during this period.

Obligation to hold scheme shares after the period of retention

9.103 The trust deed must contain a provision prohibiting the disposal of any scheme shares by trustees following the period of retention and before the release date except:

(*a*) at the direction of the participant, or of any other person in whom the beneficial interest in the participant's shares is for the time being vested; and

(*b*) by a transaction which would not involve a breach of the participant's contractual obligations under *TA 1988, 9 Sch 2(2)(c) (d)*, that is to say, to pay the trustees a sum equal to income tax at the basic rate on the appropriate percentage of the locked-in-value of the shares at the time of any direction to the trustees to the transfer the ownership of the shares into the participant's own name, and not to direct the trustees at any time before the release date in any other way except by sale for the best consideration in money that can reasonably be obtained at the time of the sale.

9.104 Profit Sharing Trust

Obligations in relation to the operation of PAYE

9.104 The trust instrument must also require the trustees to operate PAYE as follows:

(*a*) Where the trustees receive any money constituting in whole or in part:

    (i) the proceeds of a disposal of a participant's scheme shares at any time before the release date or, if earlier, the date of the participant's death; or

    (ii) a capital receipt,

the trustees must deduct an amount equal to the amount on which income tax is payable and pay that amount to the relevant company for PAYE purposes (*TA 1988, 10 Sch 7*).

(*b*) The trustees must maintain such records as may be necessary to enable the trustees to carry out their obligations under *TA 1988, 10 Sch 7* to operate PAYE.

(*c*) The trustees must inform the participants of any facts relevant to the determination of any liability to income tax under Schedule E as a result of any event giving rise to such liability in respect of his scheme shares. This would cover advising the participant of the appropriate percentage of the locked-in value on which income tax is chargeable where the participant withdraws his shares before the release date (*TA 1988, 9 Sch 34*).

Further information on the operation of PAYE is to be found at 9.112 to 9.115.

Account to the participant for dividends, etc.

9.105 The trust deed must impose on the trustees an obligation to account to the participant for any money or money's worth received in respect of his shares other than money's worth consisting of new shares issued as consideration for any scheme shares on a company reconstruction. This means that the trustees are under an obligation to account for (amongst other things):

(*a*) dividends, scrip dividends and other distributions;

(*b*) non-sale proceeds of any shares disposed of at the direction of the participant; and

(*c*) any capital receipts including the proceeds of any rights to shares sold nil paid (other than where the proceeds are used to tail-swallow by using the proceeds to take up any rights shares (*TA 1988, 10 Sch 4(2)*)).

Act on the direction of the participant in any rights issue

9.106 The trustee is under an obligation to deal on any rights issue only on the direction of the participant (or any other person in whom the shares are for the time being vested e.g. personal representatives). This requirement states that the trustees shall only deal as directed by the participant without expressly imposing an obligation on the trustees to obtain those instructions. Most schemes provide for the trustees to obtain the instructions of the participant. The Model Scheme provides that 'the Trustees shall notify each Participant concerned of the rights which are attributable to his Appropriated Shares' and states that 'the Participants shall be at liberty to accept such offer...'. The ABI Guidelines make no reference to the responsibilities of the trustees or any rights issues. In the writer's view, the best practice must be to impose an obligation on trustees to seek specific instructions from participants on each occasion and to act on them accordingly. It is not sufficient either as a term of the scheme, when an employee first participates in the scheme, merely to obtain a general standing instruction that on all future rights issues the trustees shall either sell any nil paid rights, allow them to lapse or tail-swallow.

9.107 There are a number of matters in respect of which it appears there is no obligation on the trustees to take action, although most schemes will, as a matter of good practice, cover these points. These include the question of seeking instructions from participants in relation to any rights issue or seeking directions from participants in relation to voting his shares.

Taxation of the trustees

9.108 The trustees of a profit sharing scheme hold trust assets in two capacities. First, on general trusts for directors and employees in respect of which income tax and capital gains tax will be payable on the income tax gains arising except to the extent the special reliefs mentioned below are available. Secondly, the trust holds appropriated shares but the income and gains arising from such assets belong to the scheme participants to whom the shares belong.

Income tax on the income of unappropriated assets

9.109 Income tax is chargeable in the normal way on the income of the profit sharing trust. The only exception to this rule is that the additional rate of income tax does not apply to income consisting of dividends received by the trustees on shares appropriated in accordance with an approved profit sharing scheme within 18 months of the date of their acquisition by the trustees (*TA 1988, s 186(11)*). In determining whether shares were acquired within the 18-month

9.110 *Profit Sharing Trust*

period, shares acquired at an earlier time are required to be taken as appropriated before shares of the same class which were acquired at a later time. This relief will normally be given by way of discharge or repayment of tax once it has been established that the 18 months' rule has been satisfied. This will often mean that the trustees will initially pay the tax but will be able to obtain the relief at a later date. Other sources of income such as untaxed basic interest received by the trustees will be subject to tax including the additional rate of tax by virtue of *TA 1988, s 686*.

Capital gains tax on the appropriation of shares

9.110 The trustees are exempt from capital gains tax upon any appropriation of shares to participants provided the appropriation takes place within 18 months of acquisition. In determining whether shares were acquired within the 18-month period, shares acquired at an earlier time are required to be taken as appropriated before shares of the same class which were acquired at a later time.

Inheritance tax

9.111 Property held by the trustees of an approved profit sharing scheme will not be 'relevant property' for the purposes of *IHTA 1984, s 58* and therefore will not be subject to any inheritance tax charge under *IHTA 1984, ss 64, 65*.

Operation of PAYE

9.112 *TA 1988, 10 Sch 7* sets out the machinery for the deduction of income tax under PAYE on disposals of shares or transfers of shares into the participant's own name. Basically, the machinery relies on the trustees paying the amount on which tax is chargeable through the PAYE scheme of the relevant group company.

9.113 The usual form of approval letter issued by the Inland Revenue in respect of a profit sharing trust states that the trustees shall apply to the tax office to open a special PAYE scheme as soon as they need to deduct tax through PAYE.

Occasions on which PAYE is operated

9.114 The circumstances in which PAYE is operated by the trustees are upon a disposal of shares before the release date (or the date of the death of the participant if earlier) or upon the receipt of any 'capital receipt'. For these purposes a disposal will include:

(*a*) a disposal of a participant's scheme shares;

Profit Sharing Trust **9.117**

(*b*) a disposal by the participant of the beneficial interest in his shares to the trustee (*TA 1988, 10 Sch 7(2)*); and

(*c*) a transfer before the release date of a participant's shares into his own name (*TA 1988, 10 Sch 7(7)*).

The relevant company required to operate PAYE

9.115 The legislation lays down the rules for identifying the group company through whose payroll scheme PAYE must be operated. This will normally be the employing company if employees of that company are at that time normally eligible to participate in the scheme. However, exceptional circumstances will sometimes arise, as follows:

(*a*) if there are two or more employing companies then the Inland Revenue will nominate one of them to operate PAYE (*TA 1988, 10 Sch 3*);

(*b*) if there is no employing company the trustees will normally be required to operate PAYE as if they were the employer i.e. the trustees will operate their own PAYE scheme (*TA 1988, 10 Sch 4*);

(*c*) if the Inland Revenue consider it impractical for the employing company to operate PAYE (for instance, an overseas employer) then the trustees will normally be required to operate PAYE as if they were the employer (*TA 1988, 10 Sch 4*); or

(*d*) if the Inland Revenue direct, with the consent of all the companies concerned, that a particular company which is not an employing company, would most conveniently operate PAYE (for instance, where an employee is paid by a non-participating company in the group).

Excess on unauthorised shares

9.116 The tax treatment applying to unauthorised and excess shares is explained at 9.57 above. Tax is not applied on the locked-in-value of the shares, but on their market value at the release date. Where the participant disposes of such shares before the release, or upon any capital receipt, the trustees will operate PAYE as if the excess on unauthorised shares were authorised shares. The Inland Revenue will collect the balance of the income tax on the participant by direct assessment giving credit for the tax deducted through PAYE.

Trustees PAYE scheme

9.117 A PAYE scheme will not normally be opened for the trustees before the time they first need to deduct tax. The tax district dealing

9.118 *Profit Sharing Trust*

with the company's PAYE scheme will normally arrange for a separate scheme to be opened for the trustees.

9.118 The trustees' Tax Office will supply the necessary instructions on the operation of PAYE. The trustees will be required to make the usual end of year statement in respect of any PAYE scheme operated by them.

National insurance

9.119 Although *TA 1988, 10 Sch 6* provides that any amount in respect of which a PAYE deduction is made shall be treated as an amount of income assessable to income tax under Schedule E, it is nevertheless not 'pay' for national insurance purposes (*SI 1979 No 591, s 19 (1)(l)*).

Alteration of the trusts

9.120 The terms of any trust deed cannot normally be altered except upon application to the courts in certain circumstances or if the trust deeds contains appropriate powers. Most profit sharing schemes contain appropriate powers to alter the terms of the trust usually by supplemental deed or by written resolution of the directors of the company which established the scheme. It is obviously much simpler to rely on a written resolution of the company although the trustees will obviously need to be notified of any changes which are made.

9.121 It is invariably better to alter a profit sharing scheme rather than replace it. This is because any replacement will inevitably involve the cost of maintaining and operating two scheme registers for up to five years.

Duration of the scheme

9.122 The ABI do not specify any maximum period for the duration of a profit sharing scheme. The only restriction on the duration of a scheme is the rule against perpetuities under general trust law. The rule against perpetuities is a requirement that trust property must vest absolutely within a specified period of time. The *Perpetuities and Accumulations Act 1964, s 1(1)* provides that trust instruments may provide a perpetuity period of such duration in years as may be specified in such instrument but not exceeding 80 years. In practice, to allow for the vesting of any trust property following the release date at the fifth anniversary of appropriation, most schemes will provide for appropriations to be made no later than the 74th anniversary of the execution of the trust instrument and for a perpetuity period of 80 years.

Appendix 6

PROFIT SHARING SCHEME

THIS DEED is made the ... day of ... 19

BETWEEN:

(1) ...... plc/Limited whose registered office is at ...... under registration number ...... ('the Company'); and
(2) ... TRUSTEES LIMITED whose registered office is at ...... under registration number ... ('the Trustees').

WHEREAS:

(*a*) the Company wishes to establish a profit sharing scheme approved in accordance with the provisions of *Schedule 9* to the *Income and Corporation Taxes Act 1988* constituting an 'employees' share scheme' as that expression is defined in *section 743* of the *Companies Act 1985* for the provision by the Company and any Participating Companies of funds for the purchase by the Trustees of Shares in the Company [and in particular for the purchase of such Shares from the trustees of the ESOP Trust established by the Company on ......];

(*b*) the Board of the Company by a resolution passed on ...... 19 ...... has approved the establishment of such a profit sharing scheme;

(*c*) the Trustees have agreed to be the original trustee of the profit sharing scheme.

NOW THIS DEED WITNESSETH as follows:

1. Definitions

1.1 In this Deed, the following words and expressions shall bear, unless the context otherwise requires, the meanings set forth below:

'Accounting Period'	any period for which audited accounts of the Company are made up;
'Announcement Date'	a date on which the Company makes an announcement of its final results for the preceding Accounting Period;
'the Appropriate Percentage'	in relation to any Scheme Shares, shall be construed in accordance with *paragraph 3* of *Schedule 10* to the *Taxes Act*;
'Appropriation Day'	a day on which Shares are appropriated;

9.122 Profit Sharing Trust

'Appropriation Value'	(a) in relation to any appropriation of Shares their initial market value as determined in accordance with *paragraph 30(4)* of *Schedule 9* to the *Taxes Act* (which, if and so long as Shares are listed and dealt in on the London Stock Exchange, shall be the average total acquisition price paid (exclusive of incidental expenses) in respect of them and which, if and so long as Shares are not so listed, shall be as agreed with the Shares Valuation Division of the Inland Revenue); and
	(b) any other value as agreed with the Inland Revenue;
'Appropriation Year'	a Year of Assessment during which an appropriation of Shares is or is intended to be made under the Scheme;
'the Board'	the Board of Directors of the Company or a duly authorised Committee thereof;
'Capital Receipt'	the meaning given by *section 186(3)* of the *Taxes Act*;
'the Company'	...... plc/Limited (registered in England and Wales under No ......), or where the context so requires, such other company whose shares may from time to time be Scheme Shares;
'Close Company'	the meaning given by *section 414* of the *Taxes Act*;
'Continuous Service'	the same meaning as for 'continuous employment' in the *Employment Protection (Consolidation) Act 1978*;
'Control'	control within the meaning of *section 840* of the *Taxes Act*;
'Dealing Day'	any day on which the London Stock Exchange is open for the transaction of business;
'the Deed'	this Trust Deed constituting, inter alia, the Scheme as amended from time to time;
'Deed of Adherence'	a deed substantially in the form set out in *Schedule Two* hereto;
'Eligible Employee'	(a) an individual who:

220

Profit Sharing Trust 9.122

(i) (A) is a director or employee (and is not under notice which will expire prior to the Appropriation Day) of a Participating Company on terms which require him to devote at least such minimum number of hours (between 8 and 25) a week to his duties as the Board may determine; and

(B) is chargeable to tax in respect of such office or employment under Case I of Schedule E of the *Taxes Act*; and

(C) has, on the Qualifying Date, such qualifying period (if any) of Continuous Service (being a period commencing not earlier than five years prior to the Appropriation Day) as the Board may determine; or

(ii) is nominated by the Board as an executive director or employee of a Participating Company (or is nominated as a member of a category of such executive directors and employees); or

(iii) is nominated by the Board as a former executive director or employee of a Participating Company (or is nominated as a member of a category of such former executive directors and employees) and who immediately before ceasing to be a director or employee was required to devote at least 16 hours a week to his duties and who ceased to be a director or employee within 18 months prior to the Appropriation Day;

9.122 *Profit Sharing Trust*

PROVIDED always that in each case he is not ineligible for an appropriation of Shares under the Scheme by virtue of Rules 6.1 and 6.2 of the Scheme, or because he has served a subsisting notice under Rule 6.3 of the Scheme directing the Trustees not to appropriate Shares to him;

'Employees' Share Scheme'	the meaning given by *section 743* of the *Companies Act 1985*;
'the ESOP Trustees'	...... or such other person or persons who is or are the trustee or trustees of the ESOP Trust established on ...... ;
'Locked-in-Value'	in relation to any Scheme Shares, shall be construed in accordance with *section 186(5)* of the *Taxes Act*;
'the London Stock Exchange'	The International Stock Exchange of the United Kingdom and the Republic of Ireland Limited;
'Market Value'	in relation to a Share on any day:

(a) its middle market quotation (as derived from the Daily Official List of the London Stock Exchange); or

(b) subject to (a) above, its market value, determined in accordance with *sections 272 to 274* of the *Taxation of Chargeable Gains Act 1992* and agreed in advance with the Shares Valuation Division of the Inland Revenue;

'Material Interest'	the meaning given by *section 187(3)* of the *Taxes Act*;
'Member of a Consortium'	the meaning given by *section 187(7)* of the *Taxes Act*;
'New Shares'	the meaning given by *paragraph 5(3)* of *Schedule 10* to the *Taxes Act*;
'Participant'	any person on whose behalf the Trustees hold Scheme Shares or other securities under the Scheme;
'Participating Company'	(a) the Company; and

(b) any other company which is under the Control of the Company, is a Subsidiary of the Company and with the approval of the Company participates

Profit Sharing Trust 9.122

	in the Scheme and has executed a Deed of Adherence;
'Period of Retention'	the meaning given by *paragraph 2* of *Schedule 10* to the *Taxes Act* in relation to any Participant's Scheme Shares;
'Qualifying Date'	such date as the Board may from time to time determine;
'Reconstruction or Takeover'	a transaction affecting any Scheme Shares as mentioned in *paragraphs 1(1)(a)*, *(b)* or *(c)* of *Schedule 10* to the *Taxes Act*;
'Release Date'	the meaning given by *section 187(2)* of the *Taxes Act*;
'the Relevant Amount'	the meaning given by *section 187(2)* of the *Taxes Act*;
'Scheme'	the .... Profit Sharing Scheme, the rules of which are set out in *Schedule One* hereto;
'Scheme Shares'	Shares which are held by the Trustees upon the terms of the Scheme on behalf of the Participants to whom they have been appropriated;
'Share'	a share in the capital of the Company which satisfies the conditions specified in *paragraphs 10* to *12* (inclusive) and *14* of *Schedule 9* to the *Taxes Act* or, where the context permits, in the event of a Reconstruction or Takeover of the Company, such share as forms part of any new holding as that term is defined in *paragraph 5* of *Schedule 10* to the *Taxes Act*;
'Subsidiary'	in relation to the Company, a subsidiary within the meaning given by *section 736* of the *Companies Act 1985*;
'the Taxes Act'	the *Income and Corporation Taxes Act 1988*;
'Trustees'	the original trustee referred to in the Deed or such other person or persons who is or are the trustee or trustees from time to time of the Scheme;
'Year of Assessment'	a year of assessment within the meaning given by *section 832* of the *Taxes Act*

9.122 *Profit Sharing Trust*

1.2 In this Deed unless the context requires otherwise:

(*a*) the headings are inserted for convenience only and do not affect the interpretation of any Clause or Rule;

(*b*) a reference to a Clause or Rule is a reference to a Clause or Rule of this Deed;

(*c*) a reference to a statute or statutory provision includes a reference:

   (i) to that statute or provision as from time to time consolidated, modified, re-enacted or replaced by any statute or statutory provision;

   (ii) to any repealed statute or statutory provision which it re-enacts (with or without modification); and

   (iii) to any subordinate legislation made under it;

(*d*) words in the singular include the plural, and vice versa;

(*e*) a reference to the masculine shall be treated as a reference to the feminine and vice versa;

(*f*) if a period of time is specified and starts from a given day or the day of an act or event, it is to be calculated exclusive of that day;

(*g*) a reference to a 'year' shall be a period calculated by reference to the anniversary of a particular date.

2. Trusts of the Scheme

2.1 Subject as provided in this Deed, the Trustees hereby agree with each Participating Company that they shall apply all monies received by them under the Scheme in the acquisition of Shares and in paying their expenses, taxation and other liabilities in accordance with the Rules of the Scheme.

2.2 The Trustees shall, as soon as reasonably practicable after their acquisition of Shares, appropriate the Shares to Eligible Employees in accordance with the Rules of the Scheme and shall notify each Participant of the description and number of Shares so appropriated to him, the date of the appropriation and the Appropriation Value.

2.3 If it is not possible to appropriate all the Shares so acquired, the Trustees may either retain or sell so many of the Shares as the Company shall direct and in the case of a sale shall apply the proceeds to meet any expenses of such sale and shall pay the net proceeds to the Participating Companies in the same proportion as the Participating Companies made contributions to the Trustees or as may otherwise be appropriate.

2.4 The Trustees shall hold any Shares once appropriated and all other trust property deriving therefrom UPON TRUST for the Participants respectively entitled thereto subject to the Rules of the Scheme.

2.5 If the Trustees become entitled in respect of any unappropriated Shares to any rights to be allotted, or to subscribe for, further securities in the Parent (other than an issue by way of capitalisation of shares of the same class as Shares then held by the Trustees pending an appropriation, which capitalisation shares shall be retained by the Trustees and shall form part of the Shares to be appropriated among the Participants on the relevant Appropriation Day), the Trustees may at their discretion take up those rights or sell them for the best consideration in money reasonably obtainable at the time or sell sufficient of them nil paid to enable the Trustees to subscribe in full for the balance of any unsold rights, or allow them to lapse.

2.6 The Trustees shall hold any unappropriated Shares or unutilised cash balances arising under Clause 2.3 or 2.5 above and any income arising therefrom UPON TRUST to apply towards the future acquisition of Shares for the purposes of the Scheme and their administration expenses.

3. Purchase of shares from other Trusts

The Trustees may purchase Shares from the Trustees of any other trust notwithstanding that the Trustees are the same persons as those trustees or any of them and such purchase shall be binding on all persons interested hereunder notwithstanding that it shall be effected or evidenced only by an entry in the accounts of the Trustees.

4. Application of Scheme to Subsidiaries

4.1 The Scheme may with the consent of the Board and, after notification to the Inland Revenue, be extended to any Subsidiary which is under the Control of the Company and not a party to this Deed by the execution of a Deed of Adherence, following which, the provisions of the Scheme shall apply to that Company as though it were a party to this Deed.

4.2 The Scheme shall cease to apply to any company, other than the Company, at any time when:

(a) that company ceases to be a Subsidiary of the Company or under the Control of the Company; or

(b) a notice is served by the Company upon the Trustees that the Scheme shall not apply to that company, provided that the

9.122 *Profit Sharing Trust*

conditions specified in *paragraph 2(3)* of *Schedule 9* to the *Taxes Act* continue to be satisfied.

5. Investment

5.1 The Trustees may invest any monies from time to time held by them and not immediately required for the acquisition of Shares or in paying any costs, charges, expenses, taxation and other liabilities of the Trust by placing the same on current or deposit account as they in their absolute discretion think fit.

5.2 The Trustees shall be under no duty to invest trust property.

6. Dividends

The Trustees shall, as soon as practicable following their receipt of any dividend in respect of Scheme Shares account for and pay such dividends to Participants in accordance with their respective entitlements, but otherwise may retain any dividends upon the trusts hereof.

7. Retention of Shares

7.1 The Trustees shall not dispose of any Scheme Shares for a Participant during the applicable Period of Retention except in accordance with a direction of the Participant (or his personal representatives) in the event of a Reconstruction or Takeover affecting such Shares.

7.2 The Trustees shall not dispose of any Scheme Shares after the end of the applicable Period of Retention and before the Release Date except in accordance with Rule 15.1(*b*) or (*c*) of *Schedule 1*.

8. Dealing in rights attaching to Shares

The Trustees shall deal with any right to be allotted other shares, securities or rights of any description conferred in respect of a Participant's shares only pursuant to a direction given by or on behalf of the Participant or any person in whom the beneficial interest in that Participant's Shares is for the time being vested.

9. Voting rights

9.1 If and so long as Shares held under the Scheme are registered in the names of the Trustees the Trustees shall invite the relevant Participants to direct them how to exercise any voting rights which

Profit Sharing Trust **9.122**

the Trustees shall become entitled to exercise in respect of any matter arising at a general meeting of the Company or at any class meeting.

9.2 The Trustees shall not be entitled to vote on a show of hands on a particular resolution in respect of Shares held on behalf of Participants unless all directions received from those Participants who have given directions in respect of that resolution are identical.

9.3 The Trustees are not in any circumstances under an obligation to call for a poll. In the event of any poll the Trustees shall vote only in accordance with the directions of Participants.

9.4 The Trustees may not vote in respect of Shares which have not been appropriated pursuant to the Scheme.

10. Trustees' powers of delegation

10.1 The Trustees, in the exercise of their discretions and the performance of their duties hereunder, may employ and pay a registrar, solicitor, broker, actuary, accountant, banker or any other person, and may appoint any such person as their agent to transact all or any business, and may act on the advice or opinion of any solicitor, broker, actuary, accountant or other professional or business person, and shall not be responsible for anything done or omitted or suffered in good faith in reliance on such advice or opinion.

10.2 Except as otherwise provided by *section 186* of and *Schedules 9* and *10* to the *Taxes Act*, the Trustees may delegate any of their powers and duties hereunder or any business including the exercise of any discretion to any person or company including the Company or any Subsidiary of the Company.

10.3 The Trustees may at any time, and shall if so directed by the Company, revoke any delegation or arrangement made under this Clause and/or require any trust property held by another person to be returned to the Trustees.

10.4 The Trustees may execute and authorise any of their directors, officers or employees on their behalf to execute any deeds, documents, cheques or other instruments by the impression of any signature on behalf of, or as witness of any sealing by, the Trustees of any writing, printing, photocopying and other modes of representing or reproducing words in a visible form.

11. Administration

11.1 Subject to and in accordance with the provisions of this Deed, the Trustees may convene meetings and make such regulations as they consider appropriate relating to the administration of the Scheme.

9.122 *Profit Sharing Trust*

11.2 The Trustees shall at all times comply with their obligations to make payments to any of the Participating Companies in respect of any income tax which is payable and to account to the Inland Revenue in respect of income tax or any other deductions required in accordance with *paragraph 7* of *Schedule 10* to the *Taxes Act*.

11.3 The Trustees shall maintain such records as may be necessary to comply with the *Taxes Act*, and shall give to each Participant such information as shall be in their possession to enable him to determine and quantify any liability he may have to income tax under Schedule E by reason of any event.

12. Trustees' indemnities and charges

12.1 The Participating Companies hereby covenant with the Trustees that they shall keep the Trustees and their estates and effects fully indemnified against all actions, claims, losses, demands, proceedings, charges, expenses, costs, damages, taxes, duties and other liabilities whatsoever arising out of or in connection with the Scheme, but so that no Trustee shall be indemnified or exonerated in respect of any fraud or wilful default on his or his agent's part or (in the case of a Trustee engaged in the business of providing a trustee service for a fee) his or his agent's negligence.

12.2 Neither the Trustees nor any of their officers or employees shall be liable to account to Participants for any remuneration or other benefit received in connection with the Scheme and no Trustee or officer or employee of the Trustees shall be liable to account to other Participants for any profit derived from the appropriation to him of Shares held under the Scheme.

12.3 Any person acting as a Trustee in the course of any profession or business carried on by him may charge and be paid such reasonable remuneration, charges or disbursements whether in connection with the Scheme or otherwise as shall from time to time be agreed between him and the Company.

12.4 Any Trustee (and any director or officer of a body corporate or a trust corporation acting as a Trustee) shall not on his own account be precluded from acquiring, holding or dealing with any stock, shares or securities whatsoever of the Company or any Subsidiary or any other company in the shares of which the Company or any such Subsidiary may be interested, or from entering into or being interested in any contract or other transaction with the Company, any Subsidiary or any such other company, and nor shall he be in any way liable to account to the Company, any Subsidiary, any such other company or any Participant for any profits made, fees, commissions, shares of brokerage, discounts allowed or advantages obtained by him from or in connection with such acquisition, holding, dealing, contract or transaction whether or not in connection with his duties hereunder.

12.5 The Trustees shall be entitled in the absence of manifest error to rely without further enquiry on information supplied to them by any Participating Company and on any direction, notice or document purporting to be given or executed by or with the authority of any Participating Company or any Participant or any person in whom the beneficial interest in that Participant's Shares is for the time being vested.

13. Appointment, removal and retirement of Trustees

13.1 The Company may at any time by writing under hand of a person duly authorised by a resolution of the Board:

(*a*) appoint a new or additional Trustee, including a corporate Trustee; and

(*b*) remove a Trustee from office (but not so as to leave in office less than two Trustees, unless a corporate Trustee), without assigning any reason therefor and such removal shall (in the absence of any other date specified in the notice) take place forthwith.

13.2 The powers of appointment and removal shall be vested in the Trustees in the event that the Company ceases to exist otherwise than in consequence of a Reconstruction or Takeover when the successor company (or, if more than one, such successor companies as the Company shall nominate) shall have such powers.

13.3 A Trustee may retire by giving to the Company written notice of his desire to retire and such notice shall take effect at the expiry of three months (or such other period as may be agreed with the Company) from the date of such notice. The retiring Trustee shall not be obliged to give any reason for and shall not be responsible for any costs occasioned by such retirement but shall execute all such documents and do all such things as may be necessary to give proper effect to such retirement.

13.4 Forthwith upon his removal or retirement a Trustee shall transfer all trust property held by him and deliver all documents in his possession relating to the Scheme as the Company may direct and hereby authorises the continuing Trustees, in the absence of such transfer, to effect such transfer on his behalf.

9.122 *Profit Sharing Trust*

14. Residence of the Trustees

There shall at all times be at least one trustee resident in the United Kingdom for United Kingdom tax purposes.

15. Alterations

15.1 The Board may prior to approval of the Scheme under *Schedule 9* of the *Taxes Act* by the Inland Revenue alter or add to the Scheme (including this Deed and the Schedules hereto) as may be necessary in order to obtain such approval.

15.2 After the date on which the Scheme is so approved, the Board may by written resolution alter or add to any of the provisions of this Deed and the Schedules hereto in such manner as may be thought fit (and such alterations or additions shall be binding on the Trustees, the Parent and all Participating Companies and Participants) PROVIDED THAT no such purported alteration or addition shall be effective:

(*a*) if and so long as the Scheme is desired to be approved by the Inland Revenue, until approved by the Inland Revenue;

(*b*) where the alteration or addition would cause the Scheme to cease to be an Employees' Share Scheme;

(*c*) where the alteration would affect adversely the rights of a Participant in respect of his Scheme Shares;

(*d*) where the alteration or addition would offend the rule against perpetuities.

15.3 Written notice of any alteration or addition made in accordance with Clause 15.2 shall be given to the Trustees and all Participants affected thereby.

16. Termination of Scheme

16.1 No appropriation of Shares under the Scheme may be made later than 74 years after the date of this Deed or the earlier termination of the Scheme by the Board or the Company in general meeting, and the perpetuity period applicable to this Deed shall be 80 years.

16.2 Any surplus assets of the trust shall be paid to Participating Companies so far as practicable in proportion to the total amounts provided by each of them to the Trustees.

17. Governing law

This Deed shall be governed by and construed in accordance with the law of England.

18. Construction of this Deed

The Schedules hereto shall be treated as part of this Deed.

IN WITNESS whereof this Deed has been executed by the parties hereto and is intended to be and is hereby delivered on the date first above written.

SCHEDULE ONE

The Rules of the[   ]Profit Sharing Scheme

1. Operation of the Scheme

1.1 The Board may at any time resolve that appropriations of Shares shall be made under the Scheme to Eligible Employees subject to the following limitations:

(*a*) not more than one appropriation of Shares shall be made under the Scheme in any Year of Assessment;

(*b*) any appropriation of Shares shall be made within 90 days of any relevant Announcement Date.

1.2 The Board shall notify the Trustees of the relevant Appropriation Day.

1.3 The Board may resolve that the Shares shall be acquired by purchase on the London Stock Exchange or privately (including from the ESOP Trustees) or by subscription or by any combination thereof and shall notify the Trustees accordingly.

2. Number of Shares available for appropriation under the Scheme

2.1 Unless the limit set out in Rule 2.3 is and has always been complied with, the number of Shares which may be allocated under the Scheme on any day shall not, when added to the aggregate of the number of Shares which have been allocated in the previous three years under the Scheme and any other Employees' Share Scheme adopted by the Company, exceed such number as represents 3 per cent of the ordinary share capital of the Company in issue immediately prior to that day, or 4 per cent thereof where that day falls within the

9.122 Profit Sharing Trust

period of three years commencing with the first day on which options were granted under the Company's sharesave option scheme.

2.2 The limit referred to in Rule 2.1 is that the number of Shares which may be allocated on any day shall not, when added to the aggregate of the number of Shares which have been allocated in the previous five years under the Scheme and any other Employees' Share Scheme adopted by the Company, exceed such number as represents 5 per cent of the ordinary share capital of the Company in issue immediately prior to that day.

2.3 The number of Shares which may be allocated under the Scheme on any day shall not, when added to the aggregate of the number of Shares which have been allocated in the previous ten years under the Scheme and any other Employees' Share Scheme adopted by the Company, exceed such number as represents 10 per cent of the ordinary share capital of the Company in issue immediately prior to that day.

2.4 The number of Shares which may be allocated under the Scheme on any day shall not, when added to the aggregate of the number of Shares which shall have been allocated under the Scheme prior to that day in the same Year of Assessment, exceed such number as represents 1 per cent of the ordinary share capital of the Company in issue immediately prior to that day.

2.5 In determining the above limits no account shall be taken of any Shares where the right to acquire the Shares was released, lapsed or otherwise became incapable of exercise.

2.6 References in this Rule to the 'allocation' of Shares shall mean, in the case of any share option scheme, the placing of unissued shares under option and, in relation to other types of Employees' Share Scheme, shall mean the issue and allotment of shares and references to 'allocated' shall be construed accordingly.

3. Profits limit

3.1 The Board shall in its absolute discretion determine the amount that shall be available for the acquisition of Shares for appropriation under the Scheme in any Appropriation Year and shall notify the Trustees accordingly.

3.2 Not more than 5 per cent of the aggregate consolidated profits (before tax and extraordinary items) of the Company and its Subsidiaries in the last Accounting Period (being profits which, in the opinion of the Board, are attributable to the United Kingdom operations and any overseas operations of Participating Companies whose employees participate in the Scheme) may be available for the acquisition of Shares under the Scheme in any Appropriation Year.

4. Contributions to be made by Participating Companies

4.1 The Board shall notify each Participating Company of the amount to be contributed by that Company to the Trustees to support any acquisition of Shares which shall not exceed such amount as is required to acquire the number of Shares which are to be appropriated to Eligible Employees who are for the time being directors or employees of that Participating Company or, where applicable, former directors or employees of such company.

4.2 Contributions to the Trustees to support the acquisition of Shares for appropriation on any Appropriation Day shall be paid not later than the fifth Dealing Day immediately prior to the relevant Appropriation Day.

5. Invitation to Participate

5.1 Where the Board resolves that the Scheme shall be operated, the Company shall issue a letter of invitation to each Eligible Employee who has not previously become a Participant (and, if applicable, to each Eligible Employee who has, since the Scheme was last operated, revoked a notice previously served by him under Rule 6.3).

5.2 A letter of invitation shall invite an Eligible Employee to consent to the appropriation of Shares under the Scheme and to complete and return a contract of participation (in such form as may be agreed with the Inland Revenue) by a given date which shall be prior to the relevant Appropriation Day.

5.3 A contract of participation shall bind the relevant Eligible Employee in contract with the Company:

(a) to permit all Scheme Shares appropriated to him to remain in the hands of the Trustees throughout the applicable Period of Retention; and

(b) subject as provided in Rule 5.4 below, not to assign, charge or otherwise dispose of his beneficial interest in any Scheme Shares during the applicable Period of Retention; and

(c) if he directs the Trustees to transfer the legal title of any Scheme Shares to him at any time before the applicable Release Date, to pay to the Trustees before such transfer takes place a sum equal to income tax at the basic rate on the Appropriate Percentage of the Locked-in-Value of such Scheme Shares at the time of such direction; and

9.122 *Profit Sharing Trust*

(*d*) not to direct the Trustees prior to the relevant Release Date to dispose of any Scheme Shares otherwise than as provided in Rule 5.3(*c*) above or by sale for the best consideration in money that can reasonably be obtained at the time of such sale;

5.4 No Participant by virtue of the signature of a contract of participation shall be precluded from directing the Trustees to dispose of his Shares in the event of a Reconstruction or Takeover affecting his Scheme Shares.

6. Eligibility

6.1 An individual shall not be eligible to have an appropriation of Shares in any Year of Assessment in which shares have been appropriated to him under any other profit sharing scheme approved by the Inland Revenue pursuant to the *Taxes Act* and established by:

(*a*) the Company;

(*b*) any Subsidiary of the Company;

(*c*) any company which has Control of the Company or any company which is under the Control of such a company; or

(*d*) any company which is a Member of a Consortium owning the Company or is owned in part by the Company as a member of a Consortium.

6.2 An individual shall not be eligible to have an appropriation of Shares at any time when he has (or had within the preceding twelve months) a Material Interest in:

(*a*) the Company; or

(*b*) any company which has Control of the Company; or

(*c*) a Member of a Consortium which owns the Company,

PROVIDED that this provision shall only apply if the Company is or was at relevant times a Close Company or would be or would have been a Close Company but for *section 414(1)(a)* or *415* of the *Taxes Act*.

6.3 An individual may by written notice given to the Company before an Appropriation Day direct that Shares shall not be appropriated to him on that Appropriation Day or on each subsequent Appropriation Day. A notice given by an individual under this Rule may be revoked by that individual giving written notice to the Company.

7. Acquisition of Shares for appropriation

7.1 If the Trustees are to acquire Shares for appropriation by purchase on the London Stock Exchange or privately they may not

Profit Sharing Trust **9.122**

purchase such Shares earlier than 60 days prior to the relevant Appropriation Date, and in the case of a private purchase made at a time when Shares are listed on the London Stock Exchange shall not purchase the Shares at a price which is materially more or less than the Market Value.

7.2   If the Trustees are to acquire Shares for appropriation by subscription they may not subscribe for such Shares earlier than 30 days prior to the relevant Appropriation Day and the price per share at which the Shares are subscribed shall be the greater of:

(*a*)   the nominal value of a Share on the date of subscription; and

(*b*)   the Market Value of a Share on the day immediately preceding the date of subscription.

8. Issue of Shares

8.1   Shares to be subscribed for by the Trustees (whether or not appropriated pursuant to the Scheme) will rank *pari passu* in all respects with the Shares then in issue except that they will not rank for any rights attaching to Shares by reference to a record date preceding the date of issue.

8.2   If and so long as the Shares are listed on the London Stock Exchange, the Company shall apply for a listing for any Shares issued pursuant to the Scheme as soon as practicable after the allotment thereof.

9. Basis of Allocation

9.1   The Shares to be appropriated to Eligible Employees on an Appropriation Day shall be allocated in accordance with one or more of the following formulae to be determined by the Board:

(*a*)   Eligible Employees shall receive Shares having an Appropriation Value equal to such percentage of their salary (as defined in *section 187(5)* of the *Taxes Act*) as the Board shall determine; or

(*b*)   Eligible Employees shall receive a fixed number of Shares or a number of Shares with a market value equal to a fixed sum; or

(*c*)   Eligible Employees shall receive a number of Shares proportionate to their length of service with a Participating Company; or

(*d*)   such other formula resolved on the Board and approved by the Inland Revenue.

9.122 *Profit Sharing Trust*

9.2 The aggregate of the Appropriation Value of all Shares allocated to any Participant in any Year of Assessment may not exceed the Relevant Amount.

9.3 Where the Trustees appropriate Shares a proportion of which rank for any dividend or other distribution or other rights attaching to Shares by reference to a record date preceding the relevant Appropriation Day, and a proportion of which do not, then the Shares to be appropriated to each Eligible Employee shall, as far as practicable, be in the same proportions thereto.

10. Specified age

10.1 The specified age for the purpose of the Scheme referred to in *paragraphs 2,3* and *3A* of *Schedule 10* to the *Taxes Act* is 60 years of age.

10.2 The Board may from time to time alter the age referred to in Rule 10.1 and substitute such other age as is common to men and women and is not less than 60 and not more than 75 as the Board shall think fit PROVIDED THAT no such purported alteration shall be effective:

(*a*) if and so long as the Scheme is desired to be approved by the Inland Revenue, until approved by the Inland Revenue;

(*b*) as respects any appropriation of Shares made under the Scheme before the date of such purported alteration.

11. Rights issues

11.1 Whenever any rights to acquire New Shares are granted by a company to the holders of any class of shares of which some are Scheme Shares, each Participant shall be notified by the Trustees of the rights relating to his Scheme Shares and invited to instruct the Trustees what action to take, which instructions may be of particular or of general application and relate to Scheme Shares appropriated before and after the date of the relevant rights issue.

11.2 If any Participant has not prior to five Dealing Days before the expiry of the period allowed for the exercise of any such rights given instructions to the Trustees with regard thereto and provided any funds necessary for the purpose, the Trustees shall allow such rights to lapse.

12. Reconstruction and Takeover

12.1 If there is a Reconstruction or Takeover affecting Scheme Shares, each Participant shall be notified of such event and invited

Profit Sharing Trust **9.122**

to instruct the Trustees on what action to take (and, where appropriate, exercise any right to elect to receive any particular form of consideration available thereunder) in respect of any of his Scheme Shares.

12.2 In the event of any Scheme Shares being compulsorily acquired under *sections 428* to *430F* of the *Companies Act 1985*, or if under any scheme of arrangement sanctioned by the Court pursuant to *Section 425* of the *Companies Act 1985*, Scheme Shares are transferred to another company or cancelled for a consideration consisting of cash and/or shares, each Participant shall be notified of such event as soon as practicable after such acquisition, transfer or cancellation, and be invited to instruct the Trustees in relation to such consideration.

13. Dividends

13.1 In so far as any dividend consists of cash it shall be paid to the relevant Participant by the Trustees in accordance with Clause 6 of the Deed.

13.2 Where the holders of any class of shares of which some are Scheme Shares are offered the right to elect to receive shares, credited as fully paid in whole or in part, in lieu of a cash dividend (a 'scrip dividend') each Participant shall be notified of the rights relating to his Scheme Shares and invited to instruct the Trustees what action to take, which instructions may be of particular or of general application and relate to Scheme Shares appropriated before and after the relevant date of the scrip dividend. In the absence of any such instructions, the Participant shall be deemed to have elected for cash.

13.3 Any shares taken up by the Trustees on behalf of any Participant under Rule 13.2 shall not form part of the Participant's Scheme Shares to which they relate and they shall belong to the Participant, and the Trustees shall take all reasonable steps to procure that the Shares so acquired are vested in the Participant without delay.

14. Fractional entitlements

14.1 Where a company makes an offer or invitation conferring any rights upon its members to acquire against payment additional securities in that company, or where that company allots any new securities by way of capitalisation, the Trustees shall allocate such rights or securities amongst the Participants concerned on a proportionate basis and, if such allocation shall give rise to a fraction of a security or a transferable unit thereof (in this Rule 'unit'), shall round such allocation down to the next whole unit and the Trustees shall aggregate the fractions not allocated and use their best endeavours to sell any rights or units which are not allocated and distribute

9.122 *Profit Sharing Trust*

the net proceeds of sale (after deducting therefrom any expenses of sale and any taxation which may be payable in respect thereof) proportionately among the Participants whose allocation was rounded down, provided that any sum of less than £1 otherwise distributable to a particular Participant may be retained by the Trustees.

14.2 Where the Trustees having received New Shares which form part of a Participant's Scheme Shares, allocate such New Shares to the different appropriations of Scheme Shares to which they relate and, such allocation gives rise to a fraction of a New Share, they shall, subject to the Taxes Act, round such allocation up or down to the next whole unit as they, in their discretion, think fit.

15. Disposals and payments

15.1 The Trustees shall not dispose of any Scheme Shares:

(*a*) prior to the expiry of the applicable Period of Retention in any circumstances except in the event of a Reconstruction or Takeover;

(*b*) after the expiry of the applicable Period of Retention but prior to the applicable Release Date except at the written direction of a Participant; and

(*c*) after the expiry of the applicable Period of Retention but prior to the applicable Release Date except by sale for the best consideration in money reasonably obtainable at the time of such sale.

15.2 Upon receipt of a sum of money or of money's worth not consisting of New Shares being (or being part of) the proceeds of any disposal or Capital Receipt in respect of any Scheme Shares, the Trustees shall (subject to compliance with the provisions of *paragraphs 4(2)* and *7* of *Schedule 10* to the *Taxes Act*) account as soon as reasonably practicable to the Participant for any balance remaining in their hands and relating to such Scheme Shares by paying the same to the Participating Company (if any) by which he is employed, provided that any sum of less than £1 distributable to a particular Participant may be retained by the Trustees.

15.3 Any Participating Company to which the Trustees pay or account for any part of any such sum as is referred to in Rule 15.2 shall (subject to compliance with the *Taxes Act*) forthwith account to the Participant for the balance remaining in its hands.

16. Transfer of legal title

The Trustees shall transfer the legal title to any Scheme Shares into the name of the relevant Participant (or any person nominated by him in writing) as soon as reasonably practicable after the Release

Date PROVIDED THAT in the absence of any earlier direction from the Participant the Trustees shall not be bound to effect any such transfer until 90 days after the Release Date or such other period as is permitted by regulations relating to personal equity plans in force from time to time if the Trustees are or intend seeking instructions in relation to the possible transfer of such shares to the manager of a personal equity plan as permitted by such regulations.

17. Stamp duty

Any stamp duty or other expenses involved in any transfer of Shares by the Trustees shall be payable:

(*a*) in the case of a transfer into the name of the Participant concerned, by the Trustees (and reimbursed by the Company); and

(*b*) in any other case, by the transferee concerned.

18. Notices

18.1 The Trustees shall not be bound to act upon any instructions given by or on behalf of a Participant or any person in whom the beneficial interest in his Scheme Shares is for the time being vested unless such instructions are received by the Trustees in writing signed by the relevant person.

18.2 Any notice or other communication under or in connection with the Scheme may be given by personal delivery or by sending the same by post, in the case of a company to its registered office, and in the case of an individual to his last known address, or, where he is a director or employee of the Company or a Subsidiary, either to his last known address or to the address of the place of business at which he performs the whole or substantially the whole of the duties of his office or employment, and where a notice or other communication is given by first-class post, it shall be deemed to have been received 48 hours after it was put into the post properly addressed and stamped.

19. Disputes

19.1 The decision of the Board in any dispute or question affecting any Eligible Employee or Participant under the Scheme shall be final and conclusive subject to the concurrence of the Auditors whenever required under the provisions hereof.

19.2 In any matter in which they are required to act hereunder the Auditors shall be deemed to be acting as experts and not as arbitrators.

20. Terms of employment

20.1 Nothing in this Deed or the Scheme shall in any way be construed as imposing upon a Participating Company a contractual

9.122 *Profit Sharing Trust*

obligation as between the Participating Company and an employee to contribute or to continue to contribute to the Scheme.

20.2 In no circumstances shall any person who has ceased to be an employee of the Company or any Subsidiary or any Associated Company by reason of dismissal or otherwise howsoever or who is under notice of termination of his employment be entitled to claim as against any Participating Company, Subsidiary, Associated Company or the Trustees any compensation for or in respect of any consequential loss he may suffer by reason of the operation of the terms of the Scheme or of the provisions of the *Taxes Act*.

SCHEDULE TWO

Deed of Adherence

THIS DEED is made this ...... day of ...... 19 ......

BETWEEN ...... plc ('the Company') and ...... TRUSTEES LIMITED ('the Trustees') and ...... ('New Subsidiary') and is supplemental to a Trust Deed ('the Trust Deed') of the ...... Profit Sharing Scheme ('the Scheme') executed by the Company and the Trustees on the ...... 19 ......

WHEREAS:

(a) New Subsidiary was incorporated on the ...... day of ...... 19 ...... and on the ...... day of ...... 19 ...... became a Subsidiary of the Company;

(b) New Subsidiary wishes to become a Participating Company and to invite its Eligible Employees to participate in the Scheme.

NOW THIS DEED WITNESSETH as follows:

(1) Terms and expressions used in this deed of adherence shall bear unless the context otherwise requires the same meaning as in the Trust Deed.

(2) New Subsidiary agrees to become a Participating Company and to be bound by the terms of the Trust Deed and Rules of the Scheme.

IN WITNESS whereof etc.

Chapter 10

Free and Matching Offers under a Profit Sharing Scheme

Introduction

10.1 This chapter reviews step by step the procedures for making both free and matching offers under an approved profit sharing trust. A 'free offer' is an offer of free shares subject only to the usual undertakings under *TA 1988, 9 Sch 2(2)*, that is to say, to leave the scheme shares with the trustees during the period of retention etc. (see 9.78). A 'matching offer' is an offer of one or more free shares for each share purchased by the participant. The free shares will be subject to the usual undertakings under *TA 1988, 9 Sch 2(2)* and the matching shares will also be subject to similar restrictions on disposal.

Documentation

10.2 There are only two documents which are required under the legislation to make an offer under a profit sharing trust: the undertakings given by participants under *TA 1988, 9 Sch 2(2)* and a notice of appropriation issued in the name of the trustees as required by *TA 1988, 9 Sch 31*. In addition, any company which establishes a profit sharing scheme will usually also prepare:

(*a*) an offer letter and/or an application form;

(*b*) an employee guide and any other employee communications material. The undertakings to be given by participants under *TA 1988, 9 Sch 2(2)* will normally be included in the offer letter and/or application form.

10.3 There is no need for an offer letter but many companies consider that it helps personalise the offer particularly if the letters are addressed to eligible employees individually.

10.4 It is necessary for every person who participates in an offer under a profit sharing scheme trust to first give the statutory undertakings under *TA 1988, 9 Sch 2(2)*. In free offers, the undertakings can be given at the time of the first appropriation in which the

10.5 Free & Matching Offers under a Profit Sharing Scheme

participant receives shares in respect of all future appropriations so that on future appropriations undertakings need only be sought from new eligible employees.

10.5 However, in matching offers it is necessary to prepare an application form for completion by all eligible employees on each occasion as the employees will need to decide whether to buy any qualifying shares.

10.6 Companies wish to explain the scheme to participants, particularly the statutory restrictions on their disposal of shares and the income tax consequences of any early disposal or withdrawal of the shares. This may be in the form of a separate printed guide or an article in the company newspaper or staff journals. It may also take the form of a video or team briefing or a more formal presentation.

10.7 A notice of appropriation is required to contain information specifying the number and description of shares appropriated and stating their initial market value. Any notice of appropriation under a matching offer will usually contain similar information about the purchased shares. Ideally, where notice of appropriation are issued each year in respect of annual appropriations, the notice will set out the above details in respect of each year's appropriation on a cumulative basis so that it is not necessary for employees to keep previous notices of appropriation. Any notice of appropriation will also normally set out the terms of the statutory undertakings given by participants so that they have a record of this. Some notices of appropriation also contain forms for participants to complete if they wish to dispose of their shares or have the shares transferred into their own names and other forms for the participant to return in order to notify a change of address or name. Given that the profit sharing trustees will normally continue to hold the shares of former employees it is important for the trustees to ensure their records of names and addresses are kept as complete as possible.

Trustees

10.8 The part played by the trustees in any free or matching offer is as follows:

(*a*) the trustees will receive the contributions of participating companies and hold them in such form as may be authorised by the trust instrument;

(*b*) the trustees will at the direction of the company apply the contributions of participating companies in acquiring shares;

(*c*) the trustees will appropriate the shares and hold them until the release date in accordance with the terms of the scheme;

Free & Matching Offers under a Profit Sharing Scheme 10.14

(*d*) the trustees will issue notices of appropriation, maintain the scheme register, and carry out the statutory obligations referred to at 9.101 to 9.107.

10.9 Strictly speaking, the statutory undertakings required from every participant under *TA 1988, 9 Sch 2(2)* are given to the company which established the scheme rather than the trustees and so the trustees need not be involved in the aspect, but in many cases, for completeness, the trustees are joined in as additional recipients of the undertakings.

10.10 In any matching offer, the company will make the offer of shares for purchase as the trustees will not normally have the power to hold shares in the company to sell to employees. The Inland Revenue will only approve a scheme where the trust assets, whether in cash or in shares, are held only for the purpose of providing employees and directors 'benefits' in the nature of interests in shares (*TA 1988, 9 Sch 2(1)*).

10.11 The trustees will need to open a bank account to receive contributions if participating companies are to be entitled to a tax deduction for such contributions under *TA 1988, s 85*. The tax relief is only available in respect of 'sums' paid to them and it will not, therefore, be sufficient for the participating companies to pay the contributions direct to the broker purchasing the shares with a direction to buy the shares in the name of the trustees.

10.12 Under the terms of any profit sharing scheme trust, the trustees do not have any discretion in the choice of the persons who may benefit or the amount of any appropriations. Their duties are therefore mainly custodial and administrative. In most cases, the trustees will delegate the administration to professional registrars and the trustees will be involved in name only.

10.13 The question of the persons who may be appointed trustee was considered at 9.6 to 9.10. Given the limited discretions involved, there seems little point in appointing directors or other named individuals whether directors, employees, trades union representatives or anybody else and companies which propose the establishment of a scheme will generally appoint a subsidiary company or professional registrar as trustee.

10.14 Given the limited discretions exercised by the trustees, doubts may be expressed about the need for the trustees to hold meetings. However, the trustee has a responsibility to maintain complete records of the trust and its assets and to this extent any prudent trustee will ensure that all steps taken by the trustee are fully recorded.

10.15 Free & Matching Offers under a Profit Sharing Scheme

Registrars aspects

10.15 The part played by the scheme registrar in any free or matching offer is usually as follows:

(*a*) receive the companies computer tapes of eligible employees made up to the qualifying date for any particular offer comprising the following data:

   (i) surname, forenames and title;

   (ii) national insurance number;

   (iii) home address;

   (iv) any payroll or employee number;

(*b*) prepare and despatch (usually through a mailing house) all invitations and offer documentation on behalf of the company — in matching offers all eligible employees will receive offer documentation but in free offers only new eligible employees need be sent documentation;

(*c*) receive applications from eligible employees whether directly or by post or through the company;

(*d*) process applications and make up the scheme register of free shares — in a matching offer a separate sub-register of purchased shares will also need to be prepared;

(*e*) prepare and despatch dividend vouchers and payments to participants including the preparation of scrip dividend elections and receiving and processing such elections;

(*f*) despatch annual reports and accounts, interim statements and other circulars to shareholders and participants;

(*g*) prepare any letter to participants seeking voting directions at meetings of the company and receiving, processing and advising the trustees of the results of such analysis;

(*h*) prepare letters to participants seeking instructions on any rights issue or takeover offer and receive and process such instructions;

(*i*) receive instructions on behalf of the trustees to dispose of shares, transmit instructions to any brokers, receive the sale proceeds and handle payments through the PAYE scheme and pay net sale proceeds to the participant with advice on tax liabilities;

(*j*) receive instructions on behalf of the trustees to transfer shares into the participant's own name, prepare and issue a statement of the amount of tax to be paid on account and receive such tax, prepare share transfers and register transfer, handle deductions of tax through PAYE and payment of net sale proceeds to the participant with advice on tax liabilities;

Free & Matching Offers under a Profit Sharing Scheme 10.16

(k) prepare the annual scheme tax return Form P35 on behalf of the company and the Return of Shares for each participant on Form P11 for signature by the company secretary;

(l) receive and deal with the registration of all legal documents (including probates, letters of administration, powers of attorney, certificates of death or marriage and court orders);

(m) deal with enquiries from participants.

10.16 The agreement appointing the scheme registrars is normally in the form of a letter issued by the scheme registrar detailing the services to be provided and the charges which will be made for them. Few companies are in a position to enter into detailed negotiations with prospective scheme registrars to regulate the various issues which may arise in respect of their relationship. These issues are as follows:

(i) the responsibility of the scheme register to keep back up material to reconstitute the scheme register in the event the primary records are destroyed or stolen;

(ii) the responsibility of the scheme registrar to keep accounts of monies received and expended in the course of carrying out his duties and to produce these to the company and/or the trustees;

(iii) the ownership of the register and the rights of the company and/or the trustees to a return or transfer of all records on the termination of the agreement;

(iv) the period of notice required by the company and/or the trustees for the termination of the appointment as registrars and the responsibilities of the parties on termination;

(v) the obligations of confidentiality on the registrar;

(vi) the right of the registrar to sub-contract work particularly the use of mailing houses;

(vii) the obligations on the registrar to retain records and documents;

(viii) the designation of contacts in the company and/or the trustees from whom the registrar may take instructions or receive information and the extent to which such instructions can be received by telephone (if at all);

(ix) the obligation on the registrars to produce reconciliations of movements on the scheme register (and any register of purchased shares) with the trustees total holdings on the main register;

(x) the obligation on the registrar to carry out all the duties assigned to him;

(xi) a specification of the computer tapes to be used to facilitate the transfer of tapes between the company and the registrar;

(xii) the provisions as to changes in future years.

10.17 Free & Matching Offers under a Profit Sharing Scheme

10.17 Most companies, possibly justifiably, are content to rely on the reputation of their chosen scheme registrars rather than any formal agreement for the administration of their profit sharing schemes. The principal providers of this service are:

Barclays Bank plc
Bourne House
34 Beckenham Road
Beckenham
Kent BR3 4TU

Independent Registrars
  Group Limited
Balfour House
390–398 High Road
Ilford IG1 1NQ

Lloyds Bank Registrars
The Causeway
Worthing BN12 6DA

National Westminster Bank
  PLC
Registrars Department
PO Box 82, Caxton House
Redcliffe Way
Bristol BS99 7NH

Northern Registrars Limited
Northern House
Woodstone Park
Fenny Bridge
Huddersfield HD8 0LA

Royal Bank of Scotland
Registrars Department
8 Bank Head
Crossway North
Edinburgh EH11 4BR

Towers Perrin Eagle Star Share
  Plan Services Limited
PO Box 256
Cheltenham
Glos GL50 3JP

10.18 Most companies which operate profit sharing schemes believe it is more convenient if the same person acts as both main and scheme registrar, and indeed registrar of any savings-related share option scheme as well. There are a number of reasons for this. First, transfers between the scheme register and the main register can be made more easily where only one registrar is involved. Secondly, only one posting of dividend cheques or circulars to shareholders will be necessary. Thirdly, if the registrar also maintains any savings-related share option scheme register, then a single communication of details of early leavers need be made in respect of both registers.

Preparing a board proposal

10.19 Companies vary enormously in the style of papers presented to boards in relation to the operation of employees' share schemes. In presenting a proposal for a free or matching offer under a profit sharing scheme, management will normally need to deal with the following points of detail:

(a) *Timing.* Listed companies must generally comply with ABI Guidelines under which options should only be granted in the periods following an announcement of results (see 9.44). Companies which make their allocations in or about April each year

Free & Matching Offers under a Profit Sharing Scheme **10.20**

need to ensure that two annual allocations are not made in the same tax year so that the relevant limit is inadvertently exceeded when the value of the allocations is aggregated.

(b) *Eligibility and the Companies which will participate.* Any board proposal will need to set out the eligibility criteria in particular the period of service and the minimum hours of work each week. Any period of service criteria must make it clear whether employment must have been within the relevant group, or whether a period of 'continuous' service will count if it is with a business which at the qualifying date is within the relevant group. Any eligibility criteria based on any minimum number of hours worked should be calculated by reference to the number of hours the employee is required to work under his contract rather than the number of hours he actually works since this can be difficult to establish. Finally, any board proposal needs to specify the companies which will participate in the scheme. A company may need to be excluded from participating in the scheme for any offer where its employees have participated in another scheme during that tax year since participation by an individual in more than one scheme in any tax year is prohibited (*TA 1988, 9 Sch 35(2)*). Any changes in participating companies will normally need to be made in advance with a deed of adherence or other method prescribed by the scheme.

(c) *Distributable Pool.* Any board proposal will need to specify the size of the pool of profits to be distributed, or at least the maximum amount of profits available. In the case of a group scheme, this will normally be based on the consolidated profits of the holding company.

(d) *Basis of Allocation.* The possible bases of allocation are set out in 9.59 and any board proposal will need to specify the basis to be used.

(e) *Acquisition of Shares.* Any board proposal will need to specify whether the shares are to be acquired by subscription or purchase through the market and for the detailed arrangements for the purchase of those shares by brokers.

(f) *Appointment of a Committee of Directors.* It is normally sensible for the directors to delegate the detailed implementation of the proposed offer under the profit sharing scheme to an appropriate committee of directors. This will be given the power to approve the documentation and to acquire and allocate the shares.

Free offer

Making the offer

10.20 In a free offer, the company which established the scheme only needs to ensure that all eligible employees who wish to participate

10.21 *Free & Matching Offers under a Profit Sharing Scheme*

have given the statutory undertakings required by *TA 1988, 9 Sch 2(2)* before any appropriation is made.

10.21 These undertakings may be given so that they apply either to a single appropriation or to all future appropriations unless notice is given to the contrary. Obviously, where the undertakings are given in relation to a single appropriation, each eligible employee who wishes to participate will need to sign and return the form of undertaking. In other cases where the form of undertaking applies to all future appropriations then signed undertakings are only required from those employees who have not previously been eligible or who do not have signed undertakings in place at that time.

If the form of undertaking relates to a specific appropriation, it is possible to specify the exact period of retention and the release date. The following examples show the differences involved:

Form of undertaking for a single appropriation:

'In consideration of my receiving an appropriation of shares under the profit sharing scheme on [1 May 1994], I agree with the Company that:

— until [1 May 1996] (or, if earlier, until my death or I cease employment on account of injury, disability or redundancy, or until I reach 60 years of age) and except in the event of a reconstruction on takeover of the Company, I will leave the shares appropriated to me to remain in the hands of the Trustees without any assignment, charge or other disposal of my beneficial interest in such shares; and

— until [1 May 1999], any transfer of my shares out of trust shall be either by a sale by the Trustees at the best price reasonably obtainable, or by a transfer into my own name but subject to my paying a sum equal to income tax at the basic rate in respect of the initial market value of the shares.'

Form of undertaking which will be generally applicable:

'In consideration of my receiving any future appropriations of shares whilst I remain eligible or until I give written notice to the contrary, I agree with the Company that:

— during the applicable period of retention (as defined in the Scheme) and except in the event of a reconstruction or take-over of the Company, I will leave the shares appropriated to

Free & Matching Offers under a Profit Sharing Scheme **10.25**

— me to remain in the hands of the Trustees without any assignment, charge or other disposal of my beneficial interest in such shares; and

— until the applicable release date (as defined in the Scheme), any transfer of any shares out of trust shall be either by a sale by the Trustees at the best price reasonably obtainable, or by a transfer into my own name but subject to my paying a sum equal to income tax at the basic rate in respect of the initial market value of the shares.'

10.22 Other instructions which may be incorporated in the form may include directions in relation to any rights issue and any dividend mandate. The form will often also include details of eligibility, the terms and conditions of the offer and details of the availability of the scheme documents and any telephone helpline. The trustees address will also normally be included together with a 'tear off' section for notification of any change of name or address.

Cash alternatives

10.23 A number of companies offer cash profit shares as an alternative to free shares under the profit sharing scheme. The cash may be offered as an alternative to the whole or only part of the value which may be taken in the form of shares. For instance, the offer may be for £x in shares plus £y in either shares or cash as the employee may elect. Any cash element will be subject to income tax under PAYE. It will also be taken into account for the purpose of national insurance contributions.

10.24 Strictly speaking, the Revenue will not approve a profit sharing scheme if it appears to them that there are features which are neither essential nor reasonably incidental for the purpose of providing for employees and directors benefits in the nature of rights to acquire shares or interests in shares. The inclusion of a cash alternative to shares under the terms of the trust deed will render the scheme incapable of approval. However, provided the trust deed makes clear the participant's right to receive shares, and cash is only payable at the discretion of the company if the right to receive shares is in effect waived, the Inland Revenue are usually prepared to accept such arrangements as outside the profit sharing scheme. The employee will therefore be able to choose between cash and shares by giving appropriate instructions on the form which will be returned with the signed undertakings.

10.25 It is not possible for a company to operate any cash element with the benefit of the tax reliefs available for registered profit related pay schemes under *TA 1988, ss 169–184*. These schemes confer income tax relief on employees on cash payments received under a registered

10.26   *Free & Matching Offers under a Profit Sharing Scheme*

scheme on up to one-fifth of the profit related pay for the period, or £4,000 if less. However, *TA 1988, 9 Sch 6* provides that any registered scheme must contain provisions requiring that no payments are made in respect of any profit period if the employer to whom the scheme relates constitute less than 80 per cent of all the employees in the employment unit at the beginning of that profit period. Since any such requirement will inevitably conflict with the requirement under the profit sharing schemes for all eligible employees to be entitled to receive shares on similar terms, it follows that any cash alternative to shares under an approved profit sharing scheme must be outside any registered profit related pay scheme.

Problems arising from the presentation of the offer

10.26   The logical presentation of any free offer is for the directors to determine a proportion of profits to be distributed, and for eligible employees to share in this according to the applicable basis of allocation which will usually be in proportion to salary or equally amongst the employees. However, many companies prefer to present a free offer in other terms and this can often lead to unforeseen difficulties.

10.27   One of the more common ways to present a free offer is that employees will receive 'x per cent of salary'. This means that in effect the size of the distributable pool is calculated on the basis of the total of the individual entitlements, rather than the other way around. In such cases employees tend to assume that the amount shown on their notice of appropriation as the initial market value of the shares should exactly match the percentage of salary which it has been stated will be allocated. However, the tax value of the shares does not necessarily reflect the amount of profits contributed by the participating company. As explained at 9.62 to 9.64, the tax value will usually represent the value of the shares on the appropriation day regardless of the cost of acquiring the shares. Where the shares are acquired by way of subscription it is possible to acquire the shares almost contemporareously with the appropriation. This is not usually possible where shares are acquired by purchase since the shares will usually be acquired over a longer period, and a match between the cost of the shares and the market value of the shares at appropriation will be less likely.

Matching offer

Making the offer

10.28   Whilst all eligible employees will receive an appropriation of shares under any free offer, only those who purchase shares will participate in a matching offer. It is doubtful whether the Inland Revenue would have allowed matching offers had it not been for the pressure for them in early privatisations. Matching offers were made

Free & Matching Offers under a Profit Sharing Scheme 10.32

in most privatisations by way of offers for sale in the 1980s. They have also been popular amongst the UK subsidiaries of US multinationals, for instance, IBM UK Limited, which in the mid-1980s established an approved matching offer scheme under the umbrella of the US parent company's worldwide share purchase scheme. Matching offers have also become more popular amongst UK groups in place of the annual free offers or as an alternative to the sharesave scheme where there are limited shares available for subscription.

10.29 It is the Inland Revenue's practice in relation to matching offers to require that at least one free share must be appropriated for each share acquired by the employee, and that every eligible employee must be able to obtain free shares with a payment of £100 or less, or 1 per cent of his annual salary if less. These requirements are intended to ensure that employees are not discouraged from participating in the scheme by the need to provide large sums to purchase shares. There is, of course, nothing to prevent companies offering larger numbers of shares provided the above minimum 'entry fee' is available.

10.30 ABI Guidelines require that approved profit sharing schemes should only be operated once a year after the final results. This has led to UK listed companies generally making matching offers on an annual basis rather than on a continuous savings basis.

Annual 'one off' matching offers

10.31 These are based on the principle of one or more free shares for each share purchased by the employee. The offer may take various forms as follows:

(a) an offer to match any number of shares up to a specified limit;

(b) an offer to match various specified blocks of shares e.g. blocks of 50, 100, 150 shares;

(c) an offer to match at the rate of, say, 1 for 1 in respect of 50 shares and 2 for 1 in respect of 100 shares;

(d) an offer to match on any of the above bases but subject to some form of scaling down if applications to buy exceed a specified number of shares.

10.32 In certain circumstances, such as a flotation, the offer price of the shares under a matching offer cannot be established at the time preparations for the offer are made and it may, therefore, be necessary to make the offer in terms of the monetary value of shares, for instance, £50 worth of shares for every £50 worth of shares purchased.

10.33 Free & Matching Offers under a Profit Sharing Scheme

10.33 A difficulty for any company in making a matching offer is that it cannot know in advance the number of shares which will be allocated under the offer. This is because the level of take-up by employees cannot be known in advance. However, a listed company will need to comply with ABI Guidelines and ensure the value of shares allocated does not exceed the annual limit of 5 per cent of profits (see 9.72) or the limits on the number of new shares which may be made available. A company will therefore usually make any matching offer on the basis of limiting individual offers so that there will be sufficient shares to meet all applications in full if every eligible employee were to apply.

10.34 Alternatively, a matching offer can be made on the basis that employees can apply for as many shares as they wish but applications will only be guaranteed up to some specified number and excess applications will be subject to scaling down.

10.35 The level of take-up on a matching offer may vary according to the levels of earnings, the effectiveness of employee communications and the perceived attractiveness on the part of employees of investing in the company's shares. However, as a rough guide the level of take-up will normally be about 40 to 50 per cent on a one for one offer and 50 to 60 per cent on a two for one offer. Most companies will offer between £50 and £250 in such offers, usually in £50 multiples.

Continuous savings scheme

10.36 In continuous savings scheme matching offers, the usual basis is one free share for every one share purchased where employees are allowed to save 1 or 2 per cent of their pay each month.

Administration of the offer

10.37 The essence of a matching offer is that the company offers to sell a specified number of shares which, if accepted by an eligible employee, will be matched by additional free shares appropriated by the trustees. It is, therefore, unavoidable that matching offers will involve the issue of application forms to all eligible employees.

10.38 It is Inland Revenue practice that under a matching offer, the purchased shares should normally be retained by the trustees or by some other nominee for a minimum period of one year after allocation. The purpose of this is to prevent employees obtaining large allocations of shares on the back of short-term qualifying holdings. In most matching offer schemes, including in all matching offers made in privatisations, the minimum holding period has been two years rather than one. There are a number of schemes where the holding period has been substantially longer than two years. Although the shares will

Free & Matching Offers under a Profit Sharing Scheme 10.41

normally be held by the trustee of the profit sharing scheme, the Inland Revenue have no objection to the appointment of some other nominee to hold the shares including a personal equity plan manager nominated by the company. As early as 1987, Quotient plc (now owned by ACT Group plc) operated such a matching offer scheme under which the participants had to agree to leave their purchased shares in the personal equity plan for a minimum of three years. Normally, the holding of purchased shares will be relatively small and so the economics of holding them through a personal equity plan will be questionable although as the personal equity plan holding is built up over a number of years this objection will fade.

10.39 Matching offers can present problems in relation to the acquisition of the shares and the determination of their value for tax purposes. The first problem is that the number of shares to be acquired can only be ascertained once all applications are received. This may not present any difficulty where all the shares are to be provided by way of subscription since the shares will normally only be acquired shortly before appropriation. However, where the shares are to be acquired by purchase in the market, perhaps the most common means of acquiring the shares in matching offers, the trustees may need a longer period of time than the last few days before appropriation within which to acquire the shares. The trustees may need the entire offer period. In principle, the scheme could provide for shares to be provided even earlier than the offer period out of advance contributions to the profit sharing trustees but the trustees cannot be certain that these shares will be required for appropriation or even whether they will be appropriated within the period of 18 months during which capital gains tax relief is available (see 9.105). Alternatively, the company might establish an ESOP trust which acquires shares throughout the year and sells them to the profit sharing trustees for the purposes of the annual appropriation.

10.40 The second problem presented by a matching offer, particularly where existing shares are used, is in relation to the pricing of the shares to be purchased and the determination of the value of the free shares for tax purposes. Whilst most matching offers made on continuous savings basis, and a few 'annual' matching offer schemes such as BAT Industries plc, are expressed in terms of the application of specified amounts of money in buying such number of shares as may be purchased with that sum of money at the market price on a particular date, the vast majority of matching offers are expressed in terms of 'buy 1 at a specified price and get 1 or more free'. In short, the participants in most schemes will know the offer price of the shares at the time they apply for the shares.

10.41 Normally, the offer price will be based on the market price of the company's shares shortly before invitations are issued. For tax purposes, the value of the free shares will be fixed at the same value as the offer price of the shares.

10.42 *Free & Matching Offers under a Profit Sharing Scheme*

10.42 Alternatively, the scheme may provide for the tax value of the free shares to be fixed by reference either to the market price of the shares at the time of appropriation or the average cost of the shares. Neither formula is satisfactory since the tax value will normally differ from the offer price which will be confusing to employees. Certainly there is little point in fixing the tax value by reference to the cost to the trustees of acquiring the shares since this will have no relevance to employees who are buying shares at a particular offer price.

10.43 Strictly speaking, a matching offer will usually only become a binding legal contract on the date the company accepts applications. This will often be some time after the date of invitation. It is possible, therefore, that at the time the company accepts applications the market value of the shares may have appreciated compared to the offer price. In short, by the time of the company's acceptance of applications, the offer price may represent an undervalue. Any acquisition of shares at an undervalue is under general principles subject to income tax under *Schedule E* as 'moneys worth' (*Weight v Salmon HL (1935) 19 TC 174 HC*). Although in practice the Inland Revenue do not appear to pursue this potential liability to tax particularly where the shares are purchased within 30 days of the date (i.e. the offer date) by reference to which the offer price was fixed, there is no defence for employees against any assessment. Given that the company is under an obligation within 30 days of the end of the tax year to give written particulars of any shares or interests in shares acquired by employees by reason of their employment under *FA 1988, s 85(1)*, companies should give a warning in employee communications material that any undervalue may be assessed even though it is only based on an appreciation in value of the shares over the offer period.

10.44 There is a further tax complication which arises in relation to the purchased shares. As noted above, the Inland Revenue require such shares to be held by the trustees or some other nominee for a period of at least one year although most companies usually require at least two years. This will usually mean that a participant will, in relation to his purchased shares, give similar undertakings to the trustees to those given in relation to his free shares. This also includes an undertaking to leave the shares with the trustees for at least two years or, if earlier, until he leaves employment with a participating company by reason of injury, disability, redundancy, or until he reaches retirement age. This gives rise to the question of whether any premature cessation of the restriction on disposing of the shares before the normal expiry of such period of retention will be liable to tax in respect of the accrual of value to the shares by virtue of *FA 1988, s 78(1)*. This provides that a person who acquires shares or an interest in shares shall be chargeable to income tax if a chargeable event occurs in relation to the shares at a time he has a beneficial interest

Free & Matching Offers under a Profit Sharing Scheme 10.48

in such shares. A 'chargeable event' is any increase in the value of shares as a result of (amongst other things) the removal of a restriction to which the shares are subject. It would appear that the premature removal of the restriction on sale by reason of the employee's unforeseen cessation of employment (injury, disability or redundancy) does give rise to an increase in the value of the shares although the valuation of this accrual of value will need to be agreed with Shares Valuation Division of the Inland Revenue. This will normally be valued on the basis of discount for the number of years between the cessation of employment and the expiry of the period of retention in respect of the shares. For instance, if the cessation of employment arises at least one year before the normal expiry date, then the value of the restricted shares immediately before that event might be agreed as the open market value of the shares less a discount representing one year's interest at current rates. If, therefore, current interest rates were 10 per cent then arguably the value of the shares immediately before the restriction is lifted is 90 per cent of the open market value.

10.45 The main point, however, is that a liability to tax under *FA 1988, s 78(1)* arises regardless of any disposal of the shares. It arises as a result of the lifting of the restrictions on the cessation of employment for injury, disability or redundancy (but not normal retirement since this is always foreseen).

10.46 Any potential tax liability can be avoided by providing for a fixed period of retention without any premature expiry of the period upon an employee leaving on account of any unforeseen event, namely, injury, disability or redundancy.

10.47 Alternatively, the trustees might be given a discretion to waive the restriction upon the employee leaving for any reason. The trustees would presumably only exercise this discretion if they are satisfied the participant wishes to dispose of his shares and is prepared to bear any tax liability which will arise on the premature removal of the restriction.

Registration of the purchased shares

10.48 The free shares which are appropriated under the profit sharing scheme must be registered in the name of the trustee. Any purchased shares in a matching offer may be registered in the name of the trustee, any nominee or even the employee's personal equity plan manager. The purchased shares may even be registered in the name of the participant and the certificates merely lodged with the trustee. This will mean that dividends will be payable direct to the participant with any tax voucher and the employee will be able to attend meetings of the company in his own right. Any circulars to

10.49 *Free & Matching Offers under a Profit Sharing Scheme*

shareholders and annual reports would also be sent direct to the participants.

Timetable

10.49   The timetable for an appropriation is as follows:

(*a*)   create computer tape with details of eligible employees to be kept updated up to appropriation;

(*b*)   open trustee bank account;

(*c*)   board meeting to approve:

    (i) operation of scheme;

    (ii) distributable pool of profits;

    (iii) eligibility (hours per week and period of qualifying service);

    (iv) basis of allocation (by reference to salary/length of service/equally/linked to a matching offer);

    (v) if linked to a matching offer:

        (A)   the terms of the offer (including the minimum and maximum contribution and the amounts in which applications can be made);

        (B)   fix price of purchased shares (if any);

        (C)   whether retention period is for two years;

    (vi) the appropriation timetable;

    (vii) whether trustee is to subscribe and/or purchase shares;

    (viii) appointment of a committee of any two directors to:

        (A)   fix subscription price of shares;

        (B)   fix price of purchased shares (if any);

        (C)   approve and authorise amendments to scheme documentation and the issue of application forms;

(*d*)   decide whether invitation will be:

    (i)   pre-named; or

    (ii) delivered to home addresses by Company or Registrar; or

    (iii) delivered internally;

(*e*)   review documentation with Registrar;

(*f*)   approve design of documentation and proof documents;

(*g*)   submit any revised documentation to Revenue for approval;

(*h*)   announcement of final results;

Free & Matching Offers under a Profit Sharing Scheme 10.49

(i) despatch explanatory guide and covering letter to all eligible employees announcing operation of scheme;

(j) notify trustee of appropriation timetable;

(k) employee presentations;

(l) powers of attorney available;

(m) committee of any two directors fixes price of purchased shares (if relevant) by reference to middle market quotation on day before application forms issued and authorises issue of letters;

(n) application forms issued to all eligible employees;

(o) brokers confirm middle market quotation for shares and committee of any two directors confirm this as acquisition price to trustees;

(p) company and participating companies make contribution to trustee for acquisition of shares;

(q) trustee subscribes for shares;

(r) company issues and allots shares to trustee and applies for listing;

(s) trustee appropriates shares;

(t) trustee issues notices of allocation to all participants.

Chapter 11

Subsidiary Company Profit Sharing Scheme

Introduction

11.1 A company which establishes a profit sharing scheme may use the shares of its holding company in the scheme provided the conditions of *TA 1988, 9 Sch 10–12, 14* are satisfied.

11.2 In particular, *paragraph 10* provides that shares forming part of the ordinary share capital of a company which has control of the company which established the scheme may be used as scheme shares in an approved scheme.

Single subsidiary schemes

11.3 A single subsidiary scheme is where a subsidiary establishes an approved profit sharing scheme using the shares of its parent company. The subsidiary may admit members of its own group into the scheme, but there remains only one distributable pool of profits and a common basis of allocation.

11.4 The most common situation in which a single subsidiary scheme will be established is where a UK subsidiary of a foreign parent establishes a scheme using the shares of the parent company. There are few cases of a non-listed UK subsidiary establishing a scheme using the shares of its UK listed parent as this is contrary to the ABI Guidelines (see 3.39 except in the exceptional circumstances mentioned in the 1987 ABI Guidelines, paragraph 14).

11.5 Even though the initiative for establishing such schemes will usually have been taken by the subsidiary, the approval of the parent will be required for the establishment of the scheme whether in passing a resolution of the subsidiary to establish the scheme or by giving a more informal approval.

11.6 The parent company may wish to retain control over the operation of certain aspects of the scheme and will therefore normally be brought in as a party to the trust deed, and its written approval

11.7 *Subsidiary Company Profit Sharing Scheme*

for the exercise by the subsidiary of specified powers and discretions will be necessary. Some of the matters over which the parent company may wish to exercise control are as follows:

(*a*) the making of offers;

(*b*) the size of the distributable pool and the determination of profits;

(*c*) the basis of allocation;

(*d*) the shares to be used in the scheme;

(*e*) changes to the scheme.

11.7 Schemes established by UK subsidiaries using parent company shares will usually be operated using existing shares purchased through the local overseas stock market.

11.8 Generally speaking, any scheme using new shares to be issued by a foreign listed company is likely to need the approval of shareholders in some form or other. Many US multinational company share purchase plans incorporate a general authority to establish similar arrangements overseas and this can sometimes be invoked as authority for establishing a UK approved profit sharing scheme as a sub-plan to the main international plan.

11.9 The involvement of the parent company in the operation of the scheme will be inevitable where new shares are to be newly issued. The trustees will subscribe for the shares in the appropriate local currency.

Multi-subsidiary schemes

11.10 A multi-subsidiary scheme is where different sub-groups establish separate schemes each using the shares of the parent company. Each 'satellite' scheme will have its separate distributable pool and basis of allocation. It may have different eligibility criteria and be operated independently at different times. There is no need for each scheme to be operated independently, it is merely that there is the power to do so; in practice, the 'satellite' schemes may be operated together in parallel as if they were a single scheme.

11.11 A multi-subsidiary scheme is appropriate for a conglomerate group in which different operating divisions are organised as separate sub-groups. There are various advantages in multi-subsidiary schemes for such conglomerates:

(*a*) there is greater operational flexibility in that different sub-groups can decide whether to operate their scheme in any particular year;

Subsidiary Company Profit Sharing Scheme 11.15

(b) different sub-groups can decide the appropriate size of the distributable pool, the appropriate basis of allocation and even the appropriate eligibility criteria;

(c) the existence of separate trusts for each sub-group means that the trustee administration of the scheme for any sub-group can be transferred to any purchaser. Thus avoiding the need for the vendor to continue bearing the costs of administration until all scheme shares are released.

11.12 There are objections which have sometimes been put forward to multi-subsidiary schemes, normally, greater complexity and greater costs. However, neither of these objections are substantiated. Obviously, if six separate schemes are to be established instead of one, there will be a greater amount of documentation but each of the subsidiary company schemes will usually have identical provisions except for the name of the subsidiary. Often there may be a separate parent company or head office scheme and this will, of course, have different terms since instead of joining the parent company as a third party in the scheme of one of its subsidiaries, the parent company will in such a case be the company establishing the scheme.

11.13 Consequently, any parent company scheme will simply be a standard profit sharing scheme; each 'satellite' scheme will incorporate the various restrictions on the relevant subsidiaries' exercise of their powers and discretions under the scheme.

11.14 Each 'satellite' scheme will normally incorporate the requirement on the subsidiary to obtain the prior approval of the parent company to any operation of the scheme, any determination of the size of the distributable pool or choice of the basis of allocation. Even if the documentation is more voluminous, it will not involve greater complexity. Obviously, the multiplication of schemes means that separate scheme registers will be needed, but this is unlikely to add significantly, if at all, to the administration costs. Each of the schemes can operate using a standard package of ancillary documents and employee guide. It is unusual, and certainly unnecessary, for any of the main features which may vary between different sub-schemes, the size of the distributable pool, the basis of allocation and the timing of appropriations to be set out in any employee guide.

11.15 One point which does need to be taken into account in multi-subsidiary schemes is the prohibition in *TA 1988, 9 Sch 35(2)* on participation in the same tax year of the approved share schemes of two or more group companies. If employees are transferred from one sub-group to another, then the application form should include a declaration by the employee that he has not participated in any other group scheme in the same tax year.

11.16 *Subsidiary Company Profit Sharing Scheme*

11.16 In the writer's view, multi-subsidiary schemes offer greater flexibility than single schemes for conglomerates, or other diverse groups, not only in terms of operating the scheme, but in particular in achieving administrative savings in the event of any disposal of a sub-group. Multi-subsidiary schemes have been established by a number of groups, for instance, Virgin, Caradon and BAT Industries.

Chapter 12

Takeovers, Reconstructions, Demergers and Dividends

Takeovers

12.1 Most employees' share schemes make some provision for the takeover of the company whose shares are used under the scheme. This is necessary to protect participants who might otherwise find that after a takeover they retain shares in a company which has become a dormant subsidiary and are therefore much less valuable. In a share option scheme, express provision needs to be made to protect the position of optionholders. On the other hand, in profit sharing schemes, the trustees already hold the shares and are, therefore, in a position to accept any offer which is made to shareholders generally.

Share purchase agreement v general offer

12.2 A takeover can be effected in one of two ways:

(a) by a share purchase agreement entered into by all the selling shareholders which is, therefore, normally only practicable where the offer is made for a private company with a limited number of shareholders;

(b) a 'general offer' for the shares not already owned by the offeror (or his associates) and which will usually be expressed to be conditional upon (amongst other things) the acceptance of the offer by a majority of the ordinary shareholders such as to give the offeror control.

12.3 The Inland Revenue's Model Schemes for approved executive and savings-related share option schemes deal with the rights of optionholders on a 'general offer' rather than a share purchase agreement. However, it appears that the Inland Revenue will in practice treat share purchase agreements as a 'general offer' provided identical terms are available to all shareholders of the same class. There is even a precedent for the Inland Revenue treating share purchase agreements as a 'general offer' even though the form, but not the value, of the consideration for each share to be acquired varied between different

12.4 Takeovers, Reconstructions, Demergers and Dividends

shareholders. Even if the Inland Revenue shows admirable flexibility in interpreting the term 'general offer', it is still preferable for the share option schemes of private companies to be drafted allowing for rights of exercise upon any 'change of control' rather than a general offer becoming unconditional.

Listed companies and the Takeover Code

12.4 The Takeover Code applies to offers for all listed companies. It also applies to offers for unlisted public companies considered by the Takeover Panel to be resident in the United Kingdom, the Channel Islands or the Isle of Man and to certain private companies considered to be so resident where for certain periods in the previous ten years the company has been subject to public marketing arrangements. The Takeover Code lays down both principles and procedural rules relating to all takeover and merger transactions including full takeover offers, partial offers, offers by a parent company for shares in a subsidiary and certain other transactions where control is to be obtained or consolidated.

12.5 Under General Principle 1 of the Takeover Code all shareholders of the same class of an offeree company must be treated similarly by an offeror. There is therefore no scope for an offeror to treat the trustee of an approved profit sharing scheme, or for that matter any other employee benefit trust, differently to other shareholders of the same class.

12.6 Under Rule 15 of the Takeover Code, where an offer is made for equity share capital and the offeree company has any options outstanding, the offeror must make 'an appropriate offer or proposal' to the holders of options to ensure that their interests are safeguarded. The Takeover Code requires 'equality of treatment' and the board of the offeree company must obtain competent advice on the offer or proposal and the substance of the advice made known to optionholders. In addition, details of the offer in respect of options should be despatched to the holders at the same time as the offer is despatched to shareholders, but if this is not practicable then, after consultation with the Takeover Panel, the document should be despatched as soon as possible thereafter. A copy of the offer or proposal should be lodged with the Takeover Panel at the time of issue.

12.7 Rule 21 of the Takeover Code prohibits a company, without the approval of shareholders in general meeting, from (amongst other things) granting options in respect of any unissued shares either during the course of an offer, or even before the date of an offer, if the offeree has reason to believe that a bona fide offer may be imminent. Note 7 to Rule 21 provides that where the offeree company proposes to grant options over shares, the timing and level of which are in accordance with its normal practice under an established share option scheme, the Takeover Panel will normally waive the need for shareholders' approval.

Share option schemes

12.8 There are three ways in which the rights of optionholders can be dealt with on a takeover offer:

(a) by exercise of the option so that the optionholder can accept the takeover offer;

(b) by a roll-over of options i.e. release of the existing option in consideration of the grant of a replacement option of equivalent value over the shares of the offeror;

(c) by a release of the option for a cash consideration.

Exercise and acceptance of the offer

12.9 The obligation under the Takeover Code which requires an offeror to make 'an appropriate offer or proposal' to optionholders (see 12.6) is invariably interpreted as, amongst other things, allowing optionholders to exercise any rights of exercise they may have, and then accepting the takeover offer.

Savings-related share option schemes

12.10 Whether an optionholder under an approved savings-related share option scheme will be able to exercise his option and accept the takeover offer depends on the precise terms of the scheme rules. The legislation relating to approved savings-related share option schemes allows schemes to provide for the exercise of options during (amongst other things):

(a) the six months following a change of control as a result of a general offer becoming unconditional; and

(b) during any period in which an offeror is bound or entitled to acquire shares in a company following the acquisition of 90 per cent of its shares under *CA 1985, ss 428–430*.

The scheme rules may provide for a shorter period for the exercise of options following the takeover offer becoming unconditional, but in no circumstances may the scheme rules provide for a longer period of exercise nor may the right of exercise commence earlier. As mentioned at 12.2 above, it appears to be Inland Revenue practice to allow an exercise of options even if the takeover takes the form of a share purchase agreement rather than a general offer provided all shareholders are treated in the same manner.

12.11 Takeovers, Reconstructions, Demergers and Dividends

Executive share option schemes

12.11 In the case of an approved executive share option scheme, there are no rules laid down in the legislation for the periods during which options are exercisable in the event of a takeover. In practice, however, most schemes allow for similar periods as under savings-related share option schemes.

Income tax on option gains

12.12 Gains arising on the exercise of options following a takeover under both approved savings-related and executive share option schemes are subject to income tax where the exercise takes place within three years of the grant of the option concerned (*TA 1988, 9 Sch (4)(5)*). In addition, gains arising on the exercise of approved executive share options within three years of any previous tax-exempt exercise of an option by that optionholder will be subject to income tax even if more than three years have passed since the grant of the option.

12.13 An optionholder who accepts a takeover offer will normally be able to accept any of the choices of consideration open to shareholders whether this is cash, shares in the offeror, loan notes in the offeror or otherwise. This means that if a particular form of consideration — say any cash alternative — is only open to shareholders who accept the offer until a specified date which falls before the offer has become unconditional in all respects, the optionholders will be deprived of the opportunity to elect for that particular form of consideration. However, an optionholder will be able to obtain that particular form of consideration by exercising his option and without accepting the offer. Assuming the shares arising on the exercise of the option are compulsorily acquired under the provisions of *CA 1985, s 429*, the optionholder will be entitled to elect for any particular form of consideration which was originally available to shareholders under the offer (*CA 1985, s 430(3)(4)*).

Roll-overs of options

12.14 Roll-overs of approved options were introduced in 1987 as an alternative to the exercise of options and acceptance of any takeover offer. A roll-over involves an offer by the acquiring company to grant replacement options upon the release of the existing options in the target company. The replacement options may be granted over shares in any company in the acquiring company's group. It follows, of course, that unincorporated offerors cannot offer a roll-over facility. An offeror which is under the control of a private company can only offer to replace the existing options by replacement options over its

Takeovers, Reconstructions, Demergers and Dividends   12.16

ultimate parent if the ultimate parent is so willing (which usually it is not).

12.15 There were three main reasons for the introduction of the roll-over facility. First, where a company with an approved scheme was taken over by a private company then the scheme shares in that company would immediately cease to satisfy the requirements of *TA 1988, 9 Sch 11* viz the schemes shares were in a company which has under the control of another company which was not quoted. As a result, any approved option over the shares in that company arguably ceased to be exercisable since the option is no longer subsisted over shares which satisfied the provisions of *TA 1988, 9 Sch 10–14*. The solution adopted was to allow a roll-over of options into the shares of a company in the acquiring group assuming those shares satisfy the provisions of *TA 1988, 9 Sch 10–14*. This is, therefore, the only way in which rights of exercise can be preserved in a takeover by a private company or any foreign company whose shares are not listed on a recognised stock exchange. The second reason for the introduction of roll-overs in approved schemes was to avoid the premature income tax charge which arises under both approved executive and savings-related share option schemes where options are exercised early i.e. within three years of the date of grant or, in the case of an approved executive share option scheme, three years of the date on which that optionholder last exercised an approved option in tax-exempt circumstances (see 5.77 above). The third reason for the introduction of roll-overs relates specifically to savings-related share option schemes. In such schemes, optionholders are restricted on an early exercise of options to acquiring only such number of shares as may be purchased with their accumulated savings and interest at the date of exercise. An early exercise of options, therefore, has the effect that optionholders will lose the opportunity to realise the accrued gains on the shares to the extent the savings contract is incomplete. The point of a roll-over of options, therefore, is to allow the optionholder to continue saving until the bonus date and, therefore, eventually realise the gains on all the shares assuming, of course, that the shares under option retain their value between the date of the roll-over and the eventual bonus date.

12.16 The facility for a roll-over only applies where:

(a) the acquiring company obtains control of the company whose shares are held in the scheme as a result of making a general offer to acquire either (i) all the issued ordinary share capital of the company which is made on a condition such that if it is satisfied the offeror will have control or (ii) all the shares of the same class as the shares used in the scheme;

(b) the acquiring company obtains control of a company whose shares are scheme shares in pursuance of a compromise or

12.17 *Takeovers, Reconstructions, Demergers and Dividends*

arrangement sanctioned by the court under *CA 1985, s 425* (or the equivalent Northern Ireland provisions);

(c) the acquiring company becomes bound or entitled under *CA 1985, ss 428–430* to acquire shares in a company whose shares are used under the scheme.

12.17 The maximum period during which the offer to roll-over options may be made available by the offeror is:

(a) where a general offer has become unconditional, six months;

(b) where the court sanctions a scheme or arrangement under *CA 1985, s 425*, six months;

(c) where the offeror's rights of acquisition under *CA 1985, ss 428–430* are invoked, during the period the offeror is bound or entitled to acquire the shares of the dissenting shareholders.

12.18 The shares offered under the replacement option must satisfy the conditions of *TA 1988, 9 Sch 10–14* (see 4.36 to 4.46).

12.19 The replacement option is governed by the rules of the target company scheme — it is therefore immaterial whether the offeror has any share option scheme. The replacement option must be 'equivalent' to the existing option. The total amount payable on exercise of the replacement option must be identical to the total amount payable under the existing option. The total market value of the shares under the replacement option must be equivalent to the total market value of the existing option immediately before the time of release. Where the shares in the offeror and the target company are both quoted on a recognised stock exchange and the offer is in the form of a share for share offer, then the basis of exchange of shares available to shareholders will be accepted by the Inland Revenue as 'equivalent' value and the offeror company need only notify the Board of Inland Revenue of the proposed basis of exchange; the question of valuation will not be referred to Shares Valuation Division. In all other cases, the basis of exchange must be considered by Shares Valuation Division on the basis of the market values of the shares. An appropriate basis of exchange will be agreed for a limited period which will usually be a maximum of 30 days. When applying to the Board of Inland Revenue for approval of any basis of exchange the Inland Revenue will normally require the following documents:

- the offer documentation

- a declaration given by the Secretary of the offeror company in respect of the scheme shares that they will conform to *TA 1988, 9 Sch 10–14*

- a copy of the Articles of Association of the company whose

Takeovers, Reconstructions, Demergers and Dividends 12.23

shares will be used in the scheme if the Inland Revenue have not previously reviewed them.

12.20 The tax treatment of any roll-over under an approved share option scheme (including a savings-related share option scheme) is as follows:

(a) *Income Tax.* The replacement option is treated as granted at the same time as the old option was granted, with the result that income tax will only be payable on the exercise of the replacement option in the same circumstances as applied to the old option. In practical terms this means that exercise rights and lapse provisions will be measured not from the date of the replacement option, but the date of the original option. Even if there were no express statutory provisions in *TA 1988, 9 Sch 15(4)* overriding any income tax charges at the time of the roll-over of options, *TA 1988, s 136(1)* would still have the same effect;

(b) *Capital Gains Tax.* The release of the old option in consideration of the grant of a replacement option at a lower price is, in principle, a disposal of a chargeable asset (the old option) for the purposes of capital gains tax. This is because the surrender of rights is treated as a disposal for the purpose of *TCGA 1992, s 22(1) (c).* The proceeds of the disposal is the value which accrues to the optionholder as a result of his receiving an option to buy shares at a price which is less than their current market value. However, relief is provided in *TCGA, s 238(4)* which provides for a roll-over in respect of the options so that the replacement option is treated as the same asset as the old option.

12.21 Under the *Finance Act 1987*, companies were allowed two years until 31 July 1989 to alter schemes so that roll-over provisions applied to subsisting options. Since 1 August 1989, any alteration to a scheme to allow a roll-over only applies in respect of options granted after the date of the Revenue's approval of the alteration of the scheme.

Surrender of an option for a cash consideration

12.22 The offers made to optionholders on a takeover will often include an offer to surrender their options in consideration of the payment of cash equal to any accrued gain.

12.23 The offer must be made by or on behalf of the offeror, not the target company. The reason for this is that where the payment is made by the target company, the Inland Revenue will regard this as a feature of the scheme which is 'neither essential nor reasonably incidental to the purpose of providing for employees and directors

12.24 *Takeovers, Reconstructions, Demergers and Dividends*

benefits in the nature of rights to acquire shares . . .' contrary to *TA 1988, 9 Sch 2(1)*.

12.24 In a letter to professional advisers dated 6 February 1991, the Inland Revenue accepted that a target company will often wish to advise and make recommendations to its optionholders about the various offers made by an offeror company and has indicated that it will not treat the provision of such advice and recommendations as an unacceptable feature of the scheme which might cause loss of Inland Revenue approval. In practice, the Inland Revenue will normally also accept the target company making the offers to its optionholders on behalf of the offeror. The Inland Revenue will treat any payments made by the trustees of an employee benefit trust which has a close relationship with the target company in the same way as if they were made by the company which established the scheme.

Taxation

12.25 Any sum received by an optionholder for the surrender of his option will be chargeable to income tax under Schedule E by virtue of *TA 1988, s 135(1)*. The tax charge is based on the whole of the sum received less any sum paid for the grant of the option or for its surrender. The surrender of the option is also treated as a disposal of a chargeable asset (the option) for capital gains tax, but as the amount brought into charge to income tax will be taken into account in computing the amount of any chargeable gain, no gain will in practice arise.

12.26 Where a payment is made by an offeror (or its receiving bank as agent) as consideration for the release of an option, the Inland Revenue does not in practice seek to collect tax through PAYE since the offeror will not know the employee's tax circumstances sufficient to give the appropriate tax allowances (see *Booth v Mirror Group Newspapers plc* [*1992*] STC 615 where the whole of the sum was chargeable to tax, and *IRC v Herd* [*1992*] STC 264). However, if the payment is made by the employer, PAYE would have to be operated on the whole of the payment chargeable to tax under Schedule E.

Profit sharing schemes

12.27 The basic point about a profit sharing scheme is that the scheme shares are retained by trustees subject to various restrictions on disposal. Where there is a takeover offer or reconstruction which is treated as a 'reorganisation' for capital gains tax purposes (i.e. the shareholders are entitled to a roll-over) then the legislation treats the new holding as substituted for the original shares and held accordingly under the terms of the profit sharing scheme. To the extent any such transaction is not treated as a reorganisation, it will usually be treated

Takeovers, Reconstructions, Demergers and Dividends 12.31

as a disposal of scheme shares (for instance, a cash offer for the shares), or possibly a capital receipt if the original shares have been retained and the receipt represents a capital distribution not subject to income tax e.g. an exempt demerger distribution of shares.

Takeover offers: relaxation of the trustees' obligations

12.28 *TA 1988, 9 Sch 2(2)* provides that under an approved profit sharing scheme each participant must agree that (amongst other things):

(a) during the period of retention, he will leave the shares with the trustees (*paragraph 2(2)(a)*) and he will not dispose of the beneficial interest in the shares (*paragraph 2(2)(b)*);

(b) prior to the release date, any directions he gives the trustees to sell the shares will be for the best consideration in money that can reasonably be obtained at the time of the sale (*paragraph 2(2)(d)*).

12.29 *TA 1988, 10 Sch 1(1)* provides that the above obligations shall not prevent the participant from directing the trustees in respect of his schemes shares:

(a) to accept a *cash offer* with or without any offer of shares, loan notes or other securities, if the offer forms part of a general offer which is made to the holders of the relevant class of share such that, if it is satisfied, the offeror will obtain control of the company (within the meaning of *TA 1988, s 416 (TA 1988, 10 Sch 1(1)(c)*);

(b) to accept an offer of a *new holding* (shares or loan notes) provided the transaction is treated as a 'reorganisation' for capital gains tax purposes (*paragraph 1(1)(a)*) — see 12.32 to 12.40.

Trustees' circular

12.30 As a matter of general trust law, the trustees should seek the directions of the participants in relation to any takeover offer or proposed scheme of arrangement and most trust deeds provide accordingly. This will normally involve the trustees sending copies of any offer or proposal document to shareholders to participants, together with an explanatory note, seeking their directions in writing by a date shortly before the closing date of the offer or proposal.

Cash offer

12.31 If trustees accept a cash offer for the participant's scheme shares, the participant is treated as making a disposal of those shares.

12.32 *Takeovers, Reconstructions, Demergers and Dividends*

The participant will be chargeable to income tax under Schedule E for the tax year in which the disposal takes place on the appropriate percentage of the locked-in-value of the shares, or on the disposal proceeds if less (*TA 1988, s 186(4)(6)*). For further information on the income tax treatment of disposals of scheme shares, see 9.81 to 9.84.

In addition, the participant will also be liable to capital gains tax on any chargeable gains which accrue on the disposal. A chargeable gain will arise to the extent the value of the cash offer exceeds the original market value of the shares at the time of appropriation.

Share consideration

12.32 Where a takeover offer is made involving a share consideration for the shares acquired, the transaction will be treated as a 'reorganisation' for capital gains tax purposes if the conditions of *TCGA 1992, s 135* apply, *viz*:

(*a*) the issuer holds, or in consequence of the exchange will hold, more than 25 per cent of the ordinary share capital of the target company; or

(*b*) the issuer issues the shares pursuant to a general offer for the whole of the issued share capital of the company (or all the shares of the relevant class) which is made in the first instance on a condition that, if it were satisfied, the issuer would have control of the target company; or

(*c*) the issuer holds, or will in consequence of the exchange hold, the greater part of the voting power in the target company.

Given that any takeover offer will normally involve the acquisition of at least 51 per cent of the ordinary share capital of the company, there will not usually be any difficulty in establishing that any takeover offer will be treated as a 'reorganisation' for capital gains tax purposes.

12.33 Assuming the takeover offer is treated as a 'reorganisation' for capital gains tax purposes, the trustee will be treated, after the time of such reorganisation, as holding the 'new holding' on the basis that:

(*a*) there was no disposal of the original holding as a result of the exchange (*TA 1988, 10 Sch 5(4)(a)*);

(*b*) the new holding is treated as if it were appropriated under the scheme at the time of the original holding (*TA 1988, 10 Sch 5(4)(b)*);

(*c*) the conditions related to scheme shares under *TA 1988, 9 Sch 10–12, 14*, are treated as satisfied with respect to the new shares as if they were (or were treated as) satisfied with respect to the original holding.

Takeovers, Reconstructions, Demergers and Dividends 12.36

12.34 Following any 'reorganisation' it is necessary, unless the new shares are a 'mirror image' of the old shares, to apportion the locked-in-value of the old holding amongst the new holding after the reconstruction.

Example 1

The old holding comprised 150 shares with an aggregate initial value of £300 (£2 per share). After the reorganisation, the new holding comprises 200 shares: the aggregate locked-in-value remains £300, but each new share will have a locked-in-value of £1.50 per share.

Where the new holding comprises two or more securities with different rights to the old shares (e.g. an offer of three ordinary shares and one preference share for every one old share) then the locked-in-value for each old share must be apportioned on the basis of the relative market values of the new shares immediately following the reorganisation.

Example 2

The old holding comprised 150 shares with an aggregate initial market value of £300 (£2 per share). After the reorganisation, the new holding comprises:

— 200 new ordinary shares in the offeror worth £2 each (£400 in aggregate)

— 100 new preference shares in the offeror worth 50p each (£50 in aggregate)

The locked-in-value will, therefore, be apportioned as follows:

200 new ordinary shares:

$$\frac{(£300)}{(£200)} \times \frac{(£400)}{(£450)} = £1.33 \text{ each}$$

50 new preference shares:

$$\frac{(£300)}{(£50)} \times \frac{(£50)}{(£450)} = £0.67 \text{ each}$$

12.35 If, as will usually be the case, there are shares comprised in the old holding with different appropriation prices (because they were appropriated at different times) then the apportionment of the locked-in-value must be made on each appropriation separately.

12.36 To the extent the participant takes both cash and shares for an original holding, the rules set out in 12.31 will apply to the cash and the rules set out in 12.32 to 12.34 will apply to the shares.

12.37 *Takeovers, Reconstructions, Demergers and Dividends*

Loan note consideration

12.37 Many takeover offers provide a loan note alternative to cash on the basis of £1 nominal of loan notes for every £1 cash available. In some cases the loan notes may even be convertible into shares of the offeror. Almost any loan note denominated in sterling on normal commercial terms and issued since 13 March 1984 will be a 'qualifying corporate bond' (*TCGA 1992, s 117*).

12.38 Where the consideration available in a takeover offer includes a 'qualifying corporate bond', any exchange of securities has not until *FA 1994, s 101* been treated as a 'reorganisation' for capital gains tax purposes.

12.39 Under *TA 1988, 10 Sch 5A* (as altered by *FA 1994, s 101*), the inclusion of a 'qualifying corporate bond' in the consideration for a takeover offer will not prevent the transaction being treated, so far as a participant in a profit sharing scheme is concerned, as a 'reorganisation' for capital gains tax purposes with the result that the 'qualifying corporate bond' may be held as part of the participant's new holding. Such treatment is only available in schemes approved on or after 3 May 1994 or in old schemes which are amended after that date.

12.40 Otherwise the trustees can only be directed to accept a loan note consideration if reliance is placed on *TA 1988, 10 Sch 1(1)(c)*, that is to say, the loan notes are available in part with a cash consideration. *TA 1988, 10 Sch 1(1)(c)* allows a participant to direct the trustees to 'accept an offer of cash, with or without other assets, for his shares'. The loan notes are 'other assets' and, therefore, a participant can direct the trustees to accept an offer if part cash, however small in amount, and part loan notes, even though an offer of loan notes alone could not be accepted within the scheme. Any 'qualifying corporate bond' which is received without the benefit of a roll-over is treated as a 'capital receipt'. The 'qualifying corporate bond' must be transferred to the scheme participants directly outside the scheme.

Schemes of arrangement

Share options schemes

12.41 Most share option schemes deal with the rights of optionholders upon a scheme of arrangement sanctioned by the courts under *CA 1985, s 425*.

12.42 A scheme of arrangement which is to be sanctioned by the court under *CA 1985, s 425* involves three stages:

(*a*)   the approval of shareholders by means of a special resolution;

Takeovers, Reconstructions, Demergers and Dividends **12.47**

(*b*) the sanctioning of the scheme by the court;

(*c*) the filing of the scheme with the Companies Registration Office at which point the scheme becomes effective.

12.43 *TA 1988, 9 Sch 21(1) (b)* allows optionholders under approved savings-related share option schemes to exercise their options within six months of the sanctioning of the scheme by the court; executive share option schemes may contain more flexible provisions. A roll-over facility may be included in both types of scheme in accordance with *TA 1988, 9 Sch 15* if the scheme of arrangement involves a change of control (see 12.16).

12.44 Although the legislation specifically provides for a right of exercise under savings-related share option schemes for up to six months after the scheme is sanctioned by the court, the court does not appear to have any jurisdiction to make any order in respect of unissued shares which may arise on the exercise of options particularly if, as is usual, the scheme involves the cancellation of shares (see *Re Tip Europe* and *Re Transfer Terminal* (*1987*) 3 BCC 647).

12.45 An approved executive share option scheme (but not an approved savings-related share option scheme) may provide for optionholders to be able to exercise their options between the shareholders' resolution approving a scheme of arrangement and the court's sanctioning of the scheme (or the date which is to be taken as the record date for the scheme of arrangement). In this way, the optionholder can be entered on the register in time to be included by the court under the scheme of arrangement.

12.46 An approved savings-related share option scheme cannot provide for a right of exercise before the court order sanctioning the scheme of arrangement. However, it is possible to obtain a withdrawal of the scheme approval so as to insert appropriate rights of exercise between the passing of the shareholders' resolution and the court order sanctioning the scheme of arrangement. Any withdrawal of scheme approval will involve the prior approval of the Inland Revenue and under many schemes it may also involve the prior approval of optionholders. So as not to prejudice the interests of those option-holders with mature options which may be exercised tax-free, it would normally be appropriate first to allow such optionholders to exercise their options for a period of time between the shareholders' resolution and the date on which Inland Revenue approval of the scheme is withdrawn.

12.47 Alternatively, if the scheme of arrangement involves a change of control then optionholders may exchange their existing options for replacement options over shares in the new corporate entity under a roll-over (see 12.14 to 12.21).

12.48 Takeovers, Reconstructions, Demergers and Dividends

12.48 Any such offer by the new corporate entity should be made prior to the scheme of arrangement becoming effective or the Inland Revenue would be entitled to argue that a charge to income tax arises as a result of the optionholder exchanging his existing option (which after the effective date would appear to have been worthless as it subsists over a small minority holding in a subsidiary company) for a valuable new option (over the shares of the new corporate entity).

Profit sharing schemes

12.49 A scheme of arrangement between a company and its members which is sanctioned by the court under *CA 1985, s 425* will be treated as a reorganisation for capital gains tax purposes (*TCGA 1992, s 136*). *TA 1988, 10 Sch 1(1)* provides that, notwithstanding the obligations on the participant to leave shares with the trustees during the period of retention, the participant may direct the trustees to accept a proposal affecting his scheme shares, if the proposal would be entered into pursuant to a compromise, arrangement or scheme applicable to or affecting (amongst other things) all the ordinary share capital of the company or all the shares of the relevant class.

Voluntary winding-up

Share option schemes

12.50 *TA 1988, 9 Sch 21(1) (e)* permits a right of exercise by optionholders under a savings-related share option scheme within six months of the passing of a resolution for the voluntary winding-up of the company. Executive share option schemes are also usually drafted with a similar right of exercise.

12.51 It is not clear whether any rights of exercise following a voluntary winding-up would bind a liquidator.

Profit sharing schemes

12.52 On a voluntary winding-up of a company, participants are entitled to a distribution of assets on the same basis as other shareholders. Any distribution will be treated as a capital receipt and therefore potentially subject to income tax under Schedule E for the tax year in which the distribution is declared on the appropriate percentage of so much of the value or amount of the receipt as exceeds the appropriate allowance for that year (*TA 1988, s 186(3)*).

Demerger

12.53 A demerger involves the distribution to the shareholders of a company of shares in a subsidiary. The intention is to give the

Takeovers, Reconstructions, Demergers and Dividends 12.58

shareholders of the distributing company a direct interest in the shares of the distributed business. Any such distribution must be made out of the distributing company's distributable profits unless it is made (amongst other things) in the course of a winding-up (*CA 1985, s 263(1)(2)(d)*).

12.54 A demerger distribution will normally be made in either of the following ways:

(*a*) a dividend in specie e.g. *Racal/Vodafone; Williams Holdings/ Pendragan; Trafalgar House/Hardy Oil & Gas*:

(*b*) a 'three cornered' distribution involving the transfer of a trade or 75 per cent subsidiaries to a new company which issues shares to the shareholders of the transferor pro rata e.g. *BAT/Argos & Wiggins Teape Appleton; ICI/Zeneca; Courtaulds/Courtaulds Textiles; GPG/Guinness Mahon; Racal/Chubb.*

Share option schemes

12.55 The holders of approved options are not entitled to receive dividends since they have not been entered on the register of members. For the same reason, they also have no right to any demerger distribution.

12.56 Most approved share option schemes provide for employees of any company which is transferred outside the group to exercise their options usually for a period of six months after the transfer. A demerger involves a transfer of a company outside the group and so the employees of the demerged company will usually have a right of exercise at that time. However, the value of the shares comprised in the option will depreciate as a result of the demerger perhaps rendering the options substantially less valuable.

12.57 The employees of the distributing company will not usually have any rights of exercise as a result of the demerger, but will bear the same depreciation in the value of their options over shares in the distributing group as the outgoing employees.

12.58 In principle, the fairest way to deal with a demerger in an option scheme would be to provide for an adjustment of the options to reflect the effect of the distribution. Whilst this is possible in an unapproved share option scheme, the Inland Revenue will not approve any such power of adjustment in an approved scheme on the basis that the only adjustments allowed under the legislation are in respect of 'variation in the share capital' within *TA 1988, 9 Sch 25*. In fact many schemes provide for an adjustment in the event of an exempt distribution, but only with the prior approval of the Inland Revenue and to date no such approval has been forthcoming. There are about

12.59 *Takeovers, Reconstructions, Demergers and Dividends*

12 savings-related share option schemes and about 20 executive share option schemes which were originally approved by the Inland Revenue providing specifically for an adjustment of options without the prior approval of the Inland Revenue and where an adjustment is therefore possible, but these will be eliminated in due course as the schemes either expire or the Inland Revenue takes advantage of any opportunity to remove such rights.

12.59 There are various ways in which participants in employees' share schemes have been compensated for the effects of demergers:

(a) the withdrawal of Inland Revenue approval for the scheme followed by an alteration of the rights of optionholders either by incorporating early rights of exercise (so that optionholders can be entered on the register of members before the record date) or by providing for an adjustment of options after the demerger;

(b) cash compensation;

(c) the grant of compensatory option rights.

Withdrawal of approval and the alteration of option rights

12.60 Since the Inland Revenue will not approve any alteration of subsisting rights of exercise, the company must seek a withdrawal of scheme approval as a preliminary step for any alteration of option rights to allow for their adjustment to reflect any demerger. This will itself need the prior approval of the Inland Revenue and may also, under the terms of the scheme, require the prior approval of shareholders and optionholders as well.

12.61 Alternatively, the scheme may be altered with a view to conferring on the holders of options which have not matured new rights of exercise which will enable them to be entered on the register by the record date for the demerger.

12.62 Any alteration of the scheme to provide for the adjustment of options to reflect a demerger distribution will be treated by the Inland Revenue as the grant of new rights of exercise (see *IRC v Eurocopy plc* [1991] *STC 707*). It is essential, therefore, that any such new right is restricted to a maximum of seven years duration so that there is no income tax charge at the date of grant (see *TA 1988, s 135(2)*).

12.63 Any withdrawal of Inland Revenue approval will mean that optionholders may be disadvantaged in one of the following ways:

(a) any premature exercise of options may precipitate an unexpected

Takeovers, Reconstructions, Demergers and Dividends 12.66

liability to income tax on any option gain and the consequential loss of the capital gains tax exemption;

(b) in the case of a savings-related share option scheme, any early closure of the scheme may result in the optionholder's loss of the accrued gains on the shares he has insufficient savings to buy at the time of an early exercise.

In a number of demergers, the unavoidable loss of tax relief has been the specific subject of cash compensation e.g. *ICI/Zeneca*.

Cash compensation

12.64 A sum may be paid by the company to optionholders as compensation for the depreciation in value of the shares as a result of a demerger distribution. Whereas cash compensation for the surrender of option rights is chargeable to income tax under Schedule E by virtue of *TA 1988, s 135(1)*, any payment received as compensation for the depreciation in the value of the shares comprised in the option as a result of the demerger is outside the scope of Schedule E and will be treated as the consideration for a disposal of a chargeable asset, namely the option (*TCGA, s 22(1) (a)*). As far as the company making the payment is concerned, there is unlikely to be any deduction in computing the profits of the company for corporation tax purposes. The payment arises from dealings in the capital of the company rather than a payment of earnings from an employment.

Supplementary options

12.65 A distributing company may grant parallel options at a reduced price to reflect the value distributed in the demerger. For instance if the depreciation in value of the shares distributed is £3 a share, then the exercise price of the parallel option will be reduced by £3.

12.66 The grant of the parallel option rights will normally be made under a specially established unapproved share option scheme providing for the grant of options at a price less the market value. The new scheme will normally need to be approved by shareholders if it involves the issue of new shares and this can be obtained at the same time as the demerger approval. The options under the new scheme must have a maximum duration of seven years to avoid an income tax charge at the time of grant (see *TA 1988, s 135(2)*). The new options will normally be 'linked' to the old options so that the optionholder can only acquire the original number of shares under option, whether he exercises the old or the new option, or both in part. The reason for this is that the grant of a new (lower priced) option as part of the arrangement for the surrender of old option rights would be a disposal for capital gains tax purposes as a capital

12.67 *Takeovers, Reconstructions, Demergers and Dividends*

sum derived from assets (*TCGA 1992, s 22(1)*). On the other hand, for income tax any exchange of options would attract a roll-over (*TA 1988, s 136(1)*).

Profit sharing scheme

Dividend

12.67 A distribution of shares in a subsidiary will not normally form part of a scheme of reconstruction and will be subject to income tax in the normal way for any dividend.

Distributions as part of a scheme of reconstruction

12.68 A demerger taking the form of a 'three cornered' distribution as described at 12.54 will normally qualify for a roll-over for capital gains tax purposes and as an exempt distribution for income tax purposes.

12.69 The capital gains tax roll-over is available where there is an exchange of securities as part of an arrangement between a company and its members for the purposes of a scheme or reconstruction or amalgamation (*TCGA 1992, s 136*). If the receipt of the new shares qualifies as a company reconstruction for capital gains tax purposes, the value of the new shares will not be treated as a capital receipt (*TA 1988, 10 Sch 4(1)(c)*).

12.70 A demerger distribution satisfying the conditions of *TA 1988, ss 213–218* will be treated as an 'exempt distribution' so that no income tax will be payable on the value of the distribution received by shareholders. The Inland Revenue's advance clearance that the proposed distribution will be an exempt distribution must be obtained.

Dividends

Share option schemes

12.71 Distributions are only payable to members of a company (*CA 1985, s 263(2)* and Article 102 of Table A).

12.72 The holders of options over unissued shares are not entitled to any dividends during the period of the options except as specifically provided by the scheme rules. Share option schemes will often provide that optionholders are entitled to all dividends or other rights arising by reference to record dates since the date of exercise. If the scheme rules are silent, then an optionholder will only be entitled to receive dividends and other rights arising on or after the date of allotment.

Takeovers, Reconstructions, Demergers and Dividends 12.77

12.73 In the case of options over existing shares, the entitlement to dividends or other rights belongs to the person who is the registered holder of the shares at the record date.

Profit sharing schemes

12.74 A distribution or other dividend in money or money's worth received by the trustees in respect of or by reference to any scheme shares must be paid over to the participant unless it consists of 'new shares' received in a company reconstruction (*TA 1988, 9 Sch 33(a)*).

UK dividends

12.75 As the person beneficially entitled to any dividend, the participant, if he is UK resident, is entitled to the tax credit (*TA 1988, s 231*). The Inland Revenue Guide explains that the trustees will need to split any dividend received between individual participating employees and provide them with vouchers for the amounts to which they are individually entitled using Form R185E or any substitute form which may have been agreed with Claims in Bootle. Individual vouchers should be issued in the name of the trustees regardless of any arrangement to mandate dividends directly to employees. The address for any Inland Revenue enquiries on dividends is:

Inland Revenue
Claims (Bootle)
St John's House
Merton Road
Stanley Precinct
Bootle
Merseyside L69 9BB

Foreign dividends

12.76 Where a person 'obtains payment' of a dividend paid by a foreign company, he is required to deduct tax on it at the basic rate (or at a reduced rate in certain circumstances) (*TA 1988, s 123*). Normally, this obligation to deduct tax will fall on the bank in the UK which collects payment of the dividends on behalf of the trustees. In such cases the trustees will need to supply each participant with a certificate of deduction on Form R189C showing details of the shareholding, dividend and tax deducted.

12.77 Where the trustee 'obtains' payment, it must deduct tax at the basic rate (or at the reduced rate in certain circumstances) and account of the tax to:

12.78 *Takeovers, Reconstructions, Demergers and Dividends*

Assessing Section
Inspector of Foreign Dividends Office
Lynwood Road
Thames Ditton
Surrey KT7 0DP

A tax deduction certificate on Form R189 will need to be supplied to employee participants.

12.78 An employee who is not resident in the UK may claim repayment of the UK tax deducted from dividends. Such claims should be made to the Inspector of Foreign Dividends on Form A1 together with Form R189C or Form 189 as appropriate.

Scrip dividends

12.79 Scrip dividends are commonly offered by companies as an alternative to cash at the election of the shareholder. The company's Articles of Association will normally provide for scrip dividends to be offered by the directors with the sanction of a resolution of the company. Most scrip dividends are based on shares with an equivalent value (ignoring any tax credit) to the cash dividend. However, a number of companies have offered so-called 'enhanced scrip dividends' under which the value of the shares significantly exceeds the value of the cash dividend. Scrip dividends are paid-up out of a capitalisation of reserves.

Share option schemes

12.80 Optionholders will not normally be entitled to any scrip dividend since they are not a member of the company.

12.81 Since scrip dividends are paid up out of a capitalisation of reserves, there is no obvious reason why in principle optionholders are not entitled to an adjustment of options to reflect the capitalisation of reserves. Although under an enhanced scrip dividend the interests of the non-electing shareholders (including the optionholders) are clearly prejudiced, it seems unlikely that the Inland Revenue would be prepared to approve any adjustment of options since the adverse effects on options arise from shareholders accepting the offer, rather than the terms of any variation of share capital.

Profit sharing schemes

12.82 Any scrip dividend paid by a UK company must be paid over to the scheme participant (*TA 1988, 9 Sch 33(a)*) and will be treated as income in the hands of UK recipients (*TA 1988, s 249*). On the other hand, a scrip dividend paid by a foreign company will not be treated as income in the hands of the recipient since *TA 1988, s 249* does not apply. Indeed, any scrip dividends paid by a foreign company will normally satisfy the requirements for a capital gains tax reorganisation and, accordingly, the scrip shares are held within the profit sharing trust as 'new shares'.

Chapter 13

Variations of Share Capital

13.1 Most employees' share schemes make provision for rights and capitalisation issues, sub-divisions, consolidations and reductions of share capital. Such transactions are commonly known in the context of employees' share schemes as 'variations of share capital' as a result of the use of this term in relation to share option schemes in *TA 1988, 9 Sch 25*. There is, of course, a significant difference in the impact a variation of share capital has on a profit sharing scheme and a share option scheme: whilst the shares of a participant under a profit sharing scheme are affected directly, the price and number of shares under options need to be adjusted so as to keep the optionholder in the same relative position as before the variation of share capital.

London Stock Exchange

13.2 The *1984 Yellow Book* stated that a share option scheme may provide for the adjustment of options in the event of a 'capitalisation issue, or rights issue, sub-division, consolidation of shares or reduction of capital'. This has always been interpreted strictly by the London Stock Exchange which did not permit adjustments in the event of a demerger distribution or for the discount element in an open offer, at least unless such transactions were specifically approved by shareholders at the time.

13.3 The *1993 Listing Rules* contain no reference to the adjustment of share options. Presumably the London Stock Exchange now adopts a more liberal attitude to the circumstances in which an adjustment may be made. It seems likely that scheme rules will increasingly allow for the adjustment of share options on the general grounds of any 'variation of share capital' rather than in the event of the specific transactions mentioned in 13.2.

13.4 Under the *1984 Yellow Book*, any adjustment of options (other than on a capitalisation) had to be made by the directors subject to the opinion of the company's auditors that the proposed adjustment

13.5 *Variations of Share Capital*

was in their opinion fair and reasonable. An auditor's certificate is no longer required under the *1993 Listing Rules*.

Investment Committees

13.5 The Investment Committees of the Association of British Insurers and National Association of Pension Funds do not make any specific reference to the adjustment of options in the published Guidelines. However, it is understood that any adjustments which can be justified as fair and reasonable will be acceptable to these bodies.

Inland Revenue

13.6 In the case of approved share option schemes, the Inland Revenue require any proposed adjustment (except on a capitalisation issue) to be agreed in advance. The company should write initially to the Savings and Investment Division at the address given at 4.66. Proposed adjustments following a rights issue are usually referred to the Share Valuation Division for their approval. In the case of a rights issue, therefore, it usually saves time to copy Shares Valuation Division with the application made to the Savings and Investment Division.

Rights issues

13.7 Rights issues are normally made at a discount to the market value of the shares immediately before the rights issue is announced. Participants in an approved profit sharing scheme can usually obtain the benefit of this discount by taking up the rights issue in respect of their shares. On the other hand, optionholders are not so entitled as they are not entered on the register of members, but, if the scheme so allows, an adjustment may be made in respect of the price and number of shares under option to compensate them.

Share option schemes

13.8 The adjustment which the Shares Valuation Division will agree in relation to an approved scheme using listed shares is as follows: the option price will be adjusted by the hypothetical 'ex rights' price divided by the last cum rights price; and the number of shares under individual options will be adjusted by its reciprocal i.e. the last cum rights price divided by the hypothetical ex rights price.

Example

The optionholder has an option over 1,000 shares granted at 15 pence. The company announces a rights issue of 1 rights share at 25 pence for every 4 existing shares. The last cum rights price is 32 pence.

The calculation is as follows:

(a) The hypothetical ex rights price is:

		pence
4 existing shares @ 32 pence	=	128
1 new rights share @ 25 pence	=	25
		153

$$\text{Hypothetical ex rights price} = \frac{153}{5} = 30.6 \text{ pence}$$

(b) The adjustments are as follows:

(i) to the option price

$$15 \text{ pence} \times \frac{30.6 \text{ pence (hypothetical ex rights price)}}{32.0 \text{ pence (last cum rights price)}}$$

(ii) to the number of shares:

$$= \frac{1,000 \times 32.0 \text{ pence (the reciprocal of (i) above)}}{30.6 \text{ pence}}$$

$$= 1,045 \text{ shares}$$

13.9 The last cum rights price is the closing price for the last day before the rights issue becomes effective. In a listed or USM company, this will be the last day before dealings commence in the nil paid rights shares. The Inland Revenue do not take the last dealing day before the announcement (unless it also happens to be the last cum rights price day). Any adjustment based on such a day would reflect the impact which the announcement of the rights issue had on market sentiment towards the shares rather than the actual impact of the variation of capital.

13.10 Any company seeking the Inland Revenue's approval to an adjustment to options in respect of a rights issue will need to submit a copy of the rights issue document together with a copy of the proposed adjustment calculation. In the case of an unlisted company, a copy of the last three years accounts, the scheme rules and the Memorandum and Articles of Association may also need to be submitted.

13.11 Variations of Share Capital

Profit sharing scheme

13.11 A profit sharing trust deed must contain a provision requiring the trustees to deal only pursuant to a direction given by or on behalf of the participant with any right to be allotted additional shares, securities or rights of any description (*TA 1988, 9 Sch 33(b)*). There is no corresponding obligation on trustees to seek the direction of participants in relation to any rights issue. However, most trust deeds are drafted on the basis that the trustees will seek such directions and in practice an explanatory circular will normally be prepared by registrars to send out to scheme participants contemporaneously with the despatch of the rights issue document to shareholders.

13.12 The possible courses of action which can normally be taken by a shareholder in relation to any rights issue are as follows:

(*a*) take up the rights, which involves payment at the rights issue price;

(*b*) sell the rights nil paid;

(*c*) 'tail-swallow' i.e. sell such part of the rights as realises sufficient cash proceeds to take up the balance of the rights;

(*d*) allow the rights to lapse, in which case, depending on the terms of the rights issue, the rights will usually be sold in the market at the expiry of the offer period and the net proceeds distributed to shareholders.

As best practice, participants should be given all the choices available to shareholders although the Inland Revenue will approve a scheme which provides for 'standing' instructions to be given by participants to 'tail-swallow' in the event of any rights issue. Any such agreement will, however, be subject to any contrary instructions of the participant at the relevant time.

Taking up the rights

13.13 The trust deed of an approved profit sharing scheme will normally provide that the trustees are only bound to act on the directions of the trustees to take up a rights issue if instructions and payment by the participant are received no later than a specified number of days before the last date for taking up the rights. This is normally no earlier than five days before the last date for shareholders.

13.14 A rights issue is a 'company reconstruction' within *TA 1988, 10 Sch 5* by virtue of *TA 1988, s 126(2)*: the rights shares are allotted for payment in proportion to existing holdings in the company. The legislation provides that references to a participant's shares are treated after

Variations of Share Capital 13.19

the reconstruction as including the 'new shares'. In addition, the rights issue is treated as not involving any disposal of the original holding and the new shares are treated as having been appropriated at the same time as the original holding (*TA 1988, 10 Sch 5(4)*).

13.15 A participant is liable to income tax under Schedule E on the lesser of the locked-in-value or net disposal proceeds on any disposal of the shares before the release date (*TA 1988, s 186(4)*). Where money has been paid to the trustees to take up a rights issue, the net proceeds of disposal will be reduced by this amount of money so that any income tax charge relates only to the free shares element (*TA 1988, s 186(7)*). There are provisions for apportioning the payment to take up shares where only a part disposal of the holding is involved.

13.16 There may have been more than one payment to take up rights issue shares. In such a case, the disposal proceeds are reduced by the aggregate of the payments (*TA 1988, s 186(7)*).

13.17 If there are a succession of disposals, then the amount of any payment for shares shall only be deducted once (*TA 1988, s 186(8)(b)*).

Sale of the rights nil paid

13.18 The sale of the rights nil paid is not a disposal of scheme shares — the rights were never part of the participant's holding — but they are treated as a 'capital receipt' (see 9.85 to 9.88). The trustees will sell the rights in the market for a price which broadly represents any premium in dealings over the rights issue price. The trustees cannot, therefore, guarantee any price for the rights, and for that matter, cannot guarantee any sale.

13.19 Although capital receipts are subject to income tax under Schedule E in the tax year the entitlement arises, there are relatively generous allowances which have the effect of relieving most capital receipts from income tax (see 9.86). The allowance is found by multiplying £20 by one plus the number of tax years which fall within the period of five years immediately preceding the tax year in question and in which shares were appropriated to that participant under the scheme. The maximum allowance is £100 (*TA 1988, s 186(12)*).

Example

A participant receives a capital receipt in 1994/95. He has received appropriations in each of 1993/94, 1992/93, 1991/92, 1990/91 and 1989/90 i.e. all the previous five tax years. The maximum allowance is restricted to £100.

13.20 Variations of Share Capital

Income tax is only chargeable to the extent the capital receipt exceeds the allowance for that tax year. Tax under Schedule E is chargeable on the appropriate percentage (see 9.82) of that excess value.

If in any tax year the participant is entitled to two or more capital receipts, the allowance is applied against them in the order in which they are received.

'Tail-Swallow'

13.20 A 'tail-swallow' involves the disposal of such part of the rights shares nil paid as realises sufficient cash to take up the balance of the rights. *TA 1988, 10 Sch 4(2)* provides that any proceeds of the disposal will not be a capital receipt for the purposes of *TA 1988, s 186(3)*. As a result no PAYE is deducted from such proceeds — the whole of the proceeds can be applied in taking up the balance of the shares.

13.21 The locked-in-value of the holding after the tail-swallow requires adjustment: the locked-in-value immediately before the reconstruction is apportioned amongst the total shares, both those held before the rights issue and those acquired in it (*TA 1988, 10 Sch 5(5)*).

Allow the rights to lapse

13.22 Where the rights are allowed to lapse and no payment is received, no liability to income tax arises and the locked-in-value remains unchanged.

If the rights shares are disposed of and a cash payment is received, then the cash will be dealt with as a 'capital receipt' (see 9.85 to 9.88).

13.23 A specimen of the type of document issued to participants on a rights issue is set out below:

Draft Letter to Participants from the Trustees of the [   ] Profit Sharing Scheme

[date]

Dear Participant

The [   ] Profit Sharing Scheme: Rights Issue

You will find enclosed with this letter a circular dated [   ] which gives information about a rights issue which [   ] is making. The reasons for the rights issue are explained in the circular.

Variations of Share Capital **13.23**

As a participant in the Profit Sharing Scheme (the 'Scheme') you are entitled to take part in the rights issue in the same way as other shareholders. The purpose of this letter is to explain the various courses of action which are open to you.

The terms of the rights issue are that for every [   ] shares held on your behalf by the Trustees of the Scheme (your 'scheme shares'), you have an entitlement to subscribe for [   ] new shares at a price of [   ]p per share. The number of new shares to which you are entitled is shown in box (2) on the attached Form of Direction. You may take up your rights and buy all or some of these new shares or you may sell your rights for a cash sum. The alternatives are described in detail below.

Whatever you choose to do you should instruct the Trustees of the Scheme to act on your behalf by completing and returning the enclosed Form of Direction otherwise the Trustees will take no action and your rights will be sold in accordance with the terms of the rights issue.

If the Trustees act on your behalf under one of the options set out below, you will receive a revised notice of allocation in respect of your scheme shares in due course.

A. Purchase of *all* the New Shares to which you are entitled

You may subscribe and pay for *all* of the new shares shown in box (2) on the Form of Direction. The amount you will need to pay is shown in box (3).

The new shares will be held by the Trustees on the same terms as the original shares allocated under the Scheme, and will be released to you at the same time.

The amount paid for the new shares will be taken into account when calculating any tax liability arising on a subsequent disposal of all or any of your scheme shares.

If you wish to subscribe for *all* the new shares to which you are entitled sign in box (*a*) on the Form of Direction and send it to [   ] at [   ] with a cheque for the amount set out in box (3) on the Form of Direction. The Form of Direction and cheque must arrive by [   ] a.m./p.m. on [   ]. [A pre-paid envelope is enclosed for this purpose].

B. Sale of *all* the Rights to subscribe for New Shares

You may, if you wish, instruct the Trustees to sell *all* your rights to subscribe for new shares and receive the cash proceeds.

13.23 Variations of Share Capital

If the Company's shares continue to be traded on the London Stock Exchange at a higher price than the rights issue price of [   ]p, the Trustees may be able to sell your rights to third parties. No guarantee can be given as to the price obtained for the sale of your rights to subscribe for new shares or indeed that such sale can be made. If no sale can be made by the Trustees your rights will be sold in accordance with the terms of the rights issue.

If the cash proceeds exceed a certain amount the excess will be liable to income tax. This amount will depend on the date on which you received your first appropriation of shares, as follows:

Date of First Appropriation:	Amount of Proceeds of Sale of Rights which are Tax-Free:
[ ]	£ [ ]
[ ]	£ [ ]
[ ]	£ [ ]
[ ]	£ [ ]

The balance will be subject to income tax which will be charged at your marginal rate of tax under PAYE.

You will receive the tax free amount and the net taxable amount after deducting any expenses of sale. You will also receive a sale advice note which you should retain for tax purposes.

If you wish the Trustees to arrange (where possible) a sale of *all* your rights to subscribe for new shares sign in box (*b*) on the Form of Direction and return it by [   ] **a.m./p.m.** on [   ] to [   ] at [   ]. [A pre-paid envelope is enclosed for this purpose].

C. Sale of some of the Rights and Purchase of the balance of the Shares to which you are Entitled

You may, if you wish, instruct the Trustees to sell part of your rights and to apply the cash proceeds obtained (less any expenses of sale) in acquiring as many of the new shares to which you are entitled as possible. No guarantee can be given as to the price obtained on the sale of any rights or, indeed, that such sale can be made. The number of new shares which can be acquired will depend on the price at which the rights can be sold. If no sale can be made by the Trustees your rights will be sold in accordance with the terms of the rights issue.

The new shares will be held by the Trustees on the same terms as the original shares allocated under the Scheme, and will be released to you at the same time. Any cash remaining from the sale of the rights which is insufficient to purchase a whole new share will be remitted to you.

Variations of Share Capital **13.23**

No income tax charge arises to the extent that the sale proceeds of part of the rights are used to acquire the balance of the new shares to which you are entitled.

If you wish the Trustees to sell some of your rights and to apply the proceeds to purchase as many new shares as possible sign in box (*c*) on the Form of Direction and return it by [   ] **a.m./p.m.** on [   ] to [   ] at [   ]. [A pre-paid envelope is enclosed for this purpose].

IF YOU TAKE NO ACTION IN RESPECT OF (A) BEFORE [   ] A.M./P.M. ON [   ] OR BEFORE [   ] A.M./P.M. ON [   ] IN THE CASE OF (B) OR (C), THE TRUSTEES WILL TAKE NO ACTION AND YOUR RIGHTS WILL BE SOLD IN ACCORDANCE WITH THE TERMS OF THE RIGHTS ISSUE. IF ANY NET PROFIT IN EXCESS OF £3.00 ARISES FROM A SALE OF YOUR RIGHTS (AFTER DEDUCTING THE RIGHTS ISSUE PRICE AND SELLING EXPENSES) IT WILL BE REMITTED TO YOU LESS ANY TAX WHICH IS DUE

Yours sincerely

[   ]
For and on behalf of
The Trustees of the
[   ] Profit Sharing Scheme

THIS DOCUMENT IS NOT NEGOTIABLE

[   ]
[   ] Profit Sharing Scheme (the 'Scheme')
Rights Issue of up to [   ] new ordinary shares
of [   ]p each at [   ]p per share

RIGHTS ISSUE
FORM OF DIRECTION

[   ]

[Name of Participant]
[Address]
As referred to in the Trustees' letter dated [   ], the following are the details of your entitlement in respect of the Rights Issue. You should read that letter before completing this Form of Direction.

13.23 *Variations of Share Capital*

Box (1) shows the total number of ordinary shares held on your behalf under the [ ] Profit Sharing Scheme;

Box (2) shows the number of new ordinary shares which you have the right to buy should you wish to do so;

Box (3) shows the cost to you of buying those new ordinary shares.

(1) Holding of Scheme Shares at close of business on [ ]	(2) Number of new ordinary shares of [ ]p each provisionally allocated to you	(3) Amount payable on acceptance not later than [ ] a.m./p.m. on [ ]
X X	X X	£ X

To: The Trustees of the
[ ] Profit
Sharing Scheme

THE ALTERNATIVE COURSES OF ACTION OPEN TO YOU ARE:

(A) You can ask the Trustees to take up your rights and buy all (but not part of) the new ordinary shares. To do this you should sign box (*a*) to the right of this paragraph and return this form completed together with your payment of the purchase cost (cheques only, in pounds sterling, made payable to [ ] and crossed 'Not negotiable — A/C [ ] [in the envelope enclosed] — TO REACH [ ] at [ ] BY [ ] a.m./p.m. on [ ]. These new ordinary shares bought by you will be held by the Trustees together with the ordinary shares already held on your behalf.

(*a*)

I irrevocably instruct you to take up all the new ordinary shares provisionally allocated to me and enclose my remittance for £ ...... payable on acceptance

....
Signature

Variations of Share Capital 13.24

(B) You can ask the Trustees to sell your rights to all (but not part of) the new ordinary shares. It is possible that the sale of the rights will produce a profit which will be paid to you less expenses and any tax which is deductible. To do this, please sign box (*b*) to the right of this paragraph and return this form completed, [in the envelope enclosed] — TO REACH [   ] at [   ], BY [   ] a.m./p.m. on [   ].

(*b*)

| I irrevocably instruct you to sell my rights to all of the new ordinary shares provisionally allocated to me. .... Signature |

(C) You can ask the Trustees to sell sufficient of your rights as will enable you to take up the balance of the new ordinary shares provisionally allocated to you. To do this, please sign box (*c*) to the right of this paragraph and return this form completed, [in the envelope enclosed] — TO REACH [   ] at [   ], BY [   ] a.m./p.m. on [   ].

(*c*)

| I irrevocably instruct you to sell sufficient rights to enable me to take up the balance of the new ordinary shares provisionally allocated to me. .... Signature |

N.B. You should complete only one of boxes (*a*), (*b*) or (*c*) above.

If you take no action or if this Form of Direction is wrongly completed or inconsistent instructions are given, your rights to the new ordinary shares will be sold in accordance with the terms of the rights issue and any net profit in excess of £3.00 arising from the sale of your rights (after deducting the rights issue price and selling expenses) will be paid to you.

All remittances are to be made payable to [   ] and crossed 'Not Negotiable — A/C [   ]' and this form should be returned to the Trustees c/o [   ] at [   ] [in the envelope enclosed.] The latest time for receipt is [   ] a.m./p.m. on [   ] if you have signed box (*a*) or 3.00 p.m. on [   ] if you have signed boxes (*b*) or (*c*).

Capitalisation issues

Share option schemes

13.24 A capitalisation issue is treated as a 'variation of share capital' for the purposes of *TA 1988, 9 Sch 25*. Consequently, an adjustment of options is permitted in approved share option schemes.

13.25 Variations of Share Capital

13.25 The adjustment for any capitalisation issue is normally arithmetically straightforward and the Inland Revenue do not insist that approved schemes should provide for the prior approval of the Inland Revenue to any proposed adjustment.

Profit sharing schemes

13.26 A capitalisation issue is a 'company reconstruction' within *TA 1988, 10 Sch 5* by virtue of *TA 1988, s 126(2)*: capitalisation shares are allotted without payment in proportion to existing holdings in the company. The legislation provides that, after the reconstruction, references to a participant's shares includes the 'new shares'. In addition, the rights issue is treated as not involving any disposal of the original holding and the new shares are treated as having been appropriated at the time the original holding was were appropriated (*TA 1988, 10 Sch 5(4)*).

Sub-divisions and consolidations

13.27 Although sub-divisions and consolidations are normally straightforward arithmetical adjustments, the Inland Revenue nevertheless require that schemes provide for the prior approval of the Inland Revenue to any such adjustment to options. A sub-division or consolidation is a 'company reconstruction' within *TCGA 1992, s 126(2)(b)* as an alteration of share rights. The same tax consequences apply, therefore, as for a capitalisation issue (see 13.26 above).

Reduction of share capital

13.28 A reduction of share capital is provided for by *CA 1985, s 135(2)*. A reduction may take the form of:

(*a*) the extinguishment or reduction of the liability to pay up shares;

(*b*) the cancellation of any paid-up share capital which is lost;

(*c*) repayment of share capital which is in excess of the company's requirements.

The reduction must be authorised by the company's articles.

Share option schemes

13.29 Approved share option schemes may only use fully-paid shares (*TA 1988, 9 Sch 12(1)(a)*). No reduction of share capital involving the extinguishment or reduction of a liability to pay up any share capital can, therefore, apply to shares used in an approved scheme as this would amount to the creation of partly-paid shares.

Variations of Share Capital **13.34**

13.30 It is possible that the other shares of the same class as shares used in the scheme may be only partly-paid. In this case, the liability to pay-up those other shares (but not the scheme shares) could be extinguished or reduced. In such circumstances, there would be no justification for an adjustment to the scheme shares.

13.31 Where the total issued share capital of the company is reduced by a cancellation or repayment of share capital, a corresponding reduction in the number of shares under option would normally be the appropriate adjustment to make to the share options.

Profit sharing schemes

13.32 A reduction of share capital is treated as a 'reorganisation' for capital gains tax purposes by *TCGA 1988, s 126(1)*. The only exception to this is the paying off of redeemable share capital, or where shares are redeemed by a company otherwise than by the issue of shares or debenture, or in the course of a liquidation (*TCGA 1992, s 126(3)*). It follows, therefore, that a participant's newly reduced scheme shares will normally be held by the trustees under the scheme on the same terms as the shares prior to the reduction.

Other variations of share capital

13.33 The term 'variation of share capital' in *TA 1988, 9 Sch 25* is not a legal term and its meaning will depend on the types of transaction the Inland Revenue is proposed to treat as a 'variation'. In particular, the Inland Revenue will include certain offers of shares to the shareholders of a company in proportion to their holdings provided the shares have been normally issued to a vendor or institution as consideration for the sale of some business or assets — a 'vendor placing'. Where the shareholders are offered shares at a discount to the market value, an adjustment to options might be appropriate on a similar basis to the adjustment made for a rights issue (see 13.11 to 13.23). Shares taken up in a vendor placing by the trustees of a profit sharing scheme against payment from the participants will usually be dealt with within the scheme as a reorganisation for capital gains tax purposes provided the vendor placing involves an 'issue' of shares otherwise there will be no new shares (see *TA 1988, 10 Sch 5(3)*).

13.34 At one time, the Inland Revenue seemed prepared to include exempt demerger distributions in the types of transaction which might be treated as variations of share capital but this is no longer the case (see 12.58).

Chapter 14

PEPs

Introduction

14.1 Personal Equity Plans (or PEPs) were first introduced in *FA 1986* as a way for individuals to invest and hold ordinary shares, principally UK and EC listed companies (and UK USM companies). Investment in certain authorised unit and investment trusts are now also allowed. In certain circumstances unquoted shares emerging from an approved savings-related or profit sharing scheme may be transferred to a PEP (see 14.5).

14.2 The advantages of holding ordinary shares through a PEP is that all the chargable gains on the disposal of PEP shares are exempt from capital gains tax, and all dividends on such shares are exempt from income tax, thus enabling the tax credit to be reclaimed from the Inland Revenue.

14.3 PEP shares must be held through a plan administered by a registered plan manager who must be authorised under the *Financial Services Act 1986* and who must comply with the detailed Inland Revenue regulations for PEPs. The managers will make the necessary claims for repayments of tax credits.

Types of plan

14.4 There are two types of plan:

— *General Plans*: investors may subscribe in cash up to £6,000 per tax year for investment — whether at the discretion of the PEP manager or at the discretion of the investor — in shares authorised under the Regulations (see 14.1 above)

— *Single Company Plans*: investors may subscribe in cash up to £3,000 per tax year for shares in a single company designated by the plan manager. In addition, shares released from an approved profit sharing or savings-related share option scheme (but not any executive share option scheme) may be transferred into a single company plan directly (see 14.5 below). The value

14.5 *PEPs*

of shares transferred into a plan is set off against the £3,000 limit for cash subscriptions.

An individual may transfer new issues of shares under a public offer into either type of PEP, and the subscription price of the shares counts against the appropriate subscription limit. An investor may only subscribe to one general plan and one single company plan each tax year.

Release of shares from employees' share schemes

14.5 Whilst PEPs are ordinarily available for investment in the shares of listed companies (and USM companies), investments in unquoted companies may be held in single company plans where the relevant shares were transferred into the plan following their release from an approved profit sharing or savings-related share option scheme (Regulation 4(2) of the Personal Equity Plan Regulations 1989). The investor has 90 days to transfer the shares into the plan from the date of exercise in the case of a savings-related share option scheme and 90 days from the date he directed the trustees of a profit sharing scheme to transfer the shares (or the release date if earlier) in the case of a profit sharing scheme. In the case of a profit sharing scheme, it would usually be disadvantageous for the employee to direct that any shares are transferred into a single company plan before the release date (the fifth anniversary of grant) since this would involve a charge to income tax under *TA 1988, s 186(4)*.

14.6 Some approved profit sharing schemes involve employees buying some shares as a qualifying stake for additional free shares. Whilst the free shares appropriated under the approved profit sharing scheme will qualify for a direct transfer into a single company plan, the bought shares do not since they will not have been 'appropriated' under a profit sharing scheme as required by the Personal Equity Plan Regulations 1989. However, employees may be able to subscribe cash to purchase their qualifying shares through a general or single company plan.

14.7 Where shares emerging from an approved profit sharing or savings-related share option scheme are transferred into a single company plan, it is necessary to value the shares for the purpose of the relevant subscription limit in that tax year. All valuations are based on the value at the date of transfer rather than the date of exercise or release. Quoted shares are valued by reference to the normal rules for the valuation of quoted shares in *TCGA 1992, s 272*. Unquoted shares are valued by agreement with Shares Valuation Division under the normal tax rules for valuing unquoted shares in *TCGA 1992, s 273*. Generally, a value will be agreed for a specified period although the Inland Revenue may always adjust values in the light of circumstances which come to light at a later date.

Sponsored PEPs

14.8 It is not surprising that a number of listed companies have sponsored PEP managers to offer PEPs, usually limited to the shares of the sponsoring company only, to their shareholders and employees. The object of the exercise is to reduce the managers' costs on the basis of the highest possible takeup. However, the interest in sponsored PEPs by shareholders has been patchy to say the least. Some public companies with several thousand shareholders have found only a dozen or so wishing to take advantage of the opportunity.

14.9 Given the large numbers of shares emerging from some all-employee share schemes, there is a much greater demand for sponsored PEPs from employees than from shareholders generally.

14.10 A sponsored PEP will normally be offered on the basis of both a general and a single company plan i.e. £9,000 subscription in aggregate each tax year. Whilst the single company plan can be used to take transfers of shares from an approved profit sharing or savings-related share option scheme, the general plan can only take cash subscriptions. Cash subscriptions may, of course, be made by arranging for the plan manager to dispose of the investor's holding of shares, and then investing the sale proceeds in the plan. Unfortunately, the obligations under the rules of the Securities and Investment Board ('SIB') that a seven day cooling-off period must be provided means that the number of shares disposed of and the number acquired through the PEP will rarely match each other exactly.

CA 1985, s 151: financial assistance

14.11 *CA 1985, s 151* prohibits the giving by a company of financial assistance to a person directly or indirectly for the purposes of acquisition of shares in that company. 'Financial assistance' means loans, indemnities and any other financial assistances given by a company if the net assets are thereby reduced to a material extent or if the company has no net assets.

14.12 In any sponsored PEP, the company may incur part of the marketing and the ongoing management costs of the PEP. Generally speaking, this will not be unlawful financial assistance even if the suppliers are paid direct rather than through the plan manager. The payments are unlikely to reduce the net assets of the company to any material extent. Moreover, if the sponsored PEP is established to encourage or facilitate the acquisition of shares by employees, former employees and certain relatives, it may be possible to rely on the exemption for employees' share schemes in *CA 1985, s 153(4)(b)*.

14.13 PEPs

FSA 1986: investment businesses

14.13 Any sponsoring company must ensure its activities do not amount to 'investment business' within the meaning of *FSA 1986, s 1* even if the plan documentation must be approved by the plan manager who must be a person authorised under *FSA 1986*. Arguably, the plan manager should do no more than appoint the plan manager perhaps in consideration of a one-off fee. Support of the plan manager by allowing advertising to be inserted in literature sent by the company to its shareholders has tended to be disregarded by regulatory authorities, but the companies may be exposing themselves to some risk on this. There is an exemption if the sponsored PEP is an employees' share scheme.

FSA 1986: investment advertisements

14.14 Usually the marketing material for any sponsored PEP will be issued by the plan manager who will be an authorised person under the *FSA 1986*. Any reference in the director's report and accounts to the sponsored PEP will be an investment advertisement within the meaning of *FSA 1986, s 57*. Such advertisements require the approval of an authorised person.

Chapter 15

ESOPs and Using Existing Shares

What is an ESOP?

15.1 An Employee Share Ownership Plan — or ESOP — is a trust established by a company for the benefit of its employees (and former employees and certain relatives). As a separate legal entity to the company, it is in a position, subject to satisfying all relevant legal requirements, to acquire and hold shares in the company and transfer them to employees either under the company's established employees' share schemes or directly.

15.2 Whilst the purpose of a share option or profit sharing scheme is to provide for the distribution of shares to employees, an ESOP is principally a vehicle for the acquisition and holding of shares. The establishment of an ESOP therefore involves consideration of the possible means by which it will finance its acquisition of shares (see 15.9 below).

Employees' share schemes linked to an ESOP

15.3 Many potential uses for an ESOP have been put forward including making a market in the shares of a private company, and as a vehicle for an employee or management buy-out particularly where there is uncertainty about the identity of the ultimate employee or management investors (or the relative size of their investments). However, the vast majority of ESOPs have been established to hold shares for distribution under one of the various types of approved share option scheme or under some form of unapproved scheme, for instance, a restricted share scheme (see Chapter 7).

15.4 The number of ESOPs has grown as the use of existing shares in employees' share schemes has grown more popular. One reason for this is that an allocation of existing shares under an employees' share scheme does not count against the Investment Committee's limits on the number of new shares which may be made available under employees' share schemes (see Chapter 3) so, as companies have increasingly come up against these limits, they have increasingly turned to the use of existing shares supplied through an ESOP. A

15.5 ESOPs and Using Existing Shares

number of companies have also found that in the longer term the use of existing shares can be cheaper than the issue of new equity. This is particularly the case if interest rates are relatively low and dividend yields have been maintained.

Example

Company A lends £10m to an ESOP interest-free which is used to buy 2m shares at £5 per share for the purpose of a share option grant. As consideration for the interest-free loan, dividends are waived by the trustees. In the first year, the net dividend is 17.5 pence and is assumed to grow at 10 per cent per annum. Interest rates are assumed at 6 per cent throughout the period. It is assumed the company borrows the money from the bank to lend to the ESOP.

	Interest paid by the Company to the Bank	Tax Relief @ 35 per cent on interest paid on Bank loan	Dividends waived by the Trustees	(Net cost) or net saving of ESOP
1st Year	(600,000)	210,000	350,000	(40,000)
2nd Year	(600,000)	210,000	385,000	(5,000)
3rd Year	(600,000)	210,000	423,500	33,500
4th Year	(600,000)	210,000	465,850	75,850
5th Year	(600,000)	210,000	512,435	122,435

Assuming that the interest costs of financing the acquisition of shares in the above example are fixed, any increase in dividends results in a reduction of the net cost of providing existing shares. Indeed, in the third year in the above example, there is a cross-over as a result of which there is a net saving i.e. the dividends waived exceed the interest costs of financing the acquisition of shares. The main saving in using existing shares, however, is the avoidance of dilution: there is a permanent saving every year after the exercise of options of the amount of dividend which would otherwise be payable. The amount of dividend saved in later years is likely to far exceed the cost of financing the shares between grant and exercise even on any discounted basis for timing differences.

15.5 Another reason there has been an increase in the number of employees' share schemes using existing shares through an ESOP in recent years is that it is not necessary to obtain shareholders' approval for the establishment of the scheme unless the transaction is a Related Party Transaction under the *1993 Listing Rules* (or a Class 4 transaction under the *1984 Yellow Book*). Generally speaking, the establishment and operation of an ESOP will only be regarded as a Related Party (formerly Class 4) transaction where participation is limited to directors of group companies.

Share option schemes

15.6 ESOPs may conveniently be used in connection with share option schemes including approved schemes. Bearing in mind that optionholders will pay for the shares on exercise of the options, the exercise monies can be used by the trustees to recoup any earlier outlay at the time of grant on acquiring the shares. If the options are granted at market value immediately following the acquisition of the shares, the amount payable by the optionholders should exactly match the trustees' acquisition costs. Whilst an exact match between the cost of the shares to the trustees and the exercise price payable by the optionholders may be achieved in the case of executive share option schemes where options are usually granted at market value, this will rarely be the case under a savings-related share option scheme where options are usually granted at a discount to the market value. In such cases, the company may need to fund any discounts which are given on the grant of the options.

Profit sharing schemes

15.7 ESOPs may be a convenient 'warehouse' for shares which are earmarked for appropriation under an approved profit sharing scheme. The ESOP trustees can acquire and hold the shares with loans provided by the company. At appropriation the profit sharing trustees will pay their contribution from the company to the ESOP trustees to acquire the shares; the ESOP trustees can then in turn repay their loans from the company. Profit sharing trusts have only a limited 'warehousing' capacity, partly because the Inland Revenue will not approve a scheme where the profit sharing trustees have a power to borrow money and partly because the deductibility of any contribution by the company to profit sharing trustees is conditional upon its application in the acquisition of shares for appropriation before the end of the 'relevant period' for the purposes of *TA 1988, s 85*. Basically, this is a period of nine months after the period of account in which the expenditure is charged in the accounts of the company.

Restricted share schemes

15.8 Where an ESOP is established to allocate shares to employees under a restricted share scheme, the acquisition of the shares by the ESOP trustees will also need to be financed by outright contributions as in a profit sharing scheme. Restricted share schemes usually confer substantial share benefits on a limited number of senior executives, often against specified performance targets. There is, however, no statutory deduction for payments to the ESOP trustees as there is under *TA 1988, s 85* and therefore the deductibility will depend on the normal rules (see 15.29).

15.9 ESOPs and Using Existing Shares

Qualifying Employee Share Trusts

15.9 *FA 1989, ss 67–74*, and *Schedule 5* provides for tax relief on contributions to Qualifying Employee Share Ownership Trusts (see 15.60 to 15.64).

Financing of ESOPs

15.10 The ESOP trustees acquisition of shares will generally need to be financed by the company in one form or another. The form it takes will generally be governed by the purpose for which the ESOP has been set up. Broadly speaking, if the shares acquired by the ESOP trustees are to be distributed free to employees, then the company will need to make substantial gifts. A contribution to the ESOP trustees may be given in the form of dividends on the shares, or from the sale of some of the shares at a profit, but substantially the whole of the finance will need to be provided directly by the company. On the other hand, if the shares are to be sold or transferred to employees on the exercise of share options, then the acquisition cost of the shares should be wholly or substantially recoverable by the ESOP trustees from employees on exercise of the options. In these circumstances, the ESOP trustees need only obtain interim finance until the shares are sold or transferred to the employees.

15.11 If ESOPs are analysed on the basis of whether they are primarily established to give or to sell shares to employees, they fall within the two following categories:

Established to gift shares to employees	*Established to sell shares to employees*
1. Approved profit sharing schemes (see Chapter 9)	1. ESOPs established to hold shares for share option schemes
2. Restricted share schemes (for senior executives) (see Chapter 7)	2. ESOPs established to make a market in the shares in private companies
3. Long service award schemes involving free shares under Extra-Statutory Concession A22	

The Financing of ESOPs established to gift shares

15.12 Banks and other financial institutions will have little or no part to play in the financing of an ESOP which is established to provide gifts of shares for employees. This type of ESOP will need to be funded by contributions from the company.

ESOPs and Using Existing Shares 15.17

15.13 A company which makes voluntary contributions to acquire existing shares will need to take into account that the contributions will be a charge to profit and loss and, unless applied in subscribing for new shares, will reduce the company's cash-flow. The payment and any surplus which arises on termination of the trust are irrecoverable by the company (see 15.31). The deductibility of any payments for tax purposes will be of prime importance to most companies but, except for approved profit sharing schemes and Qualifying Employee Share Ownership Trusts where a statutory deduction exists upon satisfaction of certain conditions (see 15.8 and 15.9), deductibility will depend on a line of case law authorities which will need to be considered with some care (see 15.29).

The financing of ESOPs established to sell shares

15.14 As indicated at 15.11 above, ESOPs established to sell shares will recoup the costs of acquiring the shares. The main requirement for such ESOPs is to obtain the most appropriate form of interim finance.

15.15 Any payment by the company under any guarantee of the ESOP trustees' obligations to a third party financier, or under any indemnity of the trustees, will not be deductible for tax. In managing its risks in respect of any ESOP, a company may need to consider a programme of voluntary payments to ensure that the ESOP remains solvent over the long term.

Loan by the company

15.16 A loan from the company is often the most efficient form of finance for ESOP trustees if only because the ESOP trustees will be able to borrow the required amount of funds at the right time and on as many occasions as the ESOP trustees require. There will be no need to provide security or give warranties and undertakings. In principle, interest may be payable on any loan but as the interest would only be paid out of dividends received, the ESOP trustees will probably not be in a position, initially at least, to meet the full amount of interest payable if this is charged at a commercial rate. In later years, if dividends grow, there may be a cross-over point at which the amount of dividends received exceeds the interest payments but, this will not usually happen for some time, if at all. In the meantime, any insufficiency of dividends to meet interest outgoings would need to be waived by the company.

15.17 Alternatively, it may be more advantageous for the company to waive interest on its loan to the ESOP, in consideration of the trustees waiving their right to dividends on the shares. This has the advantage that a UK resident company will not need to make any

15.18 ESOPs and Using Existing Shares

payment of advance corporation tax on the dividends. The real cost of the loan — the amount by which interest charged at a commercial rate would exceed the savings on dividend payments — is 'lost', in the sense that it does not appear as a separate item in the profit and loss.

Loans from a third party financier

15.18 The company may be unwilling to take the loans to the ESOP trustees onto its balance sheet. In these circumstances, the company may require ESOP trustees to obtain loan finance from a third party lender. Any third party lender will expect dividends to be paid and will normally require the company to guarantee the ESOP trustees obligations in respect of the loan.

15.19 It is doubtful that any UK resident ESOP trustees would be entitled to claim a deduction for interest outgoings on a loan to acquire shares since such expenditure would be to the benefit of the capital of the trust and, therefore, capital in nature (see *Carver v Duncan* HL [1985] STC 356).

Call options and UK banks

15.20 Some of the larger ESOPs have been financed by call option arrangements with a UK bank. The bank buys the shares in its own name, but grants an option in favour of the ESOP trustees who can call for the shares during an agreed period. The attraction of this type of arrangement is that the bank is able to use the tax credit attaching to dividends received against its own liability to pay ACT. In addition, a UK bank does not pay tax on dividends received from UK companies; if it buys shares with borrowed monies it is entitled to tax relief for the interest paid and obtains a largely tax-free return in the form of the tax exempt dividends. These advantages can be shared by the UK bank with the ESOP trustees in the option price payable by the ESOP trustees to acquire the shares. The way in which the UK bank determines the price payable by the ESOP trustees is to establish a model which calculates the UK bank's carrying costs plus a margin, after giving credit for all dividends and monies paid by the ESOP trustees as well as the benefit of the tax credits.

Establishment of an ESOP

Power of the company to establish an ESOP

15.21 Many companies have an express power to establish and operate employees' share trusts in their Memorandum of Association. However, the absence of any such express power will not preclude

310

ESOPs and Using Existing Shares 15.24

the establishment of an ESOP. By *CA 1985, s 3A*, where a company's memorandum states that the object of the company is to carry on business as a general commercial company, the company is treated as having the power to do all things that are incidental or conducive to the carrying on of any trade or business. Such a wide power should cover the establishment of any ESOP. If there is no power to either establish an ESOP, or the provisions of *CA 1985, s 3A* do not apply, the directors should seek the specific approval of shareholders to the establishment of any proposed ESOP in order to avoid any risk of proceedings by members to restrain the commission of an act in excess of the company's capacity (*CA 1985, s 35(2)*). A third party dealing with the company in good faith cannot be prejudiced by an act which exceeds corporate capacity (*CA 1985, s 35A*).

15.22 The directors must take care to ensure that any acts they take in relation to the establishment and operation of an ESOP are in the best interests of the company, and that any exercise of their powers and discretions is for a proper purpose. In particular, the establishment of an ESOP to prevent a bid being made for the company would not be carried out for a proper purpose (see *Hogg v Cramphorn* [*1967*] *Ch 254*). However, it would always be open to the members to pass a resolution approving or ratifying any act of the directors. Accordingly, the directors should carefully minute the reasons for establishing any ESOP.

Shareholders' approval

15.23 Any transaction between the company and an ESOP under which only directors may benefit will be a Related Party Transaction under the 1993 *Listing Rules*. Any proposed Related Party Transaction with a listed company needs to be discussed with the Stock Exchange which may require shareholders' prior approval of the proposal.

Identity of the trustees

15.24 The first decision which must normally be made in relation to the identity of any trustees to be appointed is whether they should be UK or non-UK resident. In most cases, non-UK resident trustees will be appointed for the capital gains tax advantages referred to at 15.46 and to ensure the ESOP trustees are outside the scope of the *Financial Services Act 1986*. However, UK resident trustees must be appointed for approved profit sharing schemes (see 9.6), Qualifying Employee Share Ownership Trusts and where an ESOP is established to take a gift of shares from a transferor who seeks roll-over relief under *TCGA 1992, s 165*. This applies to certain gifts of shares in an unquoted company, the transferor's personal company or the transferor's trading company. The relief is denied where the transferee

15.25 ESOPs and Using Existing Shares

is neither resident nor ordinarily resident in the UK (*TCGA 1992, s 166*).

15.25 There is no compelling reason to appoint non-UK resident trustees for many of the Restricted Share Schemes (see Chapter 7) which have been established since no capital gains tax will be payable under Extra-Statutory Concession D 35. This concession applies where shares are transferred to UK resident employees for nil payment, but in circumstances where the receipt of the shares is chargeable to income tax under Schedule E.

15.26 If UK resident trustees are appointed, the company may wish to appoint directors of the company as trustees. However, unless the ESOP trustees are to be funded with outright gifts, the appointment of directors will involve difficulties under *CA 1985, s 330* which prohibits the making by a company of loans and quasi-loans to its directors.

15.27 Where a non-UK resident trustee is to be appointed, usually the trustee will be selected from amongst the many banks offering such services in the Channel Islands or the Isle of Man. Although the costs of appointing such trustees varies depending on the nature of the activities to be performed. There will normally be a minimum of £1,000 set up and £1,000 annual fees with additional transaction fees. In some cases, the cost may be significantly greater.

15.28 Any ESOP trust which is to be non-resident in the UK, should be established as a discretionary trust in order to ensure that the non-UK residence is not challenged by the Inland Revenue on the basis that the trust is controlled by the company establishing the ESOP. However, the ESOP trustees will need to obtain information from the company about the potential beneficiaries. It is usual, therefore, for a liaison committee of directors or other senior executives to be appointed as a point of contact for the ESOP trust. In many cases, this will be a group of individuals, initially directors of the company, with the exclusive power to appoint their successors.

Tax aspects

Tax considerations for the company

Gifts

15.29 A payment by a company to ESOP trustees will be deductible in computing the company's trading profits if it is (i) revenue in nature and (ii) made wholly and exclusively for the purposes of the company's trade. Expenditure which is intended to acquire or enhance

ESOPs and Using Existing Shares 15.33

a capital asset will, therefore, not be deductible. In particular, expenditure designed as a once and for all contribution to a fund will not be revenue (*Atherton v British Insulated and Helsby Cables Ltd* (*1925*) *10 TC 155*). The second condition is that the payment is made wholly and exclusively for the purposes of its trade will usually be established where the nature for the payments is to reward employees for their efforts (*Heather v P-E Consulting Group Ltd* (*1972*) *48 TC 293*; *Jeffs v Ringtons Ltd* (*1985*) *58 TC 680*; *E Bott Ltd v Price* (*1988*) *59 TC 437*). In practice, the approach which should be adopted by a company seeking a deduction is to make a series of voluntary payments of varying amounts from year to year and avoid any 'one off' lump sums.

15.30 *FA 1989, s 67* provides a statutory tax relief for contributions made to a qualifying employee share ownership trust which satisfies the conditions set out in *FA 1989, 5 Sch*. However, little use has been made of this legislation since the tax relief is usually available for a non-qualifying ESOP anyhow, and the conditions under *FA 1989, 5 Sch* are hard to satisfy (see 15.60 to 15.64).

15.31 Where the beneficiaries include employees from a number of group companies, the trustees expenditure on shares should be carefully matched to contributions received from the different employing companies. Expenditure which is borne by one group company to buy shares for employees of another group company will not be incurred wholly and exclusively for the purposes of the payer's trade.

15.32 The company which established the ESOP should not benefit under the trust, not even as an ultimate beneficiary, if it wishes to obtain a tax deduction for any contributions (*Rutter v Charles Sharpe & Co Ltd* (*1979*) *53 TC 163*).

Loans

15.33 Close companies which advance money to ESOP trustees who are 'participants' may have difficulties under *TA 1988, s 419(5)*. This applies where a close company makes a loan which does not give rise to a liability under *section 419(1)*, and a third party either 'makes a payment or transfers property to ... an individual who is a participator' then the loan or advance is treated as made to a participator in the first place. The payment made by the ESOP trustees to buy shares from a shareholder (who will inevitably be a participator) is treated as a 'payment' within *CA 1985, s 419(5)*. Although *section 419(1)(5)* only apply to 'individuals' who are participators, or an associate of a participator, *section 419(6)* extends the reference to individual to 'a company receiving the loan or advance in a fiduciary or representative capacity, and to a company not resident in the United Kingdom'. Arguably, any subsidiary of a close company specially formed to act as the ESOP trustee will be within the section.

15.34   ESOPs and Using Existing Shares

15.34   Where the section applies to any loan made under *section 419(1)*, or deemed to be made under *section 419(5)*, the company is obliged to make an interest-free deposit of tax with the Inland Revenue which is only refundable to the extent the loan is subsequently repaid.

15.35   The question arises whether any interest-free loan used to acquire shares will give rise to a charge to income tax under Case VI, Schedule D, *TA 1988, s 786(5)*. This provides that where, under a loan transaction, a person 'agrees to waive ... income arising from any property (without a sale or transfer of the property)' then a charge to tax arises on the amount of interest foregone. It is thought that provided the waiver arises under the ESOP trust deed, rather than under any loan agreement entered into between the parties, the section should not apply.

15.36   Where interest-free loans are made by the company to a subsidiary which acts as a corporate trustee there is also a theoretical risk of the Inland Revenue making a direction under *TA 1988, s 770* so that, for tax purposes, the company is to be treated as making the loan on arms-length terms and the subsidiary is treated as receiving a market rate of interest. The Inland Revenue do not appear to make such directions in practice.

Tax considerations for the trustees

Income tax

15.37   Voluntary contributions to trustees are not income for tax purposes. On the other hand, regular payments made under a legal obligation will be treated as annual payments chargeable to income tax under Schedule D, Case III. The company is under an obligation to deduct tax at the basic rate from such payments (*TA 1988, s 349(1)*).

15.38   As in the case of any other discretionary trust, UK resident ESOP trustees are subject to a single flat rate tax of 35 per cent. They are entitled to set-off the 20 per cent tax credit on dividends against this liability. Non-UK resident trustees are liable to tax on UK dividends plus a notional, non-payable tax credit of 20 per cent which is set-off against their liability to tax at the single flat rate of 35 per cent.

15.39   Where the trustees incur revenue expenses, these are set-off against dividends in priority to other income. Dividend income used to meet expenses is treated as chargeable to tax at the lower rate of 20 per cent (and is, therefore, covered by the 20 per cent tax credit) and other income used to meet expenses is treated as chargeable to tax at 25 per cent. Trust management expenses of non-UK resident

ESOPs and Using Existing Shares 15.44

trustees are treated in a similar way except that management expenses are only allowed against income liable to UK tax.

15.40 The income tax 'settlement' provisions of *TA 1988, ss 671–682* deem income to be that of the settlor notwithstanding that it is payable to some other person. However, it is considered that these provisions only apply where the settlor is an individual.

15.41 Normally, the beneficiaries of a discretionary trust are treated as receiving the amount of any distributions after deduction of tax at the rate applicable to trusts i.e. the combined basic and additional rates of tax of 35 per cent. They are entitled to a tax credit against their own liability to pay tax. Consequently, a non-taxpayer will be able to reclaim the whole of the 35 per cent rate of tax.

However, the credit is strictly only available where the distributions to beneficiaries are treated as annual payments chargeable to tax under Case III of Schedule D rather than earnings subject to tax under Schedule E. By Extra-Statutory Concession A.68, the Inland Revenue allows the trustees to reclaim the whole or part of the tax paid by them on income which, upon payment to the employees, is treated as within the charge to tax under Schedule E. In this way the income received by the trustees and distributed as earnings to employees is not taxed twice.

15.42 Under *TA 1988, s 688* the trustees are exempt from tax under Schedule D, Case III on any interest payments received from employees under any scheme whereby the trustees borrow money from the company to lend to employees to buy shares in the company. The relief is only available to the extent the interest receivable by the trustees from employees matches the interest payable to the company.

Capital gains tax

15.43 UK resident trustees of a discretionary trust are chargeable to capital gains tax on their chargeable gains at the rate applicable to trusts i.e. 35 per cent.

15.44 Any distributions of shares by UK resident trustees to a beneficiary is a disposal for capital gains tax as far as the trustees are concerned even if it is a receipt of emoluments chargeable to tax under Schedule E as far as the employees are concerned. The trustees disposal of the shares will be treated as made for a consideration equal to the market value of the assets transferred (*TCGA 1992, s 17(1)*). It follows, therefore, that any assets transferred at an undervalue would appear to be taxed in the hands of both the ESOP trustees and the employee. However, there are a number of potential reliefs from tax:

15.45 ESOPs and Using Existing Shares

(a) by Extra-Statutory Concession D 35, the trustees will be relieved from any capital gains tax liability where the transfer of assets is made for no payment, the employee is liable to tax under Schedule E on the value of the assets received and the trust is an employee trust within *IHTA 1984, s 86* (although it is not necessary for the trust property to be held for the benefit of 'all or most employees') and the beneficiaries do not own more than 5 per cent of the share capital of the company;

(b) where Extra-Statutory Concession D 35 does not apply, a joint 'hold over' election under *TCGA 1992, s 165* might be available if the asset transferred is shares in either an unquoted trading company or group or the transferor's personal holding or his trading company or group. Generally, a company will qualify as a personal company if as little as five per cent of voting shares are held by the transferor and his associates.

15.45 A particular application of a hold over election under *TCGA 1992, s 165* is where the ESOP trustees transfer shares to profit sharing trustees. If the shares satisfy the requirement of *TCGA, s 165(2)*, then they may be transferred by the trustees at cost, and any held over gain will be absorbed into the capital gains tax exemption available for appropriations of shares by profit sharing trustees within 18 months of acquisition.

15.46 Non-UK resident trustees are exempt from UK capital gains tax even if the shares are in a UK company.

15.47 *TCGA 1992, s 87* provides for the attribution of certain trust gains accruing to non-UK resident trustees to UK beneficiaries. The provisions only apply to trusts established by settlors who are domiciled and either resident or ordinarily resident in the tax year the settlement is established. The trust's gains are only assessable on the UK beneficiaries to the extent these beneficiaries receive capital payments. However, the courts have indicated that commercial arrangements are unlikely to be settlements because they do not normally contain any element of bounty (see *IRC v Plummer* [1979] *STC 793*). It is understood the Inland Revenue take the view that employees' benefit trusts which represent normal commercial arrangements entered into to provide remuneration for employees are not 'settlements' and, therefore, any transfer of shares by such a trust is outside the scope of *section 87*.

15.48 *TCGA 1992, s 86* provides for the attribution to the settlor of certain chargeable gains accruing to non-UK resident trustees where the settlor has an 'interest' in the trust. The company which established the ESOP is potentially a settlor for these purposes if either it has a residual interest in the trust property in default of other beneficiaries or the company lends money to the ESOP. However, where the ESOP is part of a normal commercial arrangement for the remuneration of employees so that there is no element of 'bounty' involved, the Inland Revenue accept that the provisions of the section are unlikely to apply.

Inheritance tax

15.49 Discretionary trusts are subject to inheritance tax on every tenth anniversary of the trust and on any distribution out of the trust at other times. Any distribution which is income in the hands of the recipient (or would be if he were UK resident) is exempt from inheritance tax (*IHTA 1984, s 65(5)*).

15.50 The tenth anniversary charge is based on the 'value of the property'. Where the trust property has been funded by loans and income has been distributed the trust has insubstantial net worth and any tax payable will be *de minimis*.

15.51 The tenth anniversary charge and the charge on distributions do not apply where the trust property is held for the purposes described in *IHTA 1984, s 86*. Property will be held for the purpose of *IHTA 1984, s 86* if beneficiaries include 'all or most' employees and directors of (amongst other things) the particular employing company or the property is held on the trusts of an approved profit sharing scheme. The Inland Revenue do not regard the inclusion of either charitable trustees or the company's pension trustees as the ultimate beneficiary as prejudicing the 'all or most' employees' test.

15.52 Under *IHTA 1984, s 72*, an inheritance tax charge arises where property ceases to be held on employee trusts within *IHTA 1984, s 86* unless it is distributed trust property. A particular instance where this section may apply is in connection with the grant of share options at a price which is less than the market value of the shares at the date of grant.

Tax considerations of employees

15.53 Any transfer of shares or payment of cash to employee beneficiaries will be emoluments for tax purposes and chargeable to income tax under Schedule E. Where shares are transferred at an undervalue, the amount of the undervalue is an emolument (*Weight v Salmon* (*1935*) *19 TC 174*). A former employee will be within the scope of Schedule E (*Bray v Best* [*1989*] *STC 159*) but he is assessable for the last tax year of his employment (*TA 1988, s 19*). UK resident trustees must deduct tax under PAYE for payments made to employees (*Clark v Oceanic Contractors Inc* (*1982*) *56 TC 183*). A third party may also be liable to deduct tax through PAYE if it knows the exact quantum of the emoluments (*IRC v Herd* [*1993*] *STC 436*).

15.54 *ESOPs and Using Existing Shares*

15.54 Where a person acquires a chargeable asset as an employee, for capital gains tax purposes the acquisition cost will be equal to the market value at that time (*TCGA 1992, s 17*). However, the acquisition cost will be the actual price paid (which will presumably be less) when the shares are acquired pursuant to the exercise of an approved share option (*TA 1988, s 185(3)(b)*).

ESOPs and share options

15.55 ESOP trustees need a specific power in the trust deed to grant options under the company's share option scheme. The ESOP trustees will normally enter into an agreement with the company to transfer shares in satisfaction of the company's obligations under the share option scheme. Alternatively, the trustees may grant the options under the scheme, but there are capital gains tax and inheritance tax difficulties where it grants options at less than market value.

Income tax

15.56 The tax rules applying on the grant and exercise of an approved or unapproved option are identical whether the option is granted over new or existing shares.

Capital gains tax

15.57 The grant of an option is a disposal by the ESOP trustees for the purposes of capital gains tax (*TCGA 1992, s 144*). No chargeable gains arise where the option is exercisable at the market value at the date of grant; however, the grant of an option at a discounted price in principle gives rise to a chargeable gain unless the option is an approved option (*FA 1993, s 104*). Where unapproved options are to be granted at a discount the company will need to establish a non-UK resident ESOP if capital gains tax is to be avoided.

15.58 On the exercise of an option, a disposal for capital gains tax purposes arises under *TCGA, s 137(2)*. Given that any exercise of the option is pursuant to the rights as an optionholder rather than employee, *TCGA 1992, s 17* does not act to incorporate market value for the actual exercise price in determining whether a chargeable gain arises. Where the ESOP trustees' acquisition cost for the shares is not less than the option exercise price, no chargeable gain should arise.

Inheritance tax

15.59 The grant of options at open market value gives rise to no difficulties in respect of inheritance tax. However, where the option is granted at less than market value, a tax charge arises under *IHTA*

1984, s 72(2)(c) on the value of the property leaving the trust. This is because whilst distributions to employee beneficiaries are outside the scope of the tax charge, the grant of an option is not treated as an immediate distribution, but a transaction which causes a depreciation in the value of the trust. The same tax consequences apply where the trustees agree with the company to transfer shares pursuant to any obligations of the company to transfer shares on the exercise of options. The Inland Revenue have indicated that the position may be different if the trustees were under an obligation to transfer shares imposed by the trust deed.

Qualifying Employee Share Ownership Trusts

15.60 *FA 1989, ss 67–74* and *Schedule 5* (as amended by *FA 1994, 13 Sch)* provides a statutory deduction in computing profits or gains under Schedule D (or, in the case of an investment company, a management expense) where relief is claimed for contributions by a UK resident company to the trustees of a trust which at the time it was established was a Qualifying Employee Share Ownership Trust. The payments must be applied for a 'qualifying purpose' within nine months of the end of the accounting period in which they are charged (or such longer period as the Inland Revenue will allow). A 'qualifying purpose' is:

(*a*) the acquisition of shares in the company which established the trust;

(*b*) the repayment of sums borrowed;

(*c*) the payment of interest on sums borrowed;

(*d*) the payment of any sum to a person who is a beneficiary under the terms of the trust deed;

(*e*) the meeting of expenses.

15.61 The conditions for a Qualifying Employee Share Ownership Trust which must be satisfied at the time the trust is established are as follows:

Establishment

(*a*) it is established under deed by a UK resident company which is not under the control of another company;

Trustees

(*b*) the trust deed must provide for the appointment, retirement, replacement and removal of trustees including the appointment of the initial trustees;

(*c*) the trust deed must include provisions relating to the composition of the trustees. Under *FA 1989, 5 Sch* there must be provided that at all relevant times there must be at least three

15.61 ESOPs and Using Existing Shares

UK resident trustees including a trust corporation, solicitor, accountant or certain other professional persons, and that most of the trustees must be persons who are employees, but not (and never have been) directors of any company within the UK founding company group or persons who held a material interest (broadly speaking, 5 per cent) in the shares of the company. Under *FA 1989, 5 Sch* (as amended by *FA 1994, 13 Sch* with effect from 3 May 1994) two additional and alternative sets of rules are available. First, a 'paritarian' trust structure under which there are at least three UK resident trustees and at least one of them is a 'professional' trustee and there are at least two employee representatives. Secondly, a single corporate trustee may be appointed provided the directors are appointed in a similar manner to the 'paritarian' trust structure above.

(d) the trust deed must provide that the trustees in (c) above must have been appointed by either:

 (i) selection by a majority of the employees of the UK founding company group at the time of selection; or

 (ii) persons elected to represent those employees;

Beneficiaries

(e) the trust deed must provide that only employees and directors of companies within the UK founding company's group who normally work at least 20 hours a week for a qualifying period (of not less than one year and not more than five years) may be beneficiaries. However, persons with a material interest must be excluded and persons who have left employment in the previous 18 months may be excluded. A charity may be included as a residuary beneficiary on a winding-up of the trust;

Trustees' Functions

(f) the trustees functions must be expressed as the receipt of contributions or the borrowing of moneys to acquire and hold shares for:

 (i) transfer to the beneficiaries directly (gift or sale) on qualifying terms (i.e. offered to all beneficiaries on similar terms which may vary according to remuneration, length of service and similar factors) provided the shares are transferred to all who accept. (It follows that shares cannot, therefore, be made available under any form of share option scheme);

 (ii) sale to profit sharing trustees for a price not less than the market value.

The trustees must transfer the shares within seven years of acquisition (twenty years in the case of a trust established after 3 May 1994). Only fully paid shares which form part of the ordinary share capital

ESOPs and Using Existing Shares 15.65

of the founding company and are not redeemable and are not subject to any special restrictions may be used. The shares may not be acquired by the trustees for more than the market value;

(g) the trust deed must provide that any sums received by the trustees must be expended within the relevant period for a qualifying purpose (see 15.60);

(h) the trust deed must not contain features which are not essential or reasonably incidental to the qualifying purposes as set out in 15.60.

15.62 The trustees of a Qualifying Employee Share Ownership Trust are subject to income tax and capital gains tax in the normal way for the trustees of any other UK resident discretionary trust. The main tax relief available is for contributions paid to the trustees which are applied for qualifying purposes: to the extent the contributions are not applied for such purposes or there are certain other breaches of the trust, there is a clawback of tax relief on the trustees or, failing payment by the trustees, any company in the UK founding company group. In addition, roll-over relief may be available where shares are transferred by a corporation or individual vendor to a Qualifying Employee Share Ownership Trust under *TCGA 1992, s 165*, and there is a statutory deduction for expenditure in establishing a Qualifying Employee Share Ownership Trust under *TA 1988, s 85A*.

15.63 Given the absence of any relief from tax on the income and gains of the trustees, the potential liability to tax of individual trustees, the complex conditions for a Qualifying Employee Share Ownership Trust and the fact that the statutory tax deduction probably provides no greater tax relief than is available under case law ESOPs, it is not surprising that only a handful of Qualifying Employee Share Ownership Trusts have been established in the past five years.

15.64 Most companies wish to establish ESOPs to hold shares for distribution under employees' share schemes. Selective schemes such as Restricted Share Schemes are ruled out because of the wide eligibility criteria. All types of share option schemes are ruled out. This only leaves approved profit sharing schemes, but it is difficult to see any advantage in using a Qualifying Employee Share Ownership Trust as a 'feeder' for a profit sharing scheme given that the trustees of the Qualifying Employee Share Ownership Trust are required on selling any shares to the trustees of a profit sharing scheme to do so at market value, and are subject to UK capital gains tax on any gains.

Public company ESOPs

1993 Listing Rules

15.65 Under the *1993 Listing Rules*, employees' share schemes providing for the issue of new shares require the prior approval of

15.66 ESOPs and Using Existing Shares

shareholders. An ESOP which is only permitted to use existing shares will not require prior shareholders' approval.

15.66 Where the directors are discretionary beneficiaries of an ESOP, any funding of the ESOP is likely to be a Related-Party Transaction, but it will not normally be necessary to obtain the prior approval of shareholders unless only directors can benefit under the ESOP. However, in practice, ESOPs will rarely require shareholders' approval either because they are within the *de minimis* rules or because the Stock Exchange will clear the transaction where employees as well as directors will benefit. However, if the ESOP has the power to subscribe for new shares it is likely to be treated as an employees' share scheme which will require shareholders' approval (see 4.17).

15.67 The *1993 Listing Rules* impose certain disclosure requirements which may affect an ESOP:

(*a*) where any change in a director's interest is notified to the company under *CA 1985, ss 324–325* (see 15.68), an immediate corresponding notification must be made by the company to the Stock Exchange (see 15.70). In particular, this includes a grant or exercise of options whether over existing or new shares, the allocation or transfer of shares to a director under a Restricted Share Scheme (see Chapter 7) and where shares cease to be owned by a director. In addition, any acquisition or disposal of shares by ESOP trustees will be treated as a notifiable change in the directors' interests in the shares on account of their potential interest under the ESOP as discretionary beneficiaries;

(*b*) a release or surrender of an option to subscribe for shares is specifically notifiable to the Stock Exchange. The release or surrender of an option over existing shares under an ESOP is notifiable to the company under *CA 1985, s 324* (see *CA 1985, 13 Sch 6*);

(*c*) particulars of any arrangements under which a shareholder has waived or agreed to waive any dividends during a financial year must be given in the annual report and accounts unless the amount waived is *de minimis*.

Disclosure

CA 1985, s 324

15.68 Directors have an obligation to notify a company of any interest or change of interest he may have in its shares, or the shares of its subsidiary, holding company or subsidiary of a holding company (*CA 1985, s 324*). Notification must be in writing and state the number and class of shares involved and must be expressed to be in satisfaction of the directors' obligations under this section. There is an obligation

ESOPs and Using Existing Shares **15.72**

to notify the grant of a right to purchase existing shares under an ESOP as opposed to the grant of a right to subscribe for new shares since the company will already know about this (*CA 1985, 13 Sch 6*). Changes in the interests of spouses and certain family members must be notified under *CA 1985, s 325*.

CA 1985, s 325

15.69 The company has an obligation to keep a register of directors' interests in shares under *CA 1985, s 325*. Details must also be entered in the register of the grant to a director of a right to subscribe for shares in the company. The register must include details of:

(*a*) the date of grant;

(*b*) the exercise period;

(*c*) the consideration for the grant (or nil);

(*d*) details of the number and class of shares and the exercise price.

In addition, details of any exercise of the right to acquire shares by a director must be entered in the register.

15.70 Where the company is notified of any change in a directors' interest in shares under *CA 1985, s 324*, or is under an obligation to enter details in a register of the grant and exercise of options over new shares under *CA 1985, s 325*, it is under a corresponding obligation to notify the Company Announcements Office immediately and in any event no later than the end of the next business day.

CA 1985, s 198

15.71 An ESOP which acquires (or ceases to hold) at least 3 per cent of the voting shares of a public company may be under a duty to notify the company concerned within two days of the change of interest. The company is obliged to keep a register of such interests and to make this available for inspection by members and non-members. Notifiable interests do not include the interest of a discretionary beneficiary under an ESOP.

Investment Committee Guidelines

15.72 The 1991 ABI Guidelines included the first reference to ESOPs and welcomed the development so far as ESOPs genuinely result in widening share ownership. The ABI suggests that where an ESOP proposes holding more than 5 per cent of a company's issued ordinary share capital, the arrangements should first be submitted to shareholders for their prior approval. ESOPs hold shares on a

15.73 ESOPs and Using Existing Shares

revolving basis, but it is understood that the limit of 5 per cent is applied at any one time rather than over the life of the ESOP.

15.73 Informally, the ABI have made other recommendations in relation to the governance of ESOPs. In particular:

(a) the appointment of at least one independent trustee is encouraged: the ABI prefer the appointment of non-executive directors, but an independent professional trustee is acceptable;

(b) the ABI recommends that purchases of shares by the ESOP trustees are made through the market and not by a private sale, particularly if this is from a prominent founder member;

(c) the ABI recommends that dealings by ESOPs are disclosed: this may be a wider requirement than the obligation to disclose directors' share dealings to the Stock Exchange.

15.74 The National Association of Pension Funds in a Consultative Paper in September 1993 expressed similar views about ESOPs as those expressed by the ABI. In particular, it welcomed the development of ESOPs in so far as they encourage wider share ownership, but expressed concern that ESOPs should not be used to block takeover bids or to make shares available in excess of the 10 per cent in ten years limit on dilution. The NAPF also expressed concern that the NAPF might incur indebtedness to the company which might exacerbate any financial difficulties which arise for the company.

Directors' report and accounts

15.75 Where the company lends money to ESOP trustees under the authority given in *CA 1985, s 153(4)(b)(bb)* or *(c)*, then the aggregate amount of the loans included in the balance sheet must be disclosed (*CA 1985, 4 Sch 51*).

15.76 Where the company gives a guarantee of the ESOP's obligations to a third party lender to repay any loan, or to the bank under any put and call option arrangements, then this will be a contingent liability which needs to be noted in the accounts assuming no provision is made in respect of the liability (*CA 1985, 4 Sch 50*).

15.77 Under *CA 1985, Sch 6* a note in the accounts is required in respect of the aggregate amount of the directors' emoluments. Emoluments include the estimated money value of any other benefits received by him otherwise than in cash (*paragraph 1(4)*). A directors' interest in an ESOP trust as discretionary beneficiary does not appear to be a 'benefit' which can be received, but a distribution of free shares undoubtedly is such a benefit. The exercise (but not grant) of a share option may also be a 'benefit' received.

ESOPs and Using Existing Shares 15.78

15.78 *CA 1985, 7 Sch 2* provides for the disclosure of directors' interests in shares by way of a note to the accounts. These interests include the same interests as for *CA 1985, s 324* and, therefore, includes the interests of directors as discretionary beneficiaries under an ESOP. Disclosure is also required of any grant or exercise of options by each interested director during the financial year (*CA 1985, 7 Sch 2B*).

Chapter 16

Administration and Tax Returns

Administration

Making offers

16.1 The company will need to consider the terms of the scheme rules before making any offer under the scheme. In particular, scheme rules normally provide for the timing of offers, the limits on the number of shares available individually and under the scheme, eligibility and the procedure for making the offers.

16.2 A form of board resolution for making offers under approved share option schemes is set out at 5.38 (approved executive share option scheme), and 8.43 (approved savings-related share option scheme).

16.3 Specimen ancillary documentation for the grant of options is set out at 5.43 (market value approved executive share options) and at 6.39 (discounted price options under an approved executive share option scheme) and 6.47 (parallel options under an approved executive share option scheme), and 8.46 (approved savings-related share option scheme).

16.4 Specimen resolutions or timetables for making an offer are set out at 5.38 and 5.39 (approved executive share option scheme), 8.43 (approved savings-related share option scheme) and 10.49 (approved profit sharing scheme).

Maintaining registers

16.5 A register of options or interests under a profit sharing scheme needs to be maintained whether manually or by computer. There are no statutory requirements relating to the information to be retained on the register although normally the information will be retained in a form suitable for completing the annual scheme tax return.

16.6 Administration and Tax Returns

16.6 In the case of a savings-related share option scheme, the Department for National Savings and most of the building societies and banks providing sharesave contracts will maintain an option register in conjunction with the details of sharesave contracts.

16.7 Any register is only as good as the systems established for providing relevant information. The company must always ensure details of employees who leave employment and the grounds of their leaving are passed to the relevant registrar as quickly as possible.

Dividends

16.8 In profit sharing schemes, the registrar will need to ensure that dividends and the tax vouchers are mandated for payment to the participants.

Takeover offers, rights issues and other variations of share capital

16.9 The registrar will be involved in circulating circulars to shareholders in the event of any takeover offer, reconstruction proposals, rights issue or other circular to shareholders. In the case of profit sharing schemes, this will also involve seeking directions from participants in relation to their shares (see 13.23).

Voting rights

16.10 In profit sharing schemes, there are a variety of ways in which the voting rights of participants may be dealt with including taking instructions on how votes are cast on a poll or possibly appointing employees to attend and vote as proxy for the trustees.

Tax returns

Returns of share acquisitions

16.11 *FA 1988, s 85(1)* provides that where a director or employee acquires shares, or an interest in shares, a return must be made to the Inspector of Taxes. The return must be given by the company whose shares are acquired and also (if it is different) the employing company. The return must be in writing and must be given within 30 days of the end of the tax year. An interest in shares does not include an option to acquire shares.

16.12 The obligation arises where a prospective or former director or employee acquires shares in pursuance of a 'right or opportunity' conferred on him or afforded to him by reason of his employment (*FA 1988, ss 77(1), 87(1)*). In short, all acquisitions of shares by

Administration and Tax Returns **16.16**

directors and employees under employees' share schemes will need to be returned.

Return of unapproved share options

16.13 Under *TA 1988, s 136(6)*, a company must, within 30 days of the end of the relevant tax year, make a written return to the Inspector of Taxes of any of the following:

(*a*)   any grant of an unapproved share option; or

(*b*)   any allotment or transfer of shares in pursuance of an unapproved share option; or

(*c*)   any receipt of notice of the assignment of any unapproved share option; or

(*d*)   any provision by it of any benefit in money or money's worth:

  (i)   for the assignment or for the release of an unapproved share option in whole or in part;

  (ii) for or in connection with an omission or undertaking to omit to exercise an unapproved share option; or

  (iii) for, or in connection with, the grant or undertaking to grant an unapproved share option (or an interest in shares to which such a right relates).

It will be seen that, unlike *FA 1988, s 85(1)*, the obligation to make the return is imposed solely on the company involved in the transaction, and not also on the employing company (if different).

16.14 The information to be set out on any return will depend on the information needed by the Inland Revenue to raise the correct assessment. This will include details of all employees, the number and class of shares, the date of option grant or acquisition price as the case may be and the prices and values involved. The Inland Revenue operates by reference to national insurance numbers and these are best included wherever possible.

16.15 Where an overseas parent company grants an unapproved option over its own shares to an employee of its UK subsidiary, the overseas parent company is, strictly speaking, under an obligation to report the grant and to report the acquisition or transfer of the shares at the time of exercise under *section 136(6)*. It is also under an obligation to report the exercise under *FA 1985, s 85(1)* as the company whose shares are acquired.

16.16 Regardless of whether any return is made by the overseas parent, the UK subsidiary is also under an obligation to make a return in respect of the acquisition of the shares under *FA 1988, s 85(1)*.

16.17 Administration and Tax Returns

16.17 In addition, a UK resident employee is liable to make a return of his option gains. No obligation to make a return arises in respect of employees who are outside the scope of Case I of Schedule E (*FA 1988, s 77(2)* and *TA 1988, s 140(1)*).

Returns in relation to unapproved employees' share schemes

16.18 *FA 1988, s 85(2)* provides for returns to be made to the Inspector of Taxes within 60 days after the date of the event or the benefit received, where in relation to an unapproved employees' share scheme:

(*a*) a chargeable event occurs under *FA 1988, s 78* (the removal of any restrictions on shares, etc.);

(*b*) a person receives a special benefit (within the meaning of *FA 1988, s 80(1)*) in respect of shares, or an interest in shares, in a company.

The person liable to make the return is the company whose shares are involved and also (if different) the employing company.

Returns of employee benefits

16.19 The employing company is under an obligation each year to make a return of all benefits provided for the employee under *TA 1988, ss 153–168*. These returns are made on Forms P9D and P11D by 6 June following the end of the tax year (*Reg 46 Income Tax (Employments) Regs 1993, SI 1993 No 744*). The employer is under an obligation to make a return of any acquisition of shares by a director or employee at an undervalue which is chargeable to tax as an interest-free notional loan under *TA 1988, s 162(1)* or where shares are bought-back by the company, including by surrender, from the director or employee at a price greater than the market value which is chargeable to tax on the benefit received under *TA 1988, s 162(6)*. Under *TA 1988, s 161(1)* no taxable benefit will arise where the outstanding balance of all beneficial loans at any time during the tax year does not exceed £5,000.

16.20 None of the above obligations on the company whose shares are used, or the employing company, discharge the employee from his own responsibility to make a return of any income arising from shares and options on which he is chargeable to income tax (*TMA 1970, ss 7, 8*).

Approved schemes

Annual returns

16.21 The Inland Revenue Employee Shares Schemes Unit issues annual returns in respect of each approved scheme at the end of each tax year for completion and return within 30 days. The profit sharing scheme return is issued to the trustees of the scheme; the savings-related and executive share option scheme return is issued directly to the secretary of the company which established the scheme. Where that company has been taken over and options rolled-over, the Inland Revenue will normally accept a return completed and signed by the acquiring company. In some cases this may be the only company available to make the return as the company which established the scheme may have been wound-up.

16.22 Specimens of each of the approved scheme returns are set out in the explanatory booklets IR 98 (Approved SAYE share option schemes), IR 96 (Approved profit sharing schemes) and IR 100 (Approved executive share option schemes).

Power to obtain further information

16.23 *TA 1988, 9 Sch 6* contains powers under which the Inland Revenue can obtain such information as the Inland Revenue thinks necessary for the performance of their functions under the relevant statutory provisions. The Inland Revenue are entitled to ask 'any person' to give the required information. In particular, the information the Inland Revenue may require may include information enabling them to determine whether to approve or withdraw approval for any scheme and to determine any participant's income and capital gains tax liabilities. The Inland Revenue can also seek information relating to the administration of a scheme and any alteration of the terms of a scheme.

Chapter 17

Overseas Schemes and Overseas Employees

17.1 Many large US and UK companies have extended executive share options to selected executives in overseas subsidiaries, but until recently only a determined minority have attempted to extend all-employee share schemes to overseas employees. However, a growing number of UK companies wish to offer overseas employees participation in schemes on broadly similar terms to UK employees in so far as this is reasonably practicable. Consideration of these issues needs to be set against the background of the tax position of UK employees in overseas schemes, and the tax position of overseas employees in UK schemes.

The liability of non-residents to UK tax on share acquisitions

17.2 Income tax on the emoluments of an office or employment are taxed under the following three Cases:

Case I: earnings for any tax year in which the employee is resident or ordinarily resident in the UK (except certain overseas earnings);

Case II: earnings for UK duties for any tax year in which the employee is not resident (or, if resident, not ordinarily resident) in the UK (except certain overseas earnings);

Case III: earnings for any tax year in which the employee is UK resident so far as he remits the earnings to the UK.

Acquisitions of shares

17.3 The acquisition of shares by an individual as part of his earnings as a director or employee is chargeable to tax under the general principles of Schedule E on any undervalue or benefit received (*Weight v Salmon* (*1935*) *19 TC 174*). An employee is chargeable to UK tax if he is within any of Cases I, II and III of Schedule E.

333

17.4 Overseas Schemes and Overseas Employees

Share options

17.4 The residence of the optionholder at the time of grant determines the tax treatment at the time of exercise. If the employment is within Case I at the time of grant, then income tax will be chargeable under *TA 1988, s 135(1)* on any option gains which arise at exercise even if the employee has since become non-resident (although in practice liability will rarely be pursued).

17.5 If the employment was within either Case II or III at the time of grant, no liability can arise on any share option gains at the time of exercise within *TA 1988, s 135(1)* although liability may arise on the acquisition of the shares at an undervalue under *TA 1988, s 162* (employee shareholdings).

17.6 If the option was capable of exercise for more than seven years, then income tax is chargeable under the general principles of Schedule E at the time of grant, not exercise. *TA 1985, s 135(2)* provides that in respect of options not capable of exercise for more than seven years, no income tax will be payable in respect of any gains at the time of grant, but this leaves options which may last more than seven years within the general charge to tax under Schedule E. In *Abbott v Philbin (1960) 39 TC 82*, the court held that only gains which accrue on the grant of an option (because the option is granted at a discount to the market value of the shares) are to be treated as earnings of an employment; gains arising from the subsequent exercise of the option are derived not from the employment, but from the rights as optionholder.

17.7 Where an employee is within Case I of Schedule E at the time of grant, then any gains on exercise will, in principle, be chargeable to income tax but:

(*a*) any liability to tax of a director or employee who has ceased to be resident in the UK by the time of exercise will not normally be pursued if only for obvious practical reasons;

(*b*) if the employee was granted the option during only a temporary visit to the UK (so that he was within Case I of Schedule E only temporarily) then:

  (i) if he is granted an option over the shares of the overseas parent by the overseas company for which he normally works, then the option will normally be regarded as outside the scope of Case I of Schedule E (and for that matter outside the scope of Case II);

  (ii) if he is granted an option by the UK company for which he is working over the shares of the overseas parent then income tax on any option exercise will normally be pursued. This practice reflects the fact that in such a case the share

Overseas Schemes and Overseas Employees 17.11

option would probably be related to the employment for the whole group, the duties of which would mainly have been carried on outside the UK;

(c) where at the time of exercise an employee who is within Case I of Schedule E is entitled to the 100 per cent deduction for foreign earnings under *TA 1988, s 193*, the same deduction will normally apply to any option gains. If part of the tax year in which the option is exercised is a qualifying period for the foreign earnings deduction under *TA 1988, s 193*, then the option gain on exercise will only be relieved pro rata. If the optionholder qualifies for a deduction under *TA 1988, s 193* for six months of the tax year, then only one half of the gains on an exercise in that tax year will be deductible under *TA 1988, s 193*.

Approved schemes and overseas employees

17.8 *TA 1988, 9 Sch* does not exclude participation by overseas employees in any of the three types of approved schemes. However, under both approved executive share option schemes and profit sharing schemes there are limits on the value of shares available for employees whose earnings are not 'liable' to deduction of income tax through PAYE under *TA 1988, s 203*.

Executive share options

17.9 In approved executive share option schemes, the limit on the value of the shares available is the 'appropriate limit' in *TA 1988, 9 Sch 28(2)*. The appropriate limit is the greater of:

(a) £100,000; or

(b) four times the earnings liable to deduction of tax under PAYE in the current or preceding tax year;

(c) in the case of employees who only commenced employment in the current tax year, four times the earnings liable to deduction of tax under PAYE for the first twelve months employment.

17.10 An overseas employee who does not have earnings liable to deduction of tax under PAYE within paragraphs (b) and (c) in 17.9 above is only entitled to participate in an approved executive share option scheme up to the limit in paragraph (a) in 17.9 above i.e. £100,000 worth of shares.

17.11 The earnings liable to deduction of tax excludes the value of benefits in kind and other expense payments which are taxable under *TA 1988, ss 153–168*. In addition, the amount of earnings which are liable to deduction of tax are calculated by deducting certain items

17.12 Overseas Schemes and Overseas Employees

which are paid under the 'net of pay' arrangements. This includes employee contributions under approved pension schemes and self-standing AVCs and charitable payroll gifts.

Profit sharing schemes

17.12 In approved profit sharing schemes, the maximum value of shares which may be appropriated to an employee in any tax year is 'the relevant amount' (*TA 1988, 9 Sch 30(3)*). The 'relevant amount' means an amount which is not less than £3,000 and not more than £8,000, but which, subject to that, is 10 per cent of the participant's salary for the current or preceding tax years, whichever is the greater (*TA 1988, s 187(2)*). 'Salary' means emoluments liable to be paid in that tax year under deduction of tax under PAYE (*TA 1988, s 187(5)*). In the case of overseas employees who do not have earnings liable to deduction under PAYE, they will be entitled to participate only up to the £3,000 minimum for any tax year. However, this will cover allocations under most schemes anyhow.

Savings-related share option schemes

17.13 There are no specific limits on the value of shares which may be made available to overseas individuals under savings-related share option schemes other than those which apply generally.

UK approved sub-schemes to overseas parents schemes

17.14 Any participation by a UK resident employee in an employees' share scheme established by an overseas parent will normally be on 'unapproved' terms so far as UK tax is concerned. However, an overseas parent may be prepared to adapt its scheme so that the conditions for Inland Revenue approval of the scheme are satisfied, or it may be prepared to establish a separate UK approved scheme. A separate scheme largely based on an existing scheme of the parent is commonly described as a 'sub-scheme' if only to acknowledge that it is a variation of the existing overseas scheme. In practice, the most common types of sub-scheme have been UK approved share option schemes based on US share option schemes and UK profit sharing schemes based on matching offer arrangements which are common in US multinational share plans.

17.15 Many US share plans contain a power to establish appropriate arrangements for overseas employees. This will normally be accepted as giving sufficient power to establish a separate UK sub-plan. A certified resolution of the Remuneration Committee of the overseas company will normally be treated as satisfactory evidence of the establishment of the sub-scheme.

Overseas Schemes and Overseas Employees 17.20

17.16 The Inland Revenue normally prefers dealing with an appropriate UK resident. A UK subsidiary of an overseas parent which establishes an approved scheme will therefore often be asked to act as its agent for dealing with the Inland Revenue.

Extending a savings-related share option scheme to overseas employees

17.17 A UK approved savings-related share option scheme has three attractive features for UK employees: a tax-free discount in the option price, a tax-free bonus under the savings contract, and tax-free gains on the exercise of options. In virtually all overseas countries, the bonus under UK sharesave contracts and any gains accruing on the exercise of an option (as distinct from the sale of the shares) will be subject to income tax at the applicable marginal rate. Usually the discount on the grant of an option does not suffer tax at the time of grant.

Exchange differences

17.18 Overseas employees who participate in a UK approved savings-related share option scheme are exposed to an exchange risk. Savings must be made into a UK sterling savings account. If the exchange rate rises before the exercise of the option, it may be more attractive to take the bonus rather than the shares. Alternatively, if the exchange rate has fallen it may wipe out any benefits to the employee in that, after conversion into local currency, the realised proceeds may be less than the savings. These are extreme examples, but clearly the eventual gain made by overseas employees may be substantially distorted by currency fluctuations.

UK savings accounts

17.19 Strictly speaking, savings contributions under a UK savings-related share option scheme must be deducted from pay each month or week and paid into a sharesave account with a UK bank, building society or the Department for National Savings. Where overseas employees, in particular expats, are paid in UK sterling this does not cause any great difficulty but obviously the deduction may need to vary from month to month where salary is paid in foreign currency.

Overseas savings scheme legislation

17.20 There are no equivalent schemes to the UK approved savings-related share option scheme overseas except possibly the US stock

17.21 Overseas Schemes and Overseas Employees

purchase plan under *section 423* of the Internal Revenue Code but even that does not offer any beneficial savings medium.

Common overseas scheme modifications

17.21 Many of the companies which have extended their sharesave schemes overseas have done so by establishing unapproved share option schemes which provide for regular monthly savings to be made by deduction from local currency pay and held in appropriate investment media (but not necessarily a UK sharesave account) or in a choice of currencies. This removes the difficulty for companies in requiring employees to save in an inappropriate investment media or in a particular currency which may result in the erosion of benefits due to adverse exchange movements (see 17.40).

Expats

17.22 As far as expats are concerned, they will usually have UK bank accounts and it should be possible for them to make arrangements for deductions to be made each month by direct debit into the sharesave account.

Extending the profit sharing scheme to overseas employees

Advantages to UK employees

17.23 A UK profit sharing scheme has one major tax advantage for UK employees, namely, the avoidance of any tax on the value of the shares received where the employee leaves the shares with the scheme trustees for the full five years. Schemes offering similar tax advantages apply only in Eire and, to a certain extent, in the US under *section 401* of the Internal Revenue Code and in Germany where the free shares element is limited to DM 500 each year.

Employer contributions

17.24 Employers running overseas schemes will normally be entitled to a similar tax deduction for the cost of any contributions to the trustees to purchase shares for its own employees as under a UK approved profit sharing scheme.

Tax complications of overseas employees participation

17.25 Under an approved profit sharing scheme, trustees deduct tax under PAYE on the appropriate percentage of the locked-in-value of the shares on an early sale of the shares or a transfer of the shares into their own name. An overseas employee will only be entitled to a credit against his own local tax liability for the 'appropriate percentage' of the locked-in-value of the shares if the relevant double taxation treaty provides relief for quasi-employment income. Even where such relief is available, a claim needs to be made and this will involve time and effort.

Separate offshore trusts

17.26 The normal solution to extending profit sharing schemes to overseas employees, is to arrange for an unapproved profit sharing scheme trust to be established, usually offshore, so as to avoid falling within the UK tax net. An unapproved profit sharing scheme gives greater flexibility in the determination of the distributable pool, the identification of the eligible employees for any particular offer (nomination may even be restricted to individual employees) and greater flexibility in the determination of the restrictions on sale of the shares. A single trust may be established to cover a number of schemes although BP and BAT Industries have established a separate trust or sub-trust for each company. The trust will normally be established as a discretionary trust under which the employees have no entitlement to the shares until their release so as to avoid the premature tax charge in some countries on the appropriation, rather than release, of the shares. Under most overseas employees schemes, the period of restriction on sales is normally two years as in the UK.

Establishment of schemes for overseas employees

17.27 Where a UK company proposes the establishment of an employees' share scheme for overseas employees, account must still be taken of all the normal requirements which apply to the establishment of a scheme for UK employees, in particular the requirements of the *1993 Listing Rules* and the Guidelines of the Investment Committees of the ABI and the NAPF. In addition, a UK company will need to take account of the local regulations on securities laws, exchange control and tax in making any offer.

17.28 The *1993 Listing Rules* require all schemes of UK domestic companies (including overseas subsidiaries) involving the issue of new shares to be approved by shareholders of the UK company. However, where a UK company proposes the establishment of a series of schemes for overseas subsidiaries substantially based on an existing UK scheme, then the directors of the UK company may obtain a general authority to establish such overseas schemes without specific shareholders' approval in each case.

17.29 *Overseas Schemes and Overseas Employees*

17.29 The Guidelines of the Investment Committees of the ABI and NAPF are intended to apply to all companies in which their members hold shares and, therefore, shares quoted on overseas stock exchanges are in theory covered, although in practice only UK traded companies will comply to the Guidelines. The ABI expects any new shares which are allocated under any overseas scheme to be counted against the scheme limits in the UK. In addition, an allocation to an individual may not exceed the normal Guidelines limit of the four times earnings.

17.30 An appropriate form of resolution authorising directors to establish overseas schemes similar to any UK scheme is as follows:

'The Directors be hereby authorised to establish special arrangements for overseas employees to acquire shares in the Company which, although substantially based on any existing scheme of the Company, are modified to meet any relevant local securities law, tax and exchange control requirements. However, any such arrangements which are established for overseas employees will not be materially more favourable to such employees than the corresponding scheme for UK employees, and any shares allocated under such arrangements will be counted against the limits in the existing schemes on the maximum number of shares which may be newly issued. In addition, no such arrangements will be established using the shares of a local subsidiary'.

17.31 An overseas scheme which uses only existing shares supplied through an ESOP will not normally need to be submitted for shareholders' approval unless it involves a Related Party Transaction under the *1993 Listing Rules*.

Overseas laws and the making of share offers to overseas employees

17.32 Overseas laws need to be taken into account in any share offer made to overseas employees. Any company proposing an offer of shares to overseas employees should seek specific local advice before making any offer. The main points to be considered are:

(*a*) securities laws:
  (i) whether there is an obligation to file any prospectus or listing document with the local regulatory authorities before making any share offer and, if so, the nature of the information to be filed;
  (ii) whether there is an obligation to supply any particular information to the offeree at the time of making any share offer;
(*b*) taxation and social security contributions:

Overseas Schemes and Overseas Employees 17.33

- (i) whether there are liabilities to tax which arise for the employee in respect of participation in the scheme;
- (ii) whether any local subsidiary is liable to withhold tax in any circumstances;
- (iii) whether any local subsidiary is obliged to report any taxable income on gains to the regulatory authority;

(*c*) central bank requirements:
- (i) whether there are any restrictions on the holding of foreign securities or on the remittance abroad of funds for the purchase of foreign securities;
- (ii) whether the share certificates of foreign securities must be deposited with any bank or other person;
- (iii) whether there are any obligations on the repatriation of gains from investments in foreign securities;

(*d*) labour law:
- (i) whether there are any labour law requirements (such as an obligation to obtain the local works council approval of a share offer in Germany);

(*e*) data protection law:
- (i) whether there are any restrictions on the passing of personal details, particularly computer data, to a non-employer, in connection with any share offer.

Securities laws

17.33 Few overseas countries accept the view entrenched in UK law that an offer of shares to employees does not require the filing of any document with the regulatory authorities. However, many countries have introduced specific relaxations, particularly where the number of employees is limited:

— *United States*: under Rule 701, offers to employees under an employee benefit plan are allowed each year within certain limits;

— *Australia*: under Australian Securities Commission policy, offers of unissued shares on options to employees are allowed of listed shares, including foreign listed companies, in certain circumstances;

— *France*: offers to less than 300 employees are usually permitted.

One of the main countries where securities laws do not generally apply to any proposed share offer to local employees is Germany.

17.34 Overseas Schemes and Overseas Employees

Taxation

17.34 Generally speaking, income tax rates on earnings have fallen in most countries around the world over the past ten years and this has meant that offering shares and share options has become more attractive. The only comparable overseas tax relieved schemes to UK approved schemes are in the US and in the Republic of Ireland. In the Republic of Ireland, income tax relief on approved share option schemes was repealed in 1992, but approved profit sharing schemes similar to the UK approved profit sharing scheme are still popular.

Central bank requirements

17.35 Exchange controls have been dismantled in many countries over the past decade and are now rarely a hindrance to the operation of schemes except in Southern Africa and in certain other less developed countries.

Other administrative matter to be taken into account

Support of local management

17.36 Any UK group which makes a share or share option offer to employees of an overseas subsidiary will need the support of local management to communicate and handle the operation of the scheme locally. It is usually sensible to appoint a 'local co-ordinator' as a point of contact for the UK company in handling the offer.

Communications

17.37 Where an offer is made available to local employees, it may be necessary to translate all employee communications material and application forms into the local language. This is usually best done by providing a UK template of the material and leaving it for local management to translate and print locally.

Pricing of offers

17.38 Local employees will rarely have foreign currency bank accounts and any remittances to the UK will need to be converted into UK currency. Normally, the parent company will prescribe an appropriate rate of exchange for any offer and the local co-ordinator will arrange for local currency payments to be converted into UK sterling before remitted electronically to the designated branch of the UK parent company's bankers. Any currency risk may be borne by either the local company or the UK parent as may be agreed.

Offshore currency funds

17.39 A number of companies with share option schemes have established arrangements whereby employees can save the monies to exercise the option in any one of a number of possible currencies. This enables employees to switch between currencies as they consider appropriate during the option period. The most popular of these is the NM Rothschild Currency Funds which operates arrangements for, amongst others, British Vita, Enterprise Oil, Burmah Castrol, Guinness, Reuters and Reed International. This gives a choice of 18 currencies and a facility to switch between currencies with minimal cost.

Option schemes

17.40 The exercise of an option will involve the completion of notices of exercise and the remittance of the relevant funds to the UK company. Again, the local subsidiary may be able to assist in these arrangements.

Rights of shareholders

17.41 The articles of association of many companies provide that there is no obligation on a UK company to send notices of meeting to overseas members although in practice most public companies do so. As far as dividends are concerned, these will be paid in the normal way, but the local subsidiary will need to advise employees of the steps which can be taken to make any claim for repayment by the UK Inland Revenue of part of the tax credit attaching to dividends.

Some overseas schemes

17.42 Many UK public companies have established share option schemes for United States employees. These usually provide for non-qualifying options in respect of which the optionholder is chargeable to US taxes on the exercise of the option, but the local employing company may be entitled to a deduction for the option gains. Other schemes for UK employees may provide for the grant of incentive stock options which confer relief from income tax on certain option gains, but no deduction for the employing company. The favourable tax treatment of US incentive stock options is only available where the following conditions are satisfied:

(a) the plan is approved at a meeting of the parent company shareholders;

(b) the total number of shares that may be issued under the plan is specified;

17.43 *Overseas Schemes and Overseas Employees*

(c) eligibility to participate in the plan is specified;

(d) certain alterations must be approved by shareholders;

(e) options are granted within ten years of the earlier of the date of the plan and shareholders' approval of the plan;

(f) options are not capable of exercise more than ten years after grant;

(g) the exercise price is not less than the market value of a share at the time of grant;

(h) the value of the shares in respect of which the option first becomes exercisable in a calendar year is no more than US $100,000.

It will be noted that as UK shareholders' approval may need to be obtained for the scheme, the establishment of such a scheme under a general directors' authority to establish schemes for overseas employees may rule out this type of arrangement.

17.43 A number of large multinational groups have been extending their schemes to overseas employees where practical. The main multinational schemes are as follows:

Oil and Gas Sector

1. **BP:** operates profit sharing 'matching offer' schemes in Australia, Austria, France, Germany, Hong Kong, Japan, Malaysia, New Zealand, Norway, Singapore, South Africa, Thailand, Venezuela, Argentina and Brazil may be included in due course.

2. **Burmah Castrol:** extends its sharesave schemes overseas using the Rothschilds facility.

3. **Enterprise Oil:** operates schemes for Norwegian employees.

General

4. **Allied-Lyons:** is considering extending its sharesave scheme to certain overseas employees.

5. **BAT Industries:** extended its profit sharing scheme on a matching offer basis to the US and Germany and on a free offer basis to Belgium and Netherlands and to UK expats. It has in the past offered free shares to employees in Spain, France, Portugal and Denmark.

6. **BTR:** grants sharesave options to overseas employees in certain countries.

7. **Cadbury-Schweppes:** extends its SAYE scheme to employees in Ireland, Australia and New Zealand.

8. **Fisons:** extended its sharesave schemes to France, US, Germany and Eire.

Overseas Schemes and Overseas Employees 17.43

9. **Guinness:** grants sharesave options internationally using Rothschilds facility.

10. **Laporte:** extended its profit sharing scheme to employees in five European countries.

11. **LEP:** extends its sharesave schemes to Ireland, Canada, USA, Belgium, France, Netherlands, Spain, Portugal, New Zealand, Hong Kong, Japan, Malaysia, Phillipines, Taiwan, Thailand.

12. **Lonrho:** extends its sharesave scheme to selected overseas countries.

13. **NFC:** has recently established overseas 'matching offer' schemes similar to its UK scheme in US, Canada, Australia, Norway, Hong Kong, Malaysia, Germany, Spain, France out of its 15 overseas countries.

14. **Pilkington:** extends largely share option type benefits to employees in 23 countries.

15. **Reuters:** extends its sharesave scheme to 59 countries including several in Eastern Europe.

16. **Reckitt & Colman:** extends its sharesave scheme overseas.

17. **Reed International:** the SAYE scheme is extended to overseas countries using Rothschilds.

18. **Scottish & Newcastle:** extending its profit sharing scheme to Netherlands, Germany, France, Belgium, US, Eire and Jersey and the Isle of Man.

19. **Wellcome:** extends share schemes to 26 countries.

Note: The list is not exhaustive. Companies which only extend executive share options to selected executives are excluded. The list also excludes multinational companies based overseas which extend their schemes to the UK, e.g. the IBM Stock Purchase Scheme which is an approved profit sharing scheme in the UK.

Index

A

Approved share option schemes,
annual returns, 16.21, 16.22
reasons for establishment as, 5.8
tax reliefs, 4.8
valuation of shares, material time for,
–grant under seal, 5.32
–period before date of grant, in, 5.30–5.32
Association of British Insurers, guidelines, 3.1, 3.39–3.41
–concessions, 6.2
–Discounted Price Options, grant of, 6.33–6.38
–exercise of options, 5.78
–former employees, exercise of options by, 5.83–5.89
–historical development, 3.3–3.10
–individual participation limit, 5.65, 5.66
–previous guidelines, 3.3
–profit sharing schemes, subscription for shares, 9.32, 9.33
–public company ESOPs, on, 15.72, 15.73
–savings-related share option schemes, as to,
applications, timing, 8.12
eligibility criteria, 8.8–8.10
–scheme limits, 5.74–5.76
–time of grant, 5.20–5.22

B

Board resolution,
grant of options, for, 5.37, 5.38, 8.42, 8.43
offers, making, 16.2

Bridging finance,
arrangements for, 2.9, 2.10, 4.47
banks, from, 2.9
broker, from, 2.10

C

Certified contractual savings-related schemes,
savings-related share option schemes, linked to, 2.18
Close company,
material interest in,
–associate, shares of, 4.55
–exclusion of participation in scheme, 4.51
–family discretionary trust, remote interest in, 4.58
–meaning, 4.53
–option, shares under, 4.59, 4.60
–profit sharing scheme, exclusion of appropriation under, 9.53, 9.54
–rule, companies within, 4.52
–trustee, shares held by, 4.56
–unappropriated shares, disregarding, 4.57
meaning, 4.54
participants, loans to ESOP trustees being, 15.33

D

Demergers,
distributions on, 12.53, 12.54
profit sharing schemes,
–distributions, 12.68–12.70
–dividends, 12.67
share option schemes,
–adjustment of options, 12.58

Index

   –approval, withdrawal of, 12.60–12.63
   –cash compensation, 12.64
   –compensation for effects on, 12.59
   –dividends, no right to receive, 12.55
   –option rights, withdrawal of, 12.60–12.63
   –options, exercise of,
      company transferred outside group, employees of, 12.56
      distributing company, employees of, 12.57
   –parallel options, 12.65, 12.66
Directors,
   interests in shares, notification of, 9.36, 9.37
   –register of, 15.69
   reports and accounts, 15.75–15.78
Discounted Price Options,
   ABI Guidelines, 6.33–6.38
   all or nothing basis, on, 6.5
   amount of discount, 6.26, 6.27
   conditions for grant of, 6.28
   cost of, 6.33
   different groups of companies, conditions applying to, 6.30
   discretion in exercise of, 6.35
   early exercise of, 6.34
   employee guide, 6.39
   exercise, form of notice of, 6.39
   four times relevant earnings limit, 6.32
   grant of, 6.4, 6.24
   guidelines, 6.25
   intention of, 6.29
   meaning, 6.24
   method of granting, 6.39
   option certificate, form of, 6.39
   parallel options, grant of, 6.38
   participation, 6.31
   performance conditions, 6.34–6.36
   performance targets, 6.36
   price of, 6.28
   rationing, 6.37, 6.38
   replacement options, issue of, 6.38
   tax conditions, 6.28–6.32
   unapproved,
   –grant of, 6.41
   –tax aspects, 6.40
Dividends,
   mandates, 16.8
   profit sharing schemes,
   –foreign, 12.76–12.78
   –participants, payment to, 12.74
   –scrip, 12.82
   –UK, 12.75
   scrip,
   –offer of, 12.79
   –profit sharing schemes, 12.82
   –share option schemes, 12.80, 12.81
   share option schemes,
   –optionholders, no entitlement of, 12.71–12.73
   –scrip, 12.80, 12.81

E

Employee benefits,
   returns of, 16.19, 16.20
Employee Share Ownership Plan,
   beneficiaries, tax credit, 15.41
   categories of, 15.11
   company, tax considerations for,
   –close companies, 15.33
   –company not to benefit, 15.32

Index

–gifts, 15.29–15.32
–loans, 15.33–15.36
–qualifying employee share ownership trust, relief for contributions to, 15.30
–several group companies, beneficiaries including employees from, 15.31
–trustees, deduction of payments to, 15.29
contributions, deductibility, 7.14
employees' share schemes,
–holding shares under, 15.64
–linked to, 15.3–15.9
employees, tax considerations of,
–chargeable asset, acquisition of, 15.54
–transfer of shares or cash to, 15.53
establishment,
–best interests of company, in, 15.22
–power of company, 15.21, 15.22
–shareholders' approval, 15.23
–not required, where, 15.5
existing shares, use of, 15.4
financing,
–categories, 15.11
–form of, 15.10
–gift of shares, ESOP established for, 15.12, 15.13
–sale of shares, ESOP established for,
call option arrangements, 15.20
company, loan by, 15.16, 15.17
costs, recouping, 15.14
third party, loan from, 15.18, 15.19

third party, payments to, 15.15
–trustees, contributions to, 15.10
meaning, 15.1
non-resident, 15.28
number of, 15.4
overseas scheme, 17.31
potential uses for, 15.3
profit sharing schemes, use with, 15.7
public company,
–directors' interests in shares, register of, 15.69
–directors' reports and accounts, 15.75–15.78
–disclosure requirements, 15.67–15.71
–existing shares, using, 15.65
–funding, 15.66
–Investment Committee Guidelines, 15.72–15.74
–Listing Rules, 15.65–15.67
–new shares, approval of issue of, 15.65
purpose of, 15.2
Qualifying Employee Share Ownership Trusts. *See* Qualifying Employee Share Ownership Trusts
restricted share schemes as, 7.2
–use with, 15.8
settlor, attribution of chargeable gains to, 15.48
share option schemes, use with, 15.6
share options, grant of,
–capital gains tax, 15.57, 15.58
–income tax rules, 15.56
–inheritance tax, 15.59
–power of, 15.55
trustees,
–identity of, 15.24–15.28

349

Index

   –loans to, 7.16
   –non-UK resident, 15.27
   –payment to, 7.13
   –tax considerations for,
      capital gains tax,
         15.43–15.48
     distribution of shares,
        on, 15.44
     exemption from
       Schedule D Case III
       tax, 15.42
     income tax,
        15.37–15.42
     inheritance tax,
        15.49–15.52
     revenue expenses, 15.39
     voluntary contributions, 15.37
   –UK resident, 15.26
   trusts, conditions, 1.3
Employees' share schemes,
   amendments, approval
     of, 4.22–4.24
   approval, application for, 4.27–4.31
   approved,
   –jointly owned companies, App 1–4.83
   –requirements for, 4.25
   cessation of approval,
   –direction on company,
     at, 4.79–4.82
   –request on company,
     at, 4.76–4.78
   directors, fiduciary duties, 4.12
   duration, 4.71, 4.72
   establishment,
   –circular to shareholders, 4.18
   –costs of, 4.83
   –defect in, 4.25
   –memorandum and articles of association, 4.10, 4.11
   –reasons for, 4.1
   –resolution, form of, 4.26
   –shareholders' approval, 4.17

   features of, 4.19–4.21
   listed companies, in, 4.9
   material interest in close
     companies, exclusion
     of, 4.51–4.60
     See also Close company
   meaning, 4.2–4.4
   number of, 1.1
   persons outside permitted
     categories, participation
     by, 4.4
   pre-emption provisions,
     disapplication of, 4.6
   renewal,
   –Inland Revenue practice, 4.75
   –profit sharing schemes, 4.74
   –share option schemes, 4.73
   share capital, overall limit
     on, 3.5
   shares. *See* Shares
   Stock Exchange Listing
     Rules,
   –drafts, 4.16
   –features of schemes, rules
     on, 4.19
   –number of shares allocated, 4.20
   –options, adjustment of, 4.21
   –taking account of, 4.15
   types of, 2.1
ESOPS. *See* Employee share
   ownership plan
Executive share option
   schemes,
   allocations, timing, 3.24, 3.25
   approved,
   –eligibility,
     ceasing after grant of
       option, 5.15
     company establishing
       scheme,
       directorship or
        employment with, 5.14
     full-time directors, 5.12

Index

generally, 5.11
qualifying employees, 5.13
  restrictions on, 5.16
–income tax, relief from, 5.6
–tax advantages, 5.7
approved options, grant of, 6.4
bridging finance,
–arrangements for, 2.9, 2.10, 4.47
–banks, from, 2.9
–broker, from, 2.10
cap on participation, 2.8
design, timing affecting, 3.8
disclaimer of options,
–provision for, 5.45
–provisions allowing, 5.46
discounted, 3.10
Discounted Price Options. *See* Discounted Price Options
duration, 3.16
early leavers, 3.29–3.32
eligibility, 3.17
exercise of options,
–ABI Guidelines, 5.78
–employees, by,
   approved schemes, 5.79
   three-year rule, 5.80, 5.81
   unapproved schemes, 5.82
–former employees, by,
   ABI guidelines, 5.83–5.89
   approved schemes, 5.90–5.92
   dismissal without good cause, on, 5.88
   extension of period for, 5.83, 5.84
   foreign jurisdiction, on transfer to, 5.89
   involuntary circumstances, 5.85

maternity, leaving employment on, 5.87
   retirement, on, 5.86
–income tax on, 5.77
–personal representatives, by, 5.93
–takeovers, on, 5.94
fixed price, purchase of shares at, 2.4
gain, tax on,
–exercise, accruing on, 5.2
–income tax, 5.4
–instalments, payable in, 5.5
incentive, 2.4
individual participation limit, 3.18
–ABI guidelines, 5.65, 5.66
–approved schemes,
   appropriate limit, 5.53, 5.54
   market value, aggregation of, 5.55
–excess options, 5.67–5.71
–four times earnings rule, 5.52
–other approved schemes, options under, 5.56
–relevant emoluments
   calculation of, 5.62, 5.64
   definition, 5.60
   overseas earnings, 5.61
   tax year, for, 5.63
–sources of, 5.51
–£100,000 Limit, 5.57–5.59
institutional investors, 5.17
linked, 2.11
operation of, 5.1
option certificate,
–balance, 5.44
–execution of, 5.42
–form of, 5.40, 5.43
–grant under seal, 5.41
–submission of, 5.39
optionholders, selection of, 5.18

351

Index

options,
 –ABI Guidelines limiting, 6.17
 –early exercise, rights of, 3.29–3.32
 –grant of,
  board resolution, 5.37, 5.38
  discount, at, 5.29
  less than market price, at,
   approved schemes, 5.33–5.35
   unapproved schemes, 5.36
  no tax payable on, 5.3
  payment for, 5.26
  price, 5.27–5.29
  procedure for,
   grants under seal, 5.24–5.26
   offer and acceptance, 5.24–5.26
   seal, under, 5.24–5.26, 5.32, 5.41
  time of,
   ABI Guidelines, 5.20–5.22
   Model Scheme, 5.19
   Stock Exchange Model Code, 5.23
 –maximum number of shares, 2.6
 –pricing, 3.20, 3.21
 –sustained growth,
  exercisable in case of, 2.5
 –value of, 2.7
 overseas employees,
  participation by, 17.9–17.11
 Parallel Options. *See* Parallel Options
 performance targets. *See* Performance targets
 phantom, 2.16
 Remunerations Committees, 3.28
 replacement options. *See* Replacement options
 restricted,
 –financial contribution, 2.14
 –free shares, allocation of, 2.12
 –income tax, charge to, 2.13
 –scheme using, 2.15
 right to buy shares, 2.3
 rules, precedent for, App 3–5.106
 scheme limits,
 –ABI Guidelines, 5.74–5.76
 –London Stock Exchange Rules, 5.72
 –NAPF Guidelines, 5.73
 –replacement options, 3.13
 –small market capitalisation, company with, 3.14
 super options. *See* Super options
 takeover offers, 12.11
 transfer of options,
 –non-transferability, 5.47, 5.48
 –tax on, 5.49, 5.50
 unapproved, reasons for, 5.9
 valuation of shares, material time for, 5.30–5.32

G

Guidelines,
 allocations, timing, 3.24–3.28
 Association of British Insurers, 3.1, 3.39–3.41
  See also Association of British Insurers
 duration of schemes, 3.16
 early leavers, 3.29–3.33
 eligibility, 3.17
 individual participation, 3.18, 3.19
 National Association of Pension Funds, 3.1, 3.11, 3.42, 3.43
 –scheme limits, 5.73

Index

overseas employees'
    schemes, application
    to, 17.29
performance targets, 3.36
pricing, 3.20–3.23
public company ESOPs, on,
    15.72–15.74
Remunerations Committees,
    3.28
replacement options, 3.35
sources, 3.2
summary of, 3.12
super options, 3.34
underwater options, 3.37

I

Inland Revenue,
    approval of schemes
    –appeal against refusal, 4.35
    –application, documents and
        information submitted
        with, 4.29
    –documentation, submission
        of, 4.28
    –form of, 4.31
    –refusal of, 4.32–4.34
    –time limits, lack of, 4.30
    –unit dealing with, 4.27
    further information, power to
        obtain, 16.23
    renewal, practice on, 4.75

L

Legislation,
    current, meaning, 8.98
    meaning, 8.99

M

Multi-national schemes,
    overseas employees,
        for, 17.43
Multi-subsidiary schemes,
    advantages, 11.11
    conglomerate group,
        appropriate for, 11.11
    flexibility, 11.16
    meaning, 11.10

more than one, prohibition
    on participation in,
    11.15
objections to, 11.12
satellite schemes, 11.10
–approval of parent
    company, requirements
    for, 11.14
–restrictions in, 11.13

N

National Association of
    Pension Funds,
    guidelines, 3.1, 3.11,
        3.42, 3.43
–public company ESOPs,
    on, 15.72, 15.73
–scheme limits, 3.15

O

Options,
    employees, granted to, 2.17
    offers, making,
    –board resolution, 16.2
    –specimen documentation,
        16.3
    –specimen timetables, 16.4
    –terms of rules, consideration
        of, 16.1
    registers,
    –relevant information,
        systems for providing,
        16.7
    –requirements, 16.5
    –sharesave contracts, in
        relation to, 16.6
    UK tax, liability of non-
        residents to, 17.4–17.7
    unapproved, returns of,
        16.13–16.17
Overseas employees,
    approved schemes,
        participation in, 17.8
    establishment of schemes
        for,
    –ESOP, through, 17.31
    –Guidelines, application
        of, 17.29

Index

–Listing Rules, requirements of, 17.28
–normal requirements, 17.27
–resolution authorising, 17.30
executive share options, 17.9–17.11
multi-national schemes, 17.43
participation in schemes, 17.1
profit sharing schemes,
–employer contributions, 17.24
–participation in, 17.12
–separate offshore trusts for, 17.26
–tax complications, 17.25
–UK employers, advantages to, 17.23
savings-related share option schemes,
–exchange differences, 17.18
–expats, deductions from UK bank accounts, 17.22
–income tax charge, 17.17
–overseas legislation, 17.20
–overseas scheme modifications, 17.21
–participation in, 17.13
–UK savings accounts, payments into, 17.19
share offers to,
–central bank requirements, 17.35
–communications, 17.37
–local management, support of, 17.36
–offshore currency funds, 17.39
–option schemes, 17.40
–overseas laws taken into account, 17.32
–pricing, 17.38
–securities laws, 17.33
–shareholders' rights, 17.41
–taxation, 17.34

UK tax, liability to,
–acquisition of shares, on, 17.3
–income tax cases, 17.2
–Schedule E, under, 17.3
–share options, on, 17.4–17.7
Overseas parents' schemes,
approved sub-schemes, participation in, 17.14
–UK resident, Inland Revenue dealing with, 17.16
US share plans, 17.15

P
Parallel Options,
ABI attitude to, 6.46
alternative terms, 6.42
demerger, granted on, 12.65, 12.66
Discounted Price Options, and, 6.38
employee guide, 6.47
exercise,
–form of notice of, 6.47
–time of, 6.44
generally, 2.11
meaning, 6.42
option certificate, form of, 6.47
separate parts, points applying to, 6.45
uses of, 6.43
Partly-paid share schemes, income tax liability, 2.1
Pensionable age,
alteration of reference to, 8.101, 8.104
legislation, change in, 8.94
meaning, 8.93
new concept of, 8.102
new schemes, for, 8.95
options, exercise of,
–actual retirement, on, 8.105
–number of shares acquired on, 8.106
requirements, 8.93

354

Index

rules, precedent for,
    App 5–8.106
Performance targets,
  achievement of,   5.95
  additional, setting,   5.102
  approved schemes,
    5.100–5.102
  choice of,   5.99
  Discounted Price Options,
    for,   6.36
  earnings per share growth,
    based on,   5.97
  generally,   3.7
  guidance on,   5.96
  replacement options, for,
    6.3, 6.22, 6.23
  share price benchmark, based
    on,   5.98
  super options, for,
    6.11–6.13
  variations,   5.103–5.106
Personal equity plans,
  advantages of,   14.2
  employees' share schemes,
    release of shares from,
    14.5–14.7
  financial assistance for
    purchase of shares,
    14.11, 14.12
  introduction of,   14.1
  plans,
  –shares held through,   14.3
  –types of,   14.4
  qualifying shares purchased
    through,   14.6
  single company plan,
    transfer of shares to,
    14.7
  sponsored,   2.25
  –demand for,   14.9
  –financial assistance,
    14.11, 14.12
  –investment advertisements,
    14.14
  –investment business,   14.13
  –object of,   14.8
  –offer, basis of,   14.10
  unquoted companies,
    investments in,   14.5

Personal representatives,
  exercise of options by,   5.93
Profit sharing schemes,
  allocation,
  –annual, average,   9.76
  –basis of,   9.17
  –timing,   3.27
  appropriations of shares,
  –bases of allocation,
    9.58–9.61
  –close companies, material
    interests in,   9.53, 9.54
  –eligibility for,   9.45–9.52
  –legal title, trustees holding,
    9.43
  notice of,   10.7
  –resolution for,   9.42
  –statutory undertakings,
    9.55, 9.56
  –timing,   9.44
  –unauthorised,   9.57
  approval, refusal of,
    4.33, 4.34
  capitalisation issues, effect
    of,   13.26
  common distributable pool,
    9.17
  demergers,
  –distributions on,
    12.68–12.70
  –dividends on,   12.67
  disposal of shares,
  –capital gains tax,
    9.89, 9.90
  –capital receipts,   9.85–9.88
  –income tax charge,
    9.77, 9.81–9.84
  –retention, period of,
    9.78–9.80
  –retirement, relevant age for,
    9.80
  –tail-swallow,   9.87
  dividends,
  –accounting for,   9.105
  –foreign,   12.76–12.78
  –overseas companies, from,
    9.98–9.100
  –participants, payment to,
    12.74

Index

–scrip, 12.82
–trustees, paid to, 9.96, 9.97
–UK, 12.75
duration, 4.72, 9.122
early leavers, 3.33
eligibility, 3.17
Employee Share Ownership Plans, use of, 15.7
excess shares, 9.57, 9.116
explanation to participants, 10.6
free offer,
–board proposal, 10.19
–cash alternatives, 10.23–10.25
–making, 10.20–10.22
–meaning, 10.1
–percentage of salary, as, 10.27
–presentation, problems arising from, 10.26, 10.27
–registrar, role of, 10.15–10.18
–trustees, role of, 10.8–10.14
–undertakings, form of, 10.21
free shares, allocation of, 2.21
group schemes,
–anti-abuse, 9.23
–cessation of participation, generally, 9.26
scheme participants, implications for, 9.27
–meaning, 9.22
–multi-trust arrangements, 9.28–9.30
–other participating companies, admission of, 9.24, 9.25
–satellite schemes, 9.29
individual appropriations, limit on value of, 9.73–9.76
legislation, 9.1

matching offer, 2.23, 2.24
–administration, 10.37–10.47
–annual basis, on, 10.30–10.35
–application form, 10.5
issue of, 10.37
–binding legal contract, as, 10.43
–board proposal, 10.19
–company, by, 10.10
–continuous savings scheme, 10.36
–Inland Revenue practice, 10.29
–making, 10.28–10.30
–meaning, 10.1
–privatisations, in, 10.28
–purchased shares,
registration of, 10.48
retention of, 10.38
–registrar, role of, 10.15–10.18
–restriction on disposal of shares, premature cessation of, 10.44
–scaling down, 10.34
–take-up, level of, 10.35
–tax, liability to,
avoiding, 10.46
where arising, 10.45
–timetable, 10.49
–trustees, role of, 10.8–10.14
–value of shares, determining, 10.39–10.42
maximum amount of shares, 2.22
national insurance provisions, 9.119
new shares, limit on number of, 3.4
offers,
–documentation, 10.2–10.7
–letters, 10.3
–statutory undertakings, 10.4
–types of, 10.1

Index

overseas employees,
- employer contributions, 17.24
- participation by, 17.12
- separate offshore trusts for, 17.26
- tax complications, 17.25
- UK employers, advantages to, 17.23

participation, eligibility criteria,
- extension, discretion for, 9.50
- former directors and employees, 9.46
- full-time director or employee, meaning, 9.47
- other scheme, appropriation already made under, 9.52
- part-time employees, 9.49
- persons meeting, 9.45
- qualifying period of service, with reference to, 9.51
- service criteria, drafting, 9.48

PAYE,
- circumstances of operation, 9.114
- collection of tax through, 9.84
- operation of, 9.112
- relevant company required to operate, 9.115
- scheme, opening, 9.113
- trustees, operation by, 9.104
- trustees' scheme, 9.117, 9.118
- unauthorised and excess shares, 9.116

pricing, 3.22
reductions in share capital, and, 13.32
registrars,
- appointment, 10.16
- free or matching offer, role in, 10.15–10.18
- principal, 10.17

renewal, 4.74
rights issues, effect of. *See* Rights issues,
scheme allocations, limits on value of, 9.72
schemes of arrangement, 12.49
subscription for shares,
- ABI guidelines, 9.32, 9.33
- consideration for, 9.31
- directors, obligations of, 9.36
- listed companies, in, 9.34–9.38
- Model Code, 9.35
- new or existing, 9.21
- private companies, in, 9.40
- relevant securities not requiring specific authority for allotment, 9.39

subsidiary company. *See* Subsidiary company profit sharing schemes,
takeovers. *See* Takeovers
trust. *See* Profit sharing trust
unappropriated shares,
- dealings in, 9.38
- tax reliefs, 9.41
unauthorised shares, 9.57, 9.116
value of shares,
- initial market value, 9.62–9.64
- listed companies, 9.65–9.70
- private companies, 9.71
- tax purposes, for, 9.62–9.64
voluntary winding-up, 12.52
withdrawal of approval, 4.81

Profit sharing trust,
alteration of, 9.120, 9.121
takeovers. *See* Takeovers
trust deed, App 6–9.122

357

Index

trustees,
 –appointment, nature of, 9.4, 9.5
 –appropriated shares,
  retention of, 9.95
 –appropriations of shares,
  legal title, 9.43
  resolution for, 9.42
 –contributions to,
  financial assistance, 9.15, 9.16
  tax relief, 9.18–9.20
  voluntary payments, 9.14
 –custodial and administrative duties, 10.12
 –dividends paid to, 9.96, 9.97
 –establishment of, 9.3
 –fiduciary position, 9.92
 –free or matching offer, role in, 10.8–10.14
 –general powers, 9.5
 –listed companies, for, 9.8
 –meetings, 10.14
 –non-executive directors as, 9.10
 –normal duties of, 9.91, 9.92
 –participant as, 9.7
 –persons appointed as, 9.6–9.10
 –persons being, 10.13
 –powers and duties of, 9.4
 –protection of, 9.11, 9.12
 –removal, 9.13
 –retirement, 9.13
 –scheme registrars as, 9.10
 –single company as, 9.6
 –statutory duties,
  appropriation, notice of, 9.101
  dividends, accounting for, 9.105
  PAYE, operation of, 9.104, 9.117, 9.118
  period of retention,
   holding shares after, 9.103
   period of retention,
   holding shares during, 9.102
  rights issues, acting on direction of participant in, 9.106, 9.107
 –subscription for shares, 9.21, 9.31–9.40
 –subsidiary as, 9.9
 –tax vouchers, provision of, 9.97
 –taxation,
  appropriation of shares,
   capital gains tax on, 9.110
  income of unappropriated assets, income tax on, 9.109
  inheritance tax, 9.111
 –trust assets, holding, 9.108
 –unappropriated assets,
  holding, 9.93, 9.94
 –unappropriated shares,
  dealings in, 9.38

Q
Qualifying Employee Share Ownership Trusts,
 beneficiaries, 15.61
 conditions for, 15.61
 contributions to, tax relief, 15.9, 15.30, 15.60
 establishment, 15.61
 number of, 15.63
 trustees, 15.61
 –income tax, subject to, 15.62

R
Replacement options,
 ABI Guidelines, under, 6.18
 conditions, 6.19, 12.18
 Discounted Price Options, and, 6.38
 generally, 3.7
 introduction of, 6.2, 6.19

358

Index

performance of company,
    significant improvement
    in,   6.21
performance targets,
    6.3, 6.22, 6.23
takeover offers, on,   12.14
target company scheme, rules
    of,   12.19
unissued share capital, grant
    over,   6.20
Restricted share schemes,
  allocation of shares,
    –financing,   7.10–7.16
    –free,   7.4
    –generally,   7.5
    –interest in possession trusts,
      creation of,   7.28–7.30
    –loans,   7.16
    –performance target,
      contingent on,   7.15
  capital gains tax,   7.9
  companies establishing,   7.3
  contributions,
    –deductibility,   7.12–7.16
    –payment of,   7.11
  Employee Share Ownership
    Plans
    –scheme as,   7.2
    –use of,   15.8
  forfeiture,
    –capital gains tax,   7.19
    –income tax consequences,
        7.18
    –provision for,   7.17
  income tax,   7.6–7.8
  operation of,   7.1
  tax charge, deferred,   7.7
  trustees, shares held by,   7.5
  types of,   7.4
  US, imported from,   7.2
  vesting,
    –capital gains tax, 7.22, 7.23
    –income tax on,   7.20, 7.21
    –inheritance tax, 7.25–7.30
    –National Insurance,   7.24
Rights issues,
  benefit of,   13.7
  circulars to shareholders,
      16.9

profit sharing schemes,
  affecting,
  –company reconstruction,
    as,   13.14
  –disposals, succession of,
      13.17
  –income tax liability,   13.15
  –lapse of rights,
    13.22, 13.23
  –letter from trustees,   13.23
  –more than one payment,
      13.16
  –rights, taking up,
    13.13–13.17
  –sale of rights nil paid,
    13.18, 13.19
  –shareholder, courses of
    action,   13.12
  –tail-swallow,   13.20, 13.21
  –trust deed, provisions
    of,   13.11
share option schemes,
  affecting,   13.8–13.10
taking up,   13.7

S
Savings-related share option
  schemes,
allocations, timing,   3.26
applications,
  –aggregate amount,
    declaration of,   8.18
  –date for,   8.15
  –invitations, documents
    accompanying,   8.17
  –minimum age,   8.64
  –scaling down,
    application form,
      authorised by,   8.41
    application of methods
      of,   8.39
    maximum bonus,
      treatment as
      application for
      standard bonus,
        8.35
    monthly savings,
      of,   8.36
    provisions for,   8.33

Index

remuneration of
    applicants, pro rata, 8.40
selection by lot, as, 8.38
standard bonus, on basis of, 8.37
steps for, 8.34
–timing,
    ABI Guidelines, 8.12
    exceptional invitation periods, 8.13
    Model Scheme, 8.11, 8.25
    Stock Exchange Model Code, 8.14
–weekly paid employees, 8.22
approval, refusal of, 4.34
attractive features of, 8.2
bonuses, 8.74
certificate of approval, 8.62
certified contractual savings schemes, linked to, 2.18
contributions,
–death of investor, effect of, 8.75
–employees', 8.67
–postponement, 8.71–8.73
–stopping, 8.71–8.73
–weekly-paid employees, from, 8.68–8.70
discretionary participation, 8.6, 8.7
duration, 3.16
early leavers, 3.33
eligibility, 3.17
eligibility criteria,
–ABI guidelines, 8.8–8.10
–director or employee of participating company, 8.5
–Inland Revenue requirements, 8.4–8.7
–non-executive directors, 8.9
–overseas employees, 8.10
–part-time directors, 8.9

employee communications,
–annual statements, 8.52
–company newspaper articles, 8.54
–decisions, focus on, 8.48–8.50
–formal presentations, 8.55, 8.56
–importance of, 8.47
–key information, 8.48–8.50
–posters, 8.58
–team briefings, 8.55
–videos, 8.57
–written material, 8.51–8.53
individual participation, limit on, 3.19
legislation, 8.2
legislative provisions, changes taking account of, 8.100
maximum amount under, 8.16
maximum bonus, 8.20, 8.21
new shares, limit on number of, 3.6
number of, 8.3
operation of, 8.1
options,
–board resolution to grant, 8.42, 8.43
–certificate, 8.44–8.46
–consideration for, 8.24
–early exercise of,
    death, in event of, 8.85
    early retirement, on, 8.89, 8.103
    leaving employment, on, 8.86–8.91
    maternity, on, 8.89
    retirement age, at, 8.92–8.105
–exercise of,
    bonus date, at, 8.82–8.84
    changes, prior approval of, 8.97–8.99

Index

gains, income tax on, 8.81
generally, 8.80, 8.81
pensionable age,
   meaning, 8.93–8.105
–non-transferability, 8.59
–price,
   currency of, 8.32
   invitations issued without details of, 8.30
   market value, not manifestly less than 80 per cent of, 8.31
   market value of shares, fixed by reference to, 8.27
   statement of, 8.26
   sterling, expressed in, 8.32
   time for fixing, 8.29
–pricing, 3.22
–time for grant of, 8.28
options, discount for, 2.19
overseas employees,
   extension to,
–exchange differences, 17.18
–expats, deductions from UK bank accounts, 17.22
–income tax charge, 17.17
–overseas legislation, 17.20
–overseas scheme modifications, 17.21
–UK savings accounts, payments into, 17.19
overseas employees, participation by, 17.13
participation rate, 2.20
principle of, 8.80
registers, 16.6
savings contract,
–approved, 8.60
–bonuses, 8.74
–eligibility to enter into, 8.61–8.64
–employees' contributions, 8.67
–interest, payment of, 8.72, 8.73
–no transfer of, 8.76
–savings body, discretion of to enter into, 8.64
–savings contributions, 8.65
–savings period, duration of, 8.66
–selection of, 8.60
–tax relief, 8.77
–weekly-paid employees, 8.68–8.70
savings contributions, 8.65
scheme limits,
–ABI Guidelines, 8.79
–Inland Revenue requirements, 8.78
scheme rules, guide to, 8.19
shares, number of, 8.23
standard bonus, 8.20, 8.21
takeover offers, 12.10
tax relief, 8.77
UK employees, attractive features for, 17.17
unequal treatment under, 8.96
wide participation, encouragement of, 8.4
Schemes of arrangement,
profit sharing schemes, 12.49
share option schemes,
–optionholders, rights of, 12.41
–options, exercise of
   approved executive scheme, under, 12.45
   approved savings-related scheme, under, 12.43
   change of control, on, 12.47
   new corporate entity, shares in, 12.47, 12.48

Index

sanction, after
    obtaining, 12.46
unissued shares, orders
    for, 12.44
–sanctioning, stages of,
    12.42
Senior executives,
  schemes for,
  –executive share option. *See*
    Executive share option
    schemes
  –generally, 2.2
Share option schemes, *See*
    Executive share option
    schemes.
  capitalisation issues, effect
    of, 13.24, 13.25
  demergers. *See* Demergers
  dividends, 12.71–12.73
  duration, 4.71
  Employee Share Ownership
    Plans, use of, 15.6
  reductions in share capital,
    and, 13.29–13.31
  renewal, 4.73
  rights issues, effect
    of, 13.8–13.10
  schemes of arrangement. *See*
    Schemes of arrangement
  scrip dividends,
    12.80, 12.81
  takeovers. *See* Takeovers.
  US employees, for, 17.42
  voluntary winding-up,
    12.50, 12.51
  withdrawal of approval, 4.80
Share purchase schemes,
  employees' share trust, 2.26
  financial assistance, provision
    of, 2.27
  interest-free loan, tax
    on, 2.28
Shares,
  acquisitions, returns of,
    16.11, 16.12
  allotment,
  –authority for, 4.5
  –discount, at, 4.13, 4.14
  classes of, 4.38

financial assistance in
    purchase of, 4.7
ordinary share capital, 4.37
requirements, 4.36, 4.38
restrictions on,
–ancillary agreements, in,
    4.46
–collateral agreements, in,
    4.46
–discretionary refusal of
    transfer, 4.44
–Model Code, provisions of,
    4.45
–none, to be, 4.40
–pre-emption provisions,
    4.43
–special, 4.41
–transfers, applying to, 4.42
scheme limits,
–flow rate, 3.12
–National Association of
    Pension Funds
    guidelines, 3.15
–replacement options, 3.13
–rolling, 3.12–3.15
transfer,
–registration, discretionary
    refusal of, 4.44
–restrictions applied on,
    4.42
valuations,
–grant under seal, 5.32
–London Stock Exchange,
    quoted on, 4.61
–material time for, in period
    before date of grant
    5.30–5.32
–New York Stock Exchange,
    quoted on, 4.62
–partly-paid schemes, 4.70
–recognised stock exchanges,
    quoted on, 4.63
–Share Valuation Division,
    by, 4.66–4.70
–unquoted companies,
    information for,
    4.66–4.70
–unquoted shares,
    4.64, 4.67

Index

value of, 4.39
widespread ownership of, 4.48–4.50
Stock Exchange Model Code
– options, time of grant, 5.23
savings-related share option schemes, grant of options under, 8.14
recognised, App 2–4.83
Stock Exchange Listing Rules,
drafts, 4.16
features of schemes, rules on, 4.19
number of shares allocated, 4.20
options, adjustment of, 4.21
scheme limits, 5.72
Yellow Book, 4.15
Subsidiary company profit sharing schemes,
holding company, using shares of, 11.1, 11.2
multi-subsidiary,
– advantages, 11.11
– conglomerate group, appropriate for, 11.11
– flexibility, 11.16
– meaning, 11.10
– more than one, prohibition on participation in, 11.15
– objections to, 11.12
– satellite schemes, 11.10
approval of parent company, requirements for, 11.14
restrictions in, 11.13
single subsidiary,
– approval of, 11.5
– existing shares, operation using, 11.7
– foreign company, of, 11.4
– initiative for establishing, 11.5
– meaning, 11.3

– new shares, using, 11.8, 11.9
– parent company, control by, 11.6
Subsidiary company schemes,
dependent subsidiaries, 2.30
uncommon, being, 2.29
Super options,
cap on shares, 6.16
circumstances for, 6.7, 6.8
conditions, 6.9
five-year performance target, 2.6
four times earnings limit, exceeding, 6.7
generally, 3.34
introduction of, 3.9, 6.2
performance targets, 6.11–6.13
positive earnings per share figure, 6.14
separate unapproved scheme, under, 2.7
time for exercise of, 6.10
unapproved share option scheme, shares over approved scheme limit in, 6.15

T
Takeovers,
all shareholders, similar treatment of, 12.5
circulars to shareholders, 16.9
general offer, 12.2
listed companies, 12.4–12.7
means of effecting, 12.2
Model Schemes, 12.3
profit sharing schemes, 12.1
– cash offer, 12.31
– loan note consideration, 12.37–12.40
– new holding, substitution of, 12.27
– reorganisations, 12.27

Index

–share consideration,
  locked-in value of old
    holding,
    apportionment
    of,   12.34–12.36
  new holding, treatment
    of,   12.33
  reorganisation, treatment
    as,   12.32
–trustees' circular,   12.30
–trustees' obligations,
  relaxation of,
    12.28, 12.29
share option schemes,
–approved options, roll-over
  of,
  application,   12.16
  facility, reasons for
    introduction of,
    12.15
  future options, for, 12.21
  introduction of,   12.14
  maximum period for,
    12.17
  shares under,   12.18
  target company scheme,
    rules of,   12.19
  tax treatment,   12.20
–cash consideration,
  surrender of option for,
    offer of,   12.22
  offeror, offer on behalf
    of,   12.23
  target company,
    recommendations
    by,   12.24
    taxation,   12.25, 12.26
–choices of consideration,
    12.13
–gains, income tax on,
    12.12, 12.13
–offer, exercise and
  acceptance of,
  executive schemes, 12.11
  obligation under
    Takeover Code,
    12.9

  savings-related schemes,
    12.10
–optionholders, rights of,
    12.8
share purchase,   12.2
Takeover Code,   12.4–12.7
Tax returns,
  employee benefits, of,
    16.19, 16.20
  share acquisitions, of,
    16.11, 16.12
  unapproved employees'
    share schemes, in relation
    to,   16.18
  unapproved share options,
    of,   16.13–16.17

U

Unapproved employees' share
  schemes,
  returns,   16.18
Unapproved share option
  schemes,
  exercise of options,   5.82
  options, grant of,
  –less than market price, at,
    5.36
  reasons for,   5.9

V

Variations of share capital,
  adjustment of options,
  –Inland Revenue
    requirements,   13.6
  –Investment Committees,
    no reference to,   13.5
  –Listing Rules,   13.3
  –Yellow Book rules,
    13.2, 13.4
  capitalisation issues,
  –profit sharing schemes,
    effect on,   13.26
  –share option schemes, effect
    on,   13.24, 13.25
  circulars to shareholders,
    16.9
  consolidations,   13.27

Index

exempt demerger
    distributions, exclusion
    of, 13.34
meaning, 13.1
provision for, 13.1
reduction,
–form of, 13.28
–profit sharing schemes, 13.32
–share option schemes, as, 13.29–13.31
rights issues. *See* Rights issues
sub-divisions, 13.27
transactions treated as, 13.33
Voluntary winding-up,
    profit sharing schemes, 12.52
share option schemes, and, 12.50, 12.51
Voting rights,
    administration, 16.10

W

Weekly paid employees,
    savings-related share option schemes,
–applications, 8.22
–contributions, 8.68–8.70
–savings contract, 8.68–8.70

Y

Yellow Book,
    adjustment of options, rules on, 13.2, 13.4
Listing Rules, 4.15